The AMERICAN Anthology

Robert R. Potter

Globe Book Company, Inc.

New York / Cleveland / Toronto

Robert R. Potter has been a teacher of English in the New York City School System, a research associate for Project English at Hunter College, and a teacher of English at the Litchfield High School in Litchfield, Connecticut. He has held professorships at the State University of New York and at the University of Connecticut.

Dr. Potter received his B.S. from the Columbia University School of General Studies and his M.A. and Ed.D. from Teachers College, Columbia University.

Dr. Potter is the author of Globe's *Myths and Folktales Around the World, The Reading Road to Writing, Making Sense, A Better Reading Workshop, Writing Sense, Writing a Research Paper, Language Workshop, Tales of Mystery and the Unknown, The Reader's Anthology,* and co-author of *The World Anthology* and *The Collector's Anthology.*

Consultants
Jeannine Atkins, English Teacher, Housatonic Valley Regional High School, Falls Village, Connecticut
Wendy Fairbanks, English Chairperson, Venice High School, Los Angeles, California
Sandra E. Gibbs, Director of Special Programs, National Council of Teachers of English, Urbana, Illinois
Philip W. Hart, English Teacher, North High School, Phoenix, Arizona
Adrian W. McClaren, Supervisor of English, Memphis City Schools, Memphis Tennessee
Ruth D. McCubbrey, English Teacher, Tamalpais High School, Mill Valley, California

Editors: Ellen Hyman and Lauren Fedorko
Photo Editor: Adelaide Garvin Ungerland
Art Director: Lee Rosenberg
Cover Design: Bass and Goldman Associates
Text Design: Celine Brandes

Acknowledgments and credits appear on pages 399–403.

ISBN: 0-87065-037-8

PRINTED IN THE UNITED STATES OF AMERICA 9 8 7 6 5 4 3 2

CONTENTS

UNIT 1: WHO ARE YOU?

U N I T 2: FOR PEOPLE ONLY

U N I T 3:   DIFFERENT DRUMMERS

U N I T 4:   WHAT'S THE BIG IDEA?

UNIT 5: STRANGE THINGS DONE

UNIT 6: I HEAR AMERICA

SKILL DEVELOPMENT

INTRODUCTION

In this book you'll find some of the best literature you have ever read. *Literature* is a long word. Ten letters. Four syllables. But don't let it worry you. Literature is reading, yes—but with a difference.

People read for two main reasons. First they read to learn useful information. To bake a cake, you read a recipe. To fix a car, you read a repair manual. To learn a career, you read books on the subject. This is reading for its *practical* value. You read because of what the reading material can do for you.

But reading also can do things *to* you. It can make you laugh and groan and shiver and even sweat. It can introduce you to interesting people. It can stir up in you new thoughts and feelings in the same way that your own adventures do. This is why you can think of literature as an experience—*your* experience. In fact, every time you read a piece of literature, stop to think what it does to you.

In your *American Anthology* you'll read some stories and poems by famous American writers of the past. You'll also meet some exciting authors who are writing today. In addition, you'll be asked to practice the skills that will make you an even better reader than you are now. Good literature demands good readers. If you say, "That's great!" about anything in this book, you're also saying something else. You're saying, "I'm a great reader!"

You'll find the organization of this book familiar and helpful. The selections are followed by exercises to check your understanding and develop full reading appreciation. Words you may not know are defined right at the bottom of the pages where they appear. Special terms, such as **symbol**, also appear with their definitions throughout your text. Both the skills terms and the more important vocabulary words are in heavy, or **bold**, type. Pay attention to these words; most of them are tested in the "Vocabulary and Skill Reviews" that occur at intervals throughout the book. For reference, the special terms are also listed in the Glossary of Terms at the back of the book.

Remember, literature isn't simply facts or information. Literature involves *you*, the reader. The words in this book are just marks on paper until your lively mind and improving reading ability bring them to life. *You make the difference.*

THE SECRET

by Denise Levertov

Two girls discover
the secret of life
in a sudden line of poetry.

5 I who don't know the
secret wrote
the line. They
told me

10 (through a third person)
they had found it
but not what it was
not even

15 what line it was. No doubt
by now, more than a week
later, they have forgotten
the secret,

20 the line, the name of
the poem. I love them

for finding what
I can't find.

and for loving me
for the line I wrote,
and for forgetting it
so that

25 a thousand times, till death
finds them, they may
discover it again, in other
lines

30 in other
happenings. And for
wanting to know it,
for

35 assuming there is
such a secret, yes,
for that
most of all.

1. One would think that "the secret of life" (line 2), once discovered, would be too important to forget. Why, then, might the two girls "have forgotten" it not long after?
2. Why might the poet have used the adjective "sudden" in line 3?
3. Think about stanza 2. In your opinion, did the speaker "know the/secret" when she wrote the line? Explain.
4. In your own words, why does the speaker love the girls for forgetting the secret (lines 18–30)?
5. What about the girls does the speaker admire "most of all" (lines 30–36)?

U N I T · 1

WHO ARE YOU?

I'm nobody! Who are you?
Are you nobody, too?
—Emily Dickinson

Do you find these two questions puzzling, even sad? Don't despair—they're really not. For one thing, they were written not by a "nobody" but by one of our nation's most famous poets. For another, the poem from which these two lines come contains a pleasant "secret" that you'll discover in just a few pages.

Like all the units in this book, this first unit puts the spotlight on people. "Who are you?" is the sprawling question that should be at the back of your mind as you approach each selection. You'll ask it of characters as their personalities unfold. You'll ask it of famous authors as you learn a little about their lives. And most important, you'll ask it of yourself. Get ready to take a fresh look at the new person you are becoming.

THE STORY-TELLER

by Mark Van Doren

He talked, and as he talked
Wallpaper came alive;
Suddenly ghosts walked,
And four doors were five;

5 Calendars ran backward,
And maps had mouths;
Ships went tackward,
In a great drowse;

Trains climbed trees,
10 And soon dripped down
Like honey of bees
On the cold brick town.

He had wakened a worm
In the world's brain,
15 And nothing stood firm
Until day again.

● tackward (TAK wurd) slantwise against the wind

2

WAYS OF KNOWING*

1. *Who are you?* (a) What about the teller of tales so impressed the speaker of the poem? (b) What kind of a person does the speaker seem to be?

2. Think about the setting of the poem. (a) Does it take place indoors or out? How do you know? (b) What in the poem suggests that it takes place in fairly modern times and at night?

3. Clearly, much of the language in the poem does not mean *exactly* what it says. For instance, the wallpaper in line 2 did not *really* "come alive." In your opinion, what does the poet mean to suggest in lines 13–14?

4. A **stanza** is a group of lines in a poem that may be like at least one other group in (1) number of lines, (2) approximate length of lines, or (3) **rhyme scheme,** or pattern. Are the four-line groupings in "The Story-Teller" stanzas or just groups of lines?

---

*"A poem is a way of knowing."—John Hall Wheelock

THE EYE CATCHER

by Frederick Laing

▶ The question "Who are you?" can point different ways. An author can ask it of you, the reader. You can also ask an author, "Who are you? What do you stand for?" The same question can be asked of an author's characters, and the characters can ask it of themselves. We usually learn about interesting characters as they learn about themselves.

Here's a story about a girl named Genevieve. At the end, she learns something important—and maybe you will, too.

What had really brought her into Waller's department store was something definitely not romantic. She had promised her mother to get herself a new rain hat. As she wandered through she was looking wistfully at the things she couldn't afford or wouldn't be allowed to wear. That two-piece bathing suit, for instance. Renee Weston had one like it. . . .

Renee Weston, yes . . . whom Bert Howland was taking to the benefit dance this Saturday, this very night. And as for herself, who had asked her to go to the benefit dance? Why, nobody. For who was going to ask quiet Genevieve Smith?

She was walking along the aisles with her head down and her heart, to judge from the way she felt, dragging on the floor behind her. It was the sign in front of these hair ribbons that stopped her cold.

EYE CATCHERS, it said.

And around the sign was a selection of those bow ribbons for your hair. Every color of the rainbow, it said—pick a color to suit your personality.

She stood there a moment with her head down. No, her mother wouldn't let her wear a bow that big and showy, even if she had the nerve, which she hadn't. These eye catchers, they were the kind . . .

- **romantic** (roh MAN tik) fanciful; imaginative
- wistfully (WIST ful ee) longingly; in a wishful manner

4

The kind Renee Weston would wear, she had started to think, when the saleslady broke into her train of thought: "This would be a nice one for you, dearie."

"Oh, no, I'm afraid I couldn't wear anything like that," she answered. But at the same time she was reaching wistfully for the green ribbon.

The saleslady looked surprised. "With that lovely copper-colored hair and those pretty eyes? Why, child, you could wear anything."

Maybe it was only a sales talk, but the ribbon was attached to a comb, and because she didn't need much urging, she fastened it into her hair.

"No, a little farther front," the saleslady said. "One thing you have to remember, honey, if you're going to wear anything a little out of the ordinary, wear it like nobody had a better right than you. In this world, you gotta hold your head up." She looked at the position of the ribbon critically. "That's better. Why, you look positively . . . exciting."

• **critically** (KRIT ik lee) with careful judgment

She looked in the mirror and, sure enough, the green color of the ribbon and the hint of red in her hair with the green of her eyes . . .

"I'll take it," she said, a little surprised at the note of decision in her voice.

"Now if you wanted to get another for formal wear," the saleslady said, "one like this, for instance, if you were going to a party or a dance . . . "

It was the last thing she wanted to talk about. She paid for the ribbon and started to get out of there so fast that she bumped smack into a big woman with a lot of packages, and almost got knocked silly.

As she neared the door, a funny old man was staring at her. A man with black eyes and a droopy gray mustache under a green fedora hat. You could tell from his eyes that he was smiling under the gray mustache. Smiling and looking at the eye catcher.

It was a conquest, even if it wasn't much. She gave him a glance. Just the merest passing look, but . . .

But the next moment a shiver of fright went through her, for the silly old thing was actually following her. That eye catcher couldn't . . . but this was really dreadful. She started to look around and then she heard him say, "Hey, keedo!" She ran like a rabbit and didn't stop running until she was a block down the street.

Then suddenly she found herself in front of Carson's drugstore. Her girl friends might be there, she thought. Also, this was the drugstore where Bert Howland often hung around Saturday afternoons, talking with his friends or playing the pinball machine.

She hesitated just a moment before she entered the drugstore. Then she took a deep breath.

He was there all right. He was sitting at the soda counter, and the minute she saw him—the way he was hunched over a cup of coffee, not drinking it, just looking ahead—she thought, Renee turned him down. She's going to the dance with somebody else.

She sat down at the other corner of the counter facing his profile, and Harry, smiling in his white apron, came over to take her order.

"Bring me a black-and-white soda," she said.

- fedora (fi DOHR uh) kind of soft felt hat
- conquest (KON kwest) whatever is won or conquered

6

And as he went to get her the soda, she saw, out of the side of her eyelashes, that Bert Howland had turned and was staring at her.

She sat up straight, holding her head high, conscious, very conscious of that green eye catcher.

After a while he said, "Hi, Genevieve."

She turned, and did a neat little job there of looking surprised. "Why, Bert Howland," she said, "how long have you been sitting here?"

"All my life," he said. "Just waiting for you."

It was only a line, but ordinarily it would have left her stuttering. She wanted to reach up and make a few touches at her hair, just to feel the eye catcher to give her confidence, but she restrained herself.

"Flatterer," she said.

And a moment later, he was sitting on the stool beside her, looking at her in that same way, as though he'd just noticed she was alive.

"Wearing your hair a different way or something, aren't you?" he asked.

She reached for her soda and took a gulp. "Do you usually notice things like that?" she asked.

● **restrain** (ri STRAYN) hold back

"No," he said. "I guess it's just the way you're holding your head up. Like you thought I ought to notice something."

She felt a slight flush at her cheeks and the tips of her ears. "Is that meant as a crack?"

"Maybe," he said, grinning, "and maybe not. Maybe I sort of like to see you hold your head like that."

It was about ten minutes afterward that the unbelievable happened. He said, "You know, there's this benefit dance tonight."

And when he actually came across with it, the invitation and everything, it was all she could do to keep from throwing her arms around him.

They left the drugstore a little later, and he offered to walk home with her. But suddenly she remembered that formal eye catcher, the one you wore to a party or a dance. She couldn't wear the one she had on. She would have to have one to match her evening dress. And so, though only this morning she would have practically wept for joy at the chance to have Bert Howland walk home with her, she told him now that she simply had to get to Waller's before it closed.

She got there just as the doors were being shut. A man tried to keep her out, but she brushed past him and dashed to the ribbon counter.

She looked for the blue-and-gold one. Gone! If they didn't have another . . .

The saleslady smiled when she saw who it was. "I knew you'd be back."

"H . . . how?" she asked, out of breath.

The saleslady reached under the counter. "I've been saving it for you." But the eye catcher she brought out was not the blue-and-gold one. It wasn't even formal at all. In fact, it was . . .

"That's like the one I just bought," she said, puzzled.

And then she was standing with her mouth opened in amazement. Why, when the big woman had bumped into her it must have been knocked off. . . .

"It *is* the same one," the saleslady explained.

And with that knowledge a lot of things began to flash through Genevieve's mind. But suddenly she began to smile and then somehow she couldn't stop smiling. She let her head lift easily while half of her listened to the saleslady's story—a story about a man who had found his way to the ribbon counter with her eye catcher, a jolly old man in a green fedora hat.

ALL THINGS CONSIDERED ──────────────

1. As Genevieve leaves the store, she doesn't know the important fact that (a) the rain hat was really what she needed. (b) the eye catcher is not on her head. (c) the store will not refund money.
2. As the man in the fedora follows Genevieve out of the store, she experiences (a) fright. (b) a laughing fit. (c) chest pains.
3. Bert Howland suddenly notices Genevieve because (a) he admires the eye catcher. (b) she looks tired and quite ill. (c) she sits up straight and seems to have confidence.
4. At the end of the story, Genevieve receives the big surprise that (a) the man in the fedora was really Bert. (b) she hasn't been wearing the eye catcher. (c) the formal eye catchers cost more.
5. Which of these statements best expresses the meaning of the story? (a) In spite of what they say, most boys want girls to dress up once in a while. (b) Be proud of who you are. (c) Clerks in stores often give good advice.

THINKING IT THROUGH ──────────────

1. When Genevieve learns the truth, we read that "a lot of things began to flash through Genevieve's mind." What things?
2. The title of the story has a double meaning. Is the hair bow the *only* "eye catcher" in the story? Explain.
3. Who gives Genevieve the best advice in the story? What is that advice, in one sentence? (Look back if you wish.) Do you agree with the advice?
4. In your opinion, will Genevieve buy a more formal eye catcher and wear it to the dance? Explain your thinking.

Literary Skills

Literal and Figurative Language

Most words we use mean exactly what they say. For instance, if you like peanuts, you might say, "I could eat a lot of peanuts right now." Every word in that sentence means just what the dictionary says it means. Another term for such "dictionary language" is **literal** (LIT ur ul) language.

But suppose you said, "I could eat a million peanuts right now." Clearly, the word *million* doesn't really mean "1,000,000." Its real meaning is "a great many." Another term for this kind of language is **figurative** (FIG yur uh tiv) language. Figurative language says one thing and means another.

Two more points must be made about figurative language: (1) Oddly enough (and often confusing to students), one of the most common figurative expressions is the word *literally*. Think about statements such as "I was literally frozen to death." This really means, of course, "I was figuratively frozen to death." (2) Many figurative expressions are used so much that we don't recognize them as figurative. Any overused and unoriginal expression can be called a **cliché** (klee SHAY). Examples are expressions like a *million* peanuts, something *catching* the eye, and most uses of *literally*.

Five figurative expressions from the story appear in *italics* below. Explain both (a) the literal and (b) the figurative meanings. When you finish, be ready to state which expression, in your opinion, is the most original, and also which can be called cliché(s).

1. "The *Eye Catcher*."
2. . . . and her *heart*, to judge from the way she felt, *dragging on the floor behind her*.
3. "Why, child, you could wear *anything*."
4. She ran *like a rabbit*. . . .
5. It was about ten minutes later that the *unbelievable* happened.

Composition

1. Suppose you were a teacher preparing a short test on "The Eye Catcher." Write five true-false questions that might be part of such a test. At least two of your statements should be true, and at least two false.

2. Locate five completely literal sentences in the story, then rewrite them using figurative language. Write both sentences on your paper. For instance, "The saleslady looked surprised" could become "The saleslady's jaw dropped about a foot and a half" or "The saleslady's eyes were wide pools of wonder."

Emily Dickinson (1830–1886)

If I read a book," wrote Emily Dickinson, "and it makes my whole body so cold no fire can ever warm me, I know that is poetry. If I feel . . . as if the top of my head were taken off, I know that is poetry. These are the only ways I know it. Is there any other way?"

"*. . . as if the top of my head were taken off . . .* "! Those are strong words, but Emily Dickinson knew what she was talking about. Today Emily Dickinson is considered one of the greatest American poets—if not *the* greatest.

Her story is a strange one. Nearly all her life was passed in a large house in Amherst, Massachusetts. As a girl she was active and fun-loving. She had a year of college. Then, in her early 20s, something happened that changed her life. It was probably a disappointing romance, but that may not be the whole story. At any rate, she started spending more and more time alone. She read a lot. She helped with family chores. She watched the wonders of nature in a private yard and garden. She stopped going to church. By and by her parents died, and her world grew smaller still. What happened outside this private world—even the Civil War!—held little interest for her. She dressed only in white. She left chores outside the house to her unmarried sister, Vinnie. She refused to meet strangers. During the last ten years of her life she never went out.

Emily Dickinson died at the age of 55. Her relatives knew that poetry had been one of her interests. But she had written poetry mainly to please herself. During her lifetime, only seven of her poems had been printed. Her family and a few friends had seen some others, but no one had dreamed of the surprise that came following her death. Her sister Vinnie entered her room to find drawers full of poems, trunks full of poems! In all, 1,775 were found! Most of them were arranged by year. In 1862, for instance, she had written 366 poems!

In a way, Emily Dickinson's world was small. But in another way, it was huge. Her mind stretched far, far out, beyond death—even beyond the world as we know it. And for her life, our world is the richer.

In your opinion, what might have happened to make an active young woman slowly withdraw from society?

A DICKINSON SAMPLER

poems by Emily Dickinson

▶ Discoveries about other people often help us to know ourselves better. For instance, have you ever felt like a "nobody"? Have you ever felt that your life didn't amount to very much? Have you ever felt that if you suddenly vanished, you really wouldn't be missed?

    Of course you have. Everyone, once in a while, feels like a "nobody." And this knowledge about other people can help us with our own feelings. Read what Emily Dickinson has to say on this and other subjects.

I'M NOBODY!

I'm nobody! Who are you?
Are you nobody, too?
Then there's a pair of us—don't tell!
They'd banish us, you know.

How dreary to be somebody!
How public, like a frog
To tell your name the livelong day
To an admiring bog!

WAYS OF KNOWING

1. In line 1, the poet asks, "Who are you?" Does the word "you" seem to refer to the reader, to a frog, or to "somebody" else mentioned later? Explain.
2. Line 2 also contains a question. What answer does the poet seem to expect, *yes* or *no*?
3. Examine the figurative language (see page 10) in the poem. Clearly, the word "somebody" (line 5) means the opposite of the word "nobody." What kind of person does the poet mean by "somebody"?

- **dreary** (DREER ee) dull; tiresome
- **bog** (BOG) swamp; wet ground

4. Think about the rest of the figurative lan̶~̶ ̶̶~̶ in the second stanza. (a) By saying that a frog re̶n̶~̶ ̶̶ ̶e as it croaks away in a swamp, what is the po̶̶ ̶̶ ̶̶ ut a certain kind of person? (b) What does th̶̶ ̶̶ ̶ession "admiring bog" (line 8) suggest to yo̶̶

5. Explain in your own words what enj̶ ̶̶ ̶̶ ̶ets out of being a "nobody."

A WORD

A word is dead
When it is said,
Some say.
I say it just
Begins to live
That day.

I NEVER SAW A MOOR

I never saw a moor,
I never saw the sea;
Yet know I how the heather looks,
And what a wave must be.

I never spoke with God,
Nor visited in heaven;
Yet certain am I of the spot
As if the chart were given.

WAYS OF KNOWING

1. (a) In "A Word," what might make one spoken word be "dead," while another "just/Begins to live"? (b) Has history shown the words in this particular poem to be "dead" or alive?

- moor (MOOR) open wasteland
- heather (HETH ur) low evergreen plant that often grows on moors

2. Suppose another person—not a poet!—had wanted to express the thought of "I Never Saw a Moor." He or she might have written: "Although I've never seen heather or an ocean wave, I feel I know about them. In the same way, although I've never seen God or heaven, I feel I know about them, too." These two sentences make the meaning clear, but they would never have become as famous as the poem. Find at least two ways in which the poem differs from the two sentences.

3. One of the poems contains a lot of figurative language, while the other contains none, or almost none. Explain which is which, and why. (In framing your answer, remember this: An expression isn't figurative just because it refers to something imagined or unreal. For instance, you might say, "I dreamed I was a purple pig." If you really did have such a dream, nothing in that sentence is figurative. Every word means just what the dictionary says it means. It is literal language.)

4. Emily Dickinson's poems often are not printed exactly as she originally wrote them. There are several reasons for this. She used unusual spelling and punctuation. She often capitalized words she felt were important. Also, she sometimes used words that the average reader would not know.

   For instance, line 4 of "I Never Saw a Moor" was written "And what a Billow be." (A billow is a wave.) Line 8 was written "As if the Checks were given—" (Checks are markers given to train passengers to show their destinations.)

   In your opinion, is it fair to change the work of a great poet? What kinds of changes should be made, if any?

For further reading, here are two more of Emily Dickinson's best-known poems. Now it's time to stop *answering* questions and start *asking* them. For each poem, write at least two good questions on your paper. Think about the meaning behind the words, the figurative language, and the relation of the poem to the poet's life. Remember these rules:

1. Silly questions will not be counted. So forget about questions like "What was the poet's first name?"

2. Questions that can be asked of any poem are not allowed. Example: "What's the meaning of the first stanza?"

3. Questions that everyone can answer immediately are too easy; questions that stump the whole class are too hard.

4. You should be able to answer the questions yourself—but not always. If you're honestly curious about a question to which you think there is an answer, go ahead and ask it.

THE SKY IS LOW

The sky is low, the clouds are mean;
A traveling flake of snow
Across a barn or through a rut
Debates if it will go.

A narrow wind complains all day
How someone treated him.
Nature, like us, is sometimes caught
Without her diadem.

SOME KEEP THE SABBATH

Some keep the Sabbath going to church;
I keep it staying at home,
With a bobolink for a chorister,
And an orchard for a dome.

5 Some keep the Sabbath in surplice;
I just wear my wings;
And instead of tolling the bell for church,
Our little sexton sings.

God preaches—a noted clergyman—
10 And the sermon is never long;
So instead of getting to heaven at last,
I'm going all along!

- diadem (DY uh dem) crown (here, more like a halo)
- **bobolink** (BOB uh lingk) kind of songbird
- **chorister** (KOR i stur) singer in a choir
- surplice (SUR plis) loose-fitting garment worn by members of the clergy and choirs
- sexton (SEKS tun) church caretaker who rings the bell

Washington Irving (1783–1859)

The study at Sunnyside, Irving's home in Tarrytown, New York

Washington Irving has often been called America's first great writer, a title he well deserves. Even people who have not read "Rip Van Winkle" seem to know about the character of the same name, the man who slept for 20 years. Other characters are just as famous. Irving's headless horseman, some say, still rides about Sleepy Hollow on gloomy, gray days. And what would New York City be without the Knicks, or the name "Knickerbocker"? The first Knickerbocker was one "Diedrich Knickerbocker," a name Irving invented for the author of his make-believe *History of New York*.

There is a stereotyped character known as "the typical American author" whose life goes like this. The author is born poor, struggles through early hardships, risks all to be a writer, and finally achieves success. Only the last of these is true for Irving. He was born into a comfortable business family. Instead of going to college, he idled around Europe. At first his writing was just a hobby, and he always took a relaxed, comfortable approach to his work. He defined the "happy age" of life as the time when a person can be idle and not feel guilty about it. A very social man, Irving could appreciate a well-set table and a good cigar.

Yet Irving did achieve great success. His easy, effortless style transformed all that it touched. He was equally good at humor (*Knickerbocker's History*) and horror ("The Adventure of the German Student"). In addition to many short stories, he wrote travel books, histories, and biographies. He even wrote a hit play. If Mark Twain (see page 182) was "the Lincoln of our literature," Irving was definitely the Washington.

What is unusual about the way Washington Irving got his start as a writer?

THE LEGEND OF SLEEPY HOLLOW

a radio play based on the story by Washington Irving

▶ Who are you, Ichabod Crane? In the Sleepy Hollow of yesteryear, the only person who really couldn't answer that question was Ichabod Crane himself. And a person who doesn't understand himself is in for trouble—big trouble!

CHARACTERS

Announcer
Ichabod Crane, *village schoolteacher*
Master Yost Van Huten, *pupil*
Katrina Van Tassel, *daughter of a wealthy Dutch farmer*
Frow Van Tassel, *Katrina's mother*
Mynheer Van Tassel, *Katrina's father*
Brom Van Brunt, *young man*
Hans Van Ripper, *farmer* ☞ Mu59
Frow Van Ripper, *his wife*
Farmer Van Til, *neighbor* —
Two Men, a Woman, several Children, a Minister

Music: *"Memories." Fade in, then out slowly under voice.*
Announcer: Washington Irving's famous "Legend of Sleep Hollow" was first read by a delighted public more than 160 years ago. But the church mentioned in the story still stands today as Irving described it, and automobiles rattle over the Headless Horseman's Bridge near Tarrytown, New York.
Music: *An old tune takes us back in time.*
Announcer: *(With lowered voice)* Long ago the valley called Sleepy Hollow was a place bewitched.
Sound: *Indian war whoops. Fade and hold.*
Announcer: Some say that the old Indian chiefs held their meetings there, long before the explorer Henry Hudson discovered the spot.
Sound: *War whoops up briefly and out.*
Announcer: Some say it was a meeting place of witches . . .
Sound: *Odd shrieks and laughter. Fade and hold.*
Announcer: . . . after they were driven out of New England . . . and you can still hear their voices in the air . . . high above the treetops.

Sound: *Shrieks and laughter up briefly, then fade out.*

Voices: Graymalkin! Brimstone! Meet me in the forest!

Announcer: But everyone in Sleepy Hollow agreed on one thing . . . and that was the headless ghost of a Hessian* soldier on horseback.

Sound: *Wind and horse's hoofs. Fade and hold.*

Announcer: His head had been shot off by a cannonball, and he roamed the valley on windy nights.

Sound: *Wind and hoofs up briefly. Fade slowly under and out.*

Announcer: Many worthy citizens had heard the headless horseman, and not a few of them had actually seen him with their own eyes. Of all the legends that hung about—this was the favorite legend of Sleepy Hollow.

Music: *Simple country tune. Up, under, and out.*

Announcer: The schoolhouse in Sleepy Hollow was ruled over by a man named Ichabod Crane. He was tall and thin, with hands that dangled a mile out of his sleeves, and feet that might have served for shovels. He had huge ears, large glassy-green eyes, and a long nose like a bird's beak. When he walked along on a windy day, one might have taken him for a scarecrow escaped from some cornfield. But inside his own schoolroom, inside the four log walls, he ruled supreme.

Sound: *Voices of children, up and under. Up briefly between next three speeches.*

Voice: Sixty seconds make a minute. Sixty minutes make an hour. Twenty-four hours make a day. . . .

Voice: The state of Connecticut is south of Massachusetts, west of Rhode Island. . . .

Voice: The fat cat ate the rat. Run, cat, run.

Sound: *Noise of ruler hitting desk. Children's voices fade out quickly.*

Ichabod: (*A loud comedy voice that seems to come half through the nose*) Silence, children. I observe that Master Yost Van Huten is more than usually busy with his chalk and writing board. Come forward, Master Yost, and let us all admire your work.

Yost: (*Unhappily*) Please, teacher, I don't wanna.

Ichabod: You will bring me your writing board at once, Master Yost. Thank you. . . . Hmmm. . . . What have we here?

Sound: *Children laughing behind their hands.*

Ichabod: (*With sound of ruler on desk*) You would draw a funny picture of your teacher, would you, Master Yost? Read aloud what you have written.

---

*The Hessians were soldiers from Germany who fought on the side of the British during the American Revolution.

Yost: (*Unhappily*) Teacher's mad and I am glad,
                        And I know what'll please him . . .

Ichabod: Go on.

Yost: A bottle of wine to make him shine,
                        And Katrina Van Tassel to tease him.

Sound: *Laughter.*

Ichabod: I have always carried in mind that wonderful rule: "Spare the rod and spoil the child." I would not for any reason have Master Yost Van Huten spoiled. You will hold out your hand, Master Yost.

Yost: Aw, I don't wanna!

Sound: *Ruler on child's hand and child crying out. The ruler fades, but the child continues to cry.*

Ichabod: I am only doing my duty by your good parents, Master Yost! There! It may hurt now, my gifted young poet, but you will remember it and thank me for it in the longest day you have to live.

Music: *Up to close scene, then under and out.*

Announcer: Despite his rule in the classroom and his peculiar appearance, Ichabod Crane was thought of as a man of great learning. He would quote whole pages of Cotton Mather's history of witchcraft in New England. He was the singing teacher of Sleepy Hollow, and he led the singing in church every Sunday morning.

These accomplishments put Ichabod ahead of the local country boys in winning the favors of the blooming Katrina Van Tassel, daughter of the wealthiest Dutch farmer in the neighborhood. On afternoons, when his work at the schoolhouse was over, he would walk to the Van Tassel farmhouse (*Fading*) on the bank of the Hudson River in a green and . . .

Ichabod: And how are you, Miss Katrina? Hmmmm! Always busy spinning, weaving, or baking your delicious little cakes, ahem—such delicious cakes!

Katrina: It's nice of you to praise 'em, Master Crane. Won't you try some of today's baking? This honey loaf and these doughnuts. And a bit of the new cheese and a glass of father's cider.

Ichabod: (*With mouth too full, smacking lips*) Mmm! Just a bit! Just a little bit! Just a little, little bit! I'm a light eater, Miss Katrina. I take only enough to keep body and soul together!

Katrina: But you must do more than just taste my honey loaf, Master Crane. And the coffee cake. Here, let me refill your glass, too.

Ichabod: (*Speaking with difficulty through a full mouth*) Miss Katrina, your charms have made a deep impression on my heart!

Katrina: (*Giggling*) Oh, Master Crane, how you do talk!

Ichabod: (*Mouth full*) Katrina, there is something I must tell you. . . . I'll thank you to pass the peach jam. . . . Something I have long been hoping. . . . Well, just a drop more cider if you insist. . . . Katrina, I love you!

Katrina: Hist! Here comes Mother! I'll be singing!

Ichabod: Here's my tuning fork!

Sound: *Tuning fork sounds "A."*

Katrina: Do-re-mi. . . . (*Sings scale. Breaks off.*)

Mother: (*Fade in*) Good day to you, Master Crane! I see you're giving my girl a lesson.

Ichabod: Yes, indeed, Frow Van Tassel. Now give me an "A," Miss Katrina.

Sound: *Tuning fork strikes "A."*

Katrina: Ahhhhh!

Ichabod: (*Like a sheep*) Ahhh!

Katrina: (*Up one tone*) Ohhh.

Ichabod: (*Through his nose*) Ohhh! And now for the hymn for next Sunday.

Both: By the still stream we sat and wept,
While memory still to . . .

Mother: (*Interrupting*) Very nice, I'm sure. . . . Well, I must run along to my farm duties. Geese and ducks are foolish things, but girls can look after themselves. . . . (*Fading*) Do a good lesson, Katrina.

Ichabod: Miss Katrina, as I was saying . . . (*Singing scale*) do-re-me-fa-sol-la-I love you-u-u.

Katrina: (*Singing scale*) Do-re-mi-fa-sol-la. This is so sudden, Master Crane!

Ichabod: Your place forever is in my heart. . . . Just how large is this farm, Miss Katrina?

Katrina: Three hundred acres. Ahhh!

Ichabod: (*Proudly*) Three hundred acres! Miss Katrina, I adore you! Tell me you'll be Missus Ichabod Crane!

Katrina: (*Shyly*) You must give me time to think it over. I'll give you your answer—

Ichabod: When?

Katrina: Next Friday week—at our . . . at my parents' big party! Do—re—mi—fa—sol—la—a—a.

Music: *Up fast, then fade slowly under and out.*

Announcer: Next Friday week. . . . The days passed slowly for our impatient lover. Already, in his own mind, Ichabod saw himself master of the rich fields, the great barns, fat pigs, snowy geese, whole armies of turkeys! He knew, however, that there was someone else who wanted Katrina's hand in marriage. This was Brom Van Brunt, a husky young farmer who won all the neighborhood races and was the leader of a gang of mischief-makers. Brom had bragged that he would "double the schoolteacher up and lay him on a shelf in his own schoolhouse," but Ichabod did not take his words very seriously.

To pass the time until the Van Tassels' party, Ichabod reread Cotton Mather's book on witchcraft from cover to cover. He remained at his desk in the log schoolhouse one evening so late that it was pitch-dark when he at last started homeward. As he walked along through the hollow, his teeth began to chatter, and the ordinary sounds of the night took on ghostly terrors.

Music: *Notes of worry.*

Sound: *Footsteps on gravel. Crickets. Hold under.*

Ichabod: (*To self*) Ooo . . . what a spooky night. . . . J-j-just the night for the h-h-headless horseman to ride. W-w-what if I should m-m-meet him?

Sound: *Hoot of owl.*

Ichabod: It sounds like an owl . . . but it might be a witch. There was old Nance Dinwiddie of Salem and Bess o'Bedlam . . . she that makes cows' milk go sour and puts tar in the baby's hair. O-o-o-h.

Sound: *Hoot of owl.*

Ichabod: Mercy on us! What a dreadful sound! Some poor homeless ghost, I make no doubt. (*Pleading*) Get back to your grave, do, that's a good ghost!

Sound: *Hoot of owl at distance.*

Ichabod: What a black night! Not a single star. Ooooooooh! There goes one now . . . shooting across the sky. A falling star means death. Then there was that black cat I met yesterday—that's a sure sign of trouble.

Sound: *Bullfrogs croaking.*

Ichabod: Ahhh! Is that a bullfrog or a ghost?

Sound: *Fade footsteps and crickets.*

Music: *Up over fading sounds.*

Announcer: Finally came the evening of the big party at Mynheer Van Tassel's. Ichabod wanted to arrive in style at the home of his lady love, so he borrowed an old plow horse called Gunpowder from Hans Van Ripper, the farmer in whose home he was then staying. On this animal he made a curious sight indeed. His legs were so long that his bony knees came up to the top of the saddle, and the motion of his arms was like the flapping of great black wings. Such was the figure that arrived at Mynheer Van Tassel's farmhouse (*Fading*) to find the merrymaking in full swing.

Music: *Fade in dance tune of the period.*

Sound: *Fade in sounds of country dance and small crowd noise. Sounds and music fade down and hold.*

Ichabod: Ah, Mynheer Van Tassel, (*Through his nose*) this is a happy event indeed!

Van Tassel: Evenin', Ichabod, evenin'! Fall to and help yourself to the food!

Ichabod: What a feast! What a delightful feast! Apple and pumpkin pies . . . broiled fish and roasted chickens . . . jams made of plums and peaches from *my* own trees . . . ah, I should say *your* own trees, Mynheer Van Tassel!

Music: *Dance tune ending.*

Voices: (*Calling*) Ichabod, Ichabod Crane! Show us how you dance the shakedown!

Ichabod: (*Proudly*) If Miss Katrina will be my partner.

Katrina: Yes, here I am.

Music: *Fast music up, down, and hold.*

Sound: *Clapping hands and stamping feet to time of music.*

Voices: (*Together*) Go to it, Ichabod! Hooray! See the schoolmaster! *etc.*

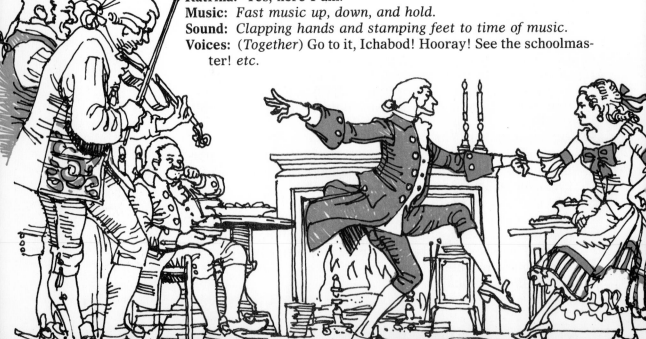

Sound: *All sound and music fade to distance.*

Announcer: But Brom Van Brunt, who also wanted to marry Katrina, did not feel so gay as the rest of the party.

Sound: *All sound and music up again.*

Van Brunt: (*Over voices, viciously*) You'd think it was Master Grasshopper himself clattering round the floor. He's put together so loose he'll fall apart if he don't watch out!

Man's Voice: (*Laughing*) Aha, Brom Van Brunt, they make a pretty pair dancing together, eh?

Woman's Voice: (*Laughing*) They say the schoolmaster is counting his chickens before they're hatched.

Another Man's Voice: Look at the schoolmaster eyeing her!

Van Brunt: (*Between teeth*) You wait and see. I'll fix him! I'll fix him!

Music: *Dance ending.*

Sound: *Clapping and stamping out with music. Hold sound of crowd low.*

Voices: (*Together*) Great, Ichabod! Wonderful, Master Crane! *etc.*

Van Tassel: (*Shouting*) Bring in the hot cider. Fall to, neighbors. You've got a cold ride home.

Sound: *Glasses rattle.*

Man: (*Smacking lips*) Ahhhh! This is the stuff to put heart into a man! Eh, Van Til?

Van Til: Give me a few mugs of friend Van Tassel's hot cider, and I'll laugh at the headless horseman himself!

Ichabod: (*Through his nose, unsteadily*) The headless horseman! (*Lowering voice*) Has he been seen of late?

Man: Yes, just t'other night old Brower met the horseman. "I hear you don't believe in me," says the ghost. "That I don't," says old Brower. "I think you're a lot of—" But just then the ghost caught him for such a ride as never was. Then with a clap of thunder he turned into a skeleton and flung Brower into the brook. "That'll teach you not to believe in honest ghosts," says he as he disappeared.

Voices: (*Together*) I hadn't heard that! Do you mean . . . *etc.*

Ichabod: (*Chattering of teeth*) W-w-what a thing to happen to a body!

Van Brunt: Ah, that's nothing! I met the headless horseman myself t'other night coming from Tarrytown. . . .

Man: (*Laughing*) Coming back from the Flowing Bowl Tavern you'd see anything!

Van Brunt: No, I hadn't been in any tavern. I offered to race the ghost to the inn for a bowl of punch. And I'd have won the race, too, but just as we got to the bridge by the churchyard (*Pause*) he vanished into a ball of fire!

Ichabod: (*Low*) A ball of fire! The Sleepy Hollow bridge, you say! And tonight I have to cross it!

Van Brunt: (*Teasing him*) If you get by Major André's hanging tree* alive, you mean, Schoolmaster. They say the goings-on around that tree, the moanings and the groanings, are terrible these nights.

Van Til: Well, ghosts or no ghosts, I've got to be getting home! I've got a barn full of cows to milk at daybreak.

All: (*Together*) That's right. Me, too. Good-by, neighbor Van Tassel! (*Fade*) Thank you. A fine party, neighbor, *etc.*

Van Tassel: Good-by, friends!

Frow Van Tassel: And thank you all for coming!

Sound: *Crowd noises fade out under.*

Ichabod: I want to speak a word to your lovely daughter before I depart, Van Tassel. You—ah—give in pretty much to her wishes, I take it?

Van Tassel: (*Laughing*) I love that girl even better than my pipe, Schoolmaster, and I've had just one rule bringing her up: Let her have her own way!

Ichabod: Good! Ah! (*Calling*) Miss Katrina! Miss Katrina! May I speak with you alone?

Katrina: (*Fade in*) Have you brought your tuning fork, Master Crane? I don't know as we would be able to talk without that! (*Giggles . . . fade out*)

Music: *Up, then under and out.*

Announcer: What was said at this interview, I wouldn't pretend to say. But something must have gone very wrong, for Ichabod came forth after a while looking like a very sad scarecrow. He went into the barn, kicked poor Gunpowder awake, and set off through the hills. . . . The hour was as gloomy as himself. Driving clouds hid the stars and the moon.

Music: *Notes of worry.*

Sound: *Crickets. One horse at walk. Crack of whip. Fade crickets and horse and hold.*

Ichabod: Get up, you crow's bait! Heaven have mercy on us! What's the matter with this animal?

Sound: *Horse at walk. Horse stops. Crack of whip.*

Ichabod: Giddap! Drat you, you one-eyed, knock-kneed, sway-backed nag!

Sound: *Horse whinnies. Hoofs begin walk, hold briefly, and stop.*

Ichabod: (*In whisper*) It's the hanging tree! It's the tree where they hanged André! Come, come, Gunpowder. If we're to get home before light, we've got to get by this tree somehow. I'll whistle to keep our courage up.

---

*Major John André was a British spy who was caught, tried, and hanged by the patriots near Tarrytown in 1780.

Sound: *Whistling of "Yankee Doodle." Horse at walk again. Add whistling of "Yankee Doodle" in higher key and out of time with first. Then whistling stops.*

Ichabod: Oooo . . . even the echo makes fun of me tonight!

Sound: *Groans.*

Ichabod: What was that?

Voice: *(Ghostly)* Ichabod! Ichabod Crane!

Ichabod: *(In whisper)* W-w-who wants Ichabod C-c-crane?

Sound: *Weird laughter.*

Ichabod: *(In whisper)* I see it now, waiting beside the road—a man on horseback. Perhaps it's just one of the people going home from the Van Tassels' party. I'll speak to him. *(In a loud, cheerful tone)* Good evening, friend!

Sound: *Add hoofs of second horse at walk more distant.*

Ichabod: *(Afraid)* W-w-who are you? Whoa, Gunpowder!

Sound: *First horse stops. Second horse approaches.*

Ichabod: If he's more than a human being, a hymn ought to drive him away. *(Singing through his nose in a shaky voice)* Praise God from whom all blessings flow. . . .

Voice: *(Distant)* Raise cod from tombs, small, large, or slow. . . .

Ichabod: There goes that echo again, making fun of me. Oh, mercy! mercy! He's riding beside me!

Sound: *As second horse grows louder, first horse begins walking again. Hold both low.*

Ichabod: *(In loud tone)* Friend, since you don't seem any too polite tonight, I'll just take my leave of you. Giddap, Gunpowder!

Sound: *Horse one, then horse two starts to trot.*

Ichabod: *(Sadly)* He's close on my heels! *(Calling)* Very well, friend, I have no mind to be polite myself, so I'll just drop behind, if you don't mind.

Sound: *Horse one, then horse two slows to walk.*

Ichabod: He won't let me lag behind. Well, here comes the moon out from under the cloud. Now I'll get a glimpse of his face! Bless me, he hasn't any head! He's the headless horseman himself! And he's carrying his head in front of him on the saddle! Giddap, Gunpowder!

Sound: *Horses begin to gallop. Fade into distance.*

Announcer: Away then they dashed, stones flying at every step. Ichabod's flimsy garments fluttered in the wind as he stretched his long, lean body over the horse's head in the eagerness of his flight.

Sound: *Two horses at gallop, fade and hold.*

Ichabod: *(Gasping)* There's the church bridge ahead, Gunpowder! Ghosts can't stand . . . churches! Just reach the bridge and we'll be safe!

Sound: *Two horses galloping on dirt road, then on bridge, then on*

road again. A rooster crows in the distance. Hold horses low.

Ichabod: A rooster! Ghosts always vanish when they hear the first crowing! Let's see . . . if he's gone. (*Gasping*) He hasn't vanished! He's right behind me! (*Shouting*) He's going to throw his head at me! (*Screaming*) Ahhhh!

Sound: *Horses fade quickly following scream to silence. Hold silence five seconds.*

Announcer: The next morning the old horse was found without his saddle, and with the bridle under his feet, quietly eating the grass at his master's gate. And where was Ichabod Crane? That worried Frow Van Ripper, too (*Fade*) as she said . . .

Frow Van Ripper: (*Fade in*) Hans Van Ripper, please to call Master Crane to breakfast. He's late for school now. And breakfast is spoiling. Hurry now!

Hans: Ja, Ja.

Sound: *Chair scraped on wood floor.*

Hans: (*Surprised*) Why, Frow, look out the window yet. That's Gunpowder. But where is my saddle? And look at that bridle!

Sound: *Footsteps on wood. Door opens.*

Hans: (*Calling*) Ichabod Crane, why didn't you put Gunpowder in the barn last night? (*Short pause*) Ichabod, why don't you answer?

Frow Van Ripper: But, Hans, has something happened to School-master? Where is he?

Music: *Up and fade out under.*

Announcer: Over at the schoolhouse the boys and girls gathered at the usual hour. As time went by and Master Crane did not appear, groups formed on the steps and in the yard. Several of the older boys strolled about the banks of the brook, while the younger ones played in the schoolyard. But still no school-master! Later in the day small groups of neighbors gathered (*Fading*) to discuss the strange disappearance.

Man 1: Ach, the poor schoolmaster. He's a strange one!

Man 2: Wasn't he now? You should'a seen him doing the shake-down with Miss Katrina. And eat—where does he put it?

Van Til: Well, then, he would have to come home by the bridge and the church road. He was on Gunpowder, wasn't he, Hans?

Hans: Ja, neighbor. I lent him my horse and my best saddle to help him win Miss Katrina. (*Laughter from group*) And it looks as if we both lost! (*Laughter up and under*)

Man 2: Let's walk down to the bridge anyhow. Maybe we can see the horse's hoofprints.

Music: *Up and fade out under.*

Announcer: And so the neighbors followed slowly after Ichabod's landlord, Hans Van Ripper, as he walked with bent head and searching eyes toward the Sleepy Hollow bridge. Hans noticed that the tracks of the horse's hoofs could be seen clearly in the road, and he knew that meant terrific speed. When he found his best saddle in the mud, he was speechless with anger. (*Fading*) But as the men reached the bridge . . .

Man 1: (*Excited*) Hans! There! On the bank near the water. It's Ichabod's hat!

Van Til: And that smashed pumpkin! Where did it come from?

Hans: (*Shocked*) Ichabod's hat! And so close to the water, too. We must look for his body. . . . (*Voice fading*) He must be buried in the proper way. . . .

Announcer: And so the good neighbors searched the brook, but the body of the schoolmaster was not to be found. When Hans Van Ripper got home, he went to Ichabod's room. His tuning fork, his books, clothes—all were there. As he was a bachelor and had no debts, no one troubled his head any more about him. But as winter approached and the time came for stories by the fireside, the story of Ichabod's disappearance was told again and again. (*Fading*) And the legend grew until one day . . .

Music: *Wedding march up and out under.*

Minister: Brom Van Brunt, wilt thou have this woman to be thy wedded wife . . . (*Fading to murmur, then up*) so long as ye both shall live?

Van Brunt: I will.

Minister: Katrina Van Tassel, wilt thou have this man to be. . . . (*Fading, then up*) I now pronounce that they are husband and wife.

Music: *Wedding march up, fade slowly and out under.*

Announcer: At the wedding breakfast at the Van Tassel home, the conversation naturally turned to Ichabod (*Fading*) as the guests thought about the past.

Sound: *Small crowd at breakfast. Fade and hold.*

Woman: Have another piece of cake, Hans.

Hans: That I will. Say, wasn't this Ichabod's favorite cake? Wonder what's become of him?

Van Til: Why, I saw Ichabod Crane in New York when I was in the city last week.

Hans: (*Amazed*) No . . . Van Til. You mean our Ichabod? Yi, yi, yi.

Van Til: You know, Hans, I've been thinking about that ride of Ichabod's. Seems to me that pumpkin we found beside his hat was more important than we thought. Whenever that story is told with Brom Van Brunt around, he always laughs fit to kill. I'm not so sure about this headless horseman. (*Fade*)

Sound: *Fade crowd noise to silence. Five seconds.*

Announcer: Although Hans Van Ripper and Farmer Van Til questioned the method of Ichabod's disappearance, a lot of people said for years that the schoolmaster had been the victim of the headless horseman. The bridge became more than ever an object of great wonder. The schoolhouse, which was never used again, was reported as haunted by Ichabod Crane's ghost. And the plowboy swore that on a still summer evening he could hear Ichabod's voice singing a sorrowful hymn among the peaceful groves of Sleepy Hollow.

Music: *Up to end.*

ALL THINGS CONSIDERED ────────────────

1. The author introduces Icabod Crane as (a) an unfortunate person who deserves sympathy. (b) a rather silly man to be laughed at. (c) an example for future teachers to follow.

2. In addition to wanting to marry Katrina, Ichabod also wants to (a) move away from the neighborhood. (b) make Katrina a famous singer. (c) become owner of the Van Tassel farm.

3. On the way home from the Van Tassels' party, Ichabod becomes the victim of (a) Brom Van Brunt. (b) a ghost. (c) Major André.

4. All things considered, Irving pictures the Dutch settlers in early New York as (a) cruel to neighbors. (b) interested only in having fun. (c) basically fine people.

5. Irving's main purpose in writing "The Legend of Sleepy Hollow" was probably to (a) warn his readers of the harm that superstitions can do. (b) share with his readers the fun of an old local legend. (c) get even with a few teachers he knew.

THINKING IT THROUGH ────────────────

1. The introduction to this book states that literary artists don't just try to transmit *information*, but instead arrange their material so that readers can experience the thrill of discovery. This is certainly true of Washington Irving. What he *leaves unsaid* is just as important as what *is said*. Explain (a) what Katrina probably told Ichabod after the party, (b) what Ichabod probably mistook for the ghost's head, and (c) what made Brom Van Brunt laugh when he later heard other people telling the story.

2. Katrina is a character about whom the average reader wants to discover more. (a) In your opinion, did she ever take the idea of marrying Ichabod Crane seriously? (b) Was she in on the trick? Explain in detail the reasons for your answers.

Literary Skills

Two Figures of Speech

An example of figurative language is called a **figure of speech.** For instance, the announcer in the play speaks of "whole armies of turkeys." Since "armies" here is figurative language, the phrase is a figure of speech.

Most figures of speech compare two things. The phrase "armies of turkeys," for example, compares a large flock of turkeys with troop after troop of soldiers. The comparison is a good one. Both the flock and the army contain large numbers of individuals that wear the same "uniform," operate as a group, and can make a lot of noise.

There are two main kinds of comparisons. A simple comparison like "whole armies of turkeys" is called a **metaphor** (MET uh for). A metaphor is simple and direct. No extra words are used to show that a comparison is being made. Instead, one expression is simply substituted for another, like "armies" for "flocks."

The other kind of comparison is called a **simile** (SIM uh lee). A simile does use a word to show that a comparison is being made. Usually this word is *like* or *as.* For instance, in the play we are told that Ichabod looked "like a very sad scarecrow." Since this comparison uses *like*, it is a simile.

Each of the following sentences contains a metaphor or a simile. For each sentence, write **M** or **S** on your paper.

1. Ichabod's nose was like a bird's beak.
2. Would Katrina marry the grasshopper?
3. Brom had dynamite in his fists.
4. The night was gloomy as a ghost.
5. A blanket of clouds made the night very dark.
6. Ichabod's face suddenly turned white as a newly washed sheet.

Composition

1. Suppose Washington Irving had wanted to tell the old legend simply as *information*. What kind of outline or summary would he have written? Try to write a summary of "The Legend of Sleepy Hollow" that tells the whole story in about ten sentences.
2. On page 24, the announcer states, "What was said at this interview, I wouldn't pretend to say. But something must have gone very wrong. . . ." What do you think was said between Katrina and Ichabod? Write the whole scene out as a dialogue (conversation). Follow the form of the radio play. Don't forget to use music and sounds that will add interest to the scene.

▶ Did you ever play the "Who are you?" game? Many people have. You see someone who interests you, say in a supermarket line or on a subway. Then you ask yourself, "Just *who* are you? What are you thinking about now? What's your life like? What's been your biggest disappointment? Your biggest joy?" Sometimes you can even go on to imagine the person's name, job, home, etc.

Suppose that right now you were walking into a public library. It's nearly closing time. Alone at a table sits a rough-looking young man with lots of curly hair. You notice some open books in front of him. They seem to be books of poetry. *Just who is he? What is he thinking about now?*

EATING POETRY

by Mark Strand

Ink runs from the corners of my mouth.
There is no happiness like mine.
I have been eating poetry.

The librarian does not believe what she sees.
5   Her eyes are sad
and she walks with her hands in her dress.

The poems are gone.
The light is dim.
The dogs are on the basement stairs and
   coming up.

10 Their eyeballs roll,
their blond legs burn like brush.
The poor librarian begins to stamp her feet
   and weep.

She does not understand.
When I get on my knees and lick her hand,
15 she screams.

I am a new man.
I snarl at her and bark.
I romp with joy in the bookish dark.

WAYS OF KNOWING

1. In your own *literal* words, what effect has the reading of poetry had on the speaker?

2. Does the librarian share the speaker's feelings? Explain your answer.

3. Think about the dogs in the poem. (a) What is the difference between the way dogs eat and the way people eat? (b) Why, then, does the speaker seem to want to join the dogs?

4. Look at the title and the first three lines. (a) Does the title contain a simile or a metaphor? (b) Which of the first three lines is the most literal?

5. You may have noticed that in these questions the person called "I" in the poem is referred to as the *speaker*. Yet in the questions on Emily Dickinson's poems (pages 12–13) the "I" is called the *poet*. When is it best to use *speaker*, and when *poet*?

6. Consider the cartoon below. How does Lucy's attitude toward books differ from that of the speaker in "Eating Poetry"?

THE CANVAS BAG

by Alan E. Nourse

> ▶ Joe Baker thought he knew himself well—until one terrible night when he started to remember. . . . This story by one of America's top science-fiction writers packs a real flip-flop.

The telephone rang just as Joe Baker got himself settled in the bathtub. He growled something nasty and dashed the length of the rooming house hallway to his little room at the end, bathrobe flying, splattering water far and wide as he reached for the telephone. Then Jeannie's voice was tinkling in his ear; his anger disappeared, and his heart skipped twice.

Jeannie was laughing. "I must have dragged you out of the shower! You sound like you've been jumping over barriers."

"Many barriers," said Joe, slapping at the water running down his leg. His feet were planted in a spreading puddle. "There's nothing wrong—is there?"

"Nothing too bad." Jeannie's voice was warm. "I'll have to be late tonight, is all. Maybe an hour or more—I don't know. Frankie's decided that *this* is the night we'll have to really clean up the diner. No other night will do. And you know Frankie."

Joe shook the water out of his ears, and cursed Frankie silently. A chill of disappointment stabbed through him. There would be an hour's delay in their dinner date. But then, he was sure he heard the same disappointment in

Jeannie's voice, and he felt somewhat better. It was almost as if she knew what a special date it was going to be. "How about nine, then? I'll meet you there."

"We should be finished by then. I'll be hungry, too."

"Sky's the limit tonight. Even on barriers to jump." He wondered how a girl who spent all day dishing out food could bear to look at it at night, much less eat it.

Jeannie's laugh was still in his ears as he hung up. He looked sadly around the room. An *extra* hour to kill. He could hardly bear it. It was an ugly room with a single window that stared out on the main street, catching the hot Indiana sun. Not a bad room, if you liked cheap boardinghouses. From the window he could see the whole town before him. He stared down for a moment before turning away, allowing his mind to go back to his first view of the small town, the day he'd dropped off the freight car six weeks before.

A grubby little dump town, he had thought. A good place to stop for the night, and move on. They probably wouldn't like drifters around here, anyway. Nothing unusual, his thinking that—the usual thoughts that went

33

through his mind when he hit a little Midwest town with its dusty streets and its dirty wooden houses. It was even an ordinary-looking diner where he had been sitting, when the girl behind the counter had come over, and he had looked up and seen Jeannie.

He gave a little laugh now, and took clean clothes from the dresser. A new shirt had always been a problem for Joe; he struggled into it bravely, grinning at himself in the mirror. So very much could happen in six short weeks! Your ideas of towns and people and everything could change so rapidly. He whistled a little tune, studying his wide tanned face and wild brown hair as he tied the tie. Not a bad face, Joe Baker. Not bad at all. You could see how a girl might go for it. And tonight, she simply *had* to go for it. He'd never asked a girl to marry him before in his whole life. She couldn't refuse, not tonight.

But the thought of marriage made him feel a bit strange. It was bound to happen sometime, he had told himself. A man can't tramp the roads forever. Someday the time would come to stop. It had always been sometime in the dim, distant future, with Joe. But it wasn't anymore. Tonight the time had come.

And then his eye fell on the little blue canvas bag on the floor in the corner.

He blinked at the bag. The bag blinked back at him. He gave a nervous laugh, and kicked the bag. It went sliding across the floor.

"Good-by, bag," he said happily. "I won't need *you* any more. Our days on the road are over."

For a girl who had worked all evening. Jeannie was bright and cheerful when Joe met her coming out of the diner. She was one of those amazing girls who never seem to run out of energy, and become the more beautiful the more work they do. She was slender and dark, with wide gray eyes set in a narrow face. Like a queen, Joe thought, as she came down the steps, or at least a princess. She kissed him lightly, and he slipped his arm around her as they walked around back to her old car.

"Let me take you away from all this," said Joe, politely. "Let me take you on the wings of the wind. The Pleasure Palace awaits."

She laughed, and Joe slipped easily into the driver's seat.

"The Spoon for dinner?" Jeannie asked.

"The Spoon? Not tonight. This is *our* night, and nothing but the best." He looked down at her and kissed her on the nose. "You know that place down by the bend of the river? Steaks an inch thick, they say, and dancing, too." He slid the car out into the road traffic. "Tonight we celebrate."

"It's very, very expensive, I've heard."

"Eat, drink, and be merry."

Worry flashed in her gray eyes. "You're—you're not heading out again, are you, Joe?"

He smiled. "Not a chance. I'm thinking of giving up life on the road."

She snuggled closer and threw her head back happily. "For good?"

"For good."

"Then we *do* have something to celebrate."

The place was crowded when they arrived, but the waiter found them a table for two looking out on the river. Across the room a band was playing quietly as they ordered, and soon they were in each other's arms, dancing gracefully to the music. It was a strange world for Joe—a warm, soft world of love and sweet smells—and he could hardly keep his mind clear as the girl pressed her soft cheek to his. He had missed so much, all these years of drifting from town to town, never satisfied, never stopping. He had waited for years, and now he was sure, beyond doubt, that the long years of waiting had been worth it. "I've got a secret, Jeannie," he whispered as they moved into the shadows.

"Don't tell me," she whispered back.

"Why not?"

"Because then it wouldn't be a secret, would it?"

"But some secrets are for two people, they aren't any good for just one." Her ear was inches from his lips. "I love you, Jeannie. Did you know that?"

She nodded.

"I want you to marry me."

He thought he felt her arms tighten for a moment, and they danced silently, close together. But when she turned her face up to him, her eyes were serious and troubled. "Are you sure you want that?" she asked.

"I'm not fooling, Jeannie."

She turned her face away. "Oh, I know you're not, Joe, but do you *know* what you want to do? Do you really want to stop drifting, take a house, settle down for good? Do you really think you could do that?"

"I wouldn't be asking you if I hadn't

thought it over, would I?" There was a puzzled note in his voice, and he frowned. Something deep inside him had gone cold, a strange sort of pain he had never felt before. "I've been on the road for a long time, I know; but a man gets tired of it after a while. Sooner or later he finds a girl that makes it all seem silly." His words stopped; somehow, he couldn't get the right ones to come out. The coldness in his chest was deeper. "Look, Jeannie, the road is a hard life, there isn't any softness or friendship or happiness out there. Why would anybody choose it? Why should I ever want to go back?"

He broke off, realizing that he was raising his voice. He looked at Jeannie, and she looked away, shaking her head and leading the way back to their seats. She looked up at him strangely. "You don't have to convince me, Joe. I believe it." She paused. "I wonder if *you* believe it."

His voice choked in his throat. "I only know how I feel, and I know it's true. I wouldn't have asked you otherwise."

She nodded, staring at the tablecloth. Then she looked him straight in the eyes. "I want you to tell me something, Joe," she said quietly. "I want you to tell me how old you are."

Joe stared at her, and very slowly set down his glass. Something was drumming in his head, a frightening sound that chilled him to the bone. "Why, I'm . . . thirty-ish, or so," he said, wondering aloud. "Thirty-one, I think, or thirty-two." He blinked at her. "I don't know, it's somewhere around there."

"But can't you *remember*, Joe?" Her eyes were wide.

"Well, of course I can, I suppose! I had a birthday last February." The drumming in his ears grew louder. "No, that was Pete Hower's birthday. We were on the road together. Funny guy, Pete. He—"

"*Please*, Joe!"

A chill ran up his back. It was as if he had suddenly looked over his shoulder and seen a huge pit opening up behind him. He saw Jeannie's worried face, and he tried hard, but his mind met with nothing except blank darkness. He stared at her in alarm. "Jeannie, *I can't remember!*"

"Oh, Joe! Think! You've got to!"

"But what difference does it make?"

"Joe—" The girl's voice was trembling, close to tears. "Think, Joe. Go back. Back to where you were before you came here, and where you were before that. Here—here's some paper. Write it down. Try to remember, Joe."

He took the pencil. Slowly, from the drumming in his head things were beginning to creep into his mind, strange things. "I—I just came East from North Dakota six weeks ago," he said. "Caught a freight train. Ran into some trouble with the cops and had a fight. And then I'd been in South Dakota for a while before that."

"How long?"

"Couple of months. I was working my way East, thought I'd work the docks for a while."

"And where were you before South Dakota?"

"California. Cab-driving job. I almost got killed; that made me want to head East. Came up from Mexico before that. And then before that there was the war."

A horrible thought flashed through Joe Baker's mind. A voice was screaming in his ear: *Which war, Joe, which war?*

Suddenly, in a flash of terror, he remembered. The muddy fog cleared from his mind, and his memory fell back and back and his face went white.

There was the fighting in Vietnam, and before that, in Korea, and, going back, the bloody beaches of World War II—

And there was the girl in Pittsburgh who'd cleaned him out that night at Jardine's—God! that seemed like a hundred years ago! And the job in the woods up in Canada before that—

And the long Depression years before that, with no money for a room—

And the job he'd lost when his boss had to go out of business—

And the run-in with the Boston cops in that liquor deal which couldn't go wrong—

And the cowboy job down through Wyoming and Colorado and Oklahoma before that—how long was that trip? Four years? Must have been, with all the time he'd wasted in Denver—

Joe Baker stared at the girl across the table from him, his mind screaming. He could almost see the blue canvas bag by his side, he could feel the excitement again as he had packed it full, ready for another move, and another, and another. . . . With a sudden rush he picked up the paper and pencil and began scratching down places, times, distances, with something digging into his chest as he wrote:

The end of World War I, and the long trip home from France—

The days of drifting through Europe right after 1900—

The bitter feelings of the Kansas farmers when the railroads went through—

The pounding of horses' hoofs on the Nevada prairie, the wild screams of the Indians—

The crash of big guns, the bitter sharp voice of Civil War rifles at Gettysburg—

He remembered them. He remembered them all.

● **depression** (di PRESH un) period when many people cannot find work

Joe Baker sat back in his chair, finally, his hands trembling. He couldn't believe it, of course. But it was true. He'd just never thought of it before. He'd drifted, from town to town, from job to job, anywhere the moment seemed to suggest. Drifted, and stopped for a while, and drifted again. He'd never thought of the past, for the past had always been filled with pain and loneliness. It had simply never occurred to him to stop and think how long he'd drifted, nor what might happen if he ever tried to stop.

And he had drifted for a hundred and fifty years.

He stared at the girl's frightened face. "You knew—somehow you knew."

She nodded. "I didn't know what it was. I knew you were *different*, somehow. At first I thought that you'd just been traveling a long time, that it was a part of a personality you'd built up on the road. I felt it the first moment I saw you. And then I began to realize that the difference was something else. But I didn't realize how long you've been going—"

"But my face!" he cried. "My body! How could it be possible? Why aren't I old, dried up, dead?"

"I don't know."

"But it couldn't happen!"

Jeannie shook her head weakly. "There's something else far more important."

"What's that?"

"What makes you do it?"

"I tell you, *I don't know.*"

"But you *must* have remembered the time passing!" she burst out.

Joe shook his head. "I just never stopped to think. Why should I have? There've never been friends, or family, or anyone to hang onto along the way. It never mattered what time it was, or what day it was. All that mattered was whether it was winter or summer, whether it was hot or cold, whether I was full or hungry. Jeannie, does it matter now? I love you, I want to stop, now, I want to marry you."

They were dancing again, and she was fighting to hold back the tears, holding on to him like a lost child. "Yes, yes—tomorrow, Joe—we can get the papers. Don't ever go away from me, Joe. Oh, I'm afraid."

"Don't be, don't be."

"I can't help it. I'm afraid tomorrow—"

He put a finger to her lips. "Tomorrow we'll get a license. Then we'll be married. I've never wanted to stop before. But I do now, more than anything on earth. And I will."

The drive back into town was very quiet.

It was late when he returned to his room. He hated to return. If there were only something they could *do*, some place to go *now*, while he knew he could! But there was nothing to do until tomorrow, and he was cold with fear. He walked into the room and snapped on the lights.

His eyes fell on the blue canvas bag.

It was old and worn and very dusty. The dust from a thousand long roads of a thousand countries was ground into it, and it seemed to be alive, a living thing with a power of its own worn deep into its dusty folds. An ordinary old-fashioned bag, really; over the years he had grown to like it with a strange fondness. It was his home, his only real connection with the world through which he had been drifting like a ghost. A good strong friend, always there, carrying the few things he owned. He had walked miles, once, to get it back when it had been left behind.

And now he hated it.

Even as he looked at it, the drums were beating in his ears again—his own heartbeat? He didn't know. He stared at the bag, and ghosts began to wander through his mind. The miles had been long and dusty, but they had been free miles. He had been lonely, very lonely, but always, he had been free. And now. . . .

He took the bag up on his lap and opened it. Inside, there were odds and ends. An old pack of cigarettes and an ancient straight razor. A couple of unused bullets, a pair of stick-on rubber soles for his shoes, a shabby torn handkerchief. Like a strong wind the memories flowed through his mind, the call of the road, the long dark nights under the glistening star blanket. And now he would stop, throw away the bag, settle down in a house, get a job to go to every day. . . . Once stopped, he could never drift again.

The coldness grew deeper. Nervously he dropped the bag on the floor, kicked it across the room. It was nonsense to think that way. He hated the road and all the loneliness it had meant. He *wouldn't* go back, not with a girl like Jeannie to keep him from ever being lonely again.

The chill grew into fear. He sat down on the bed, trembling. He was afraid. He was fighting now, and a

voice was whispering in his ear, *You've got to go, Joe, you can't stop, never, never—run now, before you hurt her any more! You can never stop drifting, Joe.*

He gripped the bed until his fingers turned white. He searched his memory, trying to think back, trying to remember how it had started, so long ago. It was as though a great hand were pushing him, drawing him toward the canvas bag, urging him to pack it up, take it and race away, like the wind, onto the road again. But he didn't want to go, he wanted a wife, a home.

Home, Joe? You hated your home!

No, no, he thought. A line of sweat was standing out on his upper lip. I didn't hate it, I was young, I didn't understand, I didn't know.

You threw a curse on your home, Joe. Remember? You screamed it in your mother's face, you swore at her and packed your canvas bag.

I didn't know what I was doing, he thought. I was foolish. I couldn't have known.

But you said it, Joe. Remember what you said?

No!

I'll never come home if I live a thousand years.

He grabbed at the bag. His hand closed on the handle, and he felt it start tugging at him. He let out a cry, and threw it on the floor. Wildly he jerked the telephone from the hook, dialed Jeannie's number, and heard her sleepy voice.

"Jeannie, you've got to help me," he choked. "Come over, please, I can't help myself."

There had been other times he'd

tried. He remembered them, now, horrible struggles that had nearly killed him until he gave up. He had never believed in ghosts and witches and curses, but something was forcing him now, something within him so cold, so dark and powerful that he could never hope to fight it. He sat on the edge of the bed, grinding his teeth together, and the voice was crying louder and louder, *You can never stop, Joe, no matter what happens, you'll never have a home again, never, never, never.*

The room was empty when she arrived. She choked back a sob, closed the door behind her, and leaned against the wall. She was too late. The dresser drawers were ripped open; a dirty sock lay under the bed. He was gone, and so was the canvas bag.

Her eye fell on a folded white paper on the floor. She picked it up with trembling fingers, and saw what it was. With a little cry she put it into her pocket, and ran down the front stairs, her coat flying behind her.

The street was dark and empty. A light shone across the street, and another, up near the end of town, made a sad yellow patch in the darkness. She ran faster, her heels snapping on the dry sidewalk, until she turned into a lighted building at the end of the street.

A sleepy clerk looked up at her and blinked.

"Was—was a young man in here?"

The clerk nodded, frowning. "Bus to Chicago. Getting ready to leave."

She threw her money down, and snatched up the little white ticket. Seconds later she was outside, running toward a large bus with CHICAGO across the front. She stumbled up the steps, and then she saw him.

He was sitting near the back, eyes closed, face deathly white. In his arms he was holding his blue canvas bag, and

his whole body was trembling. Slowly she moved back, sank down in the seat beside him. "Oh, Joe, Joe—"

"Jeannie, I'm sorry, I just can't help it."

"I know, Joe."

He looked at her, his eyes widening. She shook her head, and took his heavy hand in hers. Then he saw the ticket.

"Jeannie—"

"Hush. Don't say it."

"But you don't know what you're doing! We can never have a home, darling, *never*. No matter how hard we try. Think of the long, homeless roads, Jeannie, all over the world, on and on, maybe even to the stars."

She smiled, nodding gently. "But at least you won't be lonely now."

"Jeannie, you *can't*."

"I can," she said, and rested her head quietly against his shoulder.

ALL THINGS CONSIDERED

1. When Joe asks his big question, Jeannie seems both pleased and (a) carefree. (b) totally surprised. (c) troubled.
2. To help Joe remember his past, Jeannie gives him (a) a calendar. (b) the names of places he might have visited. (c) a pencil and paper.
3. After learning about Joe's amazing background, Jeannie (a) still wants to marry him. (b) asks for time to think things over. (c) realizes Joe can become rich.
4. Near the end of the story, a courageous decision is made by (a) Joe. (b) Jeannie. (c) Pete Hower.
5. The canvas bag seems to stand for (a) Jeannie's hopes. (b) Joe's past. (c) the happiness of married life.

THINKING IT THROUGH

1. Joe kicks the canvas bag twice in the story. (a) What makes him do this? (b) Compare Joe's feelings with yours the last time you kicked something.
2. The story illustrates the old saying about people's words coming back to haunt them. (a) What did Joe say that put a curse on his life? (b) Describe a time when you spoke angry words that you later regretted.
3. In your opinion, what will be the future of the two characters in the story? Explain your thinking.

Literary Skills

Simile, Metaphor, or Both?

Like many good short-story writers, Alan E. Nourse uses effective *figures of speech* (see page 30). The ten items below, all of which come from "The Canvas Bag," contain similes, metaphors, or both. Find each figure of speech and write **S, M,** or **SM** (for both) on a separate sheet of paper.

1. Jeannie was laughing. "I must have dragged you out of the shower! You sound like you've been jumping over barriers."

2. A chill of disappointment stabbed through him.

3. She was slender and dark. . . . Like a queen, Joe thought, as she came down the steps, or at least a princess.

4. "Let me take you away from all this," said Joe, politely. "Let me take you on the wings of the wind."

5. It was as if he had suddenly looked over his shoulder and seen a huge pit opening up behind him.

6. The muddy fog cleared from his mind, and his memory fell back and back and his face went white.

7. They were dancing again, and she was fighting to hold back the tears, holding on to him like a lost child.

8. It was his home, his only real connection with the world through which he had been drifting like a ghost.

9. Like a strong wind the memories flowed through his mind . . . the long dark nights under the glistening star blanket.

10. It was as though a great hand were pushing him, drawing him toward the canvas bag, urging him to pack it up, take it and race away, like the wind. . . .

Composition

1. Write a paragraph describing either Jeannie or Joe—as you see the character in your "mind's eye." First reread the incomplete description on page 34 or 35. Then close the book and write the description in your own words. You will have to make up details that you imagine would be true of the character.

2. When Jeannie entered Joe's room, she saw "a folded white paper on the floor" (page 40). It was important enough to make her cry out, and she stuffed it in her pocket before dashing out. What do you think was on that piece of paper? Write it out, in 50 to 75 words.

▶ Time for a short poetry break. Try out your new literary skills on the two short poems that follow here and on the next page. If the meaning of one of the titles isn't familiar to you, look up the word—to experience the joy of discovery *twice*.

SNOW

by Dorothy Aldis

The fenceposts wear marshmallow hats
On a snowy day;
Bushes in their night gowns
Are kneeling down to pray—
And all the trees have silver skirts
And want to dance away.

UMBILICAL

by Eve Merriam

You can take away my mother,
you can take away my sister,
but don't take away
my little transistor.

5　I can do without sunshine,
I can do without Spring,
but I can't do without
my ear to that thing.

I can live without water,
10　in a hole in the ground,
but I can't live without
that sound that sound that sound that sOWnd.

WAYS OF KNOWING

1. Which of the two poems do you like better? Why?
2. In your opinion, what is the major difference between the two poems?
3. **Personification** (pur son uh fuh KAY shun) is figurative language in which nonhuman subjects are given human qualities. In a personification, flowers can *smile,* clouds can *frown,* and *Mother* Nature can try to outwit *Father* Time. (a) Which of the poems contains three examples of personification? (b) What things are personified, and what is said about them?
4. One line of "Snow" does not contain a metaphor. Which one?
5. Put your answers to the last two questions together: Can a personification also be called a metaphor?
6. "Umbilical" can be called an **extended metaphor** because the figurative comparison continues throughout the whole poem. (a) What two things are being compared? (b) In what ways are those two things alike? (This is a BIG question: Think about the whole comparison and look particularly at lines 1, 5–6, 9–10, and 12.)
7. In your opinion, why is the last word written as "sOWnd"?

44

VOCABULARY AND SKILL REVIEW

Before completing the exercises that follow, you may wish to review the **bold-faced** words on pages 3 to 44.

I. On a separate sheet of paper, write the *italicized* word that best fills the blank in each sentence.

romantic   *bog*   *bobolink*   *restrain*   *cliché*
critically   *dreary*   *chorister*   *depression*   *simile*

1. "Rain cats and dogs" is a _____.
2. I had nothing to do for the whole dull, _____ day.
3. A _____ is a little smaller than a robin.
4. Winning a lottery is the _____ hope of millions of people.
5. Milagros went to the mirror and examined her hair _____.
6. A _____ is usually introduced by *like* or *as*.
7. Granddad told us about the horrible _____ in the early 1930s.
8. Jack is a _____ at St. George's Church.
9. We followed the stream to the huge _____ where it begins.
10. "Oh, those cookies smell good! I can't _____ myself!"

II. Read the poem and answer the questions that follow.

CUMULUS CLOUDS

by Sheryl Nelms

    a gallon of
    rich
    country cream

    hand-whipped
5   into stiff
    peaks

    flung
    from the beater

    into dollops
10 across a blue oilcloth

45

1. (a) Can the whole poem properly be called an extended metaphor? (b) Explain what two things are being compared.

2. In the last line, why should the oilcloth be "blue"?

3. Even if you don't know the words, the poem should help you define "cumulus" and "dollop." What do they mean?

III. Two glittering names in American literature are **Ralph Waldo Emerson** (1803–1882) and **Henry David Thoreau** (1817–1862). Both were very serious authors. Both were also geniuses with figures of speech.

Look at the ten quotations below. Some are easy to interpret. Others may be hard. Your job is to explain what they really mean, in *literal* language. And just for fun, one of the quotations does not contain a figure of speech. Which one is it?

1. "Hitch your wagon to a star." (*Emerson*)

2. "We boil at different degrees." (*Emerson*)

3. "Men have become tools of their tools." (*Thoreau*)

4. "The cart before the horse is neither beautiful nor useful." (*Thoreau*)

5. "Life is too short to waste. . . . 'Twill soon be dark." (*Emerson*)

6. "No one is so poor that he need sit on a pumpkin." (*Thoreau*)

7. "In skating over thin ice our safety is our speed." (*Emerson*)

8. "Every man is the builder of a temple, called his body." (*Thoreau*)

9. "If you have built castles in the air, your work need not be lost; that is where they should be. Now put foundations under them." (*Thoreau*)

10. "I hate quotations. Tell me what you know." (*Emerson*)

Langston Hughes (1902–1967)

125th Street west of Lenox Avenue in Harlem, early 1930s

Who are you, Langston Hughes? What do you stand for? Let's let the poet himself tell us:

> I play it cool
> And dig all jive
> That's the reason
> I stay alive.
>
> My motto,
> As I live and learn,
>   is:
> *Dig And Be Dug*
> *In Return.*

The American people have "dug" the poetry of Langston Hughes for over 60 years. And for good reason. His language is direct and uncomplicated. He catches the rhythms of jazz and the soulful sounds of the blues. In his own words, he gives us the "music of a community."

Langston Hughes was born in Joplin, Missouri, in 1902. After high school he traveled, worked at odd jobs, and polished his writing in his spare time. His first book, *The Weary Blues*, came out in 1926. Soon after graduating from Lincoln University in 1929, he settled down in the Harlem section of New York City. In addition to poetry, Hughes wrote stories, novels, plays, articles for magazines and newspapers, and even an autobiography. During his life his name appeared on the covers of about 30 books.

The short poem above is entitled "Motto." What do the last two lines mean? How is that meaning related to Langston Hughes's life and career?

MOTHER TO SON

by Langston Hughes

Well, son, I'll tell you:
Life for me ain't been no crystal stair.
It's had tacks in it,
And splinters,
5 And boards torn up,
And places with no carpet on the floor—
Bare.
But all the time
I'se been a-climbin' on,
10 And reachin' landin's,
And turnin' corners,
And sometimes goin' in the dark
Where there ain't been no light.
So boy, don't you turn back.
15 Don't set you down on the steps
'Cause you finds it's kinder hard.
Don't you fall now—
For I'se still goin', honey,
I'se still climbin',
20 And life for me ain't been no crystal stair.

WAYS OF KNOWING

1. Everyone has heard the metaphor "the road of life," but the mother in the poem compares her life to something more original. What is the comparison?
2. In lines 15–17, the mother gives the son some good advice. What is this advice, in *literal* words of your own?
3. In your opinion, about how old are the two characters in the poem?
4. After the first line, the poem becomes a long series of metaphors. For what kind of events or periods in the mother's life might the following details stand? (a) "tacks" and "splinters"? (b) "landin's"? (c) "goin' in the dark"?

• crystal (KRIS tul) fine, expensive glass

48

from MONTAGE OF A DREAM DEFERRED

by Langston Hughes

Dream Boogie

Good morning, daddy!*
Ain't you heard
The boogie-woogie rumble
Of a dream deferred?

5 Listen closely:
You'll hear their feet
Beating out and beating out a—

You think
It's a happy beat?

10 Listen to it closely:
Ain't you heard
something underneath
like a—

What did I say?

15 Sure,
I'm happy!
Take it away!

Hey, pop!
Re-bop!
20 *Mop!*

Y-e-a-h!

- montage (mon TAHZH) picture made up of a number of separate pictures
- deferred (di FURD) put off

*Here "daddy" is slang for "friend" or "brother."

Warning

Daddy,
don't let your dog
curb you!

Request

Gimme $25.00
and the change.
I'm going
where the morning
and the evening
won't bother me.

Figurette

De-daddle-dy!
De-dop!

Argument

White is right,
Yellow mellow,
Black, get back!

Do you believe that, Jack?
5   Sure do!

Tell Me

Why should it be *my* loneliness,
Why should it be *my* song,
Why should it be *my* dream
   deferred
   overlong?

Then you're a dope
for which there ain't no hope.
Black is fine!
And, God knows,
10   *It's mine!*

Blues At Dawn

I don't dare start thinking in the morning.
I don't dare start thinking in the morning.
   If I thought thoughts in bed,
   Them thoughts would bust my head—
5   So I don't dare start thinking in the morning.

I don't dare remember in the morning.
Don't dare remember in the morning.
   If I recall the day before,
   I wouldn't get up no more—
10   So I don't dare remember in the morning.

Harlem

What happens to a dream deferred?

Does it dry up
like a raisin in the sun?
Or fester like a sore—
5 And then run?
Does it stink like rotten meat?
Or crust and sugar over—
like a syrupy sweet?
Maybe it just sags
10 like a heavy load.

Or does it explode?

Island

Between two rivers,
North of the park,*
Like darker rivers
The streets are dark.

5 Black and white,
Gold and brown—
Chocolate-custard
Pie of a town.

Dream within a dream
10 Our dream deferred.

Good morning, daddy!

Ain't you heard?

WAYS OF KNOWING

1. Why might Hughes have used the word "montage" in the title of a book of poems? Identify the "dream deferred." Whose dream is it, and why has it been deferred?

2. The profile of Hughes (page 47) states that he uses (a) "the rhythms of jazz" and (b) "the soulful sounds of the blues." Which poem would you choose as the best example of each?

3. In the first section, "Dream Boogie," the speaker stops mid-sentence after lines 7 and 13. In your opinion, what might the sentences have said if the speaker had continued?

4. The short section called "Warning" is a good example of figurative language. The poet surely means more than what the words seem to say. Exactly what he means, however, is not easy to say. What does the seven-word poem mean to you?

5. Note that the section "Harlem" is filled with figures of speech: Five similes suggest ideas that finally explode in a metaphor. (a) What does at least one of the similes suggest might happen if the dream is put off too long? (b) What does the very last word suggest might happen?

*New York City's Harlem is between the East and Hudson rivers and north of Central Park.

THE TELL-TALE HEART

by Edgar Allan Poe

▶ Who are you? What are you like? People answer those questions in different ways. Some people are much easier to get to know than others. The odd genius Edgar Allan Poe (1809–1849) was in some ways a stranger even to those who knew him best. Perhaps only he could have created the mad narrator in the story that follows. Take a few deep breaths before you read this one!

True!—nervous—very, very dreadfully nervous I have been and am. But why *will* you say that I am mad? The disease has sharpened my senses—not destroyed—not dulled them. Above all was my sense of hearing acute. I heard all things in the heaven and in the earth. I heard many things in hell. How, then, am I mad? Listen! and observe how clearly—how calmly I can tell you the whole story.

It is impossible to say how the idea first entered my brain. But once conceived, it haunted me day and night. There was no good reason. There was no real hatred. I loved the old man. He had never wronged me. He had never given me insult. For his gold I had no desire. I think it was his eye! Yes, it was this! One of his eyes resembled that of a vulture—a pale blue eye, with a film over it. Whenever it fell upon me, my blood ran cold. And so little by little—very gradually—I made up my mind to take the life of the old man, and thus rid myself of the eye forever.

Now this is the point. You think I am mad. Madmen know nothing. But you should have seen *me*. You should have seen how wisely I proceeded—with what caution—with what skill—with what secrecy I went to work! I was never kinder to the old man than during the whole week before I killed him. And every night, about midnight, I turned the latch of his door and opened it—oh, so gently! And then, when I had made an opening the size of my

---

- **acute** (uh KYOOT) sharp; sensitive
- **conceived** (kun SEEVD) thought of; imagined

head, I put in a dark lantern, all closed up, closed up so that no light shone out, and then I thrust in my head. Oh, you would have laughed to see how cunningly I did it! I moved my head slowly— very, very slowly, so that I might not disturb the old man's sleep. It took me an hour to move my head so far that I could see him as he lay upon his bed. Ha!—would a madman have been so wise as this? And then, when my head was well into the room, I undid the lantern cautiously. Oh, so cautiously—cautiously (for the hinges squeaked) I undid it just so much that a single thin ray of light fell upon the vulture eye.

This I did for seven long nights—every night just at midnight—but I found the eye always closed. And so it was impossible to do the deed. For it was not the old man who vexed me, but his Evil Eye. And every morning, when the day broke, I went boldly into the room, and spoke courageously to him. I called him by name in a cheerful tone, and asked how he had passed the night. So you see he would have been a very profound old man, indeed, to suspect that every night, just at twelve, I looked in upon him while he slept.

Upon the eighth night I was more than usually cautious in opening the door. A watch's minute hand moves more quickly than did mine. Never before that night had I really *felt* just how powerful I was—just how wise. I could hardly contain my feeling of triumph. To think that there I was, opening the door, little by little. And he not even dreaming of my secret purpose or thought! I nearly chuckled at the idea—and perhaps he heard me! For he moved on the bed suddenly, as if startled. Now you may think that I drew back—but no. His room was black as pitch with the thick darkness (the shutters were fastened tight, for fear of robbers). So I knew that he could not see the opening of the door, and I kept pushing it on steadily, steadily.

I had my head in, and was about to open the lantern. All at once my thumb slipped on the tin, and the old man sprang up in the bed, crying out— "Who's there?"

I kept quite still and said nothing. For a whole hour I did not move a muscle. And in the meantime I did not hear him lie down. He was still sitting up in the bed listening—just as I have done, night after night, listening—waiting—for Death.

- **cunningly** (KUN ing lee) slyly
- vex (VEKS) bother; annoy
- profound (proh FOUND) wise; deep

Then I heard a little groan, and I knew it was the groan of mortal terror. It was not a groan of pain or of grief—oh, no! It was the low stifled sound that comes from the bottom of the soul when overfilled with fear. I knew the sound well. Many a night, just at midnight, when all the world slept, it was sprung up from the bottom of my own soul, deepening, with its dreadful echo, the terrors that held me. I say I knew it well. I knew what the old man felt, and pitied him—although I chuckled at heart. I knew that he had been lying awake ever since the first slight noise, when he had turned in the bed. His fears had ever since been growing on him. He had been trying to ignore them, but could not. He had been saying to himself— "It is nothing but the wind in the chimney," or "It is only a mouse crossing the floor." Yes, he had been trying to comfort himself with these lies. But he had found all in vain. *All in vain.* For Death, in approaching him, had walked with his black shadow before him, and surrounded the old man. And it was that unseen shadow that made him feel, yes *feel*, the presence of my head within the room.

By then I had waited a long time, very patiently, without hearing him lie down. I decided to open a little, a very, very little crack in the lantern. So I opened it—you cannot imagine how slowly, slowly. Suddenly a single dim ray, like the thread of a spider, shot out from the crack and fell upon the vulture eye.

It was open—wide, wide open. I grew furious as I gazed upon

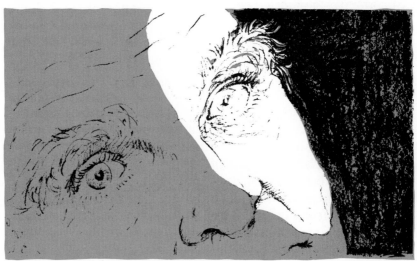

- mortal (MOR tul) deathly; causing death
- stifled (STY fuld) muffled; smothered
- **vain** (VAYN) without success; useless

it. I saw it clearly, so clearly—all a dull blue, with a hideous film over it. A hideous film that chilled me to the very bones. But I could see nothing else of the old man's face or body; for I had pointed the ray as if by instinct, exactly upon the damned spot.

And now—have I not told you about my most acute senses? Now, I say, there came to my ears a low, dull, quick sound. It was a sound such as a watch makes when enveloped in cotton. I knew *that* sound well too. It was the beating of the old man's heart. It increased my anger, as the beating of a drum increases a soldier's courage.

But even yet I held back. I kept still. I hardly breathed. I held the lantern motionless. I tried to see how steadily I could keep the ray upon the eye. Meantime the hellish drumbeat of the heart increased. It grew quicker and quicker, and louder and louder every instant. The old man's terror *must* have been great! It grew louder, I say, louder every moment! —do you hear me well? I have told you that I am nervous. So I am. And now at the dead hour of the night, in the dreadful silence of that old house, so strange a noise as this excited me to uncontrollable terror. Yet, for some minutes longer I held back and stood still. But the beating grew louder, louder! I thought the heart must burst. And now a new anxiety seized me—the sound would be heard by a neighbor! The old man's hour had come! With a loud yell, I threw open the lantern. I leaped toward him. He shrieked once—once only. In an instant I dragged him to the floor, and pulled the heavy mattress over him. I then smiled, to find the deed so far done. But for many minutes, the heart beat on with a stifled sound. This, however, did not worry me. It would not be heard through the wall. At length it stopped. The old man was dead. I removed the mattress and examined the corpse. Yes, he was stone, stone dead. I placed my hand upon the heart and held it there many minutes. There was no pulse. He was stone dead. His eye would trouble me no more.

If you still think me mad, you will think so no longer when I describe the wise steps I took to hide the body. The night went on, and I worked quickly, but in silence. First of all I cut up the corpse. I took off the head and the arms and the legs.

I then took up three wide boards from the floor of the room,

- **hideous** (HID ee us) very ugly or frightening
- **enveloped** (en VEL upt) wrapped up
- **anxiety** (ang ZY i tee) worry

and put all underneath. I then put the boards back so cleverly, so skillfully, that no human eye—not even *his*—could have noticed anything wrong. There was nothing to wash out—no stain of any kind, no blood-spot whatever. I had been too careful for that. A tub had caught all—ha! ha!

When I had made an end of these labors, it was four o'clock—still dark as midnight. As the bell sounded the hour, there came a knocking at the street door. I went to open it with a light heart—for what had I *now* to fear? There entered three men, who introduced themselves, with perfect courtesy, as officers of the police. A shriek, they said, had been heard by a neighbor during the night. The neighbor had been suspicious. The information had been brought to the police office. And now they (the officers) had been sent to search the house.

I smiled—for *what* had I to fear? I made the gentlemen welcome. The shriek, I said, was my own in a dream. The old man, I added, was absent in the country. I took my visitors all over the house. I told them to search—search *well*. I led them, finally, to *his* bedroom. I showed them his treasures, safe, undisturbed. In the excitement of my confidence, I brought chairs into the room. I asked them *here* to rest from their work, while I myself, in the wild audacity of my perfect triumph, placed my own chair upon the very spot that lay over the corpse of the victim.

The officers were satisfied. My *manner* had convinced them. I was strangely at ease. They sat there, and after I answered their questions happily, they talked about familiar things. But, before long, I felt myself growing pale. I wished them gone. My head ached, and I imagined a ringing in my ears; but still they sat, and still they chatted. The ringing became more distinct—it continued and became ever more distinct. I talked more freely to get rid of the feeling; but the ringing went on, ever louder—until, at length, I found that the noise was *not* within my own ears.

No doubt I now grew *very* pale. But I talked more fluently, and with a louder voice. Yet the sound increased—and what could I do? It was *a low, dull, quick sound—a sound such as a watch makes when enveloped in cotton.* I gasped for breath—and yet the officers heard it not. I talked more quickly—more excitedly. But the noise steadily increased. I stood up and argued about trifles, in a high voice and with wild movements. But the noise

---

- • audacity (aw DAS i tee) boldness; daring
- • **fluently** (FLOO unt lee) easily (of talking)
- • **trifle** (TRY ful) unimportant thing

steadily increased. Why *would* they not be gone? I paced the floor with heavy steps—but the noise steadily increased. Oh what *could* I do? I shouted—I swore! I took the chair upon which I had been sitting and pushed it loudly upon the boards, but the noise rose up over all and continued to increase. It grew louder—and louder—*louder!* And still the men chatted pleasantly, and smiled. Was it possible they heard it not? No, no! They heard! —they suspected—they *knew!* They were making a mockery of my horror! —this I thought, and this I think. But anything was better than this agony! Anything was better than this mockery! I could bear those hypocritical smiles no longer! I felt that I must scream or die! —and now—again! —listen! —louder! louder! *louder!*—

"Villains!" I shrieked. "Pretend no more. I admit the crime! Tear up the boards! —here, here! —it is the beating of his hideous heart!"

- **mockery** (MOK uh ree) person or thing made fun of
- hypocritical (hip uh KRIT i cul) false; not sincere

ALL THINGS CONSIDERED ───────────────

1. The very first paragraph of "The Tell-Tale Heart" indicates that the **narrator** (person who tells the story) is (a) of sound mind. (b) probably insane. (c) Edgar Allan Poe himself.
2. The narrator says that he killed the old man because of (a) his gold. (b) strange voices ordering him to do so. (c) his eye.
3. The narrator first hears the beating of the heart (a) before the crime. (b) during the killing. (c) after the crime.
4. According to the narrator, he confesses because (a) the officers frighten him with endless questions. (b) he is ashamed of his actions. (c) he hears the heart beating.
5. An interesting and unusual aspect of the story is that (a) the reader knows more about the narrator than he knows about himself. (b) horror is presented as humor. (c) Poe suggests indirectly that the narrator may be a woman.

THINKING IT THROUGH ───────────────

1. The narrator reveals himself not only in *what* he says but also in *the way* he says it, or the writing style. What is one aspect of the writing style that contributes to this effect?
2. During the scene with the officers, the narrator states that the ringing "was *not* within my own ears" (page 56). (a) What does he mean? (b) Is he correct?
3. As the narrator gets more and more excited toward the end of the story, the officers continue to talk calmly and smile. In your opinion, what are they trying to do?
4. What is the real reason for the narrator's confession? Explain as completely as possible in your own words.

Reading and Analyzing

Imagery

"The Tell-Tale Heart" has been a popular story for over a hundred years. One reason, certainly, is Edgar Allan Poe's skillful use of **imagery** (IM ij ree).

In literature, an **image** (IM ij) is something that appeals to one of the five senses. A **visual image** makes the reader form a mental picture of what is described. Other images appeal to the senses of hearing, smell, taste, and touch. At times just the suggestion of an image can have a powerful effect on some readers (like the fiendish narrator's "A tub had caught all—ha! ha!").

1. In "The Tell-Tale Heart," the old man's eye is an important visual image. Poe shows us the eye in such a way that few readers can forget it. Turn back to pages 52 and 55. What are some of the words Poe uses to effectively create the image?

2. Turn back to the first description of the old man's heartbeat (page 55). How does Poe force the reader to hear it almost "for real"?

3. Two images were considered in questions 1 and 2, above. One was something seen, the other something heard. What is another visual image in the story? What is another image that appeals to the ear?

4. Some people would rather read a good story than see the same story on TV. What does this suggest about these readers' powers of imagery?

Composition

1. Write five sentences that combine imagery with effective figurative language. Use this order: (1) sight, (2) hearing, (3) smell, (4) taste, (5) touch, or feeling. You may want to use the word *like* or *as* in forming your comparison. Example: *My tired legs felt like two frayed pieces of old clothesline.*

2. Imagery is essential to good description. Write a description of the busiest street in your town or city as you might experience it on the hottest day of the summer. Start by writing these words about two inches apart down the left margin of a sheet of paper: *sight, hearing, smell, taste, touch (feeling).* Then scribble away, writing down all the sharp sense impressions you can recall or imagine. (*Taste* will probably be the hardest one; you may have to settle for the taste of sweat from your upper lip.) When you have at least 20 images on your paper, put the best of them into an effective paragraph that will make your reader really *experience* the scene.

▶ Edgar Allan Poe was not only a gifted short-story writer; he was also a poet. "Annabel Lee" is an excellent example of his theories of poetry.

First, Poe believed that the sound of the words—"music," he called it—was the most important aspect of a poem. (Remember this when you read lines like number 32 below.) As for the subject matter, Poe asked himself what subjects interest people the most. Death, he believed, was one such subject. The other, for Poe, was beauty. The best subject matter, therefore, was obvious: the death . . . of a beautiful woman.

Not many people—in Poe's time or today—would agree that sound is more important than meaning, or that the death of a beautiful woman is the most fascinating of all possible subjects. Still, it is interesting to see what Poe did with his theories.

ANNABEL LEE

by Edgar Allan Poe

It was many and many a year ago,
    In a kingdom by the sea,
That a maiden there lived whom you may know
    By the name of Annabel Lee;
5 And this maiden she lived with no other thought
    Than to love and be loved by me.

She was a child and *I* was a child,
    In this kingdom by the sea,
But we loved with a love that was more than love—
10   I and my Annabel Lee—
With a love that the wingèd seraphs of Heaven
    Coveted her and me.

And this was the reason that, long ago,
    In this kingdom by the sea,
15 A wind blew out of a cloud, chilling
    My beautiful Annabel Lee;

- seraph (SER uf) kind of heavenly being; winged angel
- covet (KUV it) desire what belongs to another

So that her highborn kinsmen came
   And bore her away from me,
To shut her up in a sepulcher
20   In this kingdom by the sea.

The angels, not half so happy in Heaven,
   Went envying her and me:
Yes! that was the reason (as all men know,
   In this kingdom by the sea)
25 That the wind came out of the cloud by night,
   Chilling and killing my Annabel Lee.

But our love it was stronger by far than the love
   Of those who were older than we—
   Of many far wiser than we—
30 And neither the angels in Heaven above
   Nor the demons down under the sea,
Can ever dissever my soul from the soul
   Of the beautiful Annabel Lee:

For the moon never beams, without bringing me dreams
35   Of the beautiful Annabel Lee;
And the stars never rise, but I feel the bright eyes
   Of the beautiful Annabel Lee:

And so, all the night-tide, I lie down by the side
Of my darling—my darling—my life and my bride,
40   In her sepulcher there by the sea—
   In her tomb by the sounding sea.

- **highborn** (HY born) of noble birth
- sepulcher (SEP ul kur) tomb; burial place
- dissever (di SEV ur) separate
- night-tide (NYT tyd) nighttime

WAYS OF KNOWING ─────────────────────────────

1. In what two ways does "Annabel Lee" illustrate Poe's ideas about poetry?

2. (a) How might a doctor have explained Annabel Lee's death? (b) According to the speaker, what was the real reason for her death?

3. How do you think Poe would have explained the meaning of the poem? Use the terms *soul mates* and *death* in your answer.

4. The ending of line 3 must be figurative language because you, the reader, would not really "know" Annabel Lee. What do you think Poe really means by "whom you may know"?

5. Do Poe's "angels" seem to behave like angels? Explain.

6. Except for the terms "bright eyes" and "beautiful," the reader is given no description of Annabel Lee. Yet readers with good powers of imagery often make up their own visual images. Try to really see Annabel Lee in your "mind's eye." What does she look like? For instance, what color are her hair and eyes, and is she frail or strong looking?

7. Most rhymes in poetry are **end rhymes.** That is, words at the ends of lines rhyme with each other. At the beginning of the poem, for instance, "ago" (line 1) rhymes with "know" (line 3), and "sea" (line 2) rhymes with both "Lee" (line 4) and "me" (line 6). But some poets also use **internal rhymes,** or words that rhyme within single lines. In line 32, for instance, "ever" rhymes with "dissever." How many of these within-the-line rhymes can you find in the last section of the poem (lines 34–41)?

EDGAR ALLAN POE

by Robert R. Potter

> ▶ **Biography** (the story of a person's life) is one of the most important and interesting forms of literature. Here's a **nonfiction** (not made up) selection about Edgar Allan Poe, the creator of "The Tell-Tale Heart" and many other works of imaginative **fiction**.

"Truth," someone once said, "is stranger than fiction." Edgar Allan Poe himself might have made that statement. His fiction is probably the strangest ever written by an American author. Yet the facts of his luckless life seem even stranger. As he tells us in the autobiographical poem "Alone":

From childhood's hour I have not been
As others were—I have not seen
As others saw . . . I could not awaken
My heart to joy at the same tone—
And all I loved—*I* loved alone.

Alone is a good word to apply to Edgar Poe, for he was left alone at an early age. He was born in Boston on January 19, 1809, the son of David and Elizabeth Arnold Poe, both actors. When he was a baby, his father walked out on the family. Soon after that, the talented Elizabeth Arnold Poe moved with her three children to Richmond,

Virginia. Then, when Poe was two, his mother died. The children were left in indescribable poverty.

But suddenly the incredible happened. It was as if Elizabeth Poe's deathbed wish had been answered. Into the house of death walked Mrs. John Allan, the wife of a wealthy tobacco dealer. She took a liking to young Edgar. Having no children of her own, she decided to raise him as her son. At first her husband disliked the idea and foretold the worst. He knew that Edgar's parents had been actors, and actors in those days were not considered "proper" people. But finally, to prevent marital discord, he went along with his wife's wishes. The child was renamed Edgar Allan Poe, and went overnight from the poorest of rooms to one of the finest houses in Richmond.

Although the Allans did not legally adopt the child, there was nothing illegal or improper about the arrangement. In pre-Civil War America, homeless children were often just "taken-in"

- **imaginative** (i MAJ uh nuh tiv) made up; fanciful
- **marital** (MAR i tul) of a marriage
- **discord** (DIS kord) disagreement

by foster parents. And at first things went well. The child was subnormal in size, but not in ability. He learned easily; he loved fun. In 1815 the Allans went to England on business, and for five years Edgar went to a strict private school there. After their return to America, young Edgar's future seemed to have only one drawback—his foster father.

John Allan had never really accepted Edgar Poe as his son. He thought that Edgar was not thankful enough for all that had happened. He thought that Edgar was too wild, too headstrong. He complained because Edgar was constantly asking for money. And Edgar, in turn, complained because his father was such a tightwad. How could he, Edgar, lead the life of a young Virginia gentleman without enough money to keep up with his friends?

The relationship reached a breakdown in 1826, when Edgar went off to the University of Virginia. Like most of his classmates, he went to college to have fun, as well as to study. He drank too much—a habit that was long to trouble him. To get the spending money his father refused him, he tried his luck at cards. Soon he was over his head in debt. He kept on gambling, trying desperately just to get even. But his debts grew and grew. When other students complained to the University, he was forced to ask John Allan for the money. The answer was a clear NO, and Edgar's college days were over.

The break now seemed complete. Edgar considered himself an outcast. He decided to leave the Allan family for good. To support himself, he enlisted in the U.S. Army, using the name Edgar A. Perry. He quickly rose to sergeant. His fortunes were now improving, and he saw even greater chances ahead. Learning that Mrs. Allan had died, he realized that he might be named as John Allan's heir. He came to terms with his foster father, and soon won admission to West Point, the academy for army officers in New York State.

But luck never stayed with Poe for long. After three months at West Point, he received the sad news that John Allan had remarried. This meant that he would probably not become Allan's heir. And without a fortune of his own, Poe saw little future as a poorly paid Army officer. No one, however, could simply drop out of West Point. He knew that the only way was to be expelled. He stopped studying. He disobeyed orders on purpose. (There is the story that Poe once obeyed an order too literally. He read on a bulletin board that too many irregular belts were being worn for daily inspection. From then on, the order read, only one certain kind of belt was to be worn. Poe did just that: He turned out for inspection wearing *only* the belt!)

Poe's poor behavior finally got him what he wanted. He was expelled from West Point in March, 1831. His goals in life now seemed farther off than ever.

- **outcast** (OUT kast) person cast or thrown out
- **literally** (LIT ur ul ee) going by the exact words

He had tried to achieve the lifestyle of a Virginia gentleman—tried and failed. He had tried to find a place for himself in the real world—tried and failed. Now he seems to have drifted off into a dreamland of his own making. For a time he lived somewhere in New York City, where he published a small book called simply *Poems*. Then he went on to Baltimore, Maryland. We know little about his life during this period. From the outside, it must have appeared poor and lonely. We can only guess what was happening in the writer's imagination.

In Baltimore, Poe was taken in by a widowed aunt, Mrs. Maria Clemm. The sister of Edgar's father David Poe, she was a poor woman who earned her living as best she could—sewing, taking in roomers, and working here and there. But she gave Poe just what he needed—a touch of kindness, a place to come home to, and meals on the table. Moreover, she looked on him with admiration, if not adoration. It didn't really matter to her if the young man held a regular job or not. Poe had found his guardian angel.

No, *two* guardian angels! With Mrs. Clemm lived her daughter, a strange, simple-minded girl named Virginia. She, too, loved the would-be writer. She waited on him hand and foot. She called him "Eddie"; he called her "Sis" or "Sissy." They were married when Virginia was 13, but continued to live with Mrs. Clemm. Daily life in the house went on much as usual. The three people needed each other. Virginia, whose large soulful eyes and high forehead disguised a childlike mind, needed love and protection. Mrs. Clemm needed someone to love and care for, especially a young relative who happened to be a genius. And Poe, who was completely irresponsible when it came to money and other practical matters, needed someone to look after him.

Poe sold his first story in 1832. Soon he was turning out a steady stream of hair-raisers. Like "The Tell-Tale Heart," nearly all of the stories were set in an unnamed corner of the writer's dreamland. He wrote of castles, of riches, of monstrous passions, of overpowering loves. His rich imagination provided what his poor life denied him. He had no interest in stories about realistic people with real problems, like earning a living.

Yet in real life, earning a living did remain a problem. Poe was poorly paid for his stories, and he received almost nothing for his poems. For most of his life he worked as a magazine editor. He was an excellent editor. Two of the magazines he edited doubled their number of readers, and then doubled the number again. But Poe never held a job for more than a few years. His enemy was the bottle.

People who knew him well said that there were really two Edgar Allan Poes—the sober one and the drunk one. When sober, Poe charmed everybody. He had long, curly black hair, a very wide, high forehead, and large, sad-looking eyes that lit up when he spoke.

- **adoration** (ad uh RAY shun) deep love; worship
- **hair-raiser**—anything "hair-raising": terrifying or thrilling

His quick mind and clear diction could hold a whole auditorium spellbound. He was an unusually versatile man, not only a gifted writer but also a fair artist and a good athlete. But when drunk he was a different person. He turned against his friends. He lied. He seemed out to get everybody. The odd thing is that Poe was not a regular drinker, nor did he drink very much. He would often go for months without a drop. Then a single glass would make him quite drunk.

But through everything, Poe, "Sissy," and Mrs. Clemm stuck together. They went from city to city, always finding the new job suddenly lost and the wolf at the door. Troubles piled on troubles. Virginia, never in good health, seemed to be drifting slowly toward death. Doctors cost money—money which Poe didn't have. A popular poem called "The Raven," published in January, 1845, brought Poe great fame—but almost no money. A few months later he wrote a friend:

For the last three or four months I have been working 14 or 15 hours a day—and yet, Thomas, I have made no money. I am as poor now as ever I was in my life—except in hope, which is by no means bankable.

Poe's life continued its downhill journey. In 1846 the family moved to Fordham, then a small community 15 miles from New York City. Neighbors brought potatoes to keep them from starving. Friends raised money to keep Virginia alive. But the approach of winter found her lying dully on a bed in a cold room, covered only by her husband's overcoat.

Virginia died on January 30, 1847.

Edgar Allan Poe was to live for two more years. Perhaps it's not surprising that the end of such a life should again be "stranger than fiction." On June 30, 1849, Poe left New York for a trip to the South. Mrs. Clemm received few letters—and the sad news she did get was hard to fathom. Was her nephew losing his mind? Poe wrote that people were trying to kill him. He wrote that he'd been put in prison for forging a check. He wrote that he'd been very, very ill. From Richmond he wrote, "If possible, oh COME! My clothes are so horrible and I am so ill. . . . Oh do not fail. God forever bless you."

On October 3, 1849, a man was noticed lying on the floor of a tavern in Baltimore. He knew his name: Edgar A. Poe. But he seemed to know little else. Taken to a hospital, he couldn't explain where he was or who he'd been with. He had the shakes. He talked wildly to people he imagined to be in the room. At times the nurses couldn't hold him down in bed. He spoke of a wife in Richmond, and of a friend named "Reynolds" that he demanded to see.

Four days later the hellish drumbeat of the heart grew still. Edgar Allan Poe was dead.

- **diction** (DIK shun) manner of speaking
- **versatile** (VUR suh til) able to do many things well
- **bankable** (BANG kuh bul) capable of being put in a bank
- **fathom** (FATH um) understand; get to the bottom of

Yet Poe's strange story isn't quite over. He had sent a new poem, "Annabel Lee," to the New York *Herald.* It appeared two days after his death. The lines written with "Sissy" in mind now seemed to fit him, too:

And so, all the night-tide, I lie down by the side
Of my darling—my darling—my life and my bride,
In her sepulcher there by the sea—
In her tomb by the sounding sea.

ALL THINGS CONSIDERED

1. The first piece of bad luck in Poe's life was (a) his father's abandoning the family. (b) his mother's death. (c) an unhappy experience in private school.
2. Poe was forced to leave the University of Virginia because of (a) poor marks. (b) fighting. (c) gambling debts.
3. Poe was forced to leave West Point because he (a) couldn't pay his gambling debts. (b) deliberately behaved in a manner that would get him expelled. (c) drank too much.
4. Poe, "Sissy," and Mrs. Clemm (a) all helped write Poe's stories. (b) all helped support the family. (c) needed each other and stuck together for years.
5. The adjectives that best fit Poe are (a) *gifted* and *practical.* (b) *devoted* and *dependable.* (c) *talented* and *unstable.*

THINKING IT THROUGH

1. Think about the trouble between Poe and his foster father from John Allan's point of view. Considering what you know about Poe's character, do you blame John Allan for refusing to pay gambling debts or name Poe as an heir? Explain.
2. Poe's marriage was certainly an unusual one. Give at least three reasons.
3. Fiction is sometimes said to be a "form of escape." In what way did Poe's fiction provide a form of escape not only for his readers but also for the author himself?
4. Poe's life contained two periods of mystery. (a) What were they? (b) What might have happened in each case?
5. At the top of this page, you read that the ending of Poe's "Annabel Lee" "now seemed to fit him, too." Why?

Relationships

Two Methods of Organization

Written words aren't just scattered around on an author's paper in any old way, like raindrops on a flat roof. Instead, writers try to follow certain *patterns of thought* that their readers will recognize. Each of these patterns is like an invisible mold into which the writer pours whatever the subject matter happens to be.

The most common pattern of thought is probably the best-known one as well: a **main idea** followed by **supporting details** that serve as examples or reasons. Think about the organization of the selection you have just read. The main idea is presented in the first paragraph: that Poe's life was an extremely strange one. The rest of the selection, then, consists of examples of this strange life, as well as reasons that it turned out as it did.

Notice, however, that the examples and reasons also appear in ordered form. The second paragraph starts with Poe's birth; the last paragraph leaves him in his imaginary grave. In other words, the details are given in their normal sequence of time, or in **chronological** order.

Since paragraphs are smaller than complete selections, they tend to be organized in either the *main idea/details* pattern or the *details in sequence* pattern. Examine the four paragraphs from "Edgar Allan Poe" that start as shown below. Two start with a main idea that the rest of the paragraph supports. The other two simply list details in sequence. First, tell which method of organization each paragraph follows. Then either make a small informal outline (for the main-idea paragraphs) or list the details in sequence.

1. John Allan had never . . . (page 64)
2. Poe's poor behavior finally . . . (page 64)
3. People who knew him . . . (page 65)
4. On October 3, 1849 . . . (page 66)

Composition

1. With the book closed, write a paragraph starting with this main idea: *Edgar Allan Poe's life was a very strange one.* Add at least five details.

2. A newspaper story written on the occasion of a person's death is called an *obituary*. Use the most important facts from Poe's life to write an obituary (dateline: Baltimore, Oct. 7). Use obituaries from your local paper as models.

VOCABULARY AND SKILL REVIEW ―――――――――

Before completing the exercises that follow, you may wish to review the **bold-faced** words on pages 52 to 68.

I. On a separate sheet of paper, write the term in each line that means the same, or nearly the same, as the word in *italics*.

1. *acute:* shrinking, sensitive, silly, sober
2. *cunningly:* lazily, happily, slowly, slyly
3. *vain:* blood vessel, growing, useless, stomp on
4. *enveloped:* written, decided, forgotten, wrapped up
5. *anxiety:* worry, skill, legal trouble, legal skill
6. *highborn:* excitable, noble, intelligent, gracious
7. *marital:* musical, kind of herb, of war, of marriage
8. *adoration:* decoration, blame, worship, adjustment
9. *hair-raiser:* thriller, small wedge, questionable statement, soaking
10. *diction:* feeling, smell, sight, speech

II. 1. A *versatile* person is (a) usually disliked. (b) too excitable. (c) good at many things.
2. To read *literally* is to (a) skim or scan. (b) search for meaning between the lines. (c) understand only what the words usually mean.
3. A *hideous visual image* is (a) an ugly mental picture. (b) a logical explanation. (c) something experienced only by poets.
4. The *bankable* part of a worker's pay would probably be (a) spent for food. (b) saved. (c) given to charity.
5. To feel like an *outcast* is to feel (a) proud. (b) rejected. (c) fearful.
6. *Imaginative* literature is (a) best read literally. (b) expressed in pictures. (c) full of originality.
7. If others make a *mockery* of your efforts, you would probably feel (a) somewhat proud. (b) little or nothing. (c) discouraged.
8. TALK is to *FLUENTLY* as (a) LISTEN is to ACUTELY. (b) TASTE is to UNWILLINGLY. (c) ACT is to AWKWARDLY.
9. *TRIFLE* is to UNIMPORTANT as (a) FACT is to MEMORY. (b) GIANT is to HUGE. (c) SHAPE is to USEFUL.
10. TIME is to *CHRONOLOGICAL* as (a) PLACE is to OBSERVER. (b) IDEA is to PHYSICAL. (c) SPACE is to GEOGRAPHICAL.

III. Read the three poems carefully and answer the questions that follow.

NOVEMBER NIGHT

by Adelaide Crapsey

Listen . . .
With faint dry sound,
Like steps of passing ghosts,
The leaves, frost-crisped, break from the trees
And fall.

TRIAD

by Adelaide Crapsey

These be
Three silent things:
The falling snow . . . the hour
Before the dawn . . . the mouth of one
Just dead.

FOG

by Carl Sandburg

The fog comes
on little cat feet.

It sits looking
over harbor and city
on silent haunches
and then moves on.

1. Which poem of the three appeals first of all to the reader's sense of hearing?
2. To which other sense do the other two poems most appeal?
3. One of these poems is like a little outline. Which poem starts with a main heading and then goes on to list three examples?
4. Which poem most clearly uses chronological order, or details in sequence, as its organizational pattern?
5. These three poems have a record of being liked by most students. Which poem do you like best? Why? Be as specific as possible by using at least one example from that poem.

70

UNIT REVIEW

I. Match the terms in Column A with their definitions in Column B.

A

1. simile
2. metaphor
3. personification
4. imagery
5. literal language

B

a) language that appeals to the five senses

b) language that means exactly what it says

c) a figurative comparison made with a special word, usually *like* or *as*

d) a figurative comparison made directly by substituting one term for another

e) giving human qualities to non-human subjects

II. *Who are you?* Answer that question for each item below with the name of an author, a character, or someone else. Then add more facts about each person in a complete sentence of your own.

1. In my later years, I dressed in white and seldom went out into society.
2. Weird visions of my past life made me try to desert my girlfriend Jeannie.
3. I believed that the death of a beautiful woman was the most interesting of all possible subjects.
4. I learned my lesson from a fancy bow ribbon that wasn't even there!
5. I was hugely successful in using the sounds of jazz and blues to create a new kind of poetry for the twentieth century.
6. I had beautiful bright eyes and a boyfriend who loved me more than life itself.
7. I was scared out of my wits by what I thought was the ghost of a Hessian soldier.
8. I never liked my adopted son much; about all I ever gave him was his middle name.
9. I became known as America's first great writer, and I had fun doing it.
10. I married Eddie at 13 but we continued to live with Mom.

71

SPEAKING UP

Each unit in this book is followed by an exercise that will improve your ability to speak before a group. Some students, of course, love to speak—as much as others dread the very thought. But don't shake yourself silly quite yet. You won't be bothered by butterflies if you slide into speaking in an easy way.

First of all, forget about *what* you might say—or might not say—or might completely mess up saying. Don't think about *language* at all. Instead, concentrate on "body language." Your posture, attitude, and movements can tell your audience as much as words can. Remember Genevieve Smith in "The Eye Catcher"? She managed to tell Bert Howland she was a completely new person—without ever saying a word.

Right now you are asked to focus on this "silent speech," or pantomime. To **pantomime** (PAN tuh mym) is to act out silently. Begin by practicing one of the following pantomimes until it is so perfect that anyone who has read this unit can tell instantly what it is:

1. The narrator of "The Tell-Tale Heart" from the time he opens the door till he sees the old man's eye. (Go back and reread pages 53 to 54.)

2. Either Joe Baker or Jeannie as she gets on the bus, sees him, sits down, and lets some time pass before starting to speak (pages 40 to 41).

3. The hardest: Genevieve Smith as she sits down at the counter and halfway eyes Bert Howland (pages 6 to 7).

Next, present your pantomime to the group and compare it with others. Think particularly about facial expressions. Where were you the most successful? The least successful? What did you learn?

Finally, select another short scene from the unit and work up a pantomime. When you present it to the group, their job will *not* be simply to shout out the name of the character. That should be obvious. Instead, the group's responsibility will be first to praise what you did well and then to add a few suggestions for improvement. (You are free to do a scene with a partner if both of you want to.)

WRITING TO "SELL THE SIZZLE"

One of America's best wordsmiths was not a literary figure at all. His name was Elmer Wheeler. He was a top sales representative, and later a top trainer of salespersons. His most famous piece of advice was "Don't sell the steak—sell the sizzle."

Wheeler might have said, "Don't limit yourself to the dull facts—use imagery and figurative language to excite the imagination and make people say *yes*." Clearly, "sizzle" is both a zippy metaphor for "steak" and an image that grabs at least two of the five senses.

The more you strive for "sizzle" in your own writing, the more your readers will want to say *yes* to it. Except when literal language is required, as in an accident report, it's the sizzle that sells.

Prewriting: Think about how figures of speech and images add spice to or completely replace worn-out adjectives (words that describe). Consider, for instance, the common adjective *sad*. You might go on to complete a simile: *sad as a flat tire*. Or, if you wanted a metaphor, *a deflated face* would carry the idea and the image.

Writing: Write a short description of someone you know. (You will probably want to change the person's name.) Include, if you can, the way that person behaves or performs certain jobs. Every time you find yourself writing a literal, common description, try to substitute figures of speech and images. The opportunities are endless. Write *tea-kettle comforts*, not *homey comforts;* write *a frisky mind*, not *a good imagination*. Try to avoid the easy clichés (see page 10) that first come to mind. *Clean as a whistle* (whatever that means) might give way to *clean as a polished halo*.

Revising: Read your paragraph to others or let some time pass and reread it yourself. Some of your figurative language will seem original and fitting. But other expressions may sound forced or false. Drop or replace these before copying your final draft to hand in. Turn in both drafts, like the "before" and "after" pictures in a weight-loss ad.

U N I T · 2

FOR PEOPLE
ONLY

there are things sadder
than you and I. some people
do not even touch.
—"Haiku" by Sonia Sanchez

These lines were written by a popular modern poet. Read them again, thoughtfully. What do they mean to you? Why is it that "some people/do not even touch"? Why do most of us learn instead to build harmonious relationships?

The literature in this unit, like most good literature, will make you think about the way people behave. In the selections that follow, you will encounter all kinds of human behavior, including heroes who turn out to be only human and social outcasts who turn out to be heroes. You will meet characters who face life bravely and others who watch opportunities pass them by. Here— and whenever you are asked to look carefully at human nature— you will find reading helps you get a closer view.

APPOINTMENT IN BAGHDAD

traditional version

▶ "Appointment in Baghdad"* is one of the shortest stories ever told. Over the years, different authors have written many different versions. This one follows the version by Edith Wharton (1862–1937). It is presented here as a jumping-off point for a study of the elements of the short story.

Read the story carefully. It's so short that you can whiz right past the point without even saying *ouch*.

One morning the Sultan was resting in his palace in Damascus.** Suddenly the door flew open, and in rushed a young man, out of breath and wild with excitement. The Sultan sat up alarmed, for the young man was his most skillful assistant.

"I must have your best horse!" the youth cried out. "There is little time! I must fly at once to Baghdad!"

The Sultan asked why the young man was in such a rush.

"Because," came the hurried reply, "just now, as I was walking in the palace garden, I saw Death standing there. And when Death saw me, he raised his arms in a frightening motion. Oh, it was horrible! I must escape at once!"

The Sultan quickly arranged for the youth to have his fastest horse. And no sooner had the young man thundered out through the palace gate, than the Sultan himself went into the garden. Death was still there.

The Sultan was angry. "What do you mean?" he demanded. "What do you mean by raising your arms and frightening my young friend?"

"Your Majesty," Death said calmly, "I did not mean to frighten him. You see, I raised my arms only in surprise. I was astonished to see him here in your garden, for I have an appointment with him tonight in Baghdad."

---

*Baghdad: an important city in the old Middle East, now capital of Iraq.
**Damascus: another important Middle Eastern city, now capital of Syria.

Literary Skills

Elements of the Short Story

You may be familiar with the saying "The whole equals the sum of its parts." This saying applies perfectly to the short story. A story can almost always be examined by looking at four basic elements: setting, characters, plot, and theme.

Read the discussion that follows carefully. Respond to the questions about "Appointment in Baghdad" yourself before looking at the answers on page 78.

Setting

Every short story has to happen in some *place* and at some *time*. The time and place of a story are its *setting*. The setting also includes *natural events*, such as a snowstorm, a falling tree, or a beautiful sunny day. Authors usually try to make their settings very clear because certain kinds of stories seem more real in certain settings.

1. What is the setting of "Appointment in Baghdad"?
2. Why is the setting well suited to the story?

Characters

Most people in stories can be called either *flat* or *rounded* characters. Some flat characters are called **stereotypes** (STER ee uh typs)—one-dimensional characters we've met before in our reading: the kind old grandmother, the goofy teenage boy who can't do anything right, the sports hero who always manages the last-minute home run or touchdown pass. **Rounded characters,** on the other hand, are not types but distinct individuals. We haven't met them

before, and we can't predict exactly what they'll do when faced with certain problems.

The reader learns about a character in two ways. First, an author can simply tell the reader that a character is cheerful, tall, sick, . . . whatever. More usually, the author provides *character clues*. **Character clues** are speeches, thoughts, and actions that indicate indirectly what a character is like.

3. Would you call the characters in "Appointment in Baghdad" stereotypes or rounded characters?
4. (a) What is one instance of the author telling you about a character directly? (b) What is an example of a character clue in the story?

Plot

Few stories are interesting if we don't keep asking ourselves, "What will happen next?" What happens in a story is called its *plot*. Early in the story, an important **plot question** is raised. The action that answers this question can either end the story or lead to still other questions. Long stories often contain a number of implied plot questions. The **rising action** in such a story leads finally to an exciting **climax** at or near the end. Some stories continue past the climax with a section of falling action, or a **resolution.**

Another way to think about plot is in terms of **conflict,** or the meeting of opposing forces. Characters in stories can be in conflict with (1) other characters, (2) themselves ("inner conflict"), (3) things, or (4) nature.

5. What is the plot question that first interested you in "Appointment in Baghdad"?

6. The Sultan himself asks the last plot question. What is it?

7. Clearly, the story contains rising action leading to a climax. But does any resolution follow the climax?

8. In your opinion, what kind of conflict is involved in the story?

Theme

A story's *theme* is its meaning or message. It usually takes at least a sentence to state the theme of a story. Of course, some stories have more than one theme, and others have no theme of real importance.

9. In your opinion, is the theme in "Appointment in Baghdad" important?

10. What is the theme?

ANSWERS

1. The setting is the old Middle East.

2. The old Middle East is commonly associated with the supernatural—Aladdin's lamp, genies out of bottles, etc. For this reason, the reader is more likely to accept a supernatural tale as happening in the old Middle East than at other places and times.

3. The characters are stereotypes. The all-powerful Sultan, the frightening figure of Death, the worried young assistant—all are types we recognize as soon as they appear. The story is too short for the development of rounded characters.

4. (a) "The Sultan was angry" is a good example. (b) A good example is the second sentence, where expressions like "flew," "rushed," and "out of breath" reveal the young man's state of mind.

5. For most readers, the question is "Why is the young man 'wild with excitement'?" or "Why does he want the horse?"

6. It is the question in the next-to-last paragraph.

7. No, the climax—the most interesting and exciting part—is right at the end.

8. The conflict cannot be between the Sultan and the young man, for one helps the other. If Death is seen as a person, the conflict is between people. If Death is seen as a force of nature, it is between people and nature.

9. Yes.

10. The theme can be stated in several ways: "Death can't be avoided or even argued with." "When your time's up—that's it." "Death comes when it comes—period."

THE OUTCASTS OF POKER FLAT

by Bret Harte

▶ In a lifetime of writing, Bret Harte (1836–1902) produced many stories, novels, and poems. Today he's best remembered for his tales of mining-camp life in the California gold rush days. Here's one of his best short stories.

As Mr. John Oakhurst, gambler, stepped into the main street of Poker Flat on the morning of the 23rd of November, 1850, he was conscious at once that the moral atmosphere had changed. The very air felt more clear, somehow more pure. Two or three men, talking quietly together, stopped as he approached, and exchanged knowing glances. There was a Sabbath lull in the air— and in a town unused to Sabbath influences, this looked ominous.

Mr. Oakhurst's calm, handsome face showed no sign that anything had changed. Whether he was aware of any cause for the change, was another question. "I reckon they're after somebody," he told himself. "Likely it's me." He used a handkerchief to wipe away the red dust of Poker Flat from his neat boots, and he quietly put further thoughts on the subject out of his mind.

In fact, Poker Flat was "after somebody." It had lately suffered the loss of several thousand dollars, two valuable horses, and an important citizen. The town was having a spasm of "law and order"—quite as lawless and disorderly as any of the acts that had caused it. A secret committee had decided to rid the town of all improper persons. This was done permanently in the case of two men who were then hanging from a tree in the gulch. It was done in a temporary way for others who were told to leave town. I regret to say that some of these were ladies.

Mr. Oakhurst was right in thinking that he would be forced to leave. A few of the committee had wanted to hang him, a sure

- **outcast** (OUT kast) person cast or thrown out
- lull (LUL) quiet spell; peaceful period
- ominous (OM uh nus) threatening
- **spasm** (SPAZ um) fit; brief spell of activity
- **gulch** (GULCH) deep steep-sided valley

method of taking from his pockets the money he had won from them. "It's just not right," said Jim Wheeler, "to let this young man from Roaring Camp—an entire stranger—carry away our money." But an odd kind of justice among those who had been lucky enough to win from Mr. Oakhurst finally carried the day.

Mr. Oakhurst received his sentence with calmness. He may have guessed that his judges had not all agreed. At any rate, he was too much of a gambler not to accept fate. With him life was at best a game of chance, and he had long known the odds were in favor of the dealer.

A group of armed men accompanied the deported wickedness of Poker Flat to the edge of the town. Besides Mr. Oakhurst, the party included three others. One was a young woman known as "The Duchess." Another had won the title of "Mother Shipton." There was also "Uncle Billy," a known gold-mine robber and the town's worst drunk. The small group moved in silence. Only when the gulch which marked the farthest limit of Poker Flat was reached, the leader spoke briefly and to the point. The outcasts were forbidden to return. One step into Poker Flat would mean their lives.

As the escort disappeared, the feelings of the outcasts found vent in a few wild tears from the Duchess, some bad language from Mother Shipton, and a powerful volley of curses from Uncle Billy. The cool Oakhurst alone remained silent. He listened calmly to Mother Shipton's desire to cut somebody's heart out, to the repeated statements of the Duchess that she would die on the road, and he tried not to hear the alarming curses that seemed to be bumped out of Uncle Billy as his horse went forward. With easy good humor, he insisted on exchanging his own horse, "Five Spot," for the sorry mule which the Duchess rode. But even this act did not draw the party into any closer sympathy. The young woman poked at the feathers on her hat and looked at Oakhurst with flashing but tired eyes. Mother Shipton eyed the new rider of "Five Spot" with anger, and Uncle Billy included the whole party in one sweeping anathema.

The road to Sandy Bar—a wild and lawless camp that seemed to offer some invitation—lay over a steep mountain range. It was a day's hard travel. The group soon passed out of the comfortable region of the low hills into the dry, cold air of the Sierras.* The trail was narrow and difficult. At noon the Duchess climbed out of her saddle and to the ground, declaring that she would go no farther, and the party halted.

The spot was wild with raw beauty. On three sides, steep cliffs of bare granite rose gently to a towering height. It was, without a doubt, the best possible spot for a camp, had camping been the thing to do. But Mr. Oakhurst knew that hardly half the journey to Sandy Bar was over, and the party had neither equipment nor food for delay. This fact he pointed out to the others curtly, advising them not to throw up their hand before the game was played out. But soon the Duchess began to cry, and Mother Shipton snored. Mr. Oakhurst alone remained on his feet, leaning against a rock, calmly watching them.

As Mr. Oakhurst gazed at his companions, the loneliness of his profession, his habits of life, his very vices, for the first time seriously saddened him. He turned to dusting his black clothes,

---

- vent (VENT) means of expression
- volley (VOL ee) shower; many shots fired at once
- anathema (un NATH uh muh) formal curse
- curtly (KURT lee) bluntly; rudely
- **vice** (VYS) bad or evil habit

*The Sierra Nevada mountains in California.

and he washed his hands and face. He busied himself with other efforts at neatness, and for a moment forgot his worries. The thought of simply leaving his weaker companions perhaps never occurred to him. Yet he could not help feeling the lack of that excitement which, oddly enough, was most necessary for that calm behavior for which he was known. He looked at the gloomy walls that rose a thousand feet above the pines around him. He studied the clouded sky and the valley below, already deepening into shadow; and, doing so, suddenly he heard his own name called.

A horseman slowly ascended the trail. Mr. Oakhurst recognized the fresh, open face of the newcomer. It was Tom Simson, otherwise known as "The Innocent" of Sandy Bar. He had met him some months before in a "little game," and had quite easily won the entire fortune—about 40 dollars—of that inexperienced youth. After the game was finished, Mr. Oakhurst drew the boy behind a door and spoke to him: "Tommy, you're a good little man, but you can't gamble worth a cent. Don't try it over again." He then handed him his money back, pushed him gently from the room, and made a devoted slave of Tom Simson.

There was a memory of this in his boyish and friendly greeting of Mr. Oakhurst. He had started, he said, to go to Poker Flat to seek his fortune. "Alone?" No, not exactly alone. In fact (a giggle) he had run away with Piney Woods. Didn't Mr. Oakhurst remember Piney? She that used to wait tables at the one proper restaurant in Sandy Bar? They had been engaged a long time, but old Jake Woods had objected. Now they had run away and were going to Poker Flat to be married, and here they were. And they were tired out, and how lucky it was they had found a place to camp, and company. All this the Innocent delivered rapidly. Then Piney, a husky, attractive girl of 15, came out from behind a tree, where she had been blushing unseen, and rode to the side of her lover.

Mr. Oakhurst seldom troubled himself with sentiment, still less with propriety, but somehow he had the feeling that all was not fortunate. He kept, however, enough of his good judgment to kick Uncle Billy, who was about to say something—and Uncle Billy knew enough to recognize in Mr. Oakhurst's kick a superior power that could only be obeyed. He then tried to talk Tom Simson into hurrying on, but in vain. He even pointed out the fact that there was no food, nor a way to make a camp. But, unluckily, the

---

- propriety (pruh PRY i tee) decency; proper behavior
- **vain** (VAYN) useless attempt

Innocent proudly told the party that he had brought along an extra mule loaded with food. He even knew of an old log house near the trail. "Piney can stay with Mrs. Oakhurst," said the Innocent, pointing at the Duchess. "And I can take care of myself."

Nothing but Mr. Oakhurst's admonishing foot saved Uncle Billy from bursting into a roar of laughter. As it was, he felt forced to walk up the trail alone until he could come to his senses. There he told the joke to the tall pine trees, with many slaps of his leg. But when he returned to the party, he found them seated by a fire, for the air had grown chill and the sky more clouded. They were chatting together like old friends. Piney was actually talking in an impulsive youthful fashion to the Duchess, who was listening with an interest and liveliness she had not shown before. The Innocent was talking, in much the same way, to Mr. Oakhurst and Mother Shipton, who was actually relaxing into friendliness.

As the shadows crept slowly up the mountain, a light breeze rocked the tops of the pine trees and moaned through their long and gloomy aisles. The ruined cabin, patched and covered with pine branches, was set apart for the ladies. As the lovers parted, they exchanged a kiss, so honest and sincere that it might have been heard above the swaying pines. The frail Duchess and the bad-natured Mother Shipton were probably shocked by this example of true love, for they turned without a word to the hut. The fire was built up, the men lay down before the door, and in a few minutes were asleep.

Mr. Oakhurst was a light sleeper. Toward morning he woke up numb with cold. As he poked at the dying fire, suddenly the wind, which was now blowing strongly, brought to his cheek something that caused the blood to leave it—snow!

He got to his feet with the idea of awakening the sleepers, for there was no time to lose. But turning to where Uncle Billy had been lying, he found him gone. A suspicion leaped to his brain, and a curse to his lips. He ran to the spot where the horses and mules had been tied—they were no longer there. The tracks were already rapidly disappearing in the snow.

The excitement brought Mr. Oakhurst back to the fire with his usual calm. He did not awaken the others. The Innocent slept peacefully, a smile on his good-humored face. The young Piney slept beside the older women as sweetly as though protected by

---

• admonishing (ad MON ish ing) scolding; warning

• **impulsive** (im PUL siv) emotional; done with natural eagerness

celestial guardians. And Mr. Oakhurst, pulling his blanket over his shoulders, stroked his mustache and waited for the dawn. It came slowly, in a whirling cloud of snowflakes. Everything that could be seen appeared magically changed. He looked over the valley, and summed up the present and the future in two words, "Snowed in!"

Fortunately for the party, the food had been stored within the hut, and so had escaped the light fingers of Uncle Billy. With great care, thought Mr. Oakhurst, it might last ten days longer. "That is," he whispered to the Innocent, "if you're willing to share with us. If you ain't—and perhaps you'd better not—we'll have to wait till Uncle Billy gets back with food." For some strange reason, Mr. Oakhurst could not bring himself to tell everyone the truth about Uncle Billy. Instead, he offered the opinion that he had left camp with the hope of getting help, and had accidentally stampeded the animals. He dropped a warning to the Duchess and Mother Shipton, who of course knew what had really happened. "They'll find out the truth about us *all* when they find out anything," he added. "And there's no good frightening them now."

• **celestial** (suh LES chul) heavenly

Tom Simson was more than willing to share his food with everyone. He even seemed to enjoy their seclusion. "We'll have a good camp for a week," he said. "Then the snow'll melt, and we'll all go back together." The young man's cheer and Mr. Oakhurst's calm were not lost on the others. The Innocent, with the aid of pine branches, made a good roof for the cabin. The Duchess told Piney how to fix up the inside. "I reckon you're used to fine things at Poker Flat," said Piney. The Duchess turned away quickly to hide something that reddened her already red cheeks, and Mother Shipton requested Piney not to "chatter." But when Mr. Oakhurst returned from a vain search for the trail, he heard the sound of human laughter. He stopped in some alarm. Then he caught sight of the blazing fire through the still-blinding storm. Studying the group around it, he decided that the noises were all "square fun."

Whether Mr. Oakhurst had hidden his cards I cannot say. But he didn't say "cards" once during the evening. Happily, the time was spent with an accordion, produced with some pride by Tom Simson from his pack. In spite of a few difficulties, Piney Woods managed to pluck several reluctant melodies from its keys, to an accompaniment by the Innocent on a pair of bone castanets. The high point of the evening was reached in a simple camp-meeting hymn. Joining hands, the lovers sang it with loud, eager voices. I fear that a certain swing to the chorus, rather than any churchly quality, caused it speedily to spread to the others, who at last joined in:

"I'm proud to live in the service of the Lord,
And I'm bound to die in His army."

The pines rocked, the storm whirled above the miserable group, and the flames of their fire leaped toward heaven, as if joining in their song.

At midnight the storm abated, the rolling clouds parted, and the stars glittered above the sleeping camp. Mr. Oakhurst, whose profession had taught him to live on the smallest possible amount of sleep, took upon himself the greater part of the night watch. He excused himself to the Innocent by saying that he had "often been

- **seclusion** (si CLOO zhun) being shut off from others
- **reluctant** (ri LUK tunt) unwilling
- **accompaniment** (uh KUM puh ni munt) music played along with other music
- **castanets** (kas tuh NETS) simple instrument that makes clicking sounds
- abate (uh BAYT) diminish; die down

a week without sleep." "Doing what?" asked Tom. "Poker!" replied Oakhurst seriously. "When a man gets a streak of luck—real luck—he don't get tired. The luck gives in first. Luck," continued the gambler thoughtfully, "is a mighty queer thing. All you know for certain is that it's bound to change. And it's finding out when it's going to change that makes you. We've had a streak of bad luck since we left Poker Flat. You come along, and slap you get into it, too."

The third day came. Looking down through the white-curtained valley, the sun saw the outcasts divide their slowly shrinking pile of food for the morning meal. In that mountain climate, the sun's rays spread a kindly warmth over all. It was as if the sun now wanted to make up for what had happened in the past. But it revealed drift upon drift of snow piled high around the hut—a hopeless, trackless sea of white. Through the wonderfully clear air the smoke of Poker Flat rose miles away. Mother Shipton saw it, and from her mountain hurled in that direction a final curse. It was her last attempt at swearing, and perhaps for that reason was done unusually well. It did her good, she privately informed the Duchess. "Just you go out there and cuss, and see." She then set herself to amusing "the child," as she and the Duchess were pleased to call Piney. Piney was no chicken, but "child" was the only word the two women knew for a member of their sex who didn't swear and wasn't improper.

When night crept up again, the notes of the accordion again rose and fell. But they came in strange spasms and long-drawn sighs by the flickering campfire. And the music failed to fill the aching, empty space left by lack of food. Now a new activity was suggested by Piney—telling stories. As might be expected, neither Mr. Oakhurst nor his female companions cared to tell much about their personal experiences. Piney's plan would have failed, but for the Innocent. Some months before he had come upon a copy of Homer's *Iliad*.* He now wanted to tell the most important parts of that poem. And so for the rest of the night the gods of Homer again walked the earth.

So, with little food and much of Homer and the accordion, a week passed over the heads of the outcasts. The sun again forsook them, and once more from leaden skies snowflakes sifted

---

• **forsook** (for SOOK) deserted; left alone
• **leaden** (LED un) heavy and gray, like lead

*The *Iliad* is a very long poem by the ancient Greek poet Homer.

over the land. A huge, snowy circle drew day by day closer around them. At last they looked from their prison up walls of white that towered 20 feet above their heads. It became harder and harder to get wood for the fire. Even the fallen trees beside them were now half hidden in the drifts.

And yet no one complained. The lovers turned away from the world around them, looked into each other's eyes, and were happy. Mr. Oakhurst cooly studied the losing game before him. The Duchess, more cheerful than she had been, took over the care of Piney. Only Mother Shipton—once the strongest of the party—seemed to sicken and fade. At midnight on the tenth day she called Oakhurst to her side. "I'm going," she said in a weak voice. "But don't say anything about it. Don't waken the kids. Take the bundle from under my head, and open it." Mr. Oakhurst did so. It contained Mother Shipton's rations for the last week, untouched. "Give 'em to the child," she said, pointing to the sleeping Piney. "You've starved yourself," said the gambler. "That's what they call it," said the woman softly. Then she lay down again, and, turning her face to the wall, passed quietly away.

The next day Homer was forgotten, and the accordion was put away. When the body of Mother Shipton was buried in the snow, Mr. Oakhurst took the Innocent aside. He showed the young man a pair of snowshoes, which he had made from the old pack saddle. "There's one chance in a hundred to save her yet," he said, pointing to Piney. "But the town's there," he added, pointing toward Poker Flat. "If you can reach it in two days she's safe."

"And you?" asked Tom Simson.

"I'll stay here," was the curt reply.

The lovers parted with a long embrace. "You are not going, too?" asked the Duchess, as she saw Mr. Oakhurst waiting for Tom. "As far as the canyon," he replied. He turned suddenly and kissed the Duchess, leaving her face on fire, and her trembling body stiff with amazement.

Night came, but not Mr. Oakhurst. It brought the storm again and the whirling snow. Then the Duchess, feeding the fire, found that someone had quietly piled beside the hut enough wood to last a few days longer. The tears rose to her eyes, but she hid them from Piney.

The women slept but little. In the morning, looking into each other's face, they read their fate. Neither spoke. But Piney,

---

• **rations** (RAY shuns) food distributed in small quantities

87

suddenly becoming the stronger, drew near and placed her arm around the Duchess's waist. They kept this position for the rest of the day. That night the storm reached its greatest fury, and, sweeping away the protecting pine branches, tore into the very hut.

Toward morning they found themselves unable to feed the fire, which gradually died away. As the coals slowly blackened, the Duchess crept closer to Piney, and broke the silence of many hours: "Piney, can you pray?" "No, dear," said Piney simply. The Duchess, without knowing exactly why, felt better. Putting her head upon Piney's shoulder, she spoke no more. And so lying there, the younger and purer holding the head of the other tightly against her side, they fell asleep.

The wind softened, as if it feared to waken them. Feathery drifts of snow, shaken from the pine branches, flew like white-winged birds, and settled about them as they slept. The clouds broke up, and the moon looked down upon what had been the camp. But all human stain, all sign of earthly sorrow, was hidden beneath the spotless snow blanket kindly lowered from above.

They slept all that day and the next. Nor did they wake when voices and footsteps broke the silence of the camp. And when careful fingers brushed the snow from their pale faces, you could hardly have told, from the equal peace that lay upon them, which was she who had been driven from Poker Flat. Even the law recognized this, and turned away, leaving them locked in each other's arms.

But at the head of the canyon, on one of the largest pine trees, they found something else. This was a two of clubs pinned to the bark with a pocket knife. It carried the following, written in pencil in a firm hand:

†

BENEATH THIS TREE
LIES THE BODY
OF
JOHN OAKHURST
WHO STRUCK A STREAK OF BAD LUCK
ON THE 23RD OF NOVEMBER, 1850,
AND
HANDED IN HIS CHIPS
ON THE 7TH OF DECEMBER, 1850

†

And pulseless and cold, with a Derringer by his side and a bullet in his heart, though still calm as in life, beneath the snow lay he who was at once the strongest and yet the weakest of the outcasts of Poker Flat.

ALL THINGS CONSIDERED

1. The outcasts are forced to leave Poker Flat by (a) the police. (b) the town council. (c) a citizens' committee.
2. Oddly enough, Mr. Oakhurst is at his calmest (a) when women are present. (b) when faced with excitement. (c) in completely natural surroundings.
3. The outcast who could most easily be dropped from the story is (a) the Duchess. (b) Mother Shipton. (c) Uncle Billy.
4. As day follows day, the group of people in the cabin (a) argue more and more. (b) get along surprisingly well. (c) begin to steal food from each other.
5. In terms of personal sacrifice for others, the least effort is made by (a) the Duchess. (b) Mother Shipton. (c) Uncle Billy.

THINKING IT THROUGH

1. Although this story has been a popular one since it appeared in 1869, readers have always had mixed reactions to it. Some readers respond to the sentiment; others think it corny. What is your opinion? Give two examples to support your views.
2. In your judgment, what happened to Tom Simson? Did he make it to Poker Flat? Explain.
3. Think about the reasons for Oakhurst's action at the very end. In your opinion, is it more (a) a selfish, cowardly act to escape the situation, or (b) a sacrifice that might save the lives of others? Support your judgment with details about Oakhurst that appear earlier in the story.
4. Surprise endings in stories must come as sudden, unexpected events—but they cannot be *complete* surprises or no one would believe them. What does Bret Harte manage to tell the reader about Oakhurst earlier in the story that keeps the ending from coming as a total surprise?
5. Authors sometimes use people's names as character clues. What two trees does Bret Harte use in names, and what do they suggest about the characters?

• Derringer (DER in jur) kind of small pistol

Literary Skills

Story Elements: Application to Fiction

Before starting this exercise, you may wish to review the information on pages 77–78.

Setting

(1) Explain how at least three things about the setting must be as they are for the story to happen as it does. Don't forget the mountain range, the weather, the cabin, and the location of the two towns.

Characters

(2) Throughout the story, Harte uses the characters' thoughts, words, and actions as character clues. Find and explain two of these character clues in the second paragraph of the story. (3) At first, the characters in the story all appear to be stereotypes: the cool gambler, the worthless old drunk, the blushing young bride-to-be, etc. Toward the end, however, some of the characters leave the stereotype, do unexpected things, and become more rounded. Who are two of these characters, and what do they do?

Plot

(4) Explain how, in different degrees, all four kinds of conflict are involved in the story. (5) What are two or three plot questions that kept you interested as you read? (6) The story is clearly one of rising action, with the most interesting events occurring at or near the end. What are these events that form the story's climax?

Theme

(7) Here are just two of several possible meanings: (a) Hardships that draw different kinds of people together often make them like and appreciate one another; (b) even the outcasts of society are capable of performing in heroic fashion. In your opinion, which is the main theme, (a) or (b)? Explain.

Composition

1. Write five sentences about the story using these five words: (a) *cowardly;* (b) *heroic;* (c) *conflict;* (d) *calm;* (e) *sentimental.*
2. The introduction to this unit promised that the selections would make you think about the way people behave. Look through the story again, noting all mentions of Mr. Oakhurst. Then write a paragraph that explains his behavior as it changes throughout the story.

ON THE PATH OF THE POLTERGEIST

by Walter Hubbell

▶ Have you met any poltergeists (POHL tur gysts) lately? Do you know what they are? Some people call them "ghosts." Other people, trying to be scientific, call them "unexplained forces." At any rate, poltergeists are "ghosts" or "forces" that are said to haunt houses, usually by throwing small objects around, sliding furniture, and making odd rapping noises. Don't laugh yet! Walter Hubbell's strange account just might convince you.

It's a strange world, this one we live in. I don't believe in ghosts. That is, I didn't believe in ghosts before I investigated the mystery of Esther Cox. Now the only question is what to call them— ghosts, spirits, poltergeists, or what?

This selection is abridged from the book The Great Amherst Mystery.

91

My name is Walter Hubbell. By vocation, I'm an actor. By avocation, I'm an investigator of the "supernatural." During the past few years, I've investigated many people who claimed they could talk to the spirits of the dead. They were all fakes, and I exposed them. As an actor, I know all the tricks that we use on the stage. I also know most of the tricks that magicians use to fool the public. I am, beyond doubt, able to judge whether or not deception was used in the case of Esther Cox. And it was not.

Truth is often stranger than fiction. What I have written here is truth—not fiction—and it is *very strange*.

I was acting in Canada when I first heard of Esther Cox. She was 19 years old at the time. She and her sister Jennie, age 22, lived in the home of an older married sister, Olive Teed. Daniel Teed, Olive's husband, was a foreman in a shoe factory. The Teeds had two small boys. Before the trouble started, all lived together in a big old house in the town of Amherst.

Then things started to happen. One night Esther thought she heard a mouse somewhere in her bed. She awakened her sister Jennie, who slept in the same room. They listened in silence, and soon went back to sleep. But the next night, both sisters heard the noise again, louder than ever. "It's in that box, under my bed," declared Esther. Together the two sisters pulled the green cardboard box out from under the bed. It jumped, and both girls screamed. Jennie slowly took hold of the box and placed it in the middle of the room. It jumped again, rising a foot in the air and falling back on its side. The girls' screams brought Daniel Teed hurrying into the room. He listened to their story. "You're both crazy," he announced, shaking his head as he kicked the box back under the bed. "Now go to sleep and don't disturb me again!"

This was just the beginning. A few nights later, another scream echoed through the house. It was Esther: "What's happening to me? I'm swelling up! I'm going to burst!" This time the whole family ran to the bedroom, and there was Esther, confused and worried, her whole body swollen beyond belief. What had happened? What could they do? Daniel Teed was about to call a doctor, when, quite suddenly, came a loud rapping noise, as if someone were pounding with a heavy hammer on the floor under Esther's bed. The swelling started to go down. The rapping

---

- **vocation** (voh KAY shun) profession; career
- **avocation** (av uh KAY shun) hobby
- **deception** (di SEP shun) trickery; action intended to fool another person

continued, and Esther looked more comfortable. Soon she fell into a tired, troubled sleep.

The next morning Daniel Teed hurried to the family doctor. Dr. Thomas W. Carritte listened patiently, but he didn't believe a word. "I'll come this evening, and I'll stay through the night if I have to," he told Daniel. "But I guarantee you, none of this nonsense is going to happen while *I'm* in the house."

The doctor couldn't have been more wrong. After supper that evening, as he sat in Esther's room, he watched in wonder as an unseen hand seemed to slide the pillow out from under her head. A sheet and a light blanket were pulled from her bed. She began to swell up. Now the doctor had a job to do—but it was not he who cured Esther. It was, again, the loud rapping noises.

Dr. Carritte was as puzzled as everyone else. He knew the family, and he felt sure that no one was trying to fool him. As the rapping went on, he walked outside the house to see if he could discover what caused the noise. From outside the rapping sounded louder, like someone pounding on the roof. But there was no one—on the roof, in the yard, or anywhere.

Not long after, my acting job in Canada having ended, I arrived at the troubled house myself. At the time, I did not believe in ghosts, poltergeists, or spirits of any kind. I did believe that everything that happens has an explanation. From what I'd heard about Esther Cox, it didn't seem likely that she was playing tricks on people. But still, there had to be an explanation. Fortunately, I was able to rent a room from the Teeds, to be nearer the mystery I had come to investigate.

Esther Cox was a short, stout girl who could only be described as plain (her sister Jennie was the pretty one). Though far from dumb, she was not overly intelligent. She certainly didn't understand what was going on. Neither, I was soon persuaded, could she have planned it.

After I'd rented the room, I hadn't been in the house five minutes when my umbrella suddenly seemed to come to life. It flew across the living room. Soon after, Esther appeared in the kitchen doorway, carrying a plate. From behind her, something came flashing through the air—a large knife. It narrowly missed me. I rushed into the kitchen to see who had thrown it. That was my first introduction to ghosts. There was no one there.

"It looks like they don't like you," said Esther.

By "they," it turned out, Esther meant two poltergeists (or *ghosts*, as she called them). One she called "Maggie," the other "Bob." She claimed sometimes that she could see them. Once, as

Olive Teed and I looked on in amazement, Esther stared at the thin air in the middle of the living room and told us that Maggie was standing there. Even more strange, the girl swore that Maggie was wearing a pair of black and white socks that belonged to Esther. Feeling a little foolish, I shouted, "Now Maggie, take off Esther's socks—and be quick about it!" A minute later, a pair of black and white socks appeared from out of nowhere. They dropped from the air in front of us to the floor.

After that I stopped looking for explanations. The only explanation was . . . the supernatural.

Whoever—or whatever—"Maggie" and "Bob" were, they seemed to be always in action. With my own eyes, I saw a heavy ashtray leave its place on a table and come whizzing at me, crashing into the wall as I ducked. Furniture constantly slid around the floors. As I entered the dining room one time, every chair fell over with a crash. Another time, needing a light for my pipe, I remarked, "Bob, give me a few matches, if you please." Immediately, a lighted match fell out of the air.

But the poltergeists were not always so helpful. As the weeks passed, Esther's spells continued, and even grew worse. Sometimes she would lie on her bed as if dead, her body swelling up like a balloon, and then collapsing, over and over. Also, the poltergeists were ruining the furniture and damaging the walls. When they started lighting small fires, the Teeds were asked to move. The owner of the house had risked enough. The Teeds were good people, but they would have to go.

As an experiment, the Teeds decided to see what would happen if only Esther left. She was sent to live with a family named Van Amburgh on a farm in the country. And here the affair came to an end with the biggest mystery of all. With Esther out of the house, everything returned to normal. The rappings, the flying objects, the sliding furniture, the fires—all stopped at once.

And perhaps even more strangely, Esther's life in her new home was completely untroubled. Like all poltergeists, "Maggie" and "Bob" had departed as mysteriously as they had come.

It must be stated that the Teeds made no attempt to keep the strange events secret. Dr. Carritte and others were constantly in and out of the house. I have a statement signed by 16 persons who witnessed at least some of the happenings I've described. I have a letter from Olive Teed declaring that *all* I've written here is true. And Dr. Carritte writes:

"I take pen in hand to say that what Mr. Walter Hubbell has written about the mysterious Esther Cox is entirely correct. The young lady was a patient of mine both previous to and during those wonderful demonstrations. I tried various experiments, but with no satisfactory results. Honestly doubtful persons were on all occasions soon convinced that there was no fraud or deception in the case. Were I to publish the case in medical journals, as you suggest, I doubt if it would be believed by doctors generally. I am certain I could not have believed such miracles had I not witnessed them."

ALL THINGS CONSIDERED ──────────

1. According to the author, Esther Cox (a) understood what was going on. (b) could not have planned the strange events in advance. (c) must have had an unknown helper.

2. "Maggie" and "Bob" were apparently seen by (a) Esther only. (b) both Esther and the narrator. (c) at least 16 people.

3. The attitude of both the author and Dr. Carritte changes from (a) interest to boredom. (b) anger to approval. (c) doubt to belief.

4. According to the narrator, at least some of the happenings were witnessed by (a) scientists from Harvard University. (b) about 16 people. (c) hundreds of people.

5. The author tries to support his strange story by (a) including an account written by Esther Cox herself. (b) presenting himself and Dr. Carritte as experts. (c) providing proof recorded by scientific instruments.

──────────

- wonderful (WUN dur ful) curious; strange
- demonstration (dem un STRAY shun) any happening that can be observed
- **journal** (JUR nul) professional magazine

THINKING IT THROUGH ————————————————————

1. Esther is described as being "plain" and "stout." In your opinion, who would be more likely to try to fake events like the ones in the selection, a girl like Esther or a girl like her sister Jennie ("the pretty one")? Why?

2. In your opinion, could Esther have faked all the happenings? Explain why or why not.

3. If Esther working alone practiced no deception, what other possibilities are there for Walter Hubbell's strange story? Try to think of at least two. What do you suppose is the *real* story? In reaching your decision, review everything Hubbell claims is the truth as well as the following:

   (a) Newspaper stories about poltergeists appear every few years. Some of the events that occurred at Amherst are common to nearly all such stories: the rappings, flying objects, and sliding furniture. Other happenings, however, are not: Esther's swelling up, the appearance of objects out of thin air, and definite "ghosts" who even had names.

   (b) Before writing his account of Esther Cox, Walter Hubbell tried to put her on the stage. He and Esther appeared together in public several times, but the shows were total failures. Nothing unusual could be made to happen.

   (c) Reports of poltergeists usually come from homes containing at least one teenager, in most cases a girl. Some investigators believe that energy can build up inside a young person until it reaches the breaking point. Then, in some fashion, the energy breaks out with a force that can send an ashtray flying across a room or topple over a chair. This is a theory, not a proven fact.

   (d) A few years after the events concerning the poltergeist, Esther Cox was working and living on a farm. Mysterious fires started to break out. Although Esther claimed innocence, the authorities found enough proof to charge her with arson.

   (e) Once Hubbell's account was published, other investigators tried to check its accuracy. Some people in Amherst supported Hubbell; others called him the biggest liar to ever hit town. One neighbor stated that while he believed in the poltergeist, he thought that Hubbell had "dressed up the facts" to gain fame and fortune for himself.

Literary Skills

Story Elements: Application to Nonfiction

Whether "On the Path of the Poltergeist" is fact or fiction, the four story elements—setting, characters, plot, and theme—are useful tools of analysis. Indeed, the story elements often apply as well to nonfiction as they do to fiction. It might be a good idea to review pages 77–78 before answering the questions that follow.

Setting
(1) What is the better setting for a ghost story, a big old house in an out-of-the-way place or a very modern apartment in a high-rise building? (2) Why is it important that the Teeds' house happened to have an extra room that Hubbell could rent?

Characters
(3) Walter Hubbell himself is a character in the story. In the second paragraph, how does he present himself to the reader, and for what reason? (4) Hubbell seems to believe that the reader will react to "Dr. Thomas W. Carritte" as a stereotype. What qualities does the usual stereotype of a doctor have that would lend support to Hubbell's story? (5) Hubbell presents Esther Cox in both a direct and an indirect fashion. (a) Give one example of a direct statement about Esther. (b) Give one example of a character clue (or group of character clues) that presents information about Esther indirectly.

Plot
(6) The author is careful to point out that the strange events began to happen *before* he arrived on the scene. How does this plot detail affect your view of his truthfulness? (7) In your opinion, what part of the story should be called the climax? (8) What conflicts are involved? Try to name at least two.

Theme
(9) (a) What meaning or lesson do you think Walter Hubbell intended the reader to draw from the story? (b) Is this the story's meaning for you? Explain.

Composition

1. Suppose Walter Hubbell were going to visit your class tomorrow. Write three questions you would ask him to get at the truth. Try to trick him if you can!

2. Write a short composition attempting to prove that Hubbell's story is either true or untrue. Reread item 3 in "Thinking It Through" before you start.

CASEY AT THE BAT

by Ernest L. Thayer

▶ A poem that tells a story is called a **narrative poem.** Here's one of America's most popular narrative poems. "Casey at the Bat" will make you smile, then laugh, and finally think about the way certain kinds of people behave.

The outlook wasn't brilliant for the Mudville nine
    that day;
The score stood two to four, with but an inning
    left to play.
So, when Cooney died at second, and Burrows
    did the same,
A sickly silence fell upon the patrons of the
    game.

5 A straggling few got up to go, leaving there the
    rest,
With that hope that springs eternal within the
    human breast,
For they thought, "If only Casey could get a
    whack at that,"
They'd put up even money now, with Casey at
    the bat.

* **straggling** (STRAG ling) wandering off

98

But Flynn preceded Casey, and likewise so did
    Blake,
10 And the former was a puddin', and the latter was
    a fake,
So on that stricken multitude the deathlike
    silence sat,
For there seemed but little chance of Casey's
    getting to the bat.

But Flynn let drive a "single," to the
    wonderment of all,
And the much-despisèd Blakey "tore the cover
    off the ball."
15 And when the dust had lifted and they saw what
    had occurred,
There was Blakey safe at second, and Flynn a-
    huggin' third.

Then from the gladdened multitude went up a
    joyous yell,
It rumbled in the mountain-tops, it rattled in the
    dell;
It struck upon the hillside and rebounded on the
    flat;
20 For Casey, mighty Casey, was advancing to the
    bat.

There was ease in Casey's manner as he stepped
    into his place;
There was pride in Casey's bearing, and a smile
    on Casey's face.
And when, responding to the cheers, he lightly
    doffed his hat,
No stranger in the crowd could doubt 'twas
    Casey at the bat.

- puddin' (PUD un) slang term of disrespect
- **dell** (DEL) valley
- **bearing** (BAIR ing) way of carrying oneself
- **doff** (DOF) take off

25 Ten thousand eyes were on him as he rubbed
 his hands with dirt,
Five thousand tongues applauded when he wiped
 them on his shirt;
Then while the New York pitcher ground the ball
 into his hip,
Defiance gleamed in Casey's eye, a sneer curled
 Casey's lip.
And now the leather-covered sphere came
 whirling through the air,
30 And Casey stood a-watching it in haughty
 grandeur there.
Close by the sturdy batsman the ball unheeded
 sped—
"That ain't my style," said Casey. "Strike one!"
 the umpire said.

From the benches, black with people, there went
 up a muffled roar,
Like the beating of storm waves on a stern and
 distant shore.
35 "Kill him! Kill the umpire!" shouted someone on
 the stand.
And it's likely they'd have killed him had not
 Casey raised a hand.

With a smile of Christian charity great Casey's
 visage shone;
He stilled the rising tumult; he bade the game go
 on;
He signaled to the pitcher, once more the
 spheroid flew;
40 But Casey still ignored it, and the umpire said:
 "Strike two!"

- **haughty** (HAW tee) very proud
- visage (VIZ ij) face
- **tumult** (TOO mult) noisy uproar
- **bade** (BAYD) asked that
- spheroid (SFEER oid) nearly round object

"Fraud!" cried the maddened thousands, and
  echo answered "Fraud!"
But one scornful look from Casey and the
  audience was awed.
They saw his face grow stern and cold, they saw
  his muscles strain,
And they knew that Casey wouldn't let that ball
  go by again.

45 The sneer is gone from Casey's lip, his teeth are
  clenched in hate;
He pounds with cruel violence his bat upon the
  plate.
And now the pitcher holds the ball, and now he
  lets it go,
And now the air is shattered by the force of
  Casey's blow.

Ah, somewhere in this favored land the sun is
  shining bright;
50 The band is playing somewhere, and somewhere
  hearts are light.
And somewhere men are laughing, and
  somewhere children shout:
But there is no joy in Mudville—mighty Casey
  has struck out.

• **awed** (AWD) greatly impressed

ALL THINGS CONSIDERED ─────────────────

1. You are not told directly who is winning the game in stanza 1, but in fact (a) Mudville is ahead. (b) New York is winning. (c) the game is tied.
2. Lines 25–26 indicate that the game was attended by about (a) 5,000 people. (b) 10,000 fans. (c) 20,000 spectators.
3. The main conflict in the poem is between (a) the fans and Casey. (b) Casey and the umpire. (c) the pitcher and Casey as they represent the opposing teams.
4. When Casey gets his chance to hit, (a) one player is on base. (b) two players are on base. (c) the bases are loaded.
5. Perhaps better than Casey's hitting is his (a) fielding. (b) pitching. (c) acting ability.

THINKING IT THROUGH ─────────────────

1. "Casey at the Bat" has been a popular poem since its first appearance in 1888. Think of two reasons that might account for the poem's continuing fame.
2. In nearly every class there are some students who insist they "don't like poetry." But in your opinion, is there *anyone* who would prefer "Casey at the Bat" to be written out in prose sentences and paragraphs? Explain your answer.
3. On first reading, most people do not realize that about half the lines in the poem mention the crowd in the ball park. In your opinion, why does the poet give so much attention to the fans?
4. Another unnoticed point is the sudden change in tense between lines 44 and 45. Up to the last two stanzas, the verbs are in the past tense; then there is a shift to the present tense. Why do you think the poet chose to do this?

A BONUS ASSIGNMENT

Oral Interpretation. Oral interpretation means reading aloud with expression. As you might suppose, "Casey at the Bat" has long been a read-aloud favorite. Practice reading the poem until your voice perfectly reflects the gloom, the hope, the fans' excitement, Casey's grandeur, and the final sense of loss. Your teacher may prefer to assign certain stanzas or sections to particular students.

Literary Skills

Story Elements: Application to Poetry

Since a narrative poem tells a story, it can be analyzed in terms of the four story elements (pages 77–78).

Setting
(1) The name of the town is mentioned in the first line and the last. What does the name suggest about the town and the team? (2) How does the poet manage to bring the crowd to life? (3) Three lines in the last stanza take the reader outside the hometown setting. Why might the poet have done this?

Characters
(4) The mighty Casey is very much a stereotyped character. What sort of stereotype is he? What actions does the poet include as character clues? Name at least two.

Plot
(5) "Casey at the Bat" holds your interest by placing plot questions in your mind and then answering them. The first major question is answered in lines 16–20. What is that question? (6) What is the major question in the rest of the poem? (7) Where does the climax occur? (8) Can Casey be seen as in conflict with other characters, himself, things, and nature? Explain.

Theme
(9) Occasionally a humorous piece of literature has a serious theme. This is certainly true of "Casey at the Bat." The poem contains a lesson, almost a warning, about how to behave—or how *not* to. What is that lesson?

Composition

1. A **monologue** (MON uh log) is a rather long speech written in the way a person would normally talk. Suppose you had been in the Mudville ball park on that historic day. When you got home, you would certainly have gone into a long monologue about the game. Write that speech out, just as you hear yourself in your "mind's ear." Use approved spelling, but forget about formal grammar and sentence structure— you would probably use neither.

2. Write a stanza that might be inserted somewhere in the poem. Try to do as well with imagery (see page 59) as Ernest L. Thayer. Before you start, examine the rhyme pattern of Thayer's stanzas and note that each line has six or seven strong vocal stresses.

VOCABULARY AND SKILL REVIEW

Before completing the exercises that follow, you may wish to review the **bold-faced** words on pages 77 to 103.

I. On a separate sheet of paper, mark each item *true* or *false*. If it is *false*, explain what is wrong with the sentence.

1. Most people are pleased with *vain* efforts to reach their goals.
2. Angels are *celestial* beings.
3. *Leaden* skies are generally thought to be cheerful.
4. "Farmer in the *Dell*" means "farmer in the valley."
5. Stealing is a *vice*.
6. *Impulsive* behavior can get students in trouble.
7. Some people work steadily; others work in fits and *spasms*.
8. *Castanets* make a sweet, soft, purring sound.
9. The *English Journal* is probably a magazine for English teachers.
10. Many schools encourage students to think about their *vocations* early in life.

II. On a separate sheet of paper, write the *italicized* word that best fills the blank in each sentence.

outcast	*reluctant*	*awed*	*tumult*	*straggling*
haughty	*bearing*	*rations*	*gulch*	*accompaniment*

1. The earthquake was followed by hours of _____ and looting.
2. Carmen played the _____ for her older brother's vocal selection.
3. _____ behavior is often intended to make others feel inferior.
4. During World War II, the American people accepted rather small _____ of meat.
5. Tom never raises his hand and gives only _____ answers.
6. You might find a _____ filled with rushing water in the spring.
7. Most tourists are _____ when they first see the Rocky Mountains.
8. A political _____ does not live in his or her native country.

9. _____ cattle are sometimes hard to find on a large ranch.

10. "There was pride in Casey's _____, and a smile on Casey's face."

III. Study the diagram below. Each plot question rises on a slanted line until it is answered. Then the reader's interest drops off a little before rising to a higher point with the next question. Many pieces of good literature, from "Casey at the Bat" to Shakespeare's *Hamlet*, can be diagrammed in this way.

1–5 Write the correct question or answer for each of the circled numerals on the plot line. For example, the answer to the first plot question is "Yes." The answer to the second question should appear where you now see ❶. Where you see step ❷, determine the question; for ❸, give the answer; for ❹, give the question; and for ❺, give the answer.

RISING ACTION IN "CASEY AT THE BAT"

Will Casey get a hit on the first pitch?

Yes

Will Casey get up to bat?

Reader's Interest

Time of Story

IV. Suppose the cartoon on the next page had been drawn to illustrate a bit of **dialogue** (spoken language) from a story. What might that story be about? What might have already happened? What is going to happen in the near future?

"Of course I'm okay. Whose serve is it?"

Now think about the imagined story in terms of the elements: setting, characters, plot, and theme.

1. Describe the *setting* (or settings) in detail. Include different kinds of imagery (see page 59).

2. Give the *characters* names that suggest what they are like. Do you see them as rounded characters or stereotypes? Why?

3. Briefly summarize the plot of the story. Include these terms: *conflict, rising action,* and *climax.*

4. Tell what the *theme* of the story might be. Remember, an excellent story can be written on a common, unexciting theme: *pride goeth before a fall; look before you leap; actions speak louder than words;* etc.

THE FAN CLUB

by Rona Maynard

▶ Students often say that the only thing wrong with stories about teenagers is that they all seem to be written by adults. That charge certainly can't be leveled at the realistic story that follows. The author, now a successful journalist, was 15 when she wrote it. You'll recognize the insider's viewpoint at once.

It was Monday again. It was Monday and the day was damp and cold. Rain splattered the cover of *Algebra I* as Laura heaved her books higher on her arm and sighed. School was such a bore.

School. It loomed before her now, massive and dark against the sky. In a few minutes, she would have to face them again—Diane Goddard with her sleek blond hair and Terri Pierce in her candy-pink sweater. And Carol and Steve and Bill and Nancy. . . . There were so many of them, so exclusive as they stood in their tight little groups laughing and joking.

Why were they so cold and unkind? Was it because her long stringy hair hung in her eyes instead of dipping in graceful curls? Was it because she wrote poetry in algebra class and got A's in Latin without really trying? Shivering, Laura remembered how they would sit at the back of English class, passing notes and whispering. She thought of their identical brown loafers, their plastic purses, their hostile stares as they passed her in the corridors. She didn't care. They were clods, the whole lot of them.

She shoved her way through the door and there they were. They thronged the hall, streamed in and out of doors, clustered under red and yellow posters advertising the latest dance. Mohair sweaters, madras shirts, pea-green raincoats. They were all alike, all the same. And in the center of the group, as usual, Diane Goddard was saying, "It'll be a riot! I just can't wait to see her face when she finds out."

Laura flushed painfully. Were they talking about her?

"What a scream! Can't wait to hear what she says!"

- **loom** (LOOM) come into view in an indistinct form.
- **exclusive** (ik SKLOO siv) snobbish; accepting of only a select few
- **throng** (THRONG) crowd
- **mohair** (MOH hair) kind of soft goat-hair fabric
- **madras** (MAD rus) kind of fine cotton cloth, usually with a plaid pattern

Silently she hurried past and submerged herself in the stream of students heading for the lockers. It was then that she saw Rachel Horton—alone as always, her too-long skirt billowing over the white, heavy columns of her legs, her freckled face ringed with shapeless black curls. She called herself Horton, but everyone knew her father was Jacob Hortensky, the tailor. He ran that greasy little shop where you could always smell the cooked cabbage from the back rooms where the family lived.

"Oh, Laura!" Rachel was calling her. Laura turned, startled.

"Hi, Rachel."

"Laura, did you watch *World of Nature* last night? On Channel 11?"

"No—no, I didn't." Laura hesitated. "I almost never watch that kind of program."

"Well, gee, you missed something—last night, I mean. It was a real good show. Laura, it showed this fly being born!" Rachel was smiling now; she waved her hands as she talked.

"First the feelers and then the wings. And they're sort of wet at first, the wings are. Gosh, it was a good show."

"I bet it was." Laura tried to sound interested. She turned to go, but Rachel still stood there, her mouth half open, her pale, moon-like face strangely urgent. It was as if an invisible hand tugged at Laura's sleeve.

"And Laura," Rachel continued, "that was an awful good poem you read yesterday in English."

Laura remembered how Terri and Diane had laughed and whispered. "You really think so?" Well, thanks, Rachel. I mean, not too many people care about poetry."

"Yours was real nice though. I wish I could write like you. I always like those things you write."

Laura blushed. "I'm glad you do."

"Laura, can you come over sometime after school? Tomorrow maybe? It's not very far and you can stay for dinner. I told my parents all about you!"

Laura thought of the narrow, dirty street and the tattered awning in front of the tailor shop. An awful district, the kids said. But she couldn't let that matter. "Okay," she said. And then, faking enthusiasm, "I'd be glad to come."

She turned into the algebra room, sniffing at the smell of chalk and dusty erasers. In the back row, she saw the "in" group, laughing and joking and whispering.

"What a panic!"

"Here, you make the first one."

Diane and Terri had their heads together over a lot of little cards. You could see they were cooking up something.

Fumbling through the pages of her book, she tried to memorize the theorems she hadn't looked at the night before. The laughter at the back of the room rang in her ears. Also those smiles—those heartless smiles . . .

A bell buzzed in the corridors; students scrambled to their places. "We will now have the national anthem,"

- billowing (BIL oh ing) rolling like waves
- theorem (THEE uh rum) statement to be proved

said the voice on the loudspeaker. Laura shifted her weight from one foot to the other. It was so false, so pointless. How could they sing of the land of the free, when there was still discrimination. Smothered laughter behind her. Were they all looking at her?

And then it was over. Slumping in her seat, she shuffled through last week's half-finished homework papers and scribbled flowers in the margins.

"Now this one is just a direct application of the equation." The voice was hollow, distant, an echo beyond the sound of rustling papers and hushed whispers. Laura sketched a guitar on the cover of her notebook. Someday she would live in the Village* and there would be no more algebra classes and people would accept her.

She turned towards the back row. Diane was passing around one of her cards. Terri leaned over, smiling. "Hey, can I do the next one?"

". . . by using the distributive law." Would the class never end? Math was so dull, so painfully dull. They made you multiply and cancel and factor, multiply, cancel, and factor. Just like a machine. The steel sound of the bell shattered the silence. Scraping chairs, cries of "Hey wait!" The crowd moved into the hallway now, a thronging, jostling mass.

Alone in the tide of faces, Laura felt someone nudge her. It was Ellen. "Hey, how's that for a smart outfit?" She pointed to the other side of the hall.

The gaudy flowers of Rachel Horton's blouse stood out among the fluffy sweaters and pleated skirts. What a lumpish, awkward creature Rachel was. Did she have to dress like that? Her socks had fallen untidily around

---

- **equation** (i KWAY zhun) statement of equal value on both sides (=)
- distributive (di STRIB yuh tiv) having to do with a law of multiplication
- factor (FAK tur) express as a product of two or more numbers
- jostling (JOS ling) shoving; pushing
- **gaudy** (GAW dee) very showy

*Probably Greenwich (GREN ich) Village, a section of New York City known for its open-minded tolerance of all kinds of people.

her heavy ankles, and her slip showed a raggedy edge of lace. As she moved into the English room, shoelaces trailing, her books tumbled to the floor.

"Isn't that something?" Terri said. Little waves of mocking laughter swept through the crowd.

The bell rang; the laughter died away. As they hurried to their seats, Diane and Terri exchanged last-minute whispers. "Make one for Steve. He wants one, too!"

Then Miss Merrill pushed aside the book she was holding, folded her hands, and beamed. "All right, people, that will be enough. Now, today we have our speeches. Laura, would you begin please?"

So it was her turn. Her throat tightened as she thought of Diane and Carol and Steve grinning and waiting for her to stumble. Perhaps if she was careful they'd never know she hadn't thought out everything beforehand. Careful, careful, she thought. Look confident.

"Let's try to be prompt." Miss Merrill tapped the cover of her book with her fountain pen.

Laura pushed her way to the front of the class. Before her, the room was large and still. Twenty-five round, blurred faces stared blankly. Was that Diane's laughter? She folded her hands and looked at the wall, strangely distant now, its brown paint cracked and peeling. A dusty portrait of Robert Frost, a card with the seven rules for better paragraphs, last year's calendar, and the steady, hollow ticking of the clock.

Laura cleared her throat. "Well,"

she began, "my speech is on civil rights." A chorus of snickers rose from the back of the room.

"Most people," Laura continued, "most people don't care enough about others. Here in New England, they think they're pretty far removed from discrimination and violence. Lots of people sit back and fold their hands and wait for somebody else to do the work. But I think we're all responsible for people that haven't had some of the advantages. . . ."

Diane was giggling and gesturing at Steve Becker. All she ever thought about was parties and dates—and such dates! Always the president of the student council or the captain of the football team.

"A lot of people think that race prejudice is limited to the South. But most of us are prejudiced—whether we know it or not. It's not just that we don't give other people a chance; we don't give ourselves a chance either. We form narrow opinions and then we don't see the truth. We keep right on believing that we're open-minded liberals when all we're doing is deceiving ourselves."

How many of them cared about truth? Laura looked past the rows of blank, empty faces, past the bored stares and cynical grins.

"But I think we should try to forget our prejudices. We must realize now that we've done too little for too long. We must accept the fact that one person's misfortune is everyone's responsibility. We must defend the natural dignity of people—a dignity that thou-

---

• **liberal** (LIB ur ul) one who favors fairness and reform
• **cynical** (SIN i kul) doubting; lacking faith and trust

sands are denied."

None of them knew what it was like to be unwanted, unaccepted. Did Steve know? Did Diane?

"Most of us are proud to say that we live in a free country. But is this really true? Can we call the United States a free country when millions of people face prejudice and discrimination? As long as one person is forbidden to share the basic rights we take for granted, as long as we are still the victims of irrational hatreds, there can be no freedom. Only when every American learns to respect the dignity of every other American can we truly call our country free."

The class was silent. "Very nice, Laura." Things remained quiet as other students droned through their speeches. Then Miss Merrill looked briskly around the room. "Now, Rachel, I believe you're next."

There was a ripple of dry, humorless laughter—almost, Laura thought, like the sound of a rattlesnake. Rachel stood before the class now, her face red, her heavy arms piled with boxes.

Diane Goddard tossed back her head and winked at Steve.

"Well, well, don't we have lots of things to show," said Miss Merrill. "But aren't you going to put those boxes down, Rachel? No, no, not there!"

"Man, that kid's dumb," Steve muttered, and his voice could be clearly heard all through the room.

With a brisk rattle, Miss Merrill's pen tapped the desk for silence.

Rachel's slow smile twitched at the corners. She looked frightened. There was a crash and a clatter as the tower

of boxes slid to the floor. Now everyone was giggling.

"Hurry and pick them up," said Miss Merrill sharply.

Rachel crouched on her knees and began very clumsily to gather her scattered treasures. Papers and boxes lay all about, and some of the boxes had broken open, spilling their contents in wild confusion. No one went to help. At last she scrambled to her feet and began fumbling with her notes.

"My—my speech is on shells."

A cold and stony silence had settled upon the room.

"Lots of people collect shells, because they're kind of pretty—sort of, and you just find them on the beach."

"Well, whaddaya know!" It was Steve's voice, softer this time, but all mock amazement. Laura jabbed her notebook with her pencil. Why were

---

● **irrational** (i RASH uh nul)   unreasonable; senseless

they so cruel, so thoughtless? Why did they have to laugh?

"This one," Rachel was saying as she opened one of the boxes, "it's one of the best." Off came the layers of paper and there, at last, smooth and pearly and shimmering, was the shell. Rachel turned it over lovingly in her hands. White, fluted sides, like the close-curled petals of a flower; a scrolled coral back. Laura held her breath. It was beautiful. At the back of the room snickers had begun again.

"Bet she got it at Woolworth's," somebody whispered.

"Or in a trash dump." That was Diane.

Rachel pretended not to hear, but her face was getting very red and Laura could see she was flustered.

"Here's another that's kind of pretty. I found it last summer at Ogunquit." In her outstretched hand there was a small, drab, brownish object. A common snail shell. "It's called a . . . it's called . . ."

Rachel rustled through her notes. "I—I can't find it. But it was here. It was in here somewhere. I know it was." Her broad face had turned bright pink again. "Just can't find it. . . ." Miss Merrill stood up and strode toward her. "Rachel," she said sharply, "we are supposed to be prepared when we make a speech. Now, I'm sure you remember those rules on page twenty-one. I expect you to know these things. Next time you must have your material organized."

The bell sounded, ending the period. Miss Merrill collected her books.

Then, suddenly, chairs were shoved aside at the back of the room and there was the sound of many voices whispering. They were standing now, whole rows of them, their faces grinning with delight. Choked giggles, shuffling feet—and then applause—wild, sarcastic, malicious applause. That was when Laura saw that they were all wearing little white cards with a fat, frizzy-haired figure drawn on the front. What did it mean? She looked more closely. "HORTENSKY FAN CLUB," said the bright red letters.

So that was what the whispering had been about all morning. She'd been wrong. They weren't out to get her after all. It was only Rachel.

Diane was nudging her and holding out a card. "Hey, Laura, here's one for you to wear."

For a moment Laura stared at the card. She looked from Rachel's red, frightened face to Diane's mocking smile, and she heard the pulsing, frenzied rhythm of the claps and the stamping, faster and faster. Her hands trembled as she picked up the card and pinned it to her sweater. And as she turned, she saw Rachel's stricken look.

"She's a creep, isn't she?" Diane's voice was soft and intimate.

And Laura began to clap.

- fluted (FLOO tid) grooved
- scrolled (SKROHLD) decorated by a spiral design
- **sarcastic** (sahr KAS tik) mocking; scornful; bitter
- malicious (muh LISH us) cruel; with ill will
- **frenzied** (FREN zeed) frantic; very excited

ALL THINGS CONSIDERED ─────────────────────

1. Early in the story, Laura believes that the trick being planned by the "in" group (a) is probably very funny. (b) will get the whole class in trouble. (c) might be directed at her.

2. When Laura tells Rachel that she'd be "glad to come" to her house, Laura (a) never intends to go. (b) has mixed feelings. (c) can't wait to go.

3. Rachel probably feels most at home in (a) English class. (b) algebra. (c) biology.

4. The words "We must accept the fact that one person's misfortune is everyone's responsibility . . . must defend the natural dignity of people" are spoken by (a) Laura. (b) Rachel. (c) Miss Merrill.

5. At the end, Laura probably (a) feels good now that she is accepted. (b) likes Diane better than Rachel. (c) dislikes what she finds herself doing.

THINKING IT THROUGH ─────────────────────

1. (a) In a sentence or two, what is the *theme* (see page 78) of Laura's speech? (b) Does she put this theme into practice? Explain.

2. In what ways are Laura and Rachel (a) alike and (b) different? Try to think of at least two ways for each.

3. The reasons for Laura's actions at the end of the story are fairly well explained. Most readers feel they *understand* Laura's behavior. But how they *feel* about it is another question. How do you feel about her behavior? Do you think *understanding* Laura is the same as *excusing* or *pardoning* her? Explain clearly.

4. Rachel is presented as a kind of stereotype—the "hopeless kid." But in truth, could she have done some things to make her life at school more pleasant? What things?

Reading and Analyzing

Inferences and Conclusions

Authors have two main ways of getting their ideas across. Sometimes they just tell us directly what they want us to know. For instance, the author of "The Fan Club" tells us that Laura is taking both Algebra I and Latin. At other times, however, authors do not state their ideas directly. Instead, they suggest certain meanings "between the lines." They offer a little smoke in the hope that readers will say "fire" for themselves.

When readers respond to suggestions like this, they *infer* the author's meaning. In other words, they make *inferences*. An **inference** is an understanding of something that has not been stated directly.

The word *inference* covers a huge area, from a brief flash of meaning sparked by a single word to more important understandings that often require both considerable observation and some thought. Major inferences of

this kind can be called **conclusions.** For example, if you see one student yawn, you might infer that he or she is a little sleepy. But if you saw a whole class of students yawning for a half hour, you might draw a conclusion of an entirely different kind.

1. When Laura started her speech, "a chorus of snickers rose from the back of the room." What do you infer about Laura's feelings?

2. Before Laura's speech—even before her algebra class—is she herself totally free of prejudice? Go back and reread all that is said about Rachel and her family. What do you infer?

3. Think about what Laura sees in the room as she stands up to speak. Think about Miss Merrill's words, actions, and *re*actions. What would a good reader conclude about this teacher? Why?

Composition

1. Choose either (a) or (b) as the subject of a short paragraph. Explain your reasoning in each case:
   (a) When do you infer the story was written . . . last year, 10 years ago, 20 years ago?
   (b) The introduction stated that "The Fan Club" was written by a high-school student. You might have reached that conclusion yourself after reading the story.

   What details in "The Fan Club" indicate a true "student's-eye" view?

2. Suppose the story had gone on past the climax to end with a resolution (see page 77). Explain what Laura and Rachel would say to each other the next time they had a chance to talk. For extra credit, try to write the resolution out in story form.

THE WORLD IS NOT A PLEASANT PLACE TO BE

by Nikki Giovanni

the world is not a pleasant place
to be without
someone to hold and be held by

    a river would stop
5 its flow if only
    a stream were there
    to receive it

    an ocean would never laugh
    if clouds weren't there
10 to kiss her tears

the world is not
a pleasant place to be without
someone

WAYS OF KNOWING

1. Why do you think the poet feels that both "someone to hold" and "be held by" are necessary? In other words, why is either incomplete without the other?

2. Do you think the poet means the words "hold" and "held" to be taken only literally? Could *love* and *loved* be fairly substituted to expand the meaning?

3. The second group of lines, as well as the third, is a metaphorical expression of the poem's main idea. Try to explain what the poet means by each.

4. In a sentence or two, relate the poem's theme to the characters Laura and Rachel in the story "The Fan Club" (page 107).

Nathaniel Hawthorne (1804–1864)

The Turner House in Salem, Massachusetts, later renamed the House of the Seven Gables after the title of Hawthorne's famous novel

Had Nathaniel Hawthorne lived in our day, his motto would certainly have been "Hang in there." Upon graduation from Bowdoin College in 1825, Hawthorne made up his mind to be a writer. This was a courageous decision, for at the time the number of Americans who earned a living writing fiction could be counted on the fingers of one hand. Hawthorne knew what his decision would mean—practice, practice, and more practice. He returned to his mother's house in Salem, Massachusetts, and sat down to write. A year passed and he was still at it. Another year went by, and then more years. After five years of effort, he had sold only one of his stories. Then still more time passed. Hawthorne just wouldn't give up. Finally, after "twelve dark years" as he later called them, he published his first book, *Twice-Told Tales*.

But Hawthorne's practice paid off in perfection. Today he's recognized as one of the few giants in American literature. Behind his polished sentences, the reader senses a kind, thoughtful man. Hawthorne wrote about the people of his time, but first of all he wrote about ideas. What really makes a person a "criminal"? Is any person completely "good"? Which are more important to the individual, the dreams of youth or the rewards of age? Questions such as these will never die, and neither will the best of Hawthorne's stories.

Why do you think Hawthorne referred to a certain period in his life as "twelve dark years"?

▶ *The author introduces his own story:*
We can be but partially acquainted even with the events which actually affect our path through life. There are many other events—if such they may be called— which come close upon us, yet pass away. They leave no actual results. We know nothing of them. They reflect no light or shadow across our minds. Could we know all that *might* have happened, life would be too full of hope and fear to give us a single hour of true peace. This idea may be illustrated by a page from the secret history of—

DAVID SWAN
A Fantasy

by Nathaniel Hawthorne

We find David, at the age of 20, on the high road to the city of Boston, where an uncle was to take him behind the counter in his grocery store. Be it enough to say that he was a native of New Hampshire, born of good parents, and had received an ordinary school education. After traveling on foot from sunrise till nearly noon of a summer's day, his tiredness and the increasing heat forced him to rest. He looked ahead for a shady place where he could wait for the coming of the stagecoach. As if planted on purpose for him, there soon appeared a little tuft of maples. Then he noticed a fresh bubbling spring that seemed never to have sparkled for any traveler but David Swan. He kissed it with thirsty lips, and threw himself down on the bank. For a pillow he used some shirts and a pair of pants, tied up in a striped cotton handkerchief. The sunbeams could not reach him. The dust did not rise from the road after the heavy rain of yesterday. In short, his grassy bank suited the young man better than the softest of beds. The spring murmured sleepily beside him, and a deep sleep, perhaps hiding dreams within its depths, fell upon David Swan. But we are to relate events which he did not dream of.

- **fantasy** (FAN tuh see) fanciful, unreal story
- **tuft** (TUFT) small bunch
- **relate** (ri LAYT) tell

While he lay sound asleep in the shade, other people were wide awake, and passed back and forth, on foot, on horseback, and in all sorts of vehicles. Some looked neither left nor right, and never knew that David was there. Some just glanced that way, without admitting the sleeper to their busy minds. Some laughed to see how soundly he slept. And several, whose hearts were full of scorn, ejected their venomous feelings on David Swan. A middle-aged widow, when no one else was near, told herself that the young fellow looked charming in his sleep. A temperance worker cursed him as an awful example of dead drunkenness by the roadside. But praise, laughter, curses, and even indifference were all one, or rather all nothing, to David Swan.

- eject (i JEKT) force out
- **venomous** (VEN uh mus) poisonous; spiteful
- temperance (TEM pur uns) belief that no one should drink alcohol
- indifference (in DIF ur uns) lack of interest

He had slept only a few minutes when a brown carriage, drawn by a handsome pair of horses, stopped nearly in front of David's resting place. A metal pin had fallen out, so that one of the wheels had slid off. The damage was slight, and brought only a moment's worry to an elderly merchant and his wife, who were returning to Boston in the carriage. While a servant started work on the wheel, the lady and gentleman sheltered themselves beneath the maple trees. There they saw the bubbling spring, and David Swan asleep beside it. The merchant stepped as lightly as he could, and his spouse tried not to rustle her silk dress.

"How soundly he sleeps!" whispered the old gentleman. "From what a depth he draws that easy breath! Such sleep as that would be worth to me more than half my income, for it would suppose good health and a mind free from troubles."

"And youth, besides," said the lady. "Even healthy and quiet old people do not sleep like this. Our slumber is no more like his than our wakefulness.

The longer they looked, the more they felt interested in the unknown youth, to whom the grassy bank and the maple shade were as a secret room. The woman suddenly perceived that a stray sunbeam fell down upon his face. She tried to push a branch to one side, so as to catch it. And having done this little act of kindness, she began to feel like a mother to him.

"Lady Luck seems to have laid him there," she whispered, "and to have brought us here to find him, after our disappointment with our cousin's son. I think I see a likeness to our departed Henry. Shall we waken him?"

"To what purpose?" said the merchant, pausing. "We know nothing about what he's really like."

"That open, honest face!" replied his wife. "This innocent sleep!"

While these whispers were passing, the sleeper's breathing did not change, nor did his face show the least sign of interest. Yet Fortune was bending over him, just ready to let fall a shower of gold. The old merchant had lost his only son, and had no heir except a distant relative, with whose conduct he was dissatisfied. In such cases, people sometimes do stranger things than to act the magician and awaken this youth. He who fell asleep as a poor man would wake up to a rich life.

- spouse (SPOUS) husband or wife
- perceive (pur SEEV) become aware of
- **departed** (di PAHR tid) dead

"Shall we not waken him?" repeated the lady, trying again.

"The coach is ready, sir," said the servant, behind.

The old couple jumped. With red faces, they hurried away. Waken the young man? Who would ever dream of doing anything so very ridiculous! The merchant threw himself back into the carriage, and filled his mind with business. Meanwhile, David Swan enjoyed his nap.

The carriage could not have gone more than a mile, when a charming young woman came along the road. Her lively step showed just how her happy heart was dancing. Perhaps it was this merry kind of motion that caused—is there any harm in saying it?—her garter to slip its knot. Knowing that the silken strap was relaxing its hold, she turned aside into the shelter of the maple trees, and there found a young man asleep by the spring!

Finding that she had stumbled into a gentleman's bedchamber, the girl blushed as red as any rose. "And for such a purpose, too!" she thought. She was about to make her escape on tiptoe—but there was peril near the sleeper. A monster of a bee had been wandering overhead—buzz, buzz, buzz—till finally it seemed to be settling on the eyelid of David Swan. The sting of a bee is sometimes deadly. The girl attacked the bee with her handkerchief, and drove it from beneath the maples. How sweet a picture! This done, with faster breath, and a deeper blush, she stole a glance at the youthful stranger for whom she had been battling with a dragon in the air.

"He is handsome!" thought she, and blushed redder yet.

How could it be that no dream of happiness should grow strong within him? How could it be that no such dream should wake him up, and allow him to see the girl? Why, at least, did no smile brighten upon his face? She had come, the maiden whose soul, according to the old and beautiful idea, had once been separated from his own. She had come, the one that he, unknowingly, had so hoped to meet. Her, only, could he love with a perfect love. Him, only, could she receive into the depths of her heart. And now her reflection was faintly blushing in the water, by his side. Should it pass away, its happy glow would leave his life forever.

"How sound he sleeps!" murmured the girl.

She departed, but did not skip along the road so lightly as when she came.

Now, this girl's father was a thriving merchant in the

• **peril** (PER ul) danger
• **thriving** (THRYV ing) very successful

neighborhood, and at the time, he happened to be looking out for just such a man as David Swan. Had David become acquainted with the daughter, he would also have become her father's clerk—and all else in natural order. So here, again, had good Fortune come near David Swan. She had stolen so near that her garments touched him lightly, and he knew nothing of the matter.

The girl was hardly out of sight when two men turned aside beneath the maple shade. Both had evil faces, set off by cloth caps which slanted down over their foreheads. Their clothing was shabby, yet had a certain smartness. These were a couple of rascals who got their living by whatever the devil sent them. Now, having no other business, they had bet the profits of their next piece of villainy on a game of cards, which they planned to play here under the trees. But, finding David asleep by the spring, one of the rogues whispered to the other:

"Hist!—Do you see that bundle under his head?"

The other villain nodded, winked, and leered.

"I'll bet you," said the first, "that there's a nice fat wallet hidden there among his shirts. And if not there, in one of his pants pockets."

"But what if he wakes up?" asked the other.

His companion pushed aside his jacket, pointed at the handle of a large knife, and nodded.

"So be it!" muttered the second villain.

They approached the unconscious David. While one pointed the dagger towards his heart, the other reached for the bundle under his head. Their two faces, wrinkled and ghastly with guilt and fear, bent over David. They looked horrible enough to be mistaken for fiends, should he suddenly awake. But David Swan had never worn a more tranquil face, even when asleep in his mother's arms.

"I must take away the bundle," whispered one.

"If he moves, I'll strike," muttered the other.

But, at this moment, a dog, its nose to the ground, came in beneath the trees. It looked back and forth at the two evil men, and finally at the quiet sleeper. Then it lapped at the spring.

"Ah!" said one villain. "We can't do anything now. The dog's master must be close behind."

"Let's be off," said the other.

- **rogue** (ROHG) rascal; villain
- **tranquil** (TRANG kwil) peaceful; at rest

The man with the dagger put it away, and they left the spot joking together. As for David Swan, he still slept quietly, neither conscious of the shadow of death when it hung over him, nor of the glow of renewed life when the shadow departed.

He slept, but no longer so quietly as at first. An hour's repose had taken away his tiredness. Now he moved—first the lips, without a sound—and now he talked, in an inward tone, to the vanishing ghosts of his dream. But a noise of wheels came louder and louder along the road, until it smashed through the disappearing clouds of David's sleep. He jumped up, and there was the stage-coach.

"Hello, driver!" shouted he. "Take a passenger?"

"Room on top," answered the driver.

Up climbed David, and rode away toward Boston. He never glanced back at the spring. He knew not that Wealth had thrown a golden glow upon its waters, nor that Love had sighed softly to their murmurs, nor that Death had threatened to make them red with blood. Sleeping or waking, we never hear the silent footsteps of the things that almost happen. Yet these things are always right beside our paths. It is a wonder that there should still be order enough in human life to make the future even partially known.

• repose (ri POHZ) rest

ALL THINGS CONSIDERED ————————————

1. "David Swan" is an unusual story because (a) it is based on the author's own life. (b) it contains rising action. (c) the main character is asleep most of the time.
2. Another unusual feature of "David Swan" is that (a) the author correctly foretold the future. (b) its real subject is what *might have happened*, not what *did* happen. (c) some characters are not given names.
3. Hawthorne's subtitle, "A Fantasy," suggests that (a) the story is for children. (b) he wrote the story to illustrate a fanciful idea. (c) the reader can expect events to take place in the future.
4. The theme of the story (a) is stated clearly in both the introduction and the last paragraph. (b) is not likely to be clear to the average reader. (c) concerns the future more than the past.
5. Hawthorne's main purpose in writing the story was probably to make the reader (a) appreciate common people. (b) laugh. (c) think.

THINKING IT THROUGH ————————————

1. The story contains three main **episodes,** or units of action. (a) What characters appear in each episode? (b) Why did Hawthorne choose to put the episodes in this order, not in another?
2. Without looking back, try to state the theme of the story in your own words.
3. Find the words "old and beautiful idea" in paragraph 7 on page 120. What idea does the author seem to have in mind?
4. The story contains several statements that allow you to infer how David Swan spent the rest of his life. (a) What job did he probably get? (b) Did he ever find his true love?
5. "David Swan" dates back to 1837. Suppose you were asked to rewrite the story in a modern setting. What changes would you make?

Critical Thinking

Cause and Effect

People tend to think in certain patterns. Some of these patterns have already been mentioned in this book. For instance, sometimes we think of a main idea and then consider the supporting details. At other times, we first consider a group of details and then go on to a main idea they suggest. At still other times, we simply think of what happened first, second, third, and so on.

Another rather common pattern of thought—and of writing—is **cause and effect.** A *cause* is an event or idea that leads to a certain result, called an *effect.* For instance, daydreaming in class (cause) will result in low marks (effect). Putting your hand on a hot stove (cause) will result in a burn (effect).

Nathaniel Hawthorne's "David Swan" indicates that cause-effect relationships can be much more complex than low marks or an *ouch!* He suggests that most people live in a complicated world of effects, only dimly aware of the causes behind them, *and completely unaware that many events (causes) that almost happened would have made their lives quite different.*

1. Think about the episode featuring the girl with the troublesome garter. David's waking up, the author suggests, would have caused at least two effects that would lead to a completely new life. What are the two effects, and how would they have changed David's life?

2. Now consider your own life. Use your imagination to think of something that could easily have happened, yet did not. What effect would this cause have had on you?

3. Finally, think of "David Swan" itself as a *cause*—a story produced by a thoughtful, sensitive man about 150 years ago. Some modern readers find the idea behind the story exciting. Others say "ho hum." What effect does the story have on you?

Composition

1. Most short stories contain cause-effect relationships. Think back over the stories you have read so far in this book. Write the titles of three of them on your paper. After each title, write a complete sentence stating what you see as the most important cause-effect relationship in the story.

2. Paul "Bear" Bryant, "the winningest coach in football," had a sign pasted inside the lockers of all Alabama players: CAUSE SOMETHING TO HAPPEN. How did he want his players to think of themselves—as causes or effects? Do you think the advice is a good rule of life? Explain with at least one example.

VOCABULARY AND SKILL REVIEW

Before completing the exercises that follow, you may wish to review the **bold-faced** words on pages 107 to 124.

I. On a separate sheet of paper, write the term in each line that means the same, or nearly the same, as the word in *italics*.
1. *frenzied:* dried out, frantic, exhausted, trimmed
2. *tranquil:* mason's tool, Spanish fort, former, peaceful
3. *rogue:* fancy border, style, rascal, victim
4. *effect:* result, cause, reason, relationship
5. *irrational:* impossible, unreasonable, uncontrollable, defeated
6. *venomous:* oily, overly sweet, expensive, poisonous
7. *thriving:* dishonest, foolish, successful, taking advantage
8. *episode:* introduction, kind of poem, monkey, unit of action
9. *peril:* dagger, danger, garment, career
10. *relate:* tell, lie, relive, patch or repair

II. 1. A *liberal* person would probably favor (a) men's rights over women's. (b) a program to reduce poverty. (c) education only for the rich.
2. An *equation* must contain the symbol (a) ÷. (b) +. (c) =.
3. An *exclusive* club would probably (a) perform community service. (b) be hard to get into. (c) not have dancing.
4. *Departed* is a "nice" way of saying (a) silly. (b) ugly. (c) dead.
5. It's usually not hard to find a *tuft* of (a) grass. (b) clouds. (c) dogs or other animals.
6. You make an *inference* when you (a) don't tell the whole truth. (b) read between the lines. (c) take things too literally.
7. A statement of opinion based on thorough observation can be called a(n) (a) *conclusion.* (b) *equation.* (c) *episode.*
8. SCIENCE is to OBSERVATION as *FANTASY* is to (a) IMAGINATION. (b) NONFICTION. (c) STUDENT.
9. PLEASANT is to SWEET as *SARCASTIC* is to (a) FLAVOR. (b) CREAMY. (c) BITTER.
10. HUNGER is to EAT as *CAUSE* is to (a) BECAUSE. (b) REASON. (c) EFFECT.

III. Anne Bradstreet (1612–1672) and her husband Simon were among the Puritan founders of the famous Massachusetts Bay Colony. In 1630, she and her husband sailed to the New World in search of a better life. During the years that followed, Anne managed a large household and bore eight children. The amazing thing is that she found time to write the first book of poetry by an American, *The Tenth Muse Lately Sprung Up in America*.

Today most of Bradstreet's work seems stiff and formal. But the poems that speak from her heart still live on. Here is a good example. Read the poem carefully and answer the questions.

TO MY DEAR AND LOVING HUSBAND

by Anne Bradstreet

If ever two were one, then surely we;
If ever man were loved by wife, then thee;
If ever wife was happy in a man,
Compare with me, ye women, if you can.
5 I prize thy love more than whole mines of gold,
Or all the riches that the East doth hold.
My love is such that rivers cannot quench,
Nor ought but love from thee give recompense.
Thy love is such I can no way repay,
10 The heavens reward thee manifold, I pray.
Then while we live in love let's so persever
That when we live no more we may live ever.

1. The Puritans of colonial New England are often seen as having been rigid, stern, and unemotional people. Does the poem support this stereotype? Explain.

- muse (MYOOZ) goddess (or power) that inspires a poet
- quench (KWENCH) satisfy thirst or other need
- ought (AWT) anything (variation of *aught*)
- recompense (REK um pens) repayment
- manifold (MAN uh fohld) in many ways
- persever (pur SEV ur) continue to uphold; keep on trying (Today the word is spelled *persevere* and pronounced pur suh VEER.)

2. In your own words, explain the last two lines of the poem in terms of *cause* and *effect*.

3. What *inferences* can you make about the poet, her husband, and her times?

IV. Consider the cartoon below. What has probably caused Mrs. Kleindish to fall down? Is this the effect the maker of the coffee expected?

"And so Mrs. Kleindish, you'd say that you can taste the difference."

UNIT REVIEW

I. Match the terms in Column A with their definitions in Column B.

A

1. climax
2. resolution
3. theme
4. inference
5. conflict

B

a) the meaning or message of a piece of literature

b) an understanding of something not stated directly

c) the meeting of two opposing forces

d) part of a story that sometimes follows the climax

e) the most exciting part of a story, at or near the end

II. This unit has asked you to think about people, particularly about the way certain kinds of people behave in certain situations. Here are eight general statements that start with the word *People*. Try to illustrate at least *five* of the statements by referring to a selection in this unit. First copy the statement. Then start your support in this way: *For example, in "(selection)"*. . . The first has been done as an example.

1. People who think they can outwit Death are in for a big disappointment. *For example, in "Appointment in Baghdad," the young man who flees from Death doesn't know that he is fated to die that very night.*

2. People of different kinds who are drawn together by hardships often become good friends.

3. People can be forced by peer pressure to do things they know are wrong.

4. People are seldom aware that if chance events in the past had happened in other ways, their lives would have been quite different.

5. People who are boastful and haughty have a long way to fall when they finally tumble.

6. People are happiest when they have someone to love who gives love in return.

7. People who stretch the truth sometimes don't know the point at which they really start to lie.

8. People who are generally thought of as social outcasts can perform noble acts if given the chance.

SPEAKING UP

The last exercise of this kind asked you to concentrate on just one aspect of speaking in front of a group. You practiced conveying meaning through the silent speech of "body language." This lesson singles out another important aspect of "Speaking Up": finding the tone of voice that enables you to read with expression.

The remarkable poem that follows was found among the possessions of an elderly woman when she died in a nursing home. First try to find the right voice for the speaker as she starts the poem. Then try to catch the shifting voices that best express the changes in the speaker's age and mood. You may be asked to read aloud, but you can read from your seat, and the only thing judged will be your voice. Practice with a cassette if you can. It's not great poetry, but it *is* a great poem!

"CRABBY OLD WOMAN"

author's name unknown

What do you see, nurses, what do you see?
What are you thinking when you look at me?
A crabby old woman, not very wise,
Uncertain of habit, with faraway eyes,
5   Who dribbles her food and makes no reply
When you say in a loud voice, "I do wish you'd try."
Who seems not to notice the things that you do
And forever is losing a stocking or shoe.
Who, resisting or not, lets you do as you will
10   With bathing and feeding, the long day to fill.
Is that what you're thinking; is that what you see?
Then open your eyes; you're not looking at me.
I'll tell you who I am as I sit here so still,
As I move at your bidding, as I eat at your will.
15   I'm a small child of ten with father and mother,
Brothers and sisters who love one another.
A young girl at sixteen with wings on her feet,
Dreaming that soon now a lover she'll meet.

A bride soon at twenty; my heart gives a leap,
20 Remembering the vows that I promised to keep.
At twenty-five, now I have young of my own
Who need me to build a secure, happy home.
A woman of thirty, my young now grow fast,
Bound to each other with ties that should last.
25 At forty, my young now will soon be gone,
But my man stays beside me to see I don't mourn.
At fifty, once more babes play round my knee,
Again we know children, my loved one and me.
Dark days are upon me; my husband is dead.
30 I look to the future; I shudder in dread.
For my young are all busy rearing young of their own,
And I think of the years and the love that I've known.
I'm an old woman now, and nature seems cruel.
'Tis her jest to make old age look like a fool.
35 The body it crumbles; grace and vigor depart.
Now it seems like a stone where I once had a heart.
But inside this old carcass a young girl still dwells,
And now and again my battered heart swells.
I remember the joys; I remember the pain,
40 And I'm loving and living life over again.
I think of the years, all too few—gone so fast—
And accept the stark fact that nothing can last.
So open your eyes, nurses, open and see
Not a crabby old woman; look closer—see me.

WRITING A 5-PARAGRAPH THEME

The word *theme* has two related meanings. The first, as you know, is the meaning or idea of a piece of literature. The second is a composition *you* write to state and support an idea or opinion of your own.

You know, too, that people think in certain patterns and expect to discover those patterns in what they read. One pattern that works exceptionally well—and is instantly recognized by the reader—is the *five-paragraph theme:*

Paragraph 1: Start, if possible, with some kind of "hook" to catch the reader. This can be a question, an interesting fact or idea, a joke, a personal confession, a quotation, a challenge . . . anything. There is only one firm rule for this first paragraph: *The last sentence* must be *a clear statement of the theme, or main idea, of the whole paper.*

Paragraphs 2–4: Each of these paragraphs bundles together details of a particular kind that either explain or serve as examples for the main idea of the paper. Generally, the first sentence of each paragraph should let the reader know what the whole paragraph will be about. (Occasionally four, five, or only two of these paragraphs seem called for—but the old "rule of three" in writing usually works best.)

Paragraph 5: This paragraph usually restates the theme, or main idea, in slightly different words. It can also summarize the whole paper. Whatever you choose to put in this paragraph, it should give the paper a rounded-out or finished quality.

The "rule of three" applies to the *process*, or steps, of writing as well as to the *product*, or the finished paper:

Prewriting: Explore an idea and do the necessary research. Decide *exactly* what the important final sentence in the first paragraph will be. (If you don't know the main idea of your paper, your reader will never discover it.) Decide what the three supporting paragraphs will be about and determine the order. Even if you don't think a formal outline is necessary, you should make a lot of notes. If a good thought or sequence of words flashes across your mind, write it down at once. The mind is better at creating than at remembering.

Writing: If your prewriting has been done well, this step should not be at all hard. Sometimes it's a good idea not to start writing until your prewriting explorations have made you so interested that you just can't wait to begin. Don't worry too much about spelling or grammar at this point, but do follow the overall form of the five-paragraph theme.

Revising: Reread your theme several times before you copy it over, making corrections as soon as you see the need. Pay particular attention to your known weak points, whatever they may be: spelling, awkwardness, wordiness, poor usage, etc. Finally, copy or type the neatest paper you can. Research has shown that other things being equal, the neater composition gets the higher mark.

Assignment: Write a five-paragraph theme explaining why you like one of the selections in this unit. If all this is new to you, feel free to use the sample on the next page, just completing the paper as you go along. The sample shows how one good writer might approach the problem.

Let's see, a title first: *A Fan of "The Fan Club"* might be good. For a hook, I'll use a question: *What makes a good short story?* Then I might say that the question can be answered by examining a story I liked very much. Whatever I write here will have to lead directly to my last sentence in paragraph 1: *"The Fan Club" is simply my kind of story.*

For the second paragraph, I'll discuss the plot. The word *plot* will have to be in the first sentence. I'll tell what happens in a few sentences. I'll point out the plot questions that kept me interested and explain how the rising action leads to a fascinating climax.

Character should come next, for paragraph 3. *To me, Laura seems like a real person, a rounded character* might be a good opener. I'll describe her qualities and tell how the author makes the reader aware of them. I'll point out that at the end, the main conflict is *within* Laura; thus plot is influenced by character.

For paragraph 4, will I discuss setting or theme? Theme, clearly, since it's so important in this story. I might start, *The theme of this story is a problem for every teenager: How much should I let peer pressure govern what I think and do?* This paragraph doesn't have to be long. I'll just try to explain why the question is so important and why it interests me.

The last paragraph can be short: *The perfect short story has three ingredients: an interesting plot; at least one realistic, rounded character; and a truly meaningful theme. Mix these together with me as a reader, and you have a real fan of "The Fan Club."*

UNIT · 3

DIFFERENT DRUMMERS

If a man does not keep pace with his companions,
perhaps it is because he hears a different drummer.
Let him step to the music which he hears, however
measured or far away.
  —from *Walden* by Henry David Thoreau

The quotation is a famous one. It made sense when Thoreau wrote it in 1854, and it still makes sense today. Americans have always marched to different drummers, have always valued individuality, have even fought to hold on to differences. Indeed, in our nation's differences lies our nation's strength.

This unit pays tribute to some of the different voices that make up our country's literature. First you'll read an unusual folktale from our rich oral tradition. You'll move on to the personal memoir of a prize-winning Asian/American writer, the memorable words of a distinguished Native American, and a story filled with twists by perhaps the finest black writer of the 19th century. You'll find these different voices no less—and no more—"American" than that of the celebrated Mark Twain, once called "the Lincoln of our literature." Twain's work, some of which you'll encounter in this unit, is characterized by its originality. In true American fashion, he too heard a different drummer.

THE GIRL IN THE LAVENDER DRESS

(a traditional folktale, retold by Maureen Scott)

▶ Here's a popular tale told with a personal touch. Use your powers of prediction to guess at the events.

My grandmother was, I always believed, a truthful woman. She paid her taxes. She went to church. She considered the Lord's business as her own. When her children told lies, they soon saw the light of truth. They went to bed without any supper, the taste of soap still pungent on their tongues.

That's why the story that follows bothers me so much. It just *can't* be true. Of course, Grandma was 92 when she told it to me and her mind had started to fail. She might have really believed it. Who knows? Maybe you will, too.

I'll try to tell the story just the way she told it to me. She was in a nursing home then. It was late at night and the two of us were alone in the TV room. Grandma's eyelids hung low over her eyes. She worked her wrinkled jaw a few times and began:

It all happened about '42 or '43 [Grandma said]. It was during World War II. We didn't have much gas in those days. No one did. So whenever Herbert took the car somewhere, I tried to go along for the ride.

We lived in Vermont in those days. This time I'm thinking of, Herbert had some business in Claremont. That's in New Hampshire, just across the river. Well, seems Herbert had saved up the gas to go by car. About 25 miles. He said we could leave after work Friday. That night we'd have us a good restaurant meal. Maybe see a movie, too. Then we'd stay in a hotel and drive back the next day.

I don't remember the month, exactly. Sometime in the fall, 'cause it was cool. It was a misty night. I remember Herbert had to keep the wipers going. And it was after dusk when we first saw her. I know it was dark, 'cause I remember first seeing her in the lights ahead.

• pungent (PUN junt) sharp; bitter

Neither Herbert nor I spoke. He slowed down, and the girl stopped walking. She just stood there on our side of the road. Not hitching, exactly, but she sure looked like she wanted a ride. It was a lonely road, and there weren't many cars.

First Herbert passed her, going real slow. Then he backed up to where she was. I rolled down my window. She was a pretty little thing, about 18 or 20. A round face, and big round eyes. Brown hair, cut straight. The mist kind of made her face shine. But the funny thing was what she was wearing: only a thin lavender party dress. In that weather!

Well, I don't remember that anybody did any asking. I just opened the door and leaned forward. She climbed into the backseat and Herbert started up again. Finally I asked her where she was going.

"Claremont." That was all she said at first. She had a light, breathless voice, like it took a whole lungful of air to say that one word.

"You're lucky," Herbert said. "We're going all the way."

The girl didn't reply. We rode on a little ways. I turned around once or twice, but the girl just smiled, sort of sadly. Anyhow, I didn't want to stare at her. But who was she, and why was she walking on a lonely road at night? I've never been the kind to pry into other people's business. So what I did then was, well, I'd taken off my sweater when the car got warm. I offered it to her, and she put it on.

The mist turned to light rain. Just before we got to the river, Herbert broke the silence. "Where are you going in Claremont, Miss?"

There was no reply.

"It's coming on to rain," Herbert said. "And we got time to deliver you."

"Oh," the girl breathed. "Could you *really?* That would be—that would be *nice.* To my parents' house. Corner of Bond and Mason."

"Claremont must be a nice place to grow up," I said, but again, there was no sound from the back of the car. You couldn't even hear her breathing. I just settled back into my seat and enjoyed the trip. We crossed the bridge, headed into town, and Herbert turned right onto Bond Street.

We rode along, looking at the street signs. Mason was way out. There was only one house on the corner, on the opposite side. Herbert made a U-turn and stopped the car.

There was no one in the rear seat!

I looked at Herbert. He looked at me, his eyes popping. I pulled myself up so I could see the back floor. Nothing. Just a little wetness where her feet had been.

"Where'd she get out?" Herbert asked.

"At a stoplight?" I wondered. But we both knew it couldn't be. It was a two-door car, so we'd know it if a door opened. Both of us looked at the rear windows. They were closed, as they had been. Neither of us had felt a draft.

Yet there had to be some explanation. "Come," Herbert said. We hurried toward the house. It was a big, square box-like building. Lights were on in nearly every room. Splotches of brightness covered the wet lawn.

The door had a name on it: J. R. Bullard. It was opened by a long-faced man about fifty.

"Excuse me," Herbert said, "But there seems to be some mystery. You see, your daughter—"

"Daughter?" said the man. "Why, we don't have any daughter." A small woman, some years younger, now stood at his side.

"Well—" Herbert began.

"We *did* have a daughter," the woman said. "But Carol is deceased, you see. She was buried in Calhoun Cemetery four months ago."

Herbert gripped my arm. We both knew Calhoun Cemetery: it was on the Vermont side of the river. "Then who—?" Herbert wondered aloud. Suddenly he looked embarrassed. "Excuse us," he muttered. "It's all a—a mistake."

"Just a minute," I said. "Would you mind telling us what Carol looked like?"

The couple exchanged glances. If they were worried, it wasn't about Carol. It was about *us*. "A little on the short side," the woman said almost to herself. "A round face. Big round eyes. Dark straight hair, cut in bangs."

Herbert's hand was a lobster claw on my elbow. We excused ourselves in a hurry. Back in the car, we sped away through the night. Then we drove around for a long time, looking. Across the bridge. Down every little road. Back into Claremont. Near every stoplight. Along Bond Street.

But we both knew the search was futile. There was only one answer. What we'd had in our car, sitting on the backseat and even talking, was the ghost of Carol Bullard. And the amazing thing was that we had proof. A ghost, you see, cannot cross water. That was why, when we came to the river, the ghost had only one choice: to disappear!

Grandma stopped talking, and I thought that was the end of her incredible story. But no—there was more:

 • **deceased** (di SEEST) dead
 • **futile** (FYOOT ul) useless

And that isn't all [Grandma went on]. That night—the night that it happened—we were both pretty edgy. Didn't get much sleep, either. Not till the next morning did we think of my sweater. It had disappeared with the ghost.

That was a really good sweater, almost new. You see, we didn't have much money, and it was wartime. Clothes were hard to come by. But once in a while I'd blow a week's pay on something really nice, something that would last for years— like that sweater.

Now listen: it's like this. On the way home, we thought we'd swing around by Calhoun Cemetery. We wanted to find a certain gravestone, the one that would say "Carol Bullard" on it. So we did just that. It took a long time, but finally we found the new graves. And there, at last, was the stone. A small flat stone. Just "Carol Bullard" on it. No dates; nothing more. But next to the stone, neatly folded up, *was my sweater!*

True—or not? You decide.

ALL THINGS CONSIDERED ─────────────

1. During the ride to Claremont, the grandmother was a little bothered by the girl's (a) backseat driving. (b) snoring. (c) failure to speak much.
2. We learn from the story that ghosts (a) cannot talk. (b) cannot cross water. (c) never appear in winter.
3. The first real surprise in the story comes when the girl (a) disappears. (b) sees her parents. (c) accepts the sweater.
4. It is reasonable to believe that the sweater was left next to the tombstone by (a) Carol. (b) Mr. or Mrs. Bullard. (c) Herbert.
5. It is probable that Carol was buried (a) in a sweater. (b) twice. (c) in a lavender dress.

THINKING IT THROUGH ─────────────

1. In your opinion, does the grandmother really believe the story she tells? Or is she just trying to amuse her granddaughter?
2. "The Girl in the Lavender Dress" is a genuine example of American **folk literature.** The story has been told many times. Dr. Louis C. Jones of the New York State Historical Society knows of more than 75 versions (retellings). Sometimes the story goes by other titles, such as "Lavender" or "The Ghostly Hitchhiker." Certain things remain the same in all versions: the ride given the girl, her disappearance, and the interview with the parents. But other details change. Sometimes the girl is picked up by college students. Sometimes the sweater is a coat, or is simply left out of the story. (a) Why do you think this particular folktale has become popular? (b) Why do you think so many different versions exist?
3. Maureen Scott, the author, chose to use the **story-within-a-story** form for "The Girl in the Lavender Dress." This form is often used for stories involving the supernatural: one character tells the **inner story** to another. In your opinion, why do authors often use this form for ghostly tales?

LITERARY SKILLS

Using Foreshadowing to Make Predictions

A **prediction**, as you know, is a judgment about what will happen in the future. To fully enjoy "The Girl in the Lavender Dress," you had to use your knowledge at certain points in the story to make predictions about developments in the plot.

You know too that in stories that end with a twist, the surprise ending rarely occurs as a *complete* surprise. If it did, the reader would mutter "Unfair," "Foul," "Cheap ending," or "Easy way out!" For this reason, good authors usually try to **foreshadow** events, or to suggest them before they occur. Good readers use this **foreshadowing** to make predictions about what's going to happen. This is part of the fun of reading.

1. Look back at the sentence *"There was no one in the rear seat!"* on page 137. The author did not intend that sentence to come as a total surprise. Find two ways in which the so-called surprise was foreshadowed.
2. The words "But next to the stone . . . *was my sweater"* at the end of the story are also highlighted by *italics*. Did the words come as a complete surprise to you? If not, what foreshadowing did the author provide?
3. Choose another story in this book and explain how the author used foreshadowing to help prepare the reader for a twist at the end. "The Eye Catcher," "The Outcasts of Poker Flat," and "The Fan Club" are good stories to use.

COMPOSITION

1. Because the grandmother's story is presented as being spoken, parts of it are not in standard English. Find five sentences that could not be called "good written English." Then rewrite them so that they are more acceptable.
2. Every section of our country has its own folk literature. Try to think of a strange tale you have heard and write it out in your own words. If you can't think of something you have heard in your community, tell the plot of a TV show or movie you have seen. Take the time to make your version mysterious and exciting. If your story ends with a surprise, don't forget to use foreshadowing.

from

THE WOMAN WARRIOR

by Maxine Hong Kingston

▶ The gifted Maxine Hong Kingston is best known for her sensitive re-creations of life among Chinese immigrants in the United States. This episode concerns her mother, Brave Orchid. It comes from the book *The Woman Warrior: Memoirs of a Girlhood Among Ghosts*. Read it thoughtfully, for the "ghosts" you're about to meet are not the usual sort.

When she was about sixty-eight years old, Brave Orchid took a day off to wait at San Francisco International Airport for the plane that was bringing her sister to the United States. She had not seen Moon Orchid for thirty years. She had begun this waiting at home, getting up a half-hour before Moon Orchid's plane took off in Hong Kong. Brave Orchid would add her will power to the forces that keep an airplane up. Her head hurt with the concentration. The plane had to be light, so no matter how tired she felt, she dared not rest her spirit on a wing but continuously and gently pushed up on the plane's belly. She had already been waiting at the airport for nine hours. She was wakeful.

Next to Brave Orchid sat Moon Orchid's only daughter, who was helping her aunt wait. Brave Orchid had made two of her own children come too because they could drive, but they had been lured away by the magazine racks and the gift shops and coffee shops. Her American children could not sit for very long. They did not understand sitting; they had wandering feet. She hoped they would get back from the pay TV's or the pay toilets or wherever they were spending their money before the plane arrived. If they did not come back soon, she would go look for them. If her son thought he could hide in the men's room, he was wrong.

"Are you all right, Aunt?" asked her niece.

"No, this chair hurts me. Help me pull some chairs together so I can put my feet up."

She unbundled a blanket and spread it out to make a bed for herself. On the floor she had two shopping bags full of canned peaches, real peaches, beans wrapped in taro leaves, cookies, Thermos bottles, enough food for everybody, though only her niece would eat with her. Her bad boy and bad girl were probably sneaking hamburgers, wasting their money. She would scold them.

Many soldiers and sailors sat about, oddly calm, like little boys in cowboy uniforms. (She thought "cowboy" was what you would call a Boy Scout.) They should have been crying hysterically on their way to Vietnam. "If I see one that looks Chinese," she thought, "I'll go over and give him some advice." She sat up suddenly; she had forgotten about her own son, who was even now in Vietnam. Carefully she split her attention, beaming half of it to the ocean, into the water to keep him afloat. He was on a ship. He was in Vietnamese waters. She was sure of it. He and the other children were lying to her. They had said he was in Japan, and then they said he was in the Philippines. But when she sent him her help, she could feel that he was on a ship in Da Nang. Also she had seen the children hide the envelopes that his letters came in.

"Do you think my son is in Vietnam?" she asked her niece, who was dutifully eating.

"No. Didn't your children say he was in the Philippines?"

"Have you ever seen any of his letters with Philippine stamps on them?"

"Oh, yes. Your children showed me one."

"I wouldn't put it past them to send the letters to some Filipino they know. He puts Manila postmarks on them to fool me."

"Yes, I can imagine them doing that. But don't worry. Your son can take care of himself. All your children can take care of themselves."

"Not him. He's not like other people. Not normal at all. He sticks erasers in his ears, and the erasers are still attached to the pencil stubs. The captain will say, 'Abandon ship,' or, 'Watch out for bombs,' and he won't hear. He doesn't listen to orders. I told him to flee to Canada, but he wouldn't go."

She closed her eyes. After a short while, plane and ship under control, she looked again at the children in uniforms. Some of the blond ones looked like baby chicks, their crew cuts like the downy yellow on baby chicks. You had to feel sorry for them even though they were Army and Navy Ghosts.

- taro (TAHR oh) kind of tropical plant used for food
- Filipino (fil uh PEE noh) native of the Philippines
- **downy** (DOU nee) soft; fluffy

Suddenly her son and daughter came running. "Come, Mother. The plane's landed early. She's here already." They hurried, folding up their mother's encampment. She was glad her children were not useless. They must have known what this trip to San Francisco was about then. "It's a good thing I made you come early," she said.

Brave Orchid pushed to the front of the crowd. She had to be in front. The passengers were separated from the people waiting for them by glass doors and walls. Immigration Ghosts were stamping papers. The travellers crowded along some conveyor belts to have their luggage searched. Brave Orchid did not see her sister anywhere. She stood watching for four hours. Her children left and came back. "Why don't you sit down?" they asked.

"The chairs are too far away," she said.

"Why don't you sit on the floor then?"

No, she would stand, as her sister was probably standing in a line she could not see from here. Her American children had no feelings and no memory.

To while away time, she and her niece talked about the Chinese passengers. These new immigrants had it easy. On Ellis Island* the people were thin after forty days at sea and had no fancy luggage.

"That one looks like her," Brave Orchid would say.

"No, that's not her."

Ellis Island had been made out of wood and iron. Here everything was new plastic, a ghost trick to lure immigrants into feeling safe and spilling their secrets. Then the Alien Office could send them right back. Otherwise, why did they lock her out, not letting her help her sister answer questions and spell her name? At Ellis Island when the ghost asked Brave Orchid what year her husband had cut off his pigtail, a Chinese who was crouching on the floor motioned her not to talk. "I don't know," she had said. If it weren't for that Chinese man, she might not be here today, or her husband either. She hoped some Chinese, a janitor or a clerk, would look out for Moon Orchid. Luggage conveyors fooled immigrants into thinking the Gold Mountain was going to be easy.

* encampment (en KAMP munt) camp and equipment
* **conveyor (belt)** (kun VAY ur) endless moving belt or platform for carrying objects short distances
* **alien** (AYL yun) non-citizen; foreigner

*Ellis Island, in New York Harbor, served for years as an immigrant examination center.

Brave Orchid felt her heart jump—Moon Orchid. "There she is," she shouted. But her niece saw it was not her mother at all. And it shocked her to discover the woman her aunt was pointing out. This was a young woman, younger than herself, no older than Moon Orchid the day the sisters parted. "Moon Orchid will have changed a little, of course," Brave Orchid was saying. "She will have learned to wear western clothes." The woman wore a navy blue suit with a bunch of dark cherries at the shoulder.

"No, Aunt," said the niece. "That's not my mother."

"Perhaps not. It's been so many years. Yes, it is your mother. It must be. Let her come closer, and we can tell. Do you think she's too far away for me to tell, or is it my eyes getting bad?"

"It's too many years gone by," said the niece.

Brave Orchid turned suddenly—another Moon Orchid, this one a neat little woman with a bun. She was laughing at something the person ahead of her in line said. Moon Orchid was just like that, laughing at nothing. "I would be able to tell the difference if one of them would only come closer," Brave Orchid said with tears, which she did not wipe. Two children met the woman with the cherries, and she shook their hands. The other woman was met by a young man. They looked at each other gladly, then walked away side by side.

Up close neither one of those women looked like Moon Orchid at all. "Don't worry, Aunt," said the niece, "I'll know her."

"I'll know her too. I knew her before you did."

The niece said nothing, although she had seen her mother only five years ago. Her aunt liked having the last word.

Finally Brave Orchid's children quit wandering and drooped on a railing. Who knew what they were thinking? At last the niece called out, "I see her! I see her! Mother! Mother!" Whenever the doors parted, she shouted, probably embarrassing the American cousins, but she didn't care. She called out, "Mama! Mama!" until the crack in the sliding doors became too small to let in her voice. "Mama!" What a strange word in an adult voice. Many people turned to see what adult was calling, "Mama!" like a child. Brave Orchid saw an old, old woman jerk her head up, her little eyes blinking confusedly, a woman whose nerves leapt toward the sound anytime she heard "Mama!" Then she relaxed to her own business again. She was a tiny, tiny lady, very thin, with little fluttering hands, and her hair was in a gray knot. She was dressed in a gray wool suit; she wore pearls around her neck and in her earlobes. Moon Orchid *would* travel with her jewels showing. Brave Orchid momentarily saw, like a larger, younger outline around this old woman, the sister she had been waiting for. The familiar dim halo faded, leaving the woman so old, so gray. So old. Brave Orchid pressed against the glass. *That* old lady? Yes, that old lady facing the ghost who stamped her papers without questioning her was her sister. Then, without noticing her family, Moon Orchid walked smiling over to the Suitcase Inspector Ghost, who took her boxes apart, pulling out puffs of tissue. From where she was, Brave Orchid could not see what her sister had chosen to carry across the ocean. She wished her sister would look her way. Brave Orchid thought that if *she* were entering a new country, she would be at the windows. Instead Moon Orchid hovered over the unwrapping, surprised at each reappearance as if she were opening presents after a birthday party.

"Mama!" Moon Orchid's daughter kept calling. Brave Orchid said to her children, "Why don't you call your aunt too? Maybe she'll hear us if all of you call out together." But her children slunk away. Maybe that shame-face they so often wore was American politeness.

"Mama!" Moon Orchid's daughter called again, and this time her mother looked right at her. She left her bundles in a heap and came running. "Hey!" the Customs Ghost yelled at her. She went back to clear up her mess, talking inaudibly to her daughter all the while. Her daughter pointed toward Brave Orchid. And at last Moon Orchid looked at her—two old women with faces like mirrors.

Their hands reached out as if to touch the other's face, then returned to their own, the fingers checking the grooves in the forehead and along the sides of the mouth. Moon Orchid, who never understood the gravity of things, started smiling and laughing, pointing at Brave Orchid. Finally Moon Orchid gathered up her stuff, strings hanging and papers loose, and met her sister at the door, where they shook hands, oblivious to blocking the way.

"You're an old woman," said Brave Orchid.

"Aiaa. *You're* an old woman."

"But you are really old. Surely, you can't say that about me. I'm not old the way you're old."

- **hover** (HUV ur) stay nearby; linger about
- **slunk** (SLUNK) moved in a fearful or embarrassed way
- **inaudibly** (in AW duh blee) not being heard
- gravity (GRAV i tee) dignity; seriousness
- oblivious (uh BLIV ee us) unaware; unmindful

"But *you* really are old. You're one year older than I am."

"Your hair is white and your face all wrinkled."

"You're so skinny."

"You're so fat."

"Fat women are more beautiful than skinny women."

The children pulled them out of the doorway. One of Brave Orchid's children brought the car from the parking lot, and the other heaved the luggage into the trunk. They put the two old ladies and the niece in the back seat. All the way home—across the Bay Bridge, over the Diablo hills, across the San Joaquin River to the valley, the valley moon so white at dusk—all the way home, the two sisters exclaimed every time they turned to look at each other, "Aiaa! How old!"

Brave Orchid forgot that she got sick in cars, that all vehicles but palanquins made her dizzy. "You're so old," she kept saying. "How did you get so old?"

Brave Orchid had tears in her eyes. But Moon Orchid said, "You look older than I. You *are* older than I," and again she'd laugh. "You're wearing an old mask to tease me." It surprised Brave Orchid that after thirty years she could still get annoyed at her sister's silliness.

• palanquin (pal un KEEN) carriage on poles that are carried on people's shoulders

ALL THINGS CONSIDERED ─────────────────────────

1. Brave Orchid fancied that her sister's airplane was held up partly by (a) primitive gods. (b) her own will power. (c) rising currents of air.
2. Reading between the lines, you can tell that the time of the selection is (a) during the war in Vietnam. (b) about 100 years ago. (c) the early 1980s.
3. The context on page 143 makes it clear that (a) Da Nang and Manila are in Vietnam. (b) Da Nang and Manila are in the Philippines. (c) Da Nang is in Vietnam and Manila in the Philippines.
4. The adjective that best fits Brave Orchid is (a) *impatient.* (b) *understanding.* (c) *critical.*
5. Part of the charm of the selection comes from the fact that nearly everything is seen from the viewpoint of (a) Maxine Hong Kingston, the author and one of Brave Orchid's children. (b) the niece. (c) Brave Orchid herself.

THINKING IT THROUGH ─────────────────────────

1. Although they are sisters, Brave Orchid and Moon Orchid are very different people. How many differences can you name?
2. On page 144, Brave Orchid reflects that "her American children had no feelings. . . ." Give two facts from the selection that indicate Brave Orchid's opinion is wrong.
3. As used in the selection, what does "ghost" mean?
4. The selection is full of Brave Orchid's opinions of her children. Briefly, what is probably their opinion of her?
5. Maxine Hong Kingston uses *similes* (see page 30) very effectively. Explain the literal meaning of the following: (a) "Brave Orchid momentarily saw, like a larger, younger outline around this old woman, the sister she had been waiting for." (b) "And at last Moon Orchid looked at her—two old women with faces like mirrors."

LITERARY SKILLS

Chronological Order and the Flashback

One of the most important considerations in the study of literature—and one that is often overlooked—is how an author handles the whole subject of *time*. Characters live not only in the present but, through memories and the forces that have shaped their lives, in the past as well.

The term **chronological** (kron uh LOJ i kul) **order** simply means in the normal sequence of time. Event A is followed by Event B and then by Event C. On the surface, most literary selections follow strict chronological order. For instance, Brave Orchid waits for her sister, meets her sister, gets into the car, and starts home.

Quite often, however, events are not listed in exact chronological order. Sometimes characters remember past events. Also, authors often use a device called a **flashback** to skip—or "flash"—back to scenes that happened before the time frame of a given selection.

1. Turn back to the paragraph on page 144 that starts "Ellis Island. . . ." (a) What is the flashback in that paragraph? (b) Why do you suppose the author chose to include it?

2. (a) Find one other place in the selection where Brave Orchid's mind is filled with memories. (b) What do these memories tell the reader about Brave Orchid?

3. Authors can make time fly by or slow it down to a crawl. (a) Were you surprised by the terms "nine hours" and "four hours" in the selection? What do they indicate about Brave Orchid? (b) In your opinion, where does the author slow down the passage of time the most by going into great detail?

4. How does the selection illustrate the normal human tendency to think of others as they *were*, not as time has probably changed them?

COMPOSITION

1. Describe an incident when you saw someone—for example, a friend or a grandparent—whom you hadn't seen in a long time. What was your reaction to how that person looked?

2. Did reading this selection from *The Woman Warrior* make you want to read the whole book? Explain why or why not.

Chief Joseph (1840-1904)

By the end of the 1870s, nearly all Native Americans in the United States had been forced onto reservations. The famous Sitting Bull was still free—but he had escaped to Canada. The Apache chief Geronimo was also at large—but he was in Mexico. Then quite suddenly, in 1877, another great leader—called "Chief Joseph" by the white settlers—gained wide attention.

According to newspaper stories, Chief Joseph was the leader of the "unruly" Nez Percé (NEZ PURS) "troublemakers" in the northwestern United States. The papers claimed that rather than move onto a reservation, Joseph and his people decided to take on the U.S. Army. Retreating over a 1300-mile path through four western states, he fought off attack after attack, in each of which his force was greatly outnumbered. Moreover, all this was done while protecting hundreds of women and children and thousands of horses and cattle. Chief Joseph was not stopped until he was about 30 miles from his goal—Canada and freedom.

Once the Nez Percé War was over, however, quite a different story came out. Chief Joseph's people were not rebels but in the right: they had twice been guaranteed their homeland in the Wallowa Valley of Oregon (in 1855 and 1873). Moreover, Joseph was only one of several Nez Percé chiefs, and because he had always been a man of peace, he had lost much of his influence when the war started. In fact, during the months of the long march, Joseph's job had been to protect the women, children, and elderly, not to engage in combat. Only after the war did he emerge as *the* leader—a statesman, not a warrior, a fair-minded spokesman for the freedom and dignity of all people.

As "No More Forever" indicates, Joseph's voice could be a persuasive one. However, his hopes were never fully realized. Not until 1885 was he permitted to return to the Northwest, and then to a reservation in Washington, not to his Oregon homeland. He died on September 21, 1904, still dreaming of a better America for all.

How did newspaper stories about the "unruly" Nez Percé differ from the truth?

NO MORE FOREVER

by Chief Joseph (In-mut Too-yah-lat-lat)

▶ The document that follows is Chief Joseph's eloquent appeal for the rights of Native Americans. It was first published 18 months after his final defeat near Bearpaw, Montana. The famous surrender speech itself *(in italics)* is not part of the original document but was recorded by a witness at the time. Here and there helpful information has been added to the original [in brackets].

My friends, I have been asked to show you my heart. I am glad to have a chance to do so. I want the white people to understand my people. I believe much trouble and blood would be saved if we opened our hearts more. I will tell you in my way how the Indian sees things. What I have to say will come from my heart, and I will speak with a straight tongue.

My name is In-mut Too-yah-lat-lat [Thunder Traveling over the Mountains]. I am chief of a band of Nez Percé [Nose Pierced]. I was born in eastern Oregon, 38 winters ago. My father [also called Joseph by white men] was chief before me. He died a few years ago. There was no stain on his hands of the blood of a white man. He left a good name on the earth. He advised me well for my people.

Our fathers gave us many laws, which they had learned from their fathers. These laws were good. They told us to treat all men as they treated us; that we should never be the first to break a bargain; that it was a disgrace to tell a lie; that it was a shame for one man to take from another his wife, or his property without paying for it. We were taught to believe that the Great Spirit sees and hears everything, and that he never forgets. Hereafter, he will give every man a spirit-home according to his deserts: if he has been a good man, he will have a good home; if he has been a bad man, he will have a bad home. This I believe, and all my people believe the same.

We did not know there were other people besides the Indian until about 100 winters ago, when some men with white faces came to our country. They brought many things with them to trade for furs and skins. These men were French, and they called our people "Nez Percé," because some wore rings in their noses. Although very few of our people wear them now, we are still called by the same name.

- **eloquent** (EL uh kwunt) forceful; movingly expressive
- **deserts** (di ZURTS) reward or punishment; what is deserved

The first white men of your people who came to our country were named Lewis and Clark. They also brought many things that our people had never seen. They talked straight, and our people gave them a great feast, as a proof that their hearts were friendly. These men were very kind. They made presents to our chiefs and our people made presents to them. We had a great many horses, of which we gave them what they needed. They gave us guns and tobacco in return. All the Nez Percé made friends with Lewis and Clark, and agreed to let them pass through their country, and never to make war on white men. This promise the Nez Percé have never broken.

It has always been the pride of the Nez Percé that they were the friends of the white men. But about 20 winters ago, a number of white people came into our country and built houses and made farms. At first our people made no complaint. They thought there was room enough for all to live in peace, and they were learning many things from the white men that seemed to be good. But we soon found that the white men were growing rich very fast, and were greedy to possess everything the Indian had. My father was the first to see through the schemes of the white men. He warned his tribe to be careful about trading with them. He had suspicion of men who seemed so anxious to make money. I was a boy then, but I remember well my father's caution. He had sharper eyes than the rest of our people.

Next there came a white officer [Governor Stevens], who invited all the Nez Percé to a treaty council. He said there were a great many white people in the country, and many more would come. He wanted the land marked out so that the Indians and white men could be separated. If they were to live in peace, that was necessary, he said. The Indians should have a country set apart for them, and in that country they must stay. My father, who represented his band, refused to have anything to do with the council. He wished to be a free man. He claimed that no man owned any part of the earth, and a man could not sell what he did not own.

Governor Stevens urged my father to sign his treaty, but he refused. "I will not sign your paper," he said. "You go where you please, so do I. You are not a child. I am no child. I can think for my-self. No man can think for me. I have no other home than this. I will not give it up to any man. My people would have no home. Take away your paper. I will not touch it with my hand."

My father left the council. Some of the chiefs of the other bands of the Nez Percé signed the treaty. [The lands of these bands, however, were already inside the newly created reservation assigned to the Nez Percé.] Two-thirds of the Nez Percé did *not* sign. Then Governor Stevens gave them presents of blankets. My father cautioned his people to take no presents. "After a while," he said, "they will claim that you have accepted pay for your coun-try." Since that time four bands of the Nez Percé have received annuities from the United States.

Eight years later [1863] was the next treaty council. A chief called Law-yer, because he was a great talker, took the lead in this council. He sold nearly all the Nez Percé country. My father was not there. He said to me: "When you go into council with the white man, always remember your country. Do not give it away. I have taken no pay from the United States. I have never sold our land." In this treaty Lawyer acted with-out authority from our band. He had no right to sell our Wallowa River country [in Oregon]. That had always belonged to my father's own people, and the other bands had never disputed our right to it. No other Indians ever claimed Wallowa.

The United States claimed they had

bought all the Nez Percé country out-side of Lapwai Reservation [in Idaho] from Lawyer and other chiefs. But we continued to live on this land in peace until eight years ago, when many white men began to come. We warned them against this great wrong, but they would not leave our land. The United States Government again asked for a treaty council. My father had become blind and feeble. He could no longer speak for his people. It was then that I took my father's place as chief. In this council I made my first speech to white men. I said to the agent who held the council:

"I did not want to come to this coun-cil, but I came hoping that we could save blood. The white man has no right to come here and take our country. We have never accepted any presents from the government. Neither Lawyer nor any other chief had authority to sell this land. We will defend this land as long as a drop of Indian blood warms the hearts of our men."

The agent said he had orders, from the Great White Chief at Washington, for us to go upon the Lapwai Reserva-tion. If we obeyed he would help us in many ways. "You *must* move," he said. I answered him, "I will not. I do not need your help. We have plenty, and we are contented and happy if the white man will let us alone. The reservation is too small for so many people with all their stock. We are free now; we can go where we please. Our fathers were born here. Here they lived, here they died, here are their graves. We will

• annuity (uh NOO i tee) regular payment
• **stock** (STAHK) farm animals

153

never leave them." The agent went away, and we had peace for a little while.

Soon after this my father sent for me. I saw he was dying. I took his hand in mine. He said, "My son, my body is returning to my mother earth, and my spirit is going very soon to see the Great Spirit Chief. When I am gone, think of your country. You are the chief of these people. They look to you to guide them. Always remember that your father never sold his country. You must stop your ears whenever you are asked to sign a treaty selling your home. A few years more, and white men will be all around you. They have their eyes on this land. My son, never forget my dying words. This country holds your father's body. Never sell the bones of your father and your mother." I pressed my father's hand and told him I would protect his grave with my life. My father smiled and passed away to the spirit-land.

I buried him in that beautiful valley of winding waters. I love that land more than all the rest of the world. A man who would not love his father's grave is worse than a wild animal.

For a short time we lived quietly. But this could not last. White men stole a great many horses from us, and we could not get them back. The white men told lies for each other. They drove off a great many of our cattle. Some white men branded our young cattle so they could claim them. It seemed to me that some of the white men in Wallowa were doing these things on purpose to get up a war. They knew that we were not strong enough to fight them. They forgot that years before, when the white men were few and we were strong, we could have killed them all off. But the Nez Percé wished to live at peace.

Because we did not do so, we have not been to blame. I believe that the old treaty has never been correctly reported. If we ever owned the land we own it still, for we never sold it. Suppose a white man should come to me and say, "Joseph, I like your horses, and I want to buy them." I say to him, "No, my horses suit me, I will not sell them." Then he goes to my neighbor, and says to him, "Joseph has some good horses. I want to buy them, but he refuses to sell." My neighbor answers, "Pay me the money, and I will sell you Joseph's horses." The white man returns to me, and says, "Joseph, I have bought your horses, and you must let me have them." If we sold our lands to the government, this is the way they were bought.

On account of the treaty made by the other bands of the Nez Percé, the white men claimed our lands. We were troubled greatly by white men crowding over the line. Some of these were good men, and we lived on peaceful terms with them, but they were not all good.

Nearly every year the agent came over from Lapwai and ordered us on to the reservation. We always replied that we were satisfied to live in Wallowa. We were careful to refuse the presents or annuities which he offered.

Through all the years since the white men came to Wallowa we have been threatened by them. They have given us no rest. We have had a few good friends among white men, and they have always advised my people to bear these threats without fighting. Our young men were quick-tempered, and I have had great trouble in keeping them from doing rash things.

Year after year we have been threatened, but no war was made upon my people until General Howard came two years ago and told us that he was the white war-chief of all that country. He said: "I have a great many soldiers at my back. I am going to bring them up here, and then I will talk to you again. The country belongs to the government, and I intend to make you go upon the reservation."

General Howard sent out runners and called all the Indians in to a grand council. I was in that council. I said to General Howard, "I am ready to talk. I have been in a great many councils, but I am no wiser. We are all sprung from a woman, although we are unlike in many things. We cannot be made over again. You are as you were made, and as you were made you can remain. We are just as we were made, and you cannot change us. Why should children of one mother and one father quarrel—why should one try to cheat the other? I do not believe that the Great Spirit Chief gave one kind of men the right to tell another kind of men what they must do."

General Howard replied, "You deny my authority, do you? You want to dictate to me, do you?"

Then one of my chiefs—Too-hool-hool-suit—rose in the council and said to General Howard, "The Great Spirit Chief made the world as it is, and as he wanted it. He made a part of it for us to live upon. I do not see where you get authority to say that we shall not live where he placed us."

General Howard lost his temper and said, "Shut up! I don't want to hear any more of such talk. The law says you shall go upon the reservation to live, and I want you to do so."

Too-hool-hool-suit answered, "Who are you, that you ask us to talk, and then tell me I shan't talk? Are you the Great Spirit? Did you make the world? Did you make the sun? Did you make the rivers to run for us to drink? Did you make the grass to grow? Did you make all these things, that you talk to us as though we were boys? If you did, then you have the right to talk as you do."

General Howard replied, "You are an impudent fellow, and I will put you in the guardhouse."

The soldiers came forward, seized my friend, and took him to the guardhouse. My men whispered among themselves, whether they should let this thing be done. I counseled them to submit. I knew if we resisted that all the white men present, including General Howard, would be killed in a moment, and we would be blamed. While they dragged Too-hool-hool-suit to prison, I arose and said, *"I am going to talk now. I don't care whether you arrest me or not."* I turned to my people and said: "The arrest of Too-hool-hool-suit was wrong, but we will not resent the insult. We were invited to this council to express our hearts, and we have done so."

- **rash** (RASH) reckless; foolhardy
- **impudent** (IM pyuh dunt) rude; insulting

Too-hool-hool-suit was prisoner for five days before he was released.

The council broke up for that day. Next day, General Howard informed me that he would give my people *30 days* to go back home, collect all their stock, and move onto the reservation. "If you are not there in that time, I shall consider that you want to fight, and will send my soldiers to drive you on."

I said, "War can be avoided, and it ought to be avoided. I want no war. My people have always been the friends of the white man. Why are you in such a hurry? I cannot get ready to move in 30 days. Our stock is scattered, and Snake River is very high. Let us wait until fall, when the river will be low. We want time to hunt up our stock and gather supplies for winter."

General Howard replied, "If you let the time run over one day, the soldiers will be there to drive you on the reservation. And all your cattle and horses outside of the reservation at that time will fall into the hands of the white men."

I knew I had never sold my country, and that I had no land in Lapwai. But I did not want bloodshed. I did not want my people killed. I did not want anybody killed. I said in my heart that, rather than have war, I would give up my country. I would give up my father's grave. I would give up everything rather than have the blood of white men upon the hands of my people.

General Howard refused to allow me more than 30 days to move my people and their stock. I am sure that he began to prepare for war at once.

When I returned to Wallowa, I found my people very much excited. The soldiers were already in the Wallowa Valley. We held a council, and decided to move immediately, to avoid bloodshed.

Too-hool-hool-suit, who felt outraged by his imprisonment, talked for war. He made many of my young men willing to fight rather than be driven like dogs from the land where they were born. It required a strong heart to stand up against such talk, but I urged my people to be quiet, and not to begin a war.

We gathered all the stock we could find, and made an attempt to move. We left many of our horses and cattle in Wallowa, and we lost several hundred in crossing the river. All of my people succeeded in getting across in safety. Many of the Nez Percé came together in Rocky Canyon to hold a grand council. I went with all my people. This council lasted ten days. There was a great deal of war talk, and a great deal of excitement. There was one young brave present whose father had been killed by a white man five years before. This man's blood was bad against white men, and he left the council calling for revenge.

Again I counseled peace, and I thought the danger was past. We had not complied with General Howard's order because we could not, but we intended to do so as soon as possible. I was leaving the council to kill beef for

---

• outraged (OUT rayjd) insulted; made very angry

156

my family, when news came that the young man whose father had been killed had gone out with several other hot-blooded young braves and killed four white men. He rode up to the council and shouted, "Why do you sit here? The war has begun already!"

I heard then that Too-hool-hool-suit had succeeded in organizing a war party. I knew that their acts would involve all my people. I saw that the war could not then be prevented. That time had passed.

I had counseled peace from the beginning. I knew that we were too weak to fight the United States. I admit that my young men did a great wrong, but I ask, who was first to blame? They had been insulted a thousand times. Their fathers and brothers had been killed. They had been told by General Howard that all the horses and cattle they had been unable to drive out of Wallowa were to fall into the hands of white men. And, added to this, they were homeless and desperate.

I would have given my own life if I could have undone the killing of white men by my people. I blame my young men and I blame the white men. I blame General Howard for not giving my people time to get their stock away from Wallowa. I do not acknowledge that he had the right to order me to leave Wallowa at any time. I deny that either my father or myself ever sold that land. It is still our land. It may never again be our home, but my father sleeps there, and I love it as I love my mother. I left there, hoping to avoid bloodshed.

I would have taken my people to the buffalo country [Montana] without fighting, if possible. I could see no other way to avoid a war. We moved over to Whitebird Creek, 16 miles away, intending to collect our stock before leaving. But the soldiers attacked us, and the first battle was fought. We numbered in that battle 66 men, and the soldiers 100. The fight lasted but a few minutes, when the soldiers retreated before us for twelve miles. They lost 33 killed, and had seven wounded.

Seven days after the first battle, General Howard arrived, bringing more soldiers. It was now war in earnest. We crossed over Salmon River, hoping General Howard would follow. We were not disappointed. We got back between him and his supplies. The battle lasted all day, and was renewed next morning. We killed four and wounded seven or eight.

Five days later General Howard attacked us with 350 soldiers and settlers. We had 250 warriors. The fight lasted 27 hours. We lost four killed and several wounded. General Howard's loss was 29 men killed and 60 wounded.

The following day the soldiers charged upon us, and we retreated with our families and stock a few miles, leaving 80 lodges to fall into General Howard's hands.

Finding that we were outnumbered, we retreated to Bitterroot Valley. Here another body of soldiers and settlers came upon us and demanded our surrender. We refused. They said, "You cannot get by our fort [later called 'Fort Fizzle']." We answered, "We are going by it without fighting if you will let us, but we are going by anyhow." We then made a treaty with these settlers.

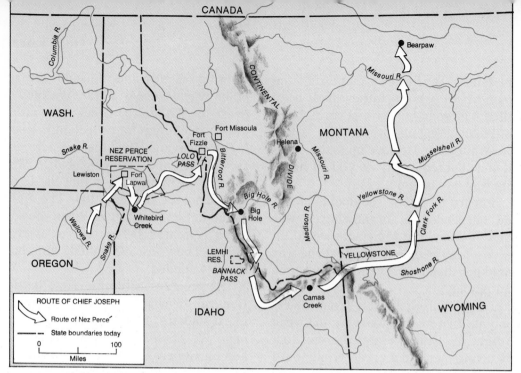

We agreed not to molest anyone, and they agreed that we might pass through the Bitterroot country in peace. We bought provisions and traded stock with white men there.

We understood that there was to be no more war. We intended to go peaceably to the buffalo country, and leave the question of returning to our country to be settled afterward.

With this understanding we traveled on for four days. Thinking that the trouble was all over, we stopped and prepared tentpoles to take with us. We started again, and at the end of two days we saw three white men passing our camp. Thinking that peace had been made, we did not molest them. We could have killed or taken them prisoners, but we did not suspect them of being spies, which they were.

That night the soldiers surrounded our camp [near Big Hole, Montana].

About daybreak one of my men went out to look after his horses. The soldiers saw him and shot him down like a coyote. I have since learned that these soldiers were not those we had left behind. They had come upon us from another direction. The new white war-chief's name was Gibbon. He charged upon us while some of my people were still asleep. We had a hard fight. Some of my men crept around and attacked the soldiers from the rear. In this battle we lost nearly all our lodges, but we finally drove General Gibbon back. In the fight we lost 50 women and children and 30 fighting men. We remained long enough to bury our dead. The Nez Percé never make war on women and children. We could have killed a great many women and children while the war lasted, but we would feel ashamed to do so cowardly an act.

We retreated as rapidly as we could

• molest (muh LEST) bother; annoy

158

toward the buffalo country. After six days General Howard came close to us, and we went out and attacked him. We captured nearly all his horses and mules [about 250 head]. We then marched on to the Yellowstone Basin [Wyoming].

On the way we captured one white man and two white women. We released them at the end of three days. They were treated kindly. The women were not insulted. Can the white soldiers tell me of one time when Indian women were taken prisoners, and held three days and then released without being insulted? Were the Nez Percé women who fell into the hands of General Howard's soldiers treated with as much respect? I deny that a Nez Percé was ever guilty of such a crime.

Nine days' march brought us to the mouth of Clark Fork of the Yellowstone. We did not know what had become of General Howard, but we supposed that he had sent for more horses and mules. He did not come up, but another new war-chief [General Sturgis] attacked us. We held him in check while we moved all our women and children and stock out of danger, leaving a few men to cover our retreat.

Several days passed, and we heard nothing of General Howard, or Gibbon, or Sturgis. We had repulsed each in turn, and began to feel secure, when another army, under General Miles, struck us [near Bearpaw, Montana]. This was the fourth army, each of which outnumbered our fighting force, that we had encountered within 60 days.

We had no knowledge of General Miles's army until a short time before he made a charge upon us. He cut our camp in two, capturing nearly all of our horses. About 70 men, myself among them, were cut off. My little daughter, 12 years of age, was with me. I gave her a rope, and told her to catch a horse and join the others who were cut off from the camp. I have not seen her since, but I have learned that she is alive and well.

I thought of my wife and children, who were now surrounded by soldiers. I resolved to go to them or die. With a prayer in my mouth, I dashed unarmed through the line of soldiers. It seemed to me that there were guns on every side, before and behind me. My clothes were cut to pieces and my horse was wounded, but I was not hurt. As I reached the door of my lodge, my wife handed me my rifle, saying: "Here's your gun. Fight!"

The soldiers kept up a continuous fire. Six of my men were killed in one spot near me. We fought at close range, not more than 20 steps apart, and drove the soldiers back, leaving their dead in our hands. We lost, the first day and night, 18 men and three women. General Miles lost 26 killed and 40 wounded. The following day General Miles sent a messenger into my camp under protection of a white flag. I sent my friend Yellow Bull to meet him.

Yellow Bull understood the messenger to say that General Miles did not want to kill my people unnecessarily. Yellow Bull understood this to be a

---

• **repulse** (ri PULS) drive back; repel
• **resolve** (ri ZOLV) determine; decide

demand for me to surrender and save blood. I sent him back with my answer, that I had not made up my mind, but would think about it and send word soon. A little later I walked to General Miles's tent. He met me and we shook hands. He said, "Come, let us sit down by the fire and talk this matter over." I remained with him all night. Next morning Yellow Bull came over to see if I was alive, and why I did not return.

General Miles would not let me leave the tent to see my friend alone.

Yellow Bull said to me, "They have got you in their power, and I am afraid they will never let you go again. I have an officer in our camp, and I will hold him until they let you go free."

I said, "I do not know what they mean to do with me, but if they kill me you must not kill the officer. It will do no good to avenge my death by killing him."

Yellow Bull returned to my camp. I did not make any agreement that day with General Miles. I was very anxious about my people. I knew that we were near Sitting Bull's camp in King George's land [Canada], and I thought maybe the Nez Percé who had escaped would return with assistance. No great damage was done to either party during the night.

On the following morning I returned to my camp by agreement, meeting the officer who had been held prisoner in my camp at the flag of truce. My people were divided about surrendering. We could have escaped from Bearpaw Mountain if we had left our wounded, old women, and children behind. We were unwilling to do this. We had never heard of a wounded Indian recovering while in the hands of white men.

On the evening of the fourth day, General Miles said to me in plain words, "If you will come out and give up your arms, I will spare your lives and send you to your reservation."

I could not bear to see my wounded men and women suffer any longer; we had lost enough already. General Miles had promised that we might return to our own country with what stock we had left. I thought we could start again.

I believed General Miles, or *I never would have surrendered.*

On the fifth day I went to General Miles, gave up my gun, and said:

Tell General Howard that I know his heart. What he told me before I have in my heart. I am tired of fighting. Our chiefs are killed. Looking Glass is dead. Too-hool-hool-suit is dead. The old men are all dead. It is the young men who say yes or no. Ollokot is dead. It is cold and we have no blankets. The little children are freezing to death. My people, some of them, have run away to the hills, and have no blankets, no food; no one knows where they are—perhaps freezing to death. I want to have time to look for my children and see how many of them I can find. Maybe I shall find them among the dead. From where the sun now stands I will fight no more forever.

I was told we could go with General Miles to Tongue River and stay there until spring, when we would be sent back to our country. We had nothing to say about it. After our arrival at Tongue River, General Miles received orders to take us to Bismarck [North Dakota]. General Miles was opposed to this order. He said, "You must not blame me. I have endeavored to keep my word, but the chief who is over me has given the order. I must obey it or resign. That would do you no good. Some other officer would carry out the order."

I believe General Miles would have kept his word if he could have done so. I do not blame him for what we have suffered since the surrender. I do not know who is to blame.

We were taken to Bismarck. Captain Johnson, who now had charge of us, received an order to take us to Fort Leavenworth [Kansas]. At Leavenworth we were placed on a low river bottom, with no water except river water to drink and cook with. We had always lived in a healthy country, where the mountains were high and the water was cold and clear. Many of my people sickened and died, and we buried them in this strange land. I cannot tell how much my heart suffered for my people, while at Leavenworth.

During the hot days [July 1878] we received notice that we were to be moved farther away from our own country. We were not asked if we were willing to go. We were ordered to get into the railroad cars. Three of my people died on the way to Baxter Springs [Kansas]. It was worse to die there than to die fighting in the mountains.

We were moved from Baxter Springs to the Indian Territory [Oklahoma]. We had but little medicine, and we were nearly all sick. Seventy of my people have died since we moved there.

We have had a great many visitors who have talked many ways. Some of the chiefs [General Fish and Colonel Stickney] from Washington, D.C., came to see us, and selected land for us to live upon. We have not moved to that land, for it is not a good place to live.

The Commissioner Chief [E. A. Hayt] came to see us. I told him, as I told everyone, that I expected General Miles's word would be carried out. He said it could not be done. White men now lived in my country, and all the land was taken up. If I returned to Wallowa, I could not live in peace, and the government could not protect my people. This talk fell like a heavy stone upon my heart. I saw that I could not gain anything by talking to him.

Then the Inspector Chief [General McNiel] came to my camp and we had a long talk. He said I ought to have a home in the mountain country north, and that he would write a letter to the Great Chief at Washington. Again the hope of seeing the mountains of Idaho and Oregon grew up in my heart.

At last I was granted permission to come to Washington, D.C., and bring my friend Yellow Bull with me. I am glad we came. I have shaken hands with a great many friends, but there are some things I want to know which no one seems able to explain. I cannot understand how the government sends a man out to fight us, as it did General Miles, and then breaks his word. Such a government has something wrong about it. I cannot understand why so many chiefs are allowed to talk so many different ways, and promise so many different things. I have seen the Great Father Chief [the President], the next Great Chief [Secretary of the Interior], and many other law chiefs [congressmen]. They all say they are my friends, and that I shall have justice. But while their mouths all talk right I do not understand why nothing is done for my people. I have heard talk and talk, but nothing is done.

If the white man wants to live in peace with the Indian, he can live in peace. There need be no trouble. Treat all men alike. Give them all the same law. Give them all an even chance to live and grow. They are all brothers. The earth is the mother of all people, and all people should have equal rights upon it. You might as well expect the rivers to run backward as that any man who was born free should be contented when penned up and denied liberty.

I only ask of the government to be treated as all other men are treated. If I cannot go to my own home, let me have a home in some country where my people will not die so fast. I would like to go to Bitterroot Valley. There my people would be healthy. Where they are now they are dying. Three have died since I left my camp to come to Washington.

We only ask an even chance to live as other men live. We ask to be recognized as men. We ask that the same law shall work alike on all men. If the Indian breaks the law, punish him by the law. If the white man breaks the law, punish him also.

Let me be a free man—free to travel, free to stop, free to work, free to trade where I choose, free to choose my own teachers, free to follow the religion of my fathers, free to think and talk and act for myself—and I will obey every law, or submit to the penalty.

Whenever the white man treats the Indian as they treat each other, then we will have no more wars. We shall all be alike—brothers of one father and one mother, with one sky above us, one country around us, and one government for all. I hope that no more groans of wounded men and women will ever go to the ear of the Great Spirit Chief above, and that all people may be one people.

In-mut Too-yah-lat-lat has spoken for his people.

ALL THINGS CONSIDERED ———————————————

1. According to Chief Joseph, since the earth cannot be considered private property (a) the government must decide who owns what. (b) no one has a right to buy or sell land. (c) the government has no right to tax people for the land they occupy.
2. The deathbed request of Chief Joseph's father was (a) "Live in peace with the white men at whatever the cost." (b) "Make war on the white men, for the time has now come." (c) "Never sell the bones of your father and your mother."
3. Chief Joseph makes the rather surprising claim that (a) the white men allowed wounded prisoners to die. (b) his own people killed wounded prisoners. (c) his people sometimes killed their own wounded.
4. At the time he wrote the account, Chief Joseph was disappointed in the government for (a) ignoring his very existence. (b) endless talk but no action. (c) refusal to pay promised annuities.
5. For some reason, Chief Joseph does *not* mention the fact that (a) his people were moved from place to place after the surrender. (b) he did not blame General Miles personally. (c) his own job was mainly to protect the women, the children, and the elderly, not to fight in the battles.

THINKING IT THROUGH ———————————————

1. What reasons does Chief Joseph give for his refusal, at first, to move to the Lapwai Reservation? Try to name at least two.
2. Throughout the document, Chief Joseph tries hard to be fair, even when it means criticizing the Nez Percé. What is one good example of such criticism?
3. Except for moving to Lapwai within the 30-day period, is there *anything* Chief Joseph could have done to avoid the war?
4. Do you believe that General Miles's promise to Chief Joseph should have been honored—*even if Miles had no authority to make it?* Explain.
5. Does Chief Joseph's account of the struggles of his people remind you of anything else in history (or in present-day events)? Explain.
6. What beliefs and customs of Chief Joseph's people do you find admirable?

RELATIONSHIPS

Comparison and Contrast

You know that people tend to think in certain patterns, and that for this reason, writers try to organize their material to harmonize with known patterns of thought. "No More Forever," for instance, makes some use of *comparison* and extensive use of *contrast*.

A **contrast** shows how two (or more) things are different. Chief Joseph was a man of peace; Too-hool-hool-suit wanted to go to war. Some Nez Percé signed the reservation treaty; others did not.

The word **comparison** unfortunately has no simple, accepted definition. A comparison always involves ways in which two (or more) things are alike. Sometimes, however, the word is used to mean differences as well as similarities. (When you see the word *compare* on an essay test, therefore, it's always a good idea to ask exactly how the word is being used.)

Prove to yourself that Chief Joseph argues his case mainly by using contrasts. First, fold a sheet of paper in half the long way so that you have two columns. Write CONTRASTS at the top, across the fold. Use the categories Chief Joseph uses. Write Nez Percé above one column and White Men above the other. Then list all the contrasts you can think of, side by side. For instance, you might start with "Never made war" in one column and "Attacked first in Nez Percé War" in the other. Don't stop until you have at least ten contrasts. Include beliefs, customs, and events, and don't forget to make reasonable inferences.

When you have finished, write COMPARISONS across the fold. Below it list all the similarities you can think of.

COMPOSITION

1. Select one of your contrasts and express it in four different ways: (1) a two-part sentence with *but* in the middle; (2) a sentence starting with the word *Although;* (3) a short two-part sentence with a semicolon (;) in the middle; (4) two sentences, the second starting with the word *However* and a comma.

2. Write a paragraph with this sentence as the leading main idea: *In "No More Forever," Chief Joseph argues his case mainly by using contrasts.* Refer to the list of contrasts you prepared earlier. Vary your sentence patterns by using the suggestions in composition question 1.

Critical Thinking

Avoiding Stereotypes

The exercise on the preceding page asked you to list *contrasts* between the Nez Percé and the white settlers. But critical thinking and analysis should not stop at that point. The process of discovering and listing contrasts can go on and on, until every individual is found to be different from every other individual. For instance, Chief Joseph speaks "for his people," but he also speaks as a "free man," who wants to be "free to think and talk and act for myself."

Unfortunately, Chief Joseph never gained his right to be treated as an individual. Instead, most of the time he was treated as a type. He was an "Indian." The government of his day, as well as the newspapers, seemed to have set ideas about how an "Indian" was supposed to think and talk and act. As a result, Chief Joseph often found himself the victim of unsound *stereotyped thinking*.

A **stereotype** (STER ee uh type) is the standard "picture in our heads" that a certain word brings to mind. Of course, since the mental picture is of no *particular* person or thing, the stereotype is almost always too general. In other words, the "picture in our heads" is usually false to fact when it comes to individual cases.

As a teenager, you have probably been the victim of unsound stereotyped thinking yourself. Think about the mental picture that many adults associate with the word *teenager*. The typical teenager is supposed to dress like this, to act like that, to have certain attitudes—in short, to be dealt with as a

teenager. As a result, many young people find themselves constantly protesting (mentally at least), "But I am not like that!" You know that each teenager can be, and usually is, quite different from the next teenager. They may all be between 12 and 20, but there is no such thing as a typical teenager.

Stereotyped thinking is a bad mental habit because it substitutes a type for the individual. *Teenagers* are often victims. So are *politicians*, *poets*, and *police officers*. So, in a way, are *city people*, *Yankees*, *Californians*, and many other groups of very different people.

1. Suppose others had made a real effort to treat Chief Joseph as an individual, not as a type. Name one or two things in his life that might have happened differently. Explain why.

2. Think about the stereotypes that these words bring to mind: cowboy, farmer, housewife. Then pick one of them and describe the false stereotype that seems to exist in the "public mind."

3. People from other nations sometimes get their ideas about "the American way of life" from American movies and TV shows. (Suppose your chief sources of information about the United States were movies and TV!) What false stereotypes of Americans do you think these people might have?

4. Explain why most prejudice is caused by sloppy and inaccurate stereotyped thinking.

165

VOCABULARY AND SKILL REVIEW

Before completing the exercises that follow, you may want to review the **bold-faced** words on pages 136 to 164.

I. On a separate sheet of paper, mark each item *true* or *false*. If it is *false*, explain what is wrong with the sentence.

1. The word *compare* sometimes includes its opposite, *contrast*.
2. An *Alien* Office would offer scientific help to farmers.
3. Baby chicks are *downy* little creatures.
4. You might see a *conveyor belt* in a fish cannery.
5. *Chronological* order is the same as size order.
6. The word *futile* is the opposite of *successful*.
7. The word *deceased* is the opposite of *dead*.
8. Good speakers know how to speak both sensibly and *inaudibly*.
9. *Impudent* remarks are usually not appreciated.
10. Good *foreshadowing* in a short story helps the reader to see what might happen.

II. On a separate sheet of paper, write the *italicized* word that best fills the blank in each sentence.

eloquent	*stock*	*resolve*	*hover*	*flashback*
repulse	*rash*	*memoir*	*slunk*	*prediction*

1. Stan's sudden, _____ actions sometimes get him into trouble.
2. The small group of soldiers managed to _____ a larger enemy force.
3. "I _____ to get better marks this term," Carmen said.
4. A _____ in a story interrupts the normal order of time.
5. Too embarrassed for words, I lowered my eyes and _____ out of the room.
6. The president of the United States should be a(n) _____ speaker.
7. In most places, farmers have to feed their _____ in the winter.
8. Weather forecasters are in the _____ business.
9. Grandfather wrote a _____ about his experiences in World War II.
10. About five o'clock each afternoon, my dog starts to _____ around the food bag.

III. Comment on the cartoon in terms of *predictions, comparisons,* and *contrasts.*

© 1978 B. Kliban. Reprinted from *Tiny Footprints* by permission of Workman Publishing Co., New York

Charles W. Chesnutt (1858–1932)

Chesnutt with his daughter, Helen

Modern American readers should remember the name Charles Waddell Chesnutt with both pride and embarrassment. On one hand, Chesnutt produced some of the best short stories in our nation's literature. One important critic has labeled them "works of art." On the other hand, magazine editors forced Chesnutt to conceal his race for much of his writing career. The editors believed that Chesnutt's reputation would suffer if the public knew that he was a black author.

Chesnutt was born in Cleveland, Ohio, where he spent most of his life. Although he had only a grade-school education, he became a teacher, a journalist, and finally a legal stenographer. He studied law and in 1887 passed the Ohio lawyer's examination with very high scores. He never successfully practiced law, however, and worked out his days as a court stenographer, not as an attorney.

Since writing was always Chesnutt's second career, it is surprising that he managed to produce so much excellent material. Today he is best remembered for three novels, a biography of the black leader Frederick Douglass, and a book of short stories, *The Wife of His Youth and Other Stories of the Color Line*. His later work deals almost entirely with the cruel effects of racial prejudice. About 1905, however, Chesnutt stopped writing for some personal reason that is not entirely clear. He wrote no fiction at all for the last 25 years of his life.

In your opinion, how might Chesnutt's career have been different if he had been born in 1958, not 1858?

BAXTER'S PROCRUSTES

by Charles W. Chesnutt

▶ The skillful story that follows must be read between the lines for full understanding. Remember to infer all you can about the narrator as you go along. Also remember that the story was written in 1904, when money was worth much more than it is today. All sums mentioned can safely be multiplied by ten.

Baxter's *Procrustes** is one of the publications of the Bodleian Club. The Bodleian Club is composed of gentlemen of culture, who are interested in books and book collecting. It was named, of course, after the famous library of the same name, and has been visited at times by pilgrims from afar. The Bodleian has entertained Mark Twain, Joseph Jefferson, and other literary celebrities. Its library contains a number of rare books, including a fine collection on chess, a game at which several of the members are experts.

The activities of the club are not, however, confined only to books. We have a very handsome clubhouse, and much taste has been exercised in its furnishing. There are many good paintings, including portraits of past presidents of the club, which decorate the entrance hall. After books, perhaps the most outstanding feature of the club is our collection of pipes. In a large rack in the sitting room is as complete an assortment of pipes as perhaps exists anywhere in the world. Indeed, it is a rule of the club that no one can join who cannot produce a new kind of pipe. This pipe is filed with his application for membership and, if he passes, is placed in the club collection.

As I have said, however, the very *reason for being* of the club and the feature upon which its fame chiefly rests, is its collection of rare books. Of these, by far the most interesting are its own publications. Early in its history it began the publication of books which should meet the club standard—books that featured those qualities that might make them valuable in the eyes of collectors. Of these, age could not, of course, be imparted. But in the matter of fine bindings, of handmade linen paper, of uncut pages, of wide margins

---

- impart (im PAHRT) give; make a part of
- uncut—not cut where pages are attached to each other at outer edges, top, or bottom (Fine books are often issued with uncut pages and then cut by hand.)

*In Greek mythology, Procrustes (proh KRUS teez) was a robber who stretched or cut off the limbs of his "guests" to make them fit the length of his bed. A *Procrustean bed* is any cruel and unfair effort to control other people.

and limited editions, the club could control its own publications. The matter of content was, it must be confessed, a less important consideration. At first it was felt by the publishing committee that nothing but the finest products of the human mind should be selected for the beautiful volumes which the club should issue. For instance, we brought out an essay by Emerson, and another by Thoreau.* Several years ago we also began to publish the works of our own members. Bascom's *Essay on Pipes* was a splendid performance. It was published in a limited edition of 100 copies, and since it had not previously appeared elsewhere, it was rare enough to be valuable at once. The second publication of local origin was Baxter's *Procrustes*.

I have omitted to say that once or twice a year, an auction is held at the Bodleian. The members of the club bring in their duplicate copies, or books they for any reason want to dispose of, which are auctioned off to the highest bidder. Three years ago, number three of Bascom's *Essay on Pipes* sold for $15—the original cost of publication was $1.75. Later in the evening, an uncut copy of the same brought $30. At the next auction, the price of the uncut copy was run up to $75. The club has always appreciated the value of uncut

copies, and this financial endorsement proved their worth. The rise in the *Essay on Pipes*, in fact, had an effect upon all the club publications. The Emerson essay rose from $3 to $17, and the Thoreau, being an author less widely read, brought a somewhat higher figure. The publication which brought the highest prices, however, was Baxter's *Procrustes*.

Baxter was, perhaps, the most scholarly member of the club. A graduate of Harvard, he had traveled and read widely. He possessed as fine a private library as any man of his age in the city. He was about 35 when he joined the club. Apparently some bitter experience—some disappointment in love or ambition—had left its mark upon his character. With light, curly hair, a healthy complexion, and gray eyes, one would have expected Baxter to be a pleasant person, indeed genial. But though he had occasional flashes of humor, his ordinary behavior was marked by a mild cynicism. This, along with his gloomy, pessimistic outlook on life, could only be accounted for by the inference of some secret sorrow such as I have suggested. What it might be no one knew. He had money and social position, and was an uncommonly handsome man.

It had occurred to me, in a vague

- endorsement (en DORS munt) approval
- **scholarly** (SKOL ur lee) like a scholar; well educated
- **genial** (JEEN yul) very cordial; cheerful
- cynicism (SIN i siz um) lack of faith in people; sneering distrust
- **pessimistic** (pes uh MIS tik) of or like a *pessimist,* one inclined to see or expect the worst

*Emerson and Thoreau—see page 46.

way, that perhaps Baxter might be an unsuccessful author. That he was a poet we knew very well. Typewritten copies of his verses had occasionally been seen. Then, slowly, the notion that Baxter was at work upon something fine became pretty well disseminated throughout our membership. At times he would read short passages to a small group of friends in the sitting room or library. These samples gave at least a few of us a pretty good idea of the theme and purpose of the poem. As I, for one, began to see, it was quite along the line of Baxter's general manner of thought. Modern society was the Procrustes which, like the Greek bandit of old, caught everyone born into the world, and then forced that person to fit some preconceived standard. Generally, the standard was one for which the person was by nature least suited. The world was full of men and women who were merely square pegs in round holes, and vice versa. Most marriages were unhappy because the two people were not properly matched. Science for the most part was superstition. Popular education was just a means of forcing the less able and holding back the bright, so that all youth of the rising generation should be forced to the same dull, dead level. Life would soon become so monotonously uniform and so uniformly monotonous as to be scarce worth the living.

It was Smith, I think, who first proposed that the club publish Baxter's *Procrustes*. The poet himself did not seem enthusiastic, protesting that the poem was not worthy of publication. But when it was proposed that the edition be limited to 50 copies, he agreed to consider the idea. At length the literary committee decided to request formally of Baxter the privilege of publishing his *Procrustes*. He consented, with obvious reluctance, upon condition that he should supervise the printing, binding, and delivery of the books. The manuscript would be submitted to the committee in advance, and Baxter would consider their views in regard to the bookmaking.

The manuscript was soon presented to the literary committee. Baxter's request was that the poem *not* be read aloud at a meeting of the club, as was the custom. He wanted, he said, "it to be given to the world clad in suitable garb." Understandably, the committee agreed—and went even farther. Having entire confidence in Baxter, they, with great courtesy, refrained from even reading the manuscript themselves. They were satisfied with Baxter's statement of the general theme and topics grouped under it. The details of the bookmaking, however, were gone into thoroughly. The paper was to be of handmade linen, from the Klemscott Mills. The cover, which was

---

- disseminated (di SEM uh nay tid) spread widely around
- preconceived (pree kun SEEVD) formed in advance
- **uniform** (YOO nuh form) unchanging; made of like parts
- **clad** (KLAD) dressed
- **garb** (GAHRB) clothing
- **refrain** (ri FRAYN) hold back from doing something

Baxter's own selection, was to be of dark green leather, with a cap-and-bells border in red inlays. Baxter was to oversee the entire publication. The whole edition of 50 numbered copies was to be sold at auction, in advance. Each member was limited to one copy, and Baxter himself was to receive one copy by way of thanks. Baxter protested at first, on the ground that his copy would probably be worth more than the usual ten percent would amount to. But he was finally persuaded to accept the author's copy.

While the *Procrustes* was under way, someone read, at one of our meetings, a note from some magazine. It stated that a sealed, airtight copy of Campanella's sonnets, published by the Grolier Club, had been sold for $300. This impressed the members greatly. It was a fresh idea. A new book, if the collector so desired, could be forever sacred, forever protected from any vulgar eyes or oily fingers. One who possessed such a work could enjoy it by the eye of imagination, knowing that he owned what was for others an unobtainable prize. The literary committee was so impressed with this idea that they presented it to Baxter. He made no objection, and members who might wish their copies delivered sealed were directed to notify the author. I sent in my name. A fine book, after all, was an investment. If there was any way of increasing its value, I was quite willing to enjoy such an advantage.

When the *Procrustes* was ready, each buyer received his copy by mail, in a strong, handsome box. Each copy was sealed in a transparent but very strong wrapping, through which the cover design and tooling were clearly visible. A label on the back of each copy bore its special number, as well as the monogram of the club.

At the next meeting of the Bodleian, a great deal was said about the *Procrustes*. It was agreed that no finer example of bookmaking had ever been published by the club. By an odd coincidence, no one had brought his copy with him, and the club's own copy was not at hand. Baxter reported that it had been kept back for some extra fine tooling. At any rate, a committee of three was appointed to review the *Procrustes* at the next literary meeting of the club. To this committee it was my doubtful fortune to be named.

In line with my duty, it soon became necessary for me to read the *Procrustes*. I was prepared to cut the pages in my own copy for this purpose. However, one of the club auctions occurred between my appointment and the date set for reading the reviews. A copy of the book, still sealed, was offered for sale. It was bought for the surprising price of $150. After this a proper regard for my own interests would not permit me to spoil my copy by opening it. I was, therefore, forced to get my information about the poem from some other source.

- cap-and-bells—fool's cap hung with bells
- inlay (IN lay) thin material (here leather) set into the surface of another material as decoration
- **sonnet** (SON it) kind of short poem
- tooling (TOOL ing) decoration made with tools

172

That chance soon presented itself. At the club one afternoon, I encountered Thompson and Davis, who were with me on the reviewing committee, in the sitting room. Both seemed anxious to get from other members their views on Baxter's masterpiece. I supposed that they wanted to review the book in a way that would reflect the opinions of those to whom the review should be presented. I assumed, of course, that Thompson and Davis had each read the book—both had purchased copies—and I wanted to get their point of view.

"What do you think," I inquired, "of the passage on social systems?"

"Well," replied Davis carefully, "I should consider it a harmonious fusion of all the best views of the best modern minds. With a strong Baxterian flavor, of course."

"Yes," said Thompson, "the charm of the passage lies in this very quality. The style is an examination of Baxter's own mind—he has written himself into the poem. Having read the book, we feel that we are so much more closely acquainted with Baxter—the real Baxter."

The talk went on, even after Baxter himself had come into the room. He stood by the fireplace smoking a pipe.

• fusion (FYOO zhun) combination; mixture

I was not quite sure if the faint smile on his face was a token of pleasure or cynicism. It was, however, *Baxterian*. I had already learned that Baxter's opinions on any subject were not always to be seen on his face. For instance, when the club porter's sick child died, Baxter remarked that the little devil was doubtless better off. He added, it seemed to me unfeelingly, that the porter himself had certainly been relieved of a burden. Then, only a week later, the porter told me privately that Baxter had paid for an expensive operation, in the hope of saving the child's life. I therefore drew no conclusions from Baxter's mysterious smile. He left the room at this point, somewhat to my relief.

"By the way," Davis said to me, "are you impressed with Baxter's view on the downward trend in modern civilization?"

"I think," I replied, "that his opinions are in harmony with the pessimistic trend, but without bitterness. Also, without flippancy. He is realistic about the world, but views it with a certain charm."

"Yes!" chimed in Davis. "The *Procrustes* answers the strongest demands of our day. It is unhappy with shallow optimism. It voices for us the courage of the human spirit facing the unknown."

"The *Procrustes*," said Thompson, "is written in beautiful lines of haunting melody. Yet the parts are so closely related, no single passage is quotable with justice to the author. To be appreciated, the poem must be read as a whole. I shall say as much in my review. What shall you say of the book itself?" The question was addressed to me, for I was supposed to discuss the printing and binding from an expert's viewpoint.

"The setting," I replied thoughtfully, "is worthy of the gem. The dark green cover and old English lettering mark this as one of our very choicest publications. The printing is of course De Vinne's best. There is nothing better this side of the Atlantic. The type is set as a beautiful, slender stream, flowing gracefully through a wide meadow of margin."

For some reason I left the room for a minute. As I stepped into the hall, I almost ran into Baxter. He was standing near the door, examining a painting. It was a very good bluff, but it did not deceive me. Baxter was anxious to learn what we thought of his poem. He had wanted to overhear our discussion without embarrassing us by his presence.

When the night came for the reviews of the *Procrustes*, there was a large attendance. Among the visitors was a young English cousin of one of the members, on his first visit to the United States. Some of us had met him in other clubs, and in society. We had found him a very jolly boy, with a youthful exuberance that made

---

- porter (POHR tur) one who does cleaning or maintenance work
- flippancy (FLIP un see) disrespectful remarks or humor
- **exuberance** (ig ZOO bur uns) high spirits; enthusiasm

his views refreshing and, at times, amusing.

The reviews were thoughtful and well expressed, if a little vague. Baxter received credit for poetic skill of a very high order.

"Our brother Baxter," said Thompson, "should no longer bury his talent. This gem, of course, belongs to the club. But the same brain from which it came can produce others to inspire and charm the entire world."

"The author's views," said Davis, "as expressed in these beautiful lines, will help us to fit our shoulders for the heavy burdens of existence. Baxter brings to life those truths that find hope in despair, and pleasure in pain. We hope he shall see fit to give to the wider world, in fuller form, the thoughts we now have in foretaste. Let us hope that some little ray of his fame may rest upon the Bodleian. It can never be taken away, that proud privilege of saying that he was one of its members."

I then pointed out the beauties of the volume. The dark green leather, I said, in summing up, symbolized the author's serious view of life. The cap-and-bells border showed just how silly were the optimists' delusions that the world was a good and pleasant place. The stern, bold type, yet with beautiful initials, showed that one might find, after all, an excuse for life and hope for humanity. I finished, "If the Bodleian had done nothing else, and if it should do nothing more, it has produced a masterpiece."

There was a sealed copy of the *Procrustes* lying on the table by which I stood. I supposed it to be the club's copy, since no one member seemed to have it under guard. I had picked it up for a moment, to emphasize one of my points. Then, I noticed, young Hunkin, the English visitor, had picked it up. He sat on the other side of the table, the *Procrustes* in his lap, examining it with interest. When the last review was read, and the generous applause had died down, there were cries for Baxter.

"Baxter!" "Baxter!" "Author!" "Author!"

Baxter had been over in a corner. He had succeeded fairly well, it seemed to me, in hiding under a mask of cynicism the joy I was sure he must feel. But this outburst of enthusiasm was too much for even Baxter. It was clear that he was struggling with strong emotion as he rose to speak.

"Gentlemen, and fellow members of the Bodleian, it gives me sincere pleasure . . . . Some day you may know how much pleasure . . . . I cannot trust myself to say it now. I see the care with which the committee has read my poor verses. I feel the sympathy with which my friends have entered into my views of life. I thank you again, and again. I'm sure you will excuse me from saying any more."

Baxter took his seat, and the applause began again, till it was broken by a loud voice.

"By Jove!" exclaimed the English visitor. "What an unusual book!"

Everyone who could gathered around him.

"You see," he exclaimed, holding up

● foretaste (FOR tayst) taste in advance

the book, "look here! You fellows said so much about this book that I wanted to see what it was like. So I took off the wrapping and cut the pages with that knife there. And I found—I found—that there isn't a single line in it!"

Blank amazement followed this announcement. It was only too true. Everyone knew at once that the club had been badly fooled. In the confusion that followed, Baxter escaped. But later he was visited by a committee, to whom he made a rather lame excuse. He said he had always thought of uncut and sealed books as a lot of nonsense. He had only been curious to see how far the thing would go. The result, he stated, proved his belief that a book with nothing in it was just as useful to a book collector as one containing the work of a genius. He offered to pay all the bills for the book, or to replace the blank copies with the real thing. Of course, after such an insult, the club did not care for the poem. However, he was permitted to pay the expense. It was hinted that his resignation from the club would be gladly accepted. He never sent it in. As he went to Europe shortly afterward, the affair had time to blow over.

In our first disgust at Baxter, most members opened and cut their copies of the *Procrustes*. Some mailed them to Baxter with nasty notes. Others threw them into the fire. A few wiser spirits held on to theirs, and this fact leaked out. It began to dawn upon the minds of the real collectors among us that the volume might be something unique—and therefore valuable.

"Baxter," said our president one evening, "was wiser than we knew, or perhaps than he knew." A select few of us were sitting around the fireplace. "His *Procrustes*, from the collector's point of view, may be an important volume. It represents a high point in the art of bookmaking. Think about the fine binding, and the paper is above criticism. The true collector loves wide margins, and the *Procrustes*, being all margin, will perhaps never be equaled. The smaller the edition, the greater the collector's eagerness to buy a copy. There are but six uncut copies left, I am told. And of these, only three are both uncut and sealed, of one of which I am the fortunate possessor."

After this speech, what happened at our next auction was not surprising. A sealed copy of Baxter's *Procrustes*, after lively bidding, was sold for $250. This was the highest price ever brought by a single volume published by the club.

ALL THINGS CONSIDERED ────────────────

1. The narrator persuades the reader early in the story that he is most concerned with (a) the content of rare books. (b) the appearance of rare books. (c) the value of rare books.

2. Early clues to Baxter's true character are best provided by the words (a) "healthy" and "genial." (b) "scholarly" and "traveled." (c) "cynicism" and "pessimistic."

3. The theme of the *Procrustes* is supposed to be (a) modern society forces people into molds they don't fit. (b) true freedom is an impossible dream. (c) you can't tell a book by its cover.

4. The story contains excellent examples of (a) flashbacks within flashbacks. (b) fine-sounding language that is really nonsense. (c) good ways to grow rich.

5. Reading between the lines, the good reader can see that Charles W. Chesnutt, the author, actually sympathizes with (a) the narrator. (b) the president at the end. (c) Baxter.

THINKING IT THROUGH ────────────────

1. A **satire** is a literary work that pokes fun at some idea or human weakness. (a) Would you call "Baxter's Procrustes" a satire? (b) If so, what is being made fun of? (You can give either a general or specific answer to this question.)

2. Many readers foresee the climax of the story before it actually happens. What are two examples of *foreshadowing* (see page 141) that might help the reader predict the young Englishman's discovery?

3. Unlike some stories, "Baxter's Procrustes" has a *resolution* after the *climax* (see page 77). (a) Where does the climax occur? (b) What is the one purpose of the resolution?

4. Explain why the author might have chosen to include the following in the story: (a) the pipes and the *Essay on Pipes*. (b) the meeting with Davis and Thompson before the final reviews are read. (c) Baxter's involvement with the porter's sick child.

5. Explain this sentence: In "Baxter's Procrustes," Chesnutt places a *rounded* character in the middle of a bunch of rather silly *stereotypes* (see page 77).

6. One of Chesnutt's aims in writing the story must have been to teach the reader a lesson. What is the lesson?

Reading and Analyzing

Mood and Tone

People read on several levels. The lowest level of all is understanding the basic or literal meaning of what words say. On a slightly higher level, the reader has to interpret figures of speech, see meaning in character clues, and make many other kinds of inferences. On quite a high level is understanding *mood* and *tone*. What do these two words mean?

The **mood** of a piece of literature is the feeling it gives the reader. For instance, some stories are depressing, others are hilarious, and still others are tender, thoughtful, disturbing, or even angry.

The word **tone** refers to the author's attitude toward both the subject matter and the reader. Sometimes an author pretends to be serious but really isn't. At other times an author presents characters who think they are very funny, but both author and reader see them as merely pitiful. The tone of a story, therefore, includes all the unstated understandings between author and reader about what the author is trying to do.

1. How would you describe the *mood* of "Baxter's Procrustes"? Look back at the *italicized* "mood words" if you have trouble.
2. Chesnutt's achievement with *tone* is what makes "Baxter's Procrustes" the superior story it is. After the first couple of pages, the reader begins to see what the author is up to. A few more pages, and the reader can almost see Chesnutt's face grinning between the lines: "Hey, I'm really having fun with this stuffy, pompous fool I've created as the narrator. And the rest of the bunch—except Baxter—aren't they delightful phonies?" (a) Look back at the story. Where did you begin to realize that you were supposed to laugh at the narrator, not take him as seriously as he takes himself? (b) When were you *sure* of the tone of the story? (c) Clues to the tone are provided by the narrator's style with words, by what he thinks as well as by what he says. What are one or two sentences that seem stuffy and overblown?

Composition

1. The terms *mood* and *tone* are sometimes carelessly used to mean nearly the same thing. In your own words, state the difference between them.
2. Try to write a review of "Baxter's Procrustes" that is as phony and empty of specific meaning as the nonsense spouted by Davis, Thompson, and the narrator. The idea is to sound impressive but really say very little.

Edna St. Vincent Millay (1892–1950)

The story of American literature contains some bleak chapters—chapters that this book has made no attempt to hide. You know, for instance, that the talented Charles W. Chesnutt once thought it necessary to conceal his race. Perhaps as bad is the fact that Edna St. Vincent Millay once thought that being a woman would jinx her chances for success as a poet.

And what a poet! She is not just a major voice in literature, but a major among the majors. Readers have been marching to her music now for more than 60 years.

Edna St. Vincent Millay grew up in Maine. Her parents were divorced when she was a little girl, and her mother supported the children by working as a nurse. Although money was scarce, life was as happy as Cora Millay and her three daughters could make it. The house was full of music and books. When Edna graduated from high school, she wanted to go on to college, but the money couldn't be found. She cheerfully turned to other things.

Then, when she had just turned 20, she submitted a poem to an important national contest. Two of the judges wanted to give it the first prize of $500. But the other judge disagreed. Why should the first-prize money go to an unknown person named E. St. Vincent Millay? Because the judges disagreed, they decided to ignore the Millay poem. The prize went to a well-known poet. But news of the disagreement among the judges spread across the country. People grew curious about the poem, and—when it was discovered that the "E." stood for "Edna"—about the poet. Edna St. Vincent Millay failed to win the prize, but she did win people's hearts.

From then on, her life took a different path. People who met the small woman with reddish hair liked her at once. They gave her money for college. The year she graduated, she published her first book of poems. Later she married, traveled around the world, and read her poetry to thousands of eager listeners across the country. She published book after book of poems that were tender yet strong, sometimes sad, sometimes bittersweet, but always honest.

What was the big turning point in Edna St. Vincent Millay's life?

LAMENT

by Edna St. Vincent Millay

Listen, children:
Your father is dead.
From his old coats
I'll make you little jackets;
5 I'll make you little trousers
From his old pants.
There'll be in his pockets
Things he used to put there,
Keys and pennies
10 Covered with tobacco;
Dan shall have the pennies
To save in his bank;
Anne shall have the keys
To make a pretty noise with.
15 Life must go on,
And the dead be forgotten;
Life must go on,
Though good men die;
Anne, eat your breakfast;
20 Dan, take your medicine;
Life must go on;
I forget just why.

WAYS OF KNOWING

1. Read both "Lament" and "Afternoon on a Hill." Why does it seem reasonable to call the "I" in the first poem the *speaker,* yet use *poet* for the "I" in the second?

2. Why do you infer that the speaker in "Lament" is the mother, rather than a doctor, nurse, or member of the clergy?

3. (a) Explain in your own words how the speaker in "Lament" is struggling with her feelings. (b) How successful is this struggle? (c) Which line in the poem tells you so?

• lament (luh MENT) speech of grief or sorrow

AFTERNOON ON A HILL

by Edna St. Vincent Millay

I will be the gladdest thing
   Under the sun!
I will touch a hundred flowers
   And not pick one.

5 I will look at cliffs and clouds
   With quiet eyes,
Watch the wind bow down the grass,
   And the grass rise.

And when lights begin to show
10   Up from the town,
I will mark which must be mine,
   And then start down!

---

4. In a word or two, how would you describe the *mood* (see page 178) of "Afternoon on a Hill"?

5. Line 6 of "Afternoon on a Hill" contains the term "quiet eyes." Of course, eyes don't usually make much noise. What does the word "quiet" suggest here?

6. Most poems deal with the past or the present, not with the future. Why might the poet have chosen the future tense for "Afternoon on a Hill"?

● **mark** (MARK) take note of

Mark Twain (1835–1910)

"The difference between the right word and the almost right word," wrote Mark Twain, "is the difference between lightning and the lightning bug."

Finding—catching—seizing—pinning down that *just-right* word was Mark Twain's specialty. It was he who defined a *classic* as "something that everybody wants to have read and nobody wants to read." It was also he who defined *cauliflower* as "nothing but cabbage with a college education."

America's favorite humorist was born as Samuel Langhorne Clemens in 1835. He grew up in the "little one-horse town" (a Twain term) of Hannibal, Missouri, on the west bank of the Mississippi River. His father died when he was 11, and "Sam'l" quit school to go to work for a printer. That was the first of his four careers. In the late 1850s he became a steamboat pilot, and in the 1860s he turned to newspaper work. Sketches and stories written for newspapers soon made him known across the country.

During his steamboating days, Sam Clemens often had to measure the depth of the water. This was done with a weighted rope that had knot markers tied six feet apart. The second mark, called "mark twain," showed that the water was deep enough for easy sailing. This may have been in his mind when he chose his pen name, for writing, too, soon became easy sailing. Working on *The Adventures of Tom Sawyer,* for instance, he often wrote 50 pages a day. After that book he went on to such classics as *Life on the Mississippi* and *The Adventures of Huckleberry Finn.*

Twain had many friends and was a concerned family man. He traveled often, to many parts of the world. He made, lost, and then remade a fortune in business. But the shock of his wife's death in 1904 left him a troubled man, and his last years were not happy ones. His birth had been signaled by the appearance of Halley's comet in 1835. Knowing that the comet's next visit was due in 1910, Twain told his friends that he would "go out with it," too.

Twain was right about his death. This self-educated genius, this "Lincoln of our literature," died peacefully on the night of April 21, 1910.

In your opinion, why has Mark Twain been called "the Lincoln of our literature"?

▶ After Mark Twain's books had made him one of the most famous authors in America, he grew even more popular as a public speaker. He carried in his head hundreds of stories and thousands of jokes. It took him only a minute or two to find the funny bone of an audience, and even convulsions of laughter would not make him let go of it. As a writer who was also an actor, he has never been equaled. No one but Mark Twain could better tell us—

HOW TO TELL A STORY

by Mark Twain

I do not claim that I can tell a story as it ought to be told. I only claim to know how a story ought to be told, for I have been almost daily in the company of the most expert storytellers for many years.

There are several kinds of stories, but only one difficult kind—the humorous. I will talk mainly about that one. The humorous story is American; the comic story is English; the witty story is French. The humorous story depends for its effect upon the *manner* of the telling; the comic story and the witty story upon the *matter*.

The humorous story may be spun out to great length, and may wander around as much as it pleases, and arrive nowhere in particular; but the comic and witty stories must be brief and end with a point. The humorous story bubbles gently along; the others burst.

The humorous story is strictly a work of art—high and delicate art—and only an artist can tell it. But no art is necessary in telling the comic and the witty story; anybody can do it. The art of telling a humorous story—understand, I mean by word of mouth, not print—was created in America, and has remained at home.

The humorous story is told gravely. The teller does his best to conceal the fact that he even dimly suspects that there is anything funny about it. But the teller of the comic story tells you beforehand that it is one of the funniest things he has ever heard, then tells it with eager delight, and is the first person to laugh when he gets through. Sometimes, if he has had good success, he is so glad and happy that he will repeat the "nub" of it and glance around from face to face, collecting applause, and then repeat it again. It is a pathetic thing to see.

Very often, of course, the rambling humorous story also finishes with a nub, point, snapper, or whatever you like to call it. Then the listener must be alert, for in many cases, the teller will divert attention from that nub by dropping it in a carefully casual and indifferent way, as though he does not even know it is a nub.

But the teller of the comic story does not slur the nub; he shouts it at you—every time. And when he prints it, in England, France, Germany, and Italy, he *italicizes* it, puts some whooping exclamation points after it, and sometimes explains it in a parenthesis. All of which is very depressing, and makes one want to renounce joking and lead a better life.

Let me set down an instance of the comic method, using a story which has been popular all over the world for twelve or fifteen hundred years. The teller tells it in this way:

THE WOUNDED SOLDIER

In a certain battle a soldier whose leg had been shot off appealed to another soldier who was hurrying by to carry him to the rear, informing him at the same time of the loss which he had sustained. The generous son of Mars,* shouldering the unfortunate, proceeded to carry out his desire. The bullets and cannonballs were flying in all directions, and presently one of the latter took the wounded man's head off—without, however, his deliverer being aware of it. In no long time he was hailed by an officer, who said:

"Where are you going with that carcass?"

- **pathetic** (puh THET ik) pitiful
- **divert** (di VURT) turn aside
- **indifferent** (in DIF ur unt) not caring
- **slur** (SLUR) make unclear; pass over carelessly
- **renounce** (ri NOUNS) reject; abandon with disgust
- **sustained** (sus TAYND) experienced; suffered
- **carcass** (KAHR kus) dead body, usually of an animal

*In ancient Roman mythology, Mars was the god of war.

184

"To the rear, sir—he's lost his leg!"

"His leg, really?" responded the astonished officer; "you mean his head, you fool."

At that the soldier relieved himself of his burden, and stood looking down upon it in great perplexity. At length he said:

"It is true, sir, just as you have said." Then after a pause he added, "*But he* TOLD *me* IT WAS HIS LEG! ! ! !"

Here the narrator bursts into explosion after explosion of horse-laughter, repeating that nub from time to time through his gaspings and shriekings and suffocatings.

It takes only a minute and a half to tell that in its comic story form, and isn't worth the telling after all. Put into the humorous story form, it takes ten minutes, and is about the funniest thing I have ever listened to—as James Whitcomb Riley* tells it.

He tells it in the character of a dull-witted old farmer who has just heard it for the first time, thinks it is unspeakably funny, and is trying to repeat it to a neighbor. But he can't remember it, so he gets all mixed up and wanders helplessly round and round, putting in tedious details that don't belong in the tale and only retard it; taking them out and putting in others that are just as useless; making minor mistakes now and then and stopping to correct them and explain how he came to make them; remembering things which he forgot to put in their proper place and going back to put them in there; stopping his narrative a good while in order to try to recall the name of the soldier that was hurt, and finally remembering that the soldier's name was not mentioned, and remarking thoughtfully that the name is of no real importance, anyway—better, of course, if one knew it, but not essential, after all—and so on, and so on, and so on.

To string incongruities and absurdities together in a wandering and sometimes purposeless way, and seem innocently unaware that they are absurdities, is the basis of the American art, if my position is correct. Another feature is the slurring of the point. A third is the dropping of a studied remark apparently

---

- **perplexity** (pur PLEK si tee) confusion; uncertainty
- tedious (TEE dee us) boring; tiresome
- incongruity (in kong GROO i tee) something not fitting or in harmony
- **absurdity** (ab SUR di tee) something absurd or ridiculous

*James Whitcomb Riley (1849–1916) was a popular poet and speaker at the time.

without knowing it, as if one were thinking aloud. The fourth and last is the pause.

The pause is a very important feature in any kind of story, and a frequently recurring feature, too. It is a dainty thing, and delicate, and also uncertain and treacherous; for it must be exactly the right length—no more and no less—or it fails of its purpose and makes trouble.

On the platform I used to tell a story about a man who came to interview me once to get a sketch of my life. I consulted with a friend—a practical man—before he came, to know how I should treat him.

"Whenever you give the interviewer a fact," he said, "give him another fact that will contradict it. Then he'll go away with a jumble that he can't use at all. Be gentle, be sweet, smile like an idiot—just be natural." That's what my friend told me to do, and I did it:

AN ENCOUNTER WITH AN INTERVIEWER

The nervous, dapper young man took the chair I offered him, and said he was connected with the *Daily Thunderstorm*, and added:

"Hoping it's no harm, I've come to interview you."

"Come to what?"

"*Interview* you."

"Ah! I see. Yes—yes. Um! Yes—yes."

I was not feeling bright that morning. Indeed, my powers seemed a bit under a cloud. However, I went to the bookcase, and when I had been looking six or seven minutes, I said:

"How do you spell it?"

"Spell what?"

"Interview."

"Oh, my goodness! What do you want to spell it for?"

"I don't want just to spell it; I want to spell it to see what it means."

"In, *in*, ter, *ter*, inter—"

"Then you spell it with an *I*?"

"Why, certainly!"

- **recurring** (ri KUR ing) occurring again and again
- dapper (DAP ur) neat; trim

"Oh, that is what took me so long."

"Why, my *dear* sir, what did *you* propose to spell it with?"

"Well, I—I—hardly know. I had the Unabridged, and I was looking around in the back end, among the pictures. But it's a very old edition."

"Why, my friend, they wouldn't have a *picture* of it in even the latest e— My dear sir, I beg your pardon, I mean no harm in the world, but you do not look as—as—intelligent as I had expected you would. No harm—I mean no harm at all."

"Oh, don't mention it! It has often been said, and by people who would not flatter me, that I am quite remarkable in that way. Yes—yes; they always speak of it with pleasure."

"I can easily imagine it. But about this interview. You know it is the custom, now, to interview any man who has become famous."

"Indeed, I had not heard of it before. It must be very interesting. What do you do it with?"

"Ah, well—well—well—it *ought* to be done with a club in some cases. But usually the interviewer asks questions and the interviewed answers them. It is all the rage now. Will you let me ask you certain questions to bring out the salient points of your public and private history?"

"Oh, with pleasure—with pleasure. I have a very bad memory, but I hope you will not mind that. That is to say, it is an irregular memory—very irregular. Sometimes it goes in a gallop, and then again it will be as much as a week passing a given point. This is a great grief to me."

"Oh, it is no matter, so you will try to do the best you can."

"I will. I will put my whole mind on it."

"Thanks. Are you ready to begin?"

"Ready."

Q. How old are you?

A. Nineteen, in June.

Q. Indeed. I would have taken you to be thirty-five or -six. Where were you born?

A. In Missouri.

Q. When did you begin to write?

A. In 1836.

Q. Why, how could that be, if you are only nineteen now?

A. I don't know. It does seem curious, somehow.

Q. It does, indeed. Whom do you consider the most remarkable man you ever met?

A. Aaron Burr.*

Q. But you never could have met Aaron Burr, if you are only nineteen years—

A. Now, if you know more about me than I do, what do you ask me for?

Q. Well, it was only a suggestion; nothing more. How did you happen to meet Burr?

A. Well, I happened to be at his funeral one day, and he asked me to make less noise, and—

Q. But, good heavens! If you were at his funeral, he must have been dead, and if he was dead how could he care whether you made a noise or not?

A. I don't know. He was always a particular kind of man that way.

Q. Still, I don't understand it at all. You say he spoke to you, and that he was dead.

A. I didn't say he was dead.

• salient (SAY lee unt) important; remarkable

*Aaron Burr, U.S. Vice President 1801–1805, died in 1836, the year after Twain was born.

Q. But wasn't he dead?

A. Well, some said he was, some said he wasn't.

Q. What did you think?

A. Oh, it was none of my business! It wasn't any of my funeral.

Q. Did you— However, we can never get this matter straight. Let me ask about something else. What was the date of your birth?

A. Monday. October 31, 1693.

Q. What! Impossible! That would make you a hundred and eighty years old. How do you account for that?

A. I don't account for it at all.

Q. But you said at first you were only nineteen, and now you make yourself out to be one hundred and eighty. It is an awful discrepancy.

A. Why, have you noticed that? (Shaking hands.) Many a time it has seemed to me like a descrepancy, but somehow I couldn't make up my mind. How quick you notice a thing!

Q. Thank you for the compliment, as far as it goes. Had you, or have you, any brothers or sisters?

A. Eh! I—I—I think so—yes—but I don't remember.

Q. Well, that is the most extraordinary statement I ever heard!

A. Why, what makes you think that?

Q. How could I think otherwise? Why, look here! Who is this a picture of on the wall? Isn't that a brother of yours?

A. Oh, yes, yes, yes! Now you remind me of it; that *was* a brother of mine. That's William—*Bill* we called him. Poor old Bill!

Q. Why? Is he dead, then?

A. Ah! Well, I suppose so. We never could tell. There was a great mystery about it.

Q. That is sad, very sad. He disappeared, then?

A. Well, yes, in a sort of general way. We buried him.

Q. *Buried* him! *Buried* him, without knowing whether he was dead or not?

A. Oh, no! Not that. He was dead enough.

Q. Well, I confess that I can't understand this. If you buried him, and you knew he was dead—

A. No! no! We only thought he was.

Q. Oh, I see! He came to life again?

A. I bet he didn't.

• discrepancy (di SKREP un see) difference; variation

Q. Well, I never heard anything like this. *Somebody* was dead. *Somebody* was buried. Now, where was the mystery?

A. Ah! That's just it! That's it exactly. You see, we were twins—defunct and I—and we got mixed in the bathtub when we were only two weeks old, and one of us was drowned. But we didn't know which. Some think it was Bill. Some think it was me.

Q. Well, that *is* remarkable. What do *you* think?

A. Goodness knows! I would give whole worlds to know. This solemn, this awful mystery has cast a gloom over my whole life. But I will tell you a secret now, which I never have revealed to any creature before. One of us had a peculiar mark—a large mole on the back of his left hand; that was *me. That child was the one that was drowned!*

Q. Very well, then, I don't see that there is any mystery about it, after all.

A. You don't? Well, *I* do. Anyway, I don't see how they could ever have been such a blundering lot as to go and bury the wrong child. But, 'sh!—don't mention it where the family can hear of it. Heaven knows they have heartbreaking troubles enough without adding this.

Q. Well, I believe I have got material enough for the present, and I am very much obliged to you for the pains you have taken. But I was a good deal interested in that account of Aaron Burr's funeral. Would you mind telling me what it was that made you think Burr was such a remarkable man?

A. Oh! It was a mere trifle! Not one man in fifty would have noticed it at all. When the sermon was over, and the procession all ready to start for the cemetery, and the body all arranged nice in the hearse, he said he wanted to take a last look at the scenery, and so he *got up and rode with the driver.*

Then the young man reverently withdrew. He was very pleasant company, and I was sorry to see him go.

• defunct (di FUNGKT) dead person
• **hearse** (HURS) carriage for taking the dead to the grave

ALL THINGS CONSIDERED

1. According to Twain, the *humorous* story (a) should be told quickly. (b) depends on the *manner* of the telling more than on the *matter*. (c) came originally from England.

2. Twain uses "The Wounded Soldier" (a) to illustrate both the comic and the humorous manner. (b) as an example of poor taste in subject matter. (c) to prove there are stories no one can tell well.

3. Twain uses "An Encounter with an Interviewer" (a) to illustrate what he calls the humorous manner. (b) as an example of poor taste. (c) to present factual details about his own life.

4. The character who answers the questions in "An Encounter with an Interviewer" is (a) Mark Twain as he would naturally act. (b) Mark Twain playing an imagined version of himself. (c) probably James Whitcomb Riley or someone else.

5. You can tell from the context that what Twain means by the "nub" of a story is the (a) theme or meaning. (b) punch line or point. (c) central conflict.

THINKING IT THROUGH

1. (a) Be honest—which do you prefer, what Twain calls the "comic" or the "humorous" story? (b) Can you explain what in your own experience—or *not* in it—led you to answer (a) as you did?

2. "The humorous story is told gravely," Twain says on page 183. But aren't the words *humorous* and *grave* opposites? Explain what Twain means by the sentence.

3. How do you explain the fact that most stories in joke books are comic, not humorous?

4. The two stories contained in the selection were probably not the only things that made you laugh. What else made you smile or chuckle as you read (a single sentence will do). Can you explain why?

5. Find the paragraph on page 185 that begins "He tells it in . . . ." The second sentence in that paragraph is 144 words long. In your opinion, why did the author deliberately let the sentence go on and on?

Oral Interpretation

Reading with Expression

Oral interpretation, or reading aloud with expression, is a vital reading skill that is losing ground in our fast-paced modern world. So for a few minutes, forget all you ever heard about the so-called advantages of speed reading. Mark Twain would ask you to renounce the practice and try to lead a better life.

1. Turn back to Twain's four rules for the humorous performance (the paragraph on page 185 that begins "To string incongruities . . ."). Write them on a sheet of paper, using your own words if you wish.
2. Now read through "An Encounter with an Interviewer" with the first rule in mind. Note how Mark Twain's story thoroughly illustrates the rule. Try to make a mental note of each example.
3. Do the same for rules 2, 3, and 4.

Where are the examples? Pay particular attention to the last rule—the pause. At what places would a pause make the next line funnier? And how long should that pause be? (Note that these first three steps can be done silently—even in a study hall—if you try to hear the words in your "mind's ear.")

4. Finally, practice reading "An Encounter with an Interviewer" aloud, exactly as you imagine Twain himself might have told the story on the stage.

(Hal Holbrook, a modern actor, has become famous for his "Mark Twain Tonight" performances across the country. Tapes and records of these performances are available in many schools and libraries. "An Encounter with an Interviewer" is on Columbia record OL 5440.)

Composition

1. Think of the funniest story you have heard recently. Write it out in what Twain would call the comic story form. Don't forget to finish with *italics*, CAPITALS, and a row of bowling pins—!!!!!!
2. The short profile of Mark Twain on page 182 contains only a few of the interesting facts about "the Lincoln of our literature." Look in reference books until you find at least two other aspects of Twain's life you think would be of general interest to the class. Write them in your own words on a separate sheet of paper.

VOCABULARY AND SKILL REVIEW ⸻

Before completing the exercises that follow, you may wish to review the **bold-faced** words on pages 169 to 190.

I. On a separate sheet of paper, write the term in each line that means the same, or nearly the same, as the word in *italics*.
1. *garb:* seize, drab, clothing, money
2. *exuberance:* enthusiasm, great strength, breaking point, endurance
3. *pathetic:* sympathetic, diseased, pitiful, barely alive
4. *divert:* disobey, turn aside, destroy, annoy
5. *genial:* elderly, stingy, uncontrolled, cheerful
6. *perplexity:* generosity, mental power, prejudice, confusion
7. *clad:* dressed, defeated, well fed, cheered up
8. *uniform:* unique, unchanging, unhealthy, unknown
9. *refrain:* replace, repair, hold back, think again
10. *scholarly:* serious, sober, strict, studious

II. 1. The *mood* of a poem is (a) the feeling it gives the reader. (b) its most depressing part. (c) whether the rhythm seems fast or slow.
2. You could easily find a *sonnet* (a) on a seashore. (b) in a library. (c) on a four-cycle engine.
3. A *pessimistic* person tends to (a) take advantage of most opportunities. (b) spread cheer. (c) be doubtful.
4. A *satire* (a) is a heavenly being. (b) makes fun of some idea or human weakness. (c) exists only in mythology.
5. To *slur* is to (a) support. (b) fill with air. (c) make unclear.
6. The *tone* of a literary work is the (a) author's attitude toward both subject and reader. (b) clarity of expression. (c) feeling it gives most readers.
7. A piece of *absurdity* is a piece of (a) wisdom. (b) nonsense. (c) reassurance.
8. WEEK is to DAY as *RECURRING* is to (a) NEVER. (b) ONCE. (c) ALWAYS.
9. SPEAK is to TALK as *MARK* is to (a) NOTICE. (b) PENCIL. (c) READ.
10. CRADLE is to BIRTH as *HEARSE* is to (a) MARRIAGE. (b) ILLNESS. (c) DEATH.

193

III.   Leroy "Satchel" Paige was a black baseball player whose whip-like pitching arm seemed to last forever. He was a star in the powerful Negro League for more than 20 years. Late in Paige's career the major leagues began to accept black players, and he became a star there, too. Paige pitched until he was nearly 50 years old and was elected to the Baseball Hall of Fame in 1971.

    Read the poem carefully before starting the review exercise that follows.

TO SATCH

by Samuel Allen

Sometimes I feel like I will *never* stop
Just go on forever
Til one fine mornin'
I'm gonna reach up and grab me a handfulla
    stars
5   Swing out my long lean leg
And whip three hot strikes burnin' down the
    heavens
And look over at God and say
How about that!

1. What is the *mood* of the poem? In other words, what feeling does it give you as a reader? Try to think of at least two words that express the mood.

2. What is the *tone* of the poem, particularly the poet's attitude toward "Satch"? Is Samuel Allen admiring the pitcher or making fun of him?

3. Explain how the tone of the poem is both humorous and serious at the same time.

4. Can you use oral interpretation to convey the author's tone? Remember the following points:
   a) Words can be made to sound like what they mean. For instance, you may want to make your voice a little higher for the words "reach up" in line 4. The phrase "long lean leg" in line 5 can be made to sound like a windup. Slow down for these words and pause a little on "leg," the instant of balance before the ball is released.
   b) The word "whip" in line 6 really does sound like what it means. Stress it.
   c) Read the poem triumphantly, especially the *"How about that!"*

UNIT REVIEW

I. Match the terms in Column A with their definitions in Column B.

A	**B**
1. satire	**a)** author's (usually inferred) attitude toward both subject and reader
2. foreshadowing	**b)** a piece of literature that pokes fun at some idea or human weakness
3. tone	**c)** a word that is sometimes used to include its opposite: *contrast*
4. compare	**d)** an interruption of chronological order to insert a scene that happened before the time frame of a story
5. flashback	**e)** clues deliberately planted by an author to enable the reader to predict what may or will happen

II. Here are seven statements about American literature. Some are clearly right or wrong; others depend on your opinion. First, read through the list and note your reactions: *true, false,* or *maybe*. Then pick the five statements you find you know the most about. On your paper, first write the numeral of the statement. Then write **T** (true), **F** (false), or **?** (maybe). Finally, write at least one sentence supporting your opinion. Note that if you so choose, all your support can come from this unit.

1. Almost all good American literature was written by bearded gentlemen.
2. Native Americans are best represented by simple poems of the people, not by the significant statements of recognized leaders.
3. American literature is best represented by Mark Twain.
4. Black writers have always been given the same opportunities as white writers to present their works to the public.
5. Some good literature has come from the common people in the form of folktales.
6. In general, it's safe to think of women as poets and men as writers of prose.
7. The best American literature has come from the imaginative minds of people like C. W. Chesnutt, not from authors who never leave the realistic world.

SPEAKING UP

This exercise could be thought of as *your* encounter with an interviewer. It works best if you pair up with another student, although it is not absolutely necessary. One person can play the roles of both the interviewer and the person being interviewed, as Mark Twain did on the stage.

1. As the person being interviewed, you can be anyone you choose to be—except yourself. Try to pick someone whose voice and manner the whole class knows well. TV celebrities or characters in the stories you've read are good choices.

2. Write at least five questions that a newspaper or TV interviewer might ask the person whose role you will play. Try for questions that get at the person's opinions and private life.

3. Make some notes on—*but do not fully write out*—answers to the questions. Your job here is to use a lot of words and seem willing to provide good answers, but in reality to confuse the interviewer and say almost nothing. If you want to, go back and review two examples in this unit: (1) the speeches of Davis, Thompson, and the narrator in "Baxter's Procrustes," and (2) Twain's responses in "An Encounter with an Interviewer."

4. Practice the answers until they seem perfect. Use all the notes you need, but no more than that. You can't sound spontaneous if a prepared statement is at hand to read. Notice, for example, that you wouldn't really need many notes to give the nearly meaningless answer that follows:

Q: Mr. Twain, which of your books did you most enjoy writing?

A: I'm glad you asked me that question, very glad. In fact, it's a question I'm asked frequently, and one that I take not only pleasure, but also some pride, if I may say so, in answering. . . . Which of my books did I enjoy writing the most? . . . You know, the last person who asked me that question—in Lincoln, Nebraska, it was; no, Omaha . . . well, Lincoln or Omaha, one or the other; it's not the vital thing I'm trying to get at here—refused to believe that I gave her an honest answer. But why wouldn't I? There's no reason to avoid that question, or to greet it with an untruthful response. I've always been a truthful person, and I've lived by my principles. Of course, I was born without principles, but along the way I've picked up six—no, seven, I think—that have served me well. Now, next question?

WRITING A 5-PARAGRAPH THEME

Assignment: Write a five-paragraph composition using this sentence, or one very like it, as the theme or main idea: *American literature is not any single kind of writing but a chorus of different voices.*

Prewriting: First, turn back to the organization of a five-paragraph theme on pages 131–133. Review the information up to the paragraph that starts with the word *Assignment.* Then apply what you have reviewed to this assignment. You know the sentence that contains the controlling idea of the whole composition, and you know exactly where that sentence has to be.

Now you have to find some kind of "hook" to start the paper. *Don't* begin with something like "In this composition I am going to . . ." *Of course* you are writing a composition, and *of course* you are going to do something in it. *Just do it.* Several ways to begin are given on page 131. You might think of beginning with the Thoreau quotation on page 135. Then simply point out that American writers have often followed this advice, with each following his or her own music. That idea leads right to the main idea of the paper.

Decide on the three examples you will use in the central paragraphs. You don't have to confine your search to this unit, but you easily can. Ethnic voices suggest themselves: Maxine Hong Kingston, Chief Joseph, Charles W. Chesnutt. Or you might want to make distinctions based on authors' purposes: to be funny, to be serious, to be suspenseful. There are other possibilities as well.

Writing: Your first paragraph is now so well planned that you simply have to put it on paper. Each of the next three paragraphs should begin with a sentence that indicates what the whole paragraph will be about. If you can, try to link the paragraphs together by starting with expressions like "One major voice . . . ," "A second voice . . . ," and "Still another voice. . . ." As you write, be alert for some good phrases to use in the final, concluding paragraph.

Revision: Follow the procedures given on page 132. With more practice, you should have less to revise.

197

UNIT · 4

WHAT'S THE BIG IDEA?

I care,
I understand,
I long to be wanted,
I cry, I laugh—I am very
Human
—Vivian Velasquez (high school student)

What's the big idea? That's a question that most readers should ask more often than they do. Literature is full of BIG IDEAS—thoughts about right and wrong, courage, wisdom, sacrifice, and even death. Even the shortest of poems can make a powerful statement about life.

Serious ideas, however, don't have to be presented in boring ways. Good authors can deliver serious messages in literature that is thrilling, amusing, heartrending, or fanciful. You'll begin this unit with a sober, highly symbolic story in which death is exchanged for life, and you'll go on to read a real cliff-hanger about a man whose life is threatened by a terrifying, unexplainable force. In these selections, as in the others, the "big ideas" are determined not by the length of the reading, but by how much your mind can measure.

O. Henry (1862-1910)

A Times Square street scene in New York City, 1908

Few authors have had a stranger life than William Sydney Porter, or "O. Henry," as he signed his stories. He was born in Greensboro, North Carolina. He had little formal education. As a young man he drifted to Texas, where he worked on a ranch, in a bank, and on a newspaper. Charged with stealing money from the bank, he fled to Central America. But news of his wife's illness brought him back, and he was forced to face the bank robbery charges. He served a three-year prison term in Ohio.

Strangely enough, being sent to prison was the big break in O. Henry's life. With time on his hands, he practiced writing short stories. Soon he won the success he desired. After his release, he moved to New York City, and for several years he wrote a story a week for popular magazines. He made a lot of money—but his life was to have an early end. He died before he was 50, of a liver disease associated with alcoholism.

Today O. Henry is remembered as the master of the surprise ending. His writing style, once thought fresh and clever, now seems old-fashioned and artificial at times, but his fast-moving plots and last-page surprises still hold the reader's attention. Among his best-known stories are "The Last Leaf," "The Furnished Room," "Mammon and the Archer," and "The Gift of the Magi."

O. Henry's stories are notable for their surprising turns and trick endings. What was one surprising turn in the author's life?

200

► When Johnsy fell ill, the doctor said her chances of living were only one in ten. She herself thought she was going to die. It was only a question of *when*—and everything depended on . . .

THE LAST LEAF

by O. Henry

Just west of New York City's Washington Square, the streets have run crazy and broken themselves into small strips called "places." These "places" make strange angles and curves. One street crosses itself a time or two. A poor artist once discovered that this was *just* the place to live. Suppose a bill collector came. On streets like these, he might suddenly meet himself coming back, without a cent having been paid on any of his bills!

So here, years ago, the art people came in great numbers. The area was—and still is—called Greenwich Village. Young artists poured in from all over the country, looking for north windows and 18th-century gables and Dutch attics and low rents.

And here, Sue and Johnsy had their art studio. "Johnsy" was a nickname for *Joanna*. They rented the top of a three-story brick building. One was from Maine; the other from California. The girls had met at an Eighth Street cafeteria. Their tastes in art were the same. Their tastes in food were the same. So the shared studio was a natural result.

That was in May. In November a cold, unseen stranger, whom the doctors called Pneumonia, stalked about the city. With icy fingers, he touched one here, one there. Over on the East Side, this ravager strode boldly, smiting his victims by scores. But he had to walk slowly through the crooked, narrow streets of Greenwich Village.

Mr. Pneumonia was hardly a kind old man. He was red fisted and short of breath. And a young woman from California was

- gable (GAY bul) end of peaked roof
- ravager (RAV ij ur) one who *ravages*, or does bad damage
- smiting (SMYT ing) hitting hard; punishing with force
- **scores** (SKORZ) a great many

201

hardly fair game for him. But Johnsy he smote. Soon she lay, scarcely moving, on her bed. She grew even more ill. Day after day she lay staring through the window at the blank wall of an old brick house.

One morning the busy doctor paid a visit. He looked at Johnsy; then he invited Sue into the hallway by raising his shaggy gray eyebrow.

"I could put her in the hospital," the doctor said. "But beds are scarce. And besides, she's just as well off here."

Sue nodded.

"She has one chance in—let us say, ten," the doctor went on. "And that chance is for her to want to live. You see, she's joined the crowd lining up for the funeral director. That kind of thing makes us doctors look silly. She's decided for herself that she's not going to get well. Has she anything on her mind?"

"She used to," Sue replied. "She—she wanted to paint the Bay of Naples* someday."

"Paint? Bosh! Has she anything on her mind worth thinking about twice? A man, for instance?"

"A man?" said Sue, with a twang in her voice. "Is a man worth—? But no, doctor. Nothing of the kind."

"Well, it's the illness, then," said the doctor. "I will do all that science can accomplish. But that girl is already counting the people at her funeral. When that happens, I subtract fifty percent from the powers of our medicines. You just get her to ask one question about something she really likes. Just one question. Then I'll promise you a one-in-five chance for her, instead of one in ten."

The doctor left, and Sue went into their workroom. She cried a napkin soggy with tears. Then she walked brightly into Johnsy's room, carrying her drawing board and whistling a jazz tune.

Johnsy lay with her face toward the window. Was she asleep? Sue thought so. She stopped whistling and sat down to work on her drawing, a picture for a magazine story.

For a while Sue worked on the figure of the hero, an Idaho cowboy. Then she heard a low sound, several times repeated. She went quickly to the bedside.

Johnsy's eyes were wide open. She was looking out the window and counting—counting backward.

"Twelve," she said. Then, a little later, "Eleven." Next came

---

• **twang** (TWANG) sharp, vibrating sound

*Naples (NAY pulz) is a large city in Italy, just south of Rome.

ten and nine. Finally she said, "Eight, seven," almost together.

Sue was worried. She glanced out the window. What was there to count? There was only a bare, dreary yard to be seen, and the side of the brick house 20 feet away. An old, old ivy vine, gnarled and decayed at the roots, crawled up the brick wall. The cold breath of autumn had touched the vine, leaving its skeleton branches almost bare.

"What is it, Johnsy?" asked Sue.

"Seven now," said Johnsy, in almost a whisper. "They're falling faster now. Three days ago there were almost a hundred. It made my head ache to count them. But now it's easy. There goes another one. There are only six left now."

"Six *what*, Johnsy? Tell me!"

"Leaves. On the ivy vine. When the last one falls, I must go, too. I've known that for three days. Didn't the doctor tell you?"

"Oh, that's nonsense!" complained Sue. "What have those old ivy leaves to do with *you*? With your getting well? And you used to love that vine so. Don't be a goose. Why, your chances are good, Johnsy. The doctor told me just now—let's see exactly what he said—he said the chances were ten to one! There's really no reason to worry, Johnsy. Try to take some soup now. And let Sue get back to her drawing. I've got to sell it to that magazine. Then we'll have money for—for pork chops!"

• **gnarled** (NAHRLD) badly twisted

"You needn't get any pork chops for me," said Johnsy, keeping her eyes fixed out the window. "There goes another. No, I don't want any soup. The last one will fall before it gets dark. Then I'll go, too."

"Johnsy, dear!" exclaimed Sue. "Look, I want you to promise me something. Promise to keep your eyes closed, and not look out the window till I'm done working. My drawings are due tomorrow. I need the light, or I'd pull the shade down."

"Couldn't you draw in the other room?" Johnsy's voice was cold.

"I'd rather be here by you," said Sue. "Besides, I don't want you to keep looking at those silly ivy leaves."

"Tell me when you're done," said Johnsy, closing her eyes. Her face was white, and she lay still as a fallen statue. "You see, I want to see that last leaf fall. I'm tired of waiting. I'm tired of thinking. I want to turn loose my hold on everything. Then I'll go sailing down, down, just like one of those poor, tired leaves."

"Try to sleep," said Sue. "I must go see Behrman. He's to be my model for the older cowboy. I'll not be gone a minute. Try not to move till I come back."

Old Behrman was a painter who lived downstairs, on the ground floor. He was past 60. He was a failure in art. For 40 years he had wielded the brush, without success. He'd been always about to paint a masterpiece, but he'd never yet begun it. Now he earned a little money by working as a model, and he still talked of his masterpiece. For the rest, he was a fierce little old man, who scoffed terribly at softness in anyone. He thought of himself as the protector of the two young artists in the studio above.

Sue found Behrman at home. In one corner of his den was a blank canvas on an easel that had been waiting 25 years for the first line of his masterpiece. She told him of Johnsy's thoughts: "She's as light as a leaf herself, and she might really float away. Her hold on the world gets weaker and weaker."

Old Behrman's red eyes went wet. He waved his arms and shouted his contempt and derision for such idiotic imaginings.

"What!" he cried. "Is there people in the world with such foolishness? To die because a leaf drops off a vine? I have not heard of such a thing! No, I will not pose as model for you. Why do you

---

- wield (WEELD) hold and use
- contempt (kun TEMPT) scorn; disrespect
- derision (di RIZH un) ridicule; mockery

allow this silly business to come into the brain of her? Huh? Ach, poor little Miss Johnsy!"

"She's very ill and weak," said Sue. "The fever has left her mind morbid and filled with strange thoughts. Very well, Mr. Behrman. If you don't want to pose, you needn't. But I think you're a horrible old—"

"You are just like a woman!" yelled Behrman. "Who says I not pose. Go on. I come with you. What a place is this city! One so good as Miss Johnsy should not lie sick. Someday I paint a masterpiece, and then we shall all go away. Yes?"

Johnsy was sleeping when they went upstairs. Sue pulled the shade down and led Behrman into the other room. There they stared out the window at the ivy vine. They looked at each other for a moment without speaking. A cold rain was now falling, mixed with snow. Behrman, in his old blue shirt, sat down to pose on an upturned kettle for a rock.

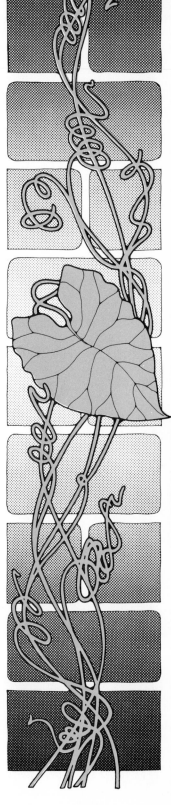

Sue slept badly that night. In the morning, when she awoke from only an hour's sleep, she found Johnsy with dull, wide-open eyes, staring at the dawn green shade.

"Pull the shade up," Johnsy ordered, in almost a whisper. "I want to see."

Wearily, Sue obeyed.

But, there! A fierce wind had blown all night, and the rain had beat down. Yet one ivy leaf stood out against the brick wall. Just one. It was still dark green near its stem, and its sawtooth edge was tinted with yellow. It hung bravely about twenty feet from the ground.

"It's the last one," said Johnsy. "I thought it would fall during the night. I heard the wind. It will surely fall today, and I will die at the same time."

"No, no!" said Sue, leaning her worried face down to the pillow. "Think of me, if you won't think of yourself. What would I do?"

But Johnsy did not answer. She seemed to be making ready to go on a mysterious, far journey. One by one, the ties that bound her to friendship and to earth were breaking.

The day wore away. At last came the twilight, and they could still see the lone ivy leaf clinging to its stem. And then, with the coming of night, they could see it against the wall no longer. The north wind was again set free, and the rain still beat against the windows.

• **morbid** (MOR bid) gloomy; mentally unhealthy

The night passed slowly. When it was light enough, Johnsy, the merciless, commanded that the shade be raised.

The ivy leaf was still there.

Johnsy lay for a long time looking at it. Sue finally left for the kitchen. And then Johnsy called to Sue, who stopped stirring the chicken soup at once.

"I've been a bad girl, Susie," Johnsy said. "Something has made that last leaf stay there. Why? To show me how wicked I was. It's a sin to want to die. You can bring me a little soup now, and some milk. No! Bring me a hand mirror first. Then pack some pillows behind me. I want to sit up."

An hour later she said:

"Susie, someday I'm going to paint the Bay of Naples."

The doctor came in the afternoon. Again, Sue followed him into the hallway as he left.

"Even chances," said the doctor, taking Sue's thin, shaking hand in his. "With good nursing you'll win. And now I must see another case downstairs. Behrman, his name is. Some kind of an artist, I think. Pneumonia, too. He's an old, weak man, and the disease is too much for him. There's no hope. But he goes to the hospital today to be more comfortable."

The next day the doctor returned. "She's out of danger," he said to Sue. "You've won. Nutrition and care now—that's all."

And that afternoon Sue came to the bed where Johnsy lay. "I have something to tell you, white mouse," she said. Johnsy looked up from her knitting.

"Mr. Behrman died of pneumonia today in the hospital," Sue went on. "He was ill only two days. They found him on the morning of the first day. He was in his room, helpless with pain. His clothes were wet and cold. They couldn't imagine where he'd been on such a bad night. And then, outside, they found a lantern, still lighted. Near it was a ladder. They found some scattered brushes, and a palette with green and yellow paint. . . . Look out the window, Johnsy. Look at the last ivy leaf on the wall. Didn't you wonder why it never moved when the wind blew? Yes, it's Behrman's masterpiece—he painted it there the night that the last leaf fell."

• **palette** (PAL it) artist's hand-held board for mixing colors

ALL THINGS CONSIDERED ────────────────────

1. At first, the doctor thinks that Johnsy's chances to live are (a) very poor. (b) about 50–50. (c) quite good.
2. Sue immediately tells Johnsy that her chances are (a) very poor. (b) about 50–50. (c) quite good.
3. The term that *best* describes Johnsy's behavior toward the end of the story is (a) *accidental.* (b) *strong-willed.* (c) *self-sacrificing.*
4. The term that *best* describes Behrman's behavior toward the end of the story is (a) *accidental.* (b) *weak-willed.* (c) *self-sacrificing.*
5. The *least* important of the three characters is (a) Behrman. (b) Sue. (c) Johnsy.

THINKING IT THROUGH ────────────────────

1. At the end of the story, Sue calls the leaf "Behrman's masterpiece." What does she mean?
2. If you were Johnsy, what would be your feelings at the end?
3. Although the last paragraph comes as a surprise to most readers, it at least seems like a *possible* ending to the story. This is due to O. Henry's careful *foreshadowing* (see page 141). List two things the reader is told about Behrman that help foreshadow the ending.
4. "The Last Leaf" deals with not one but several BIG IDEAS about life. In your opinion, what is an important theme in the story? These key terms may guide your thinking: *love, faith, sacrifice, will power, courage.*
5. As you know, the technique of giving human qualities to non-human subjects is known as *personification* (see p. 44). For instance, people often speak of *Mother Nature* and *Father Time.* How does O. Henry use personification on page 201 of the story?

Reading and Analyzing

Symbols and Symbolic Action

One of the most misused terms in the study of literature is *symbol*. This confusion is unnecessary, for there is really nothing hard about the word.

The simplest definition of **symbol** is something in a story or poem that stands for something else. For instance, in "The Last Leaf" it is no accident that Sue goes into the kitchen and prepares *chicken soup*. Chicken soup, or broth, is a common symbol of love and concern for a person who is sick. Sue's preparation of the soup can be seen as a **symbolic action**: The act tells us something about Sue herself.

You won't have trouble with the term *symbol* if you remember two things about the definition:

- A symbol must REALLY BE THERE in a story or poem. Think about the doctor's statement that Johnsy is "already counting the people at her funeral." In fact, Johnsy is probably doing no such thing. There is no real "funeral" in the story. "Funeral" is not a symbol here but part of a *metaphor* (see page 30). Now consider Johnsy's lying in bed, "still as a fallen statue." Is there any real statue in the story? Of course not. "Statue" is not a symbol but part of a *simile* (see page 30).

- The "something else" that a symbol stands for is usually not the kind of real thing one can see and touch. More often, the symbol is the real thing and what it "stands for" is an idea, feeling, or quality.

1. What fact about Behrman does the blank canvas in his den symbolize?
2. What does the last leaf symbolize to Johnsy, both (a) before and (b) after the second stormy night?
3. Consider the painting of the leaf in terms of symbolic action. What does the act tell us about the actor—old Behrman?

Composition

1. Suppose that soon after the end of the story, Johnsy had written a letter to a good friend back in California. Pretend to be Johnsy yourself and write the letter. Include not only what happened but also how you now feel and what you learned from the experience.

2. Identify and explain two symbols you have encountered in other selections in this book. If you have trouble, think particularly about "The Eye Catcher" (page 4), "The Canvas Bag" (page 33), "The Fan Club" (page 107), and "No More Forever" (page 151).

Critical Thinking

Supporting Hypotheses with Facts

Some of the terms used in critical thinking come originally from the sciences. One such term is **hypothesis** (hy POTH uh sis). When faced with a problem, or with a set of events to explain, a scientist often tries to think of several **hypotheses** (hy POTH uh seez—the plural form). These hypotheses are possible solutions to the problem or explanations of the events.

Suppose, for example, that you were a scientist trying to discover why birds migrate south in the winter. You might reason that the migration has something to do with hours of sunlight, temperature, availability of food, or safety provided by dense leaves and grass. Are there other hypotheses you could make?

Next, you would test each hypothesis against the facts. In the case of bird migration, it might be found that one, a few, or all of the hypotheses are correct to some degree. It might also be determined that different hypotheses are involved for different kinds of birds.

The process of finding hypotheses and then seeking facts to support them is a useful one, not only in science but in other fields as well. Problems in the study of literature can often be approached in this way. For instance, it's easy to say that a certain short story is "interesting," "so-so," or "boring"— but it's often far from easy to explain *why*. To do this, you might start by making several hypotheses about what makes a short story a "good" one. Then you would go on to test each hypothesis against the facts provided by your own reading.

Below are ten hypotheses that may or may not help explain your reaction to "The Last Leaf." Ask two questions about each hypothesis: (1) Can it be properly applied to this story? (2) If so, exactly *what* in the story supports the hypothesis?

1. The characters are presented so skillfully that the reader gets to "know" them as real people, not as *stereotypes* (see page 77).
2. The characters are a lot like me, making it my kind of story.
3. The characters are different from me, providing opportunities for new discoveries about people.
4. The writing is crisp, fast, and easy to read.
5. The plot is formed so that the reader is constantly curious about what will happen next.
6. The setting is familiar, one in which I feel at home.
7. The setting is unfamiliar and therefore interesting.
8. Humor adds a pleasant mood to the story.
9. The imagery in the story is so powerful that I have the sense of really *being there* as I read.
10. The story makes the reader think about an important theme.

Now explain your overall reaction to "The Last Leaf" by using some or all of the hypotheses listed above. You can be either positive or negative, but you must use *facts* from the story (or note their absence) to support your views.

209

from TREES

by Joyce Kilmer

I think that I shall never see
A poem lovely as a tree. . . .

A tree that looks at God all day
And lifts her leafy arms to pray;

5　A tree that may in summer wear
A nest of robins in her hair;

Upon whose bosom snow has lain;
Who intimately lives with rain.

Poems are made by fools like me,
10　But only God can make a tree.

SONG OF THE OPEN ROAD

by Ogden Nash

I think that I shall never see
A billboard lovely as a tree.
Perhaps, unless the billboards fall,
I'll never see a tree at all.

WAYS OF KNOWING

1. In "Trees," what two things are contrasted with each other in both the first and last stanzas?
2. Now look at stanzas 2–4 of "Trees." How is *personification* (see page 44) used in the stanzas?
3. The BIG IDEA of "Trees" is one that goes way beyond poems and trees. Try to state the theme in a complete sentence. The following key terms may help: *nature, creation, human effort.*
4. Do you think that the two poems illustrate a basic difference in attitude between men and women?
5. Even without looking up the dates of the two poets, you should be able to guess which poem was written first. (a) Which is the earlier poem? (b) What is the relationship between the two poems?

Read the information below and then look back at your answer to Item 4 above. Does this information affect your answer?

It may interest you to know that (Alfred) Joyce Kilmer (1886–1918) was a man. He lost his life as an American soldier in World War I, five years after writing his famous poem "Trees." Don't be too quick in finding "differences" between men and women or in assuming too much about the "I" speaking voice in a poem.

▶ The law says 55 MPH, but fair warning—your reading speed is about to go out of control. This story traces a zigzag between reality and fantasy and then picks up speed as it races toward a thrilling finish. PROCEED WITH CAUTION!

DUEL

by Richard Matheson

At 11:32 A.M., Mann passed the truck.

He was heading west, en route to San Francisco. He had his suit coat off and shirt collar opened. There was sunlight on his left arm and on part of his lap. He could feel the heat of it through his dark trousers as he drove along the two-lane highway. For the past 20 minutes, he had not seen another vehicle going in either direction.

Then he saw the truck ahead, moving up a curving grade between two high green hills. He heard the grinding strain of its motor and saw a double shadow on the road. The truck was pulling a trailer. As he drew behind it, he edged his car toward the opposite lane. He didn't pass until the truck had crossed the ridge. He waited until he could see the truck front in his rearview mirror before he turned back into the proper lane.

The highway ahead was straight now. Mann drifted into a reverie. He wondered what Ruth was doing. The kids, of course, were in school. Maybe Ruth was shopping; Thursday was the day she usually went. He wished he were with her instead of starting on another sales trip. Hours of driving yet before he'd reach San Francisco. Then three days of hotel sleeping and restaurant eating.

He started as the truck roared past him on the left, causing his car to shudder slightly. He watched the truck and trailer cut in abruptly for the westbound lane and frowned as he had to brake. What's with you? he thought.

He eyed the truck with disapproval. It was a huge gasoline tanker pulling a tank trailer, each of them having six pairs of wheels. He could see that it was not a new rig but was dented and

---

• reverie (REV uh ree) dreamlike state

in need of renovation. The driver must be an independent trucker, he decided.

Mann checked his speedometer. He was holding steady at 55 an hour, as he did when he drove without thinking on the open highway. The truck driver must have done a good 70 to pass him so quickly. This seemed a little odd. Weren't truck drivers supposed to be cautious?

He grimaced at the smell of the truck's exhaust and looked at the vertical pipe to the left of the cab. It was spewing smoke. He scowled at the fumes. They'd make him nauseated in a little while, he knew. He couldn't lag back here like this. Either he slowed down or he passed the truck again. He didn't have the time to slow down. He'd gotten a late start. Keeping it at 55 all the way, he'd just about make his afternoon appointment. No, he'd have to pass. He pushed down hard on the accelerator and steered all the way into the eastbound lane.

As he passed the truck, he glanced at it. The cab was too high for him to see into. All he caught sight of was the back of the truck driver's left hand on the steering wheel. It was darkly tanned and square-looking, with large veins knotted on its surface.

- **renovation** (ren uh VAY shun) complete rebuilding; full repair
- grimace (GRIM us) make an ugly and disapproving expression
- spewing (SYOO ing) sending forth; vomiting out

When Mann could see the truck reflected in the rearview mirror, he pulled back over to the proper lane and looked ahead again. The truck driver gave him an extended horn blast. What was that? he wondered. A greeting or a curse? The unexpected roar of the truck motor made his gaze jump to the side mirror. The guy was passing him *again*! He tried to see into the cab but couldn't because of its height. What's with him, anyway? he wondered. What are we having here, a contest?

His scowl deepened as the odor of the truck's exhaust reached his nostrils again. Irritably, he cranked up the window on his left. Was he going to have to breathe that all the way to San Francisco? He couldn't afford to slow down. He had to meet Forbes at a quarter after three, and that was that.

He looked ahead. At least there was no traffic. When the highway curved enough to the left to give him a completely open view, he jarred down on the pedal, steering out into the opposite lane.

The truck edged over, blocking his way.

For several moments, all Mann could do was stare at it in confusion. Then he braked, returning to the proper lane. The truck moved back in front of him.

Mann could not allow himself to accept what had taken place. It had to be a coincidence. The truck driver couldn't have blocked his way on purpose. He waited for more than a minute, then steered again into the eastbound lane.

Immediately, the truck shifted, barring his way.

Mann was astounded. This was unbelievable. He'd never seen such a thing in 26 years of driving. He returned to the westbound lane, shaking his head as the truck swung back in front of him.

He eased up on the gas pedal, falling back to avoid the truck's exhaust. Now what? he wondered. He still had to make San Francisco on schedule. Impulsively, he sped into the eastbound lane again. To his surprise, the truck driver stuck his left arm out and waved him on. Mann started pushing down on the accelerator. Suddenly, he let up on the pedal and jerked the steering wheel around, raking back behind the truck so quickly that his car began to fishtail. He was fighting to control it when a blue convertible shot by him in the opposite lane. Mann was sucking breath in through his mouth. His heart was pounding almost pain-

---

- **impulsively** (im PUL siv lee) with sudden desire; without thinking
- raking (RAYK ing) sweeping; moving sideways
- fishtail (FISH tayl) slide from side to side

214

fully. *He wanted me to hit that car head-on*, he thought. To wave him on. . . . Mann felt sickened. This was really one for the books.

Mann tried to calm himself. Maybe it's the heat, he thought. Maybe the truck driver had a headache or an upset stomach. Maybe he'd had a fight with his wife. Mann tried in vain to smile. There could be any number of reasons. He drove behind the truck for several minutes.

Unexpectedly, the car began to bounce. Mann thought that one of his tires had gone flat. Then he noticed that the paving along this section of highway consisted of slabs with gaps between them. He saw the truck and trailer jolting up and down and thought: I hope it shakes your brains loose.

"Ah," he said. A long, steep hill was looming up ahead. The truck would have to climb it slowly. Mann pressed down on the accelerator pedal, drawing as close behind the truck as safety would allow.

Halfway up the slope, Mann saw a turnout for the eastbound lane with no oncoming traffic. Flooring the accelerator pedal, he shot into the opposite lane. The slow-moving truck began to angle out in front of him. Face stiffening, Mann steered his speeding car across the highway edge and curved it sharply on the turnout. Clouds of dust went billowing up behind his car, making him lose sight of the truck. His tires buzzed and crackled on the dirt, then were humming on the pavement once again.

He glanced at the rearview mirror, and a laugh erupted from his throat. He'd only meant to pass. The dust had been an unexpected bonus. He swept across the summit of the hill. A striking vista lay ahead: sunlit hills and flatland, a corridor of dark trees and bright-green vegetable patches. Lovely, he thought. Reaching out, he turned the radio on and started humming cheerfully with the music.

Seven minutes later, Mann passed a billboard advertising CHUCK'S CAFÉ. No thanks, Chuck, he thought. Hearing the noise behind him, he looked at the rearview mirror and felt himself go cold with fear. The truck was hurtling down the hill, pursuing him.

His mouth fell open and he threw a glance at the speedometer. He was doing more than 60! On a curving downgrade, that was

---

- looming (LOOM ing) rising into view
- **billowing** (BIL oh ing) moving in waves
- **vista** (VIS tuh) long view

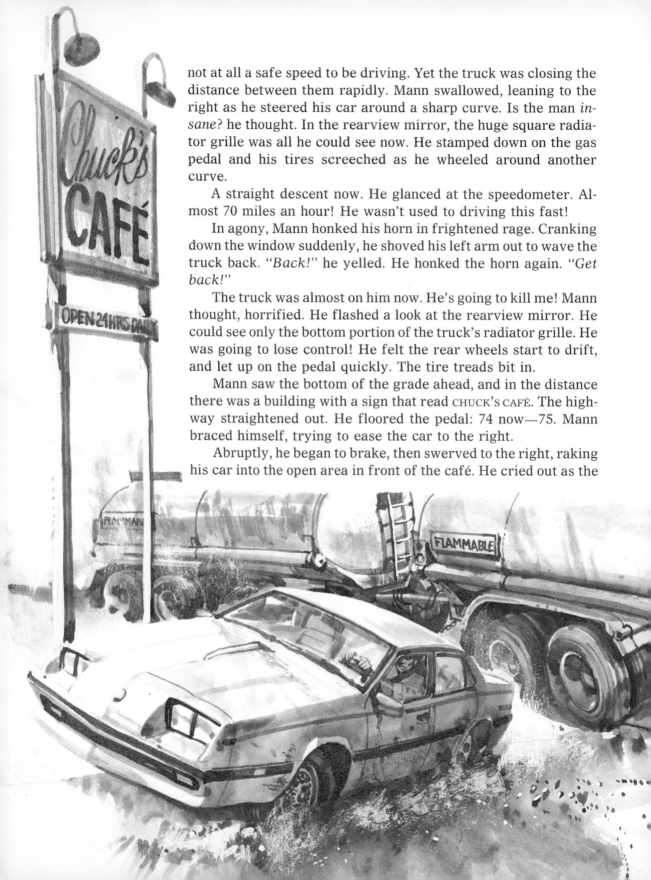

not at all a safe speed to be driving. Yet the truck was closing the distance between them rapidly. Mann swallowed, leaning to the right as he steered his car around a sharp curve. Is the man *insane?* he thought. In the rearview mirror, the huge square radiator grille was all he could see now. He stamped down on the gas pedal and his tires screeched as he wheeled around another curve.

A straight descent now. He glanced at the speedometer. Almost 70 miles an hour! He wasn't used to driving this fast!

In agony, Mann honked his horn in frightened rage. Cranking down the window suddenly, he shoved his left arm out to wave the truck back. *"Back!"* he yelled. He honked the horn again. *"Get back!"*

The truck was almost on him now. He's going to kill me! Mann thought, horrified. He flashed a look at the rearview mirror. He could see only the bottom portion of the truck's radiator grille. He was going to lose control! He felt the rear wheels start to drift, and let up on the pedal quickly. The tire treads bit in.

Mann saw the bottom of the grade ahead, and in the distance there was a building with a sign that read CHUCK'S CAFÉ. The highway straightened out. He floored the pedal: 74 now—75. Mann braced himself, trying to ease the car to the right.

Abruptly, he began to brake, then swerved to the right, raking his car into the open area in front of the café. He cried out as the car careened into a skid. *Steer with it!* screamed a voice in his mind. Mann pressed harder on the brake pedal, turning further into the skid. He braked harder yet, conscious of the truck and trailer roaring by on the highway. He nearly sideswiped one of the cars parked in front of the café. The rear end broke to the right and the car spun half around to a neck-wrenching halt 30 yards beyond the café.

Mann sat in pulsing silence, eyes closed. His heartbeats felt like club blows in his chest. If he were ever going to have a heart attack, it would be now. After a while, he opened his eyes and pressed his right palm against his chest. His heart was still throbbing. No wonder, he thought. It isn't every day I'm almost murdered by a truck.

He stumbled as he walked to the front door of the café. TRUCK-ERS WELCOME, read a sign in the window. Shivering, he pulled open the door and went inside, avoiding the sight of its customers. Keeping his gaze fixed straight ahead, he moved to the rear and opened the door marked GENTS.

Moving to the sink, he leaned over to cup cold water in his palms and splash it on his face. There was a fluttering of his stomach muscles he could not control. Straightening up, he tugged down several towels and patted them against his face. Dropping the soggy towels into a wastebasket beside the sink, he regarded himself in the wall mirror. Still with us, Mann, he thought. He nodded, swallowing. Drawing out his metal comb, he neatened his hair. You never know, he thought. You just never know. You drift along, year after year, presuming certain values to be fixed; like being able to drive on a public thoroughfare without somebody trying to murder you. You come to depend on that sort of thing. Then something occurs and all bets are off. All the years of logic are displaced and, suddenly, the jungle is in front of you again. *Man, part animal, part angel.* Where had he come across the phrase? He shivered.

It was entirely an animal in that truck out there.

His breath was almost back to normal now. Mann forced a smile at his reflection. All right, boy, he told himself. It's over now. It was a nightmare, but it's over. You are on your way to San Francisco. You'll get yourself a nice hotel room, soak your body in a hot bath, and forget. He turned and walked out of the washroom.

- careen (kuh REEN) sway or lean while in motion
- **values** (VAL yooz) approved customs; things believed in
- thoroughfare (THUR oh fair) road; highway

He jolted to a halt, his breath cut off. Standing rooted, he gaped through the front window of the café.

The truck and trailer were parked outside.

Mann stared at them in unbelieving shock. It wasn't possible. He'd seen them roaring by at top speed. The driver had won; he'd *won!* He'd had the whole highway to himself! *Why had he turned back?*

Mann looked around with sudden dread. There were five men eating, three along the counter, two in booths. He cursed himself for having failed to look at faces when he'd entered. Now there was no way of knowing who it was. Mann felt his legs begin to shake.

Abruptly, he walked to the nearest booth and slid in clumsily. Now wait, he told himself; just wait. Surely, he could tell which one it was. Masking his face with the menu, he glanced across its top. Was it that one in the khaki work shirt? That one in the front booth, square-faced, black-haired? One of the two others at the counter?

The woman behind the counter came over, and Mann ordered a ham sandwich on rye toast. He tried to calm himself. He looked deliberately at the men. Either of two seemed a likely possibility as the driver of the truck: the square-faced one in the front booth and the chunky one in the jump suit sitting at the counter. He glanced at the pay telephone on the front wall. What was to prevent him from calling the local police and telling them the situation? But, then, he'd have to stay here, lose time, make Forbes angry, probably lose the sale. And what if the truck driver stayed to face them? Naturally, he'd deny the whole thing. What if the police believed him and didn't do anything about it? After they'd gone, the truck driver would undoubtedly take it out on him again, only worse.

The sandwich tasted flat. Mann stared at the table as he ate. Why was he just *sitting* here like this? He was a grown man, wasn't he? Why didn't he settle the thing once and for all?

His left hand twitched unexpectedly. The man in the jump suit had risen from the counter and was strolling toward the front of the café. Mann felt his heartbeat thumping as the man gave money to the waitress, took his change and a toothpick, and went outside. Mann watched in anxious silence.

The man did not get into the cab of the tanker truck.

It had to be the one in the front booth, then: square, with dark eyes, dark hair; the man who'd tried to kill him.

Mann stood up abruptly, letting impulse conquer fear. Eyes fixed ahead, he started toward the entrance. He stopped by the cash register. Was the man observing him? he wondered. He swallowed, pulling out a clip of dollar bills. He glanced toward the waitress. Come *on*, he thought. He looked at his check. Seeing the amount, he reached shakily into his trouser pocket for change. He heard a coin fall onto the floor and roll away. Ignoring it, he dropped a dollar and a quarter onto the counter.

As he did, he heard the man in the front booth get up. Turning quickly to the door, he shoved it open. He started toward his car with long strides. His mouth was dry again. The pounding of his heart was painful in his chest.

Suddenly, he started running. He heard the café door bang shut and fought away the urge to look across his shoulder. Reaching his car, Mann yanked open the door and jarred in awkwardly behind the steering wheel. He reached into his trouser pocket for the keys. His hand was shaking so badly he couldn't get the ignition key into its slot. Come on! he thought.

The key slid in; he twisted it. The motor started. He raked the car around and steered it toward the highway. From the corners of his eyes, he saw the truck and trailer being backed away from the café.

Reaction burst inside him. "No!" he raged and slammed his foot down on the brake pedal. This was idiotic! Why should he run away? His car slid sideways to a rocking halt. Shouldering out the door, he lurched to his feet and started toward the truck with angry strides. *All right, Jack*, he thought. He glared at the man inside the truck. You want to punch my nose, O.K. But no more tournament on the highway.

The truck began to pick up speed. Mann raised his right arm. "Hey!" he yelled. He knew the driver saw him. "*Hey!*" He started running as the truck kept moving, engine grinding loudly. It was on the highway now. He sprinted toward it. The driver shifted gears; the truck moved faster. "Stop!" Mann shouted. "*Stop!*"

He got into his car and was about to drive onto the highway when he changed his mind and switched the motor off. He'd sit here for a while and let the nut get out of range, let him think he'd won the day. He grinned. He really should have done this earlier, pulled over, waited. Then the truck driver would have *picked on someone else*, he thought. He looked at the dashboard clock. It was just past 12:30. Wow, he thought. All that in less than an hour.

• **lurch** (LURCH) move awkwardly

He shifted on the seat and stretched his legs out. Leaning against the door, he closed his eyes. Today was shot, as far as he could see.

When he opened his eyes, almost 11 minutes had passed. The nut must be an ample distance off by now, he thought. Good enough. He wasn't going to try to make San Francisco on schedule now, anyway. He'd take it real easy.

Mann adjusted his safety belt, switched on the motor, and pulled onto the highway. Not a car in sight. Everybody was staying at home. That nut must have a reputation around here. When Crazy Jack is on the highway, lock your car in the garage. Mann chuckled at the notion as his car began to turn the curve ahead.

Mindless reflex drove his right foot down against the brake pedal. Suddenly, his car had skidded to a halt, and he was staring down the highway. The truck and trailer were parked on the shoulder less than 90 yards away.

Mann couldn't seem to function. His head was aching again. What was he to do? He knew very well that if he left his car to walk to the truck, the driver would pull away and repark farther down the highway. He might as well face the fact that he was dealing with a madman. He felt the tremor in his stomach muscles starting up again. His heartbeat thudded slowly, striking at his chest wall. Now what?

With a sudden, angry impulse, Mann stepped down hard on the accelerator pedal. The tires of the car spun; the car shot out onto the highway. Instantly, the truck began to move. He even had the motor on! Mann thought in raging fear. He floored the pedal, then realized he couldn't make it. The truck would block his way and he'd collide with its trailer. He started braking fast, trying to decelerate evenly, so he wouldn't lose control.

When he'd slowed down enough, he steered the car onto the shoulder and stopped it again.

Approximately 80 yards ahead, the truck pulled off the highway and stopped.

Mann tapped his fingers on the steering wheel. *Now* what? he thought. Turn around and head east until he reached a cutoff that would take him to San Francisco by another route? How did he know the truck driver wouldn't follow him even then? His cheeks

---

- **reflex** (REE fleks) impulse; thoughtless action
- **tremor** (TREM ur) shudder; shaking
- **decelerate** (dee SEL uh rayt) slow down

220

twitched as he bit his lips together angrily. No! He wasn't going to turn around!

His expression hardened suddenly. Well, he wasn't going to *sit* here all day, that was certain. Reaching out, he tapped the gearshift into drive and steered his car onto the highway once again. The truck driver had his left arm out the cab window and was waving him on. What did that mean? Had he changed his mind?

Abruptly, Mann decided. *Right*, he thought. He checked ahead, then pressed down hard on the accelerator pedal. As he neared the truck, he tensed, then glanced at the cab and saw the name KELLER printed on its door. For a shocking instant, he thought it read KILLER. He depressed the pedal sharply. When he saw the truck reflected in the rearview mirror, he steered his car into the westbound lane.

He shuddered, dread and satisfaction mixed together, as he saw that the truck driver was starting up. It was strangely comforting to know the man's intentions definitely again. That plus the knowledge of his face and name seemed, somehow, to reduce his stature. Before, he had been faceless, nameless, an embodiment of unknown terror. Now, at least, he was an individual. All right, Keller, said his mind, let's see you beat me with that relic now. He pressed down harder on the pedal. *Here we go*, he thought.

After several moments, he glanced into the rearview mirror again. Was the truck getting closer? Stunned, he checked the speedometer. He forced in the accelerator pedal angrily. *He mustn't go less than 80!*

Mann's eyes shifted. Up ahead were hills and mountains. He tried to reassure himself that upgrades were on his side, that he could climb them at the same speed he was going now. Yet all he could imagine were the downgrades, the immense truck close behind him, slamming violently into his car and knocking it across some cliff edge. He had a horrifying vision of dozens of broken, rusted cars lying unseen in the canyons ahead, corpses in every one of them, all flung to shattering deaths by Keller.

The hills were closer now. There would be slopes directly,

- stature (STACH ur) degree of importance; rank
- embodiment (em BAHD ee munt) representative; symbol
- **relic** (REL ik) something very old

long steep grades. He was sure to gain a lot of distance on the truck. No matter how he tried, Keller couldn't manage 80 miles an hour on a hill. But I can! cried his mind with fierce elation. He looked at the rearview mirror. *Square,* he thought, everything about the truck was square: the radiator grille, the fender shapes, the bumper ends, the outline of the cab, even the shape of Keller's hands and face. He visualized the truck as something brutish, chasing him with instinct only.

Mann cried out, horror-stricken, as he saw the ROAD REPAIRS sign up ahead. Both lanes blocked. A huge black arrow pointing toward the alternate route! He groaned, seeing it was dirt. His foot jumped automatically to the brake pedal. He threw a dazed look at the rearview mirror. The truck was moving as fast as ever! It *couldn't,* though! Mann's expression froze in terror as he started turning to the right.

He stiffened as the front wheels hit the dirt road. Abruptly, he was jarring down the dirt road, elbows braced against his sides, trying to keep from losing control. His tires battered at the ruts, almost tearing the wheel from his grip. The windows rattled noisily. His neck snapped back and forth with painful jerks. He felt the bouncing of the car drive up his spine. His clenching teeth slipped and he cried out hoarsely as his upper teeth gouged deep into his lip. His head was pounding like his heart now, with gigantic, throbbing spasms. He started coughing as he gagged on dripping blood.

The dirt road ended suddenly, and he dared to look at the rearview mirror. The truck was slowed down but was still behind him, rocking like a freighter on a storm-tossed sea, its huge tires scouring up dust. Mann shoved in the accelerator pedal and his car surged forward. A good, steep upgrade lay just ahead. He swallowed blood, grimacing at the taste, then fumbled in his trouser pocket and tugged out his handkerchief. He pressed it to his bleeding lip, eyes fixed on the slope ahead. Another 50 yards or so. His undershirt was soaking wet. He glanced at the rearview mirror. The truck had just regained the highway.

His car was on the first yards of the upgrade when steam began to issue from beneath its hood. Mann stiffened suddenly, eyes widening with shock. The steam increased. Mann's gaze

---

- **elation** (i LAY shun) joy; gladness
- **spasm** (SPAZ um) sudden and uncontrolled muscular movements
- issue (ISH oo) come forth; flow out

222

jumped down. The red light hadn't flashed on yet but had to in a moment. How could this be happening? Just as he was set to get away! The slope ahead was long and gradual, with many curves. He knew he couldn't go back down.

He was going to die.

He stared ahead with stricken eyes, his view increasingly obscured by steam. He sobbed in terror as the dashboard light flashed on. He glanced at it and read the word HOT, black on red. He looked ahead. The slope seemed endless. Already, he could hear a boiling throb inside the radiator. How much coolant was there left? Steam was clouding faster, hazing up the windshield. Reaching out, he twisted at a dashboard knob. The wipers started flicking back and forth in fan-shaped sweeps. Yard by yard, his car was slowing down. Make it, make it, pleaded his mind, even though he thought that it was futile. The car was running more and more unevenly. Any moment now, the motor would be choked off and the car would shudder to a stop, leaving him a sitting target. *No*, he thought. He tried to blank his mind.

He was almost to the top, but in the mirror he could see the truck drawing up on him. He jammed down on the pedal and the motor made a grinding noise. He groaned. It had to make the top! The ridge was just ahead. Closer. Closer. Make it. "Make it." The car was shuddering and clanking, slowing down—oil, smoke, and steam gushing from beneath the hood. The windshield wipers swept from side to side. Mann's head throbbed. Both his hands felt numb. Make it. *Make it!*

● coolant (KOO lunt) liquid in a motor's cooling system

Over! Mann's lips opened in a cry of triumph as the car began descending. He shoved the transmission into neutral and let the car go into a glide. The triumph strangled in his throat as he saw that there was nothing in sight but hills and more hills. Never mind! He was on a downgrade now, a long one. He passed a sign that read TRUCKS USE LOW GEARS NEXT 12 MILES. Twelve miles! Something would come up. It had to.

The car began to pick up speed. Mann glanced at the speedometer. Forty-seven miles an hour. He'd save the motor; let it cool for 12 miles, if the truck was far enough behind.

His speed increased: 50 . . . 51. Mann watched the needle turning slowly toward the right. He glanced at the rearview mirror. The truck had not appeared yet. With a little luck, he might still get a good lead. The needle edged past 55 and started toward the 60 mark.

Again, he looked at the rearview mirror, jolting as he saw that the truck had topped the ridge and was on its way down. His gaze jumped fitfully between the steam-obscured highway and the mirror. The truck was accelerating rapidly. Keller doubtless had the gas pedal floored. The car's velocity had just passed 60. Not enough! He had to use the motor now! He reached out desperately.

His right hand froze in midair as the motor stalled. Then, shooting out the hand, he twisted the ignition key. The motor made a grinding noise but wouldn't start. Mann glanced up, saw that he was almost on the shoulder, jerked the steering wheel around. Again, he turned the key, but there was no response. He looked up at the rearview mirror. The truck was gaining on him swiftly. He glanced at the speedometer. The car's speed was fixed at 62. Mann felt himself crushed in a vise of panic. He stared ahead with haunted eyes.

Then he saw it, several hundred yards ahead: an escape route for trucks with burned-out brakes. Either he took the turnout or his car would be rammed from behind. The truck was frighteningly close. He heard the high-pitched wailing of its motor. Unconsciously, he started easing to the right, then jerked the wheel back suddenly. He mustn't give the move away! He had to wait until the last possible moment. Otherwise, Keller would follow him in.

Just before he reached the escape route, Mann wrenched the steering wheel around. The car rear started breaking to the left,

---

• **fitfully** (FIT ful ee) by fits or spells; nervously

tires shrieking on the pavement. Mann steered with the skid, braking just enough to keep from losing all control. The rear tires grabbed. At 60 miles an hour, the car shot up the dirt trail, tires slinging up a cloud of dust. Mann began to hit the brakes. The rear wheels sideslipped, and the car slammed hard to the right. He drove his foot down on the brake pedal with all his might. The car skidded to the right and slammed against the bank. Mann heard a grinding of metal and felt himself heaved downward suddenly, as the car plowed to a violent halt.

As in a dream, Mann turned to see the truck and trailer swerving off the highway. Paralyzed, he watched the massive vehicle hurtle toward him, knowing he was going to die but so stupefied by the sight of the looming truck that he couldn't react. The shape roared closer, blotting out the sky. Mann felt a strange sensation in his throat, unaware that he was screaming.

• **hurtle** (HUR tul) rush wildly

Suddenly, the truck began to tilt. Mann stared at it in choked-off silence as it started tipping over like some ponderous beast in slow motion.

Hands palsied, Mann undid the safety belt and opened the door. Struggling from the car, he stumbled to the trail edge, staring downward. He was just in time to see the truck capsize. The tanker followed, huge wheels spinning as it overturned.

The storage tank on the truck exploded first, the violence causing Mann to stagger back and sit down clumsily on the dirt. A second explosion roared below, making his ears hurt. His glazed eyes saw a fiery column shoot up toward the sky in front of him, then another.

Mann crawled slowly to the trail edge and peered down at the canyon. Enormous flames were towering upward, topped by thick, black, oily smoke. He couldn't see the truck or trailer, only flames. He gaped at them in shock, all feeling drained from him.

Then, unexpectedly, emotion came. Not dread, at first, and not regret; not the nausea that followed soon. It was a primeval tumult in his mind: the cry of some ancestral beast above the body of its vanquished foe.

ALL THINGS CONSIDERED

1. Mann knows the truck driver wants to kill him when the driver (a) blows his horn. (b) refuses to let him pass. (c) waves him by although a car is coming.
2. Several clues in the story allow the reader to infer that Mann is (a) in his 30s. (b) usually a careful driver. (c) happy to be away from his family.
3. Mann encounters a big surprise when he (a) turns on the radio. (b) enters the café washroom. (c) leaves the café washroom.
4. Tension mounts toward the end when something happens to (a) the car's cooling system. (b) Mann's left wrist. (c) the truck's steering mechanism.
5. At the end, Mann is saved by (a) flagging down a police car. (b) turning onto an escape route for trucks. (c) outriding his pursuer.

- ponderous (PAHN dur us) heavy; awkward
- palsied (PAWL zeed) shaking
- **primeval** (pry MEE vul) primitive; from the earliest age of humanity
- tumult (TOO mult) unrest; violent action
- **vanquished** (VAN kwisht) defeated; conquered

226

THINKING IT THROUGH

1. The story proceeds down a thin line between reality and fantasy. In your opinion, could the events really happen? Explain your answer.

2. (a) What is the overall plot question in the story? (b) What are three minor plot questions that hold the reader's interest at different points in the story?

3. At least twice, Mann thinks of possible solutions that either aren't tried or don't work out. (a) What are two of these possible solutions? (b) What happens in each case?

4. By page 221, Mann has seen the truck driver and learned his name. Mann finds that this knowledge produces "satisfaction" and is "strangely comforting." Why?

5. Some readers think the story has a very serious *theme*. One critic described the theme in this way: "Every human being on earth feels in vague but constant danger from some unnamed, unexplainable, and overpowering force that will suddenly unleash its fury." What details in "Duel" might suggest such a theme? Think about the names of the main characters, what the truck (and driver) might represent, and the last paragraph.

6. Explain how the writer of the following letter would probably react to the story.

A monster at the wheel

DEAR ANN LANDERS:

My husband is a kind, considerate person—a perfect, gentleman—until he gets behind the wheel. Then he becomes a hateful, frightening monster. He drives a tanker for a living.

He has told me many times that one of these days he is going to get even with all those "idiots" out there and kill somebody. I realize that people do stupid things, but I don't believe anyone deserves to be ground up like hamburger under the wheels of a truck just because he did something dumb.

I was shocked to learn that some of my husband's colleagues are of the same mind. They, too, he says, are waiting for a chance to "get" some driver who has given them a hard time.

Last week, my husband chased a small truck with every intention of smashing into it because the driver was guilty of a traffic violation. My husband got a speeding ticket before he caught the small truck. Thank God.

I beg of you small-truck drivers, don't challenge the big boys. Let them have their way, even if they are wrong. It could mean your life.—**No Name In California**

DEAR NO NAME:

A shocking letter, but thanks for writing it.

Literary Skills

Point of View

In ordinary use, the expression *point of view* means "opinion." In the study of literature, however, **point of view** means the position from which a story (or other work) is presented.

In the **first-person** point of view, the storyteller (or narrator) is one of the characters. This character (called *I* or *me,* of course) can have either a large role or a small one. The important point is that *everything* in the story has to be presented as if from the observations and thoughts of this particular character.

In the **third-person** point of view, the storyteller is completely outside the story. The narrator is not an *I/me* character. The characters are called *he* or *she* (except, of course, when speaking about themselves).

The distinction between first- and third-person is not a simple one, however. Some third-person storytellers are **omniscient** (om NISH unt), or "all knowing." The omniscient narrator can enter the minds of any of the characters when convenient, reporting on the feelings and thoughts of now one character, now another. Other third-person storytellers take a **limited third-person** point of view, limiting themselves to the feelings and thoughts of a single character, usually the main character. Because of the focus on a single character, the limited third person is in many ways like the first person.

1. (a) Is "Duel" told from a first-person or third-person point of view? (b) If third person, is it omniscient or limited?

2. The omniscient third-person point of view is giving way among modern writers to the limited third person. Yet so far in this book, you have read some good examples of the omniscient point of view. What is one example? (Hint: Unit 2 is a good place to look.)

3. This book also contains several examples of the limited third-person point of view. What is one example?

Composition

1. Write a paragraph that describes another student in your class from a first-person point of view. There are only three rules: You cannot (1) use the person's name, (2) be deliberately unkind, or (3) write anything you are not sure is true.

2. Some years ago, "Duel" was turned into a TV drama. Explain at least three of the changes you would need to make to have the story work on screen or stage. For instance, you couldn't just tell the reader about Mann's family or his appointment with Forbes. How might information like this be revealed in dramatic form?

VOCABULARY AND SKILL REVIEW

Before completing the exercises that follow, you may wish to review the **bold-faced** words on pages 201 to 228.

I. On a separate sheet of paper, mark each item *true* or *false*. If it is *false*, explain what is wrong with the sentence.

1. A really successful school dance would be attended by *scores* of people.
2. The United States was a *vanquished* nation after World War II.
3. The hands of some elderly people are *gnarled* with years of work.
4. America's *primeval* forests were here at the time of Columbus.
5. It's a good idea to start each day by repeating a few *morbid* sentences to yourself.
6. The Pledge of Allegiance is a statement of American *values*.
7. The Super Bowl results in joy for the fans of one city, and *elation* for the fans of the other.
8. Pulling your hand off a hot stove is an example of a *reflex*.
9. Most *reflexes* are done *impulsively*.
10. One would rarely find a *vista* on a mountaintop.

II. On a separate sheet of paper, write the *italicized* word that best fills the blank in each sentence.

twang	palette	renovation	hurtle	relic
lurch	billowing	decelerate	fitfully	spasm

1. The first runner in a race would probably _____ across the finish line.
2. The last runner in a race might well _____ across the finish line.
3. _____ waves of heat can sometimes be seen in the summer.
4. It's not at all rare for a sleeping person to have a _____.
5. Too many, however, will make a person sleep _____.
6. CASTANET is to CLICK as BANJO is to _____.
7. COMPUTER is to NOVELTY as STAGECOACH is to _____.
8. CARPENTER is to HAMMER as ARTIST is to _____.
9. GROW is to SHRINK as ACCELERATE is to _____.
10. HOUSE is to REBUILDING as CAR is to _____.

III. Read the short poems carefully before answering the questions that follow.

ON SEEING WEATHER-BEATEN TREES

by Adelaide Crapsey

Is it as plainly in our living shown,
By slant and twist, which way the wind hath blown?

THE HIPPOPOTAMUS

by Ogden Nash

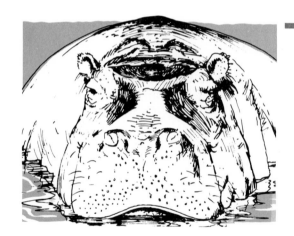

Beyond the hippopotamus!
We laugh at how he looks to us,
And yet in moments dank and grim
I wonder how we look to him.
Peace, peace, thou hippopotamus!
We really look all right to us,
As you no doubt delight the eye
Of other hippopotami.

1. (a) Which poem did you like more? (b) Which poem did you find easier? (c) Are your answers to (a) and (b) the same?
2. Although "On Seeing Weather-Beaten Trees" compares trees with people, the trees are *not* examples of personification. Explain why not.
3. "The Hippopotamus" is written, at least partly, in the *first person*, since it contains the word "I." Is the other poem also written in the first person? Explain.
4. The second poem suggests that the hippopotamus is viewed as a kind of symbol by many people. In your opinion, what does a hippopotamus represent?

THE SHEEP OF SAN CRISTÓBAL

a Mexican-American folktale, retold by Terri Bueno

▶ Soon after Columbus's voyage in 1492, people from Spain started to come to the New World. First they settled in Puerto Rico, Cuba, and other nearby islands. Then they entered Florida, Central America, and South America. Finally they pushed up through Mexico into what is now the U.S. Southwest.

"The Sheep of San Cristóbal" is a very old folktale from New Mexico. At the time of the story New Mexico was the northern part of Mexico, and it belonged to Spain.

No! No!" screamed Felipa. "Not Carlos. Not my Carlos! It cannot be!"

The young woman stood in the doorway of her little two-room house. Before her, on the dirt floor, lay the body of her husband. He had just been killed by Ute Indians in a sneak raid. The dust raised by their horses still hung in the air outside.

In tears, Felipa sank to her knees and covered her face with her hands. Why hadn't she been home? Why had she picked that hour—that minute even—to go for water? Together, she and Carlos might have driven the Utes away. . . . And where was Manuel?

"Manuel!" she cried. Jumping to her feet, she dashed outside to look for her seven-year-old son. Her nearest neighbors were coming on the run, and behind them, the village priest. Surprisingly, no one had seen the Utes until their damage had been done. The neighbors searched the small field next to the house for the boy, but before long everyone guessed the truth: He had been carried off by the Indians. That was the same as death.

The priest held Felipa's sobbing face in his old brown hands. "Come," he said. "Come, Felipa Sandoval. Come to the shrine of Our Lady of Light. And may the Lord have mercy."

Felipa followed the old man to the church. Prayer did not fill the void in her heart, but it did help her to go on living. And she knew what it would mean to go on living: She would have to work

---

• void (VOID) empty space

the little farm herself. She would have to plant all the squash and hoe all the beans and pick all the corn. There was no other way.

In the days that followed, deep sorrow never left Felipa. She could not forget the Ute raid. But little by little, she learned to do what she had to do. She had always been very religious, and now she spent at least an hour a day on her knees at the shrine. The rest of the time she worked in her field—digging, planting, hoeing, picking. Sometimes she carried a basket of vegetables to the center of Las Colonias to sell. The people of the little town had always liked Felipa, and now they felt sorry for her. They would buy from her first. Men who cut firewood often dropped off a few pieces as they went by her doorstep. Other people did her other little favors, and Felipa always remembered to thank them.

There was one man, however, whose favors Felipa did not want. This was Don José Vigil. From his father, Don José had inherited a huge flock of sheep. People said he was the richest man in town, but people also knew that he never gave anything to the poor. It was not Don José's habit to help anyone but himself. Felipa soon learned the reason for his favors to her: He was a young man without a wife, and she was a young woman without a husband.

At night Don José kept his sheep in a corral beside his house in town. In the daytime he took them to the top of a huge mesa to eat grass. This meant that twice a day, morning and evening, Don José had to pass Felipa's house with his sheep. Felipa would groan when she saw them coming up the dirt road. Leading the way would be Sancho, Don José's big dog; then would come the sheep, and finally Don José himself. Always he would smile and stop to talk.

Felipa did nothing to lead Don José on—but he would not be stopped. If she would not talk to him, he would talk for both of them. If she refused a present, he would leave it on the ground. If she hid in the house, he would simply open the door and walk in. Only if she locked the door would Don José leave, angry and silent. Felipa didn't like making *anyone* mad, but locking the door was better than listening to all his fatuous talk of marriage.

Soon Felipa found herself locking the door twice a day. And to her surprise, she sometimes found herself thinking evil thoughts about Don José. "If only Don José would fall off the mesa and

---

- mesa (MAY suh) Spanish for flat-topped hill with steep sides
- fatuous (FACH oo us) foolish; silly

break his neck!" she would think. Then, realizing how mean her thoughts had been, she would sigh and pray to Our Lady for forgiveness.

Before long, however, Don José found a way to get Felipa out of her house. He changed places with Sancho, the big brown dog. Instead of having Sancho lead the sheep, he led them himself. When he got to Felipa's house, he stopped. For a few minutes the sheep would stand still on the road. But soon, left to themselves, they would wander into Felipa's field. They would begin to eat her half-grown bean plants. Felipa had no choice. She would come tearing out of the house, shouting and waving her arms at the sheep, as Don José stood in the road and laughed.

The same thing happened every morning for a week. Felipa was puzzled. What was Don José trying to do? Was he trying to punish her for not liking him? Was he trying to force her to marry him? Without the beans to sell, Felipa would soon have no money. Then what would she do? What *could* she do?

One morning Don José's sheep arrived very early. Waking up to hear them already in her field, Felipa quickly looked out the window. They were eating the last of the beans.

Wild with anger, Felipa bolted out of the house. First she screamed at the sheep. But what was the use? Her beans had already disappeared. Then she screamed at Don José:

"You are a bad man, Don José Vigil! A bad man! May San Cristóbal throw you off the mesa today! May he break your neck! May you—"

Bursting into tears, Felipa ran back into the house. The door slammed behind her. She didn't watch as Don José shook his head, laughed once, and followed the last of his sheep toward the mesa. The peaceful dog Sancho was already way ahead.

Four hours later, the body of Don José Vigil was carried past Felipa's house. His foot had landed on the wrong small round stone on the narrow path up the side of the mesa. He had slipped, fallen to the plain far below, and broken his neck.

The news made Felipa feel dead herself. Her anger turned inward, toward herself. She was sure that her curse had caused Don José's death. All day long she prayed to Nuestra Señora de los Dolores, Our Lady of Sorrows. She could eat nothing, and that night she could not sleep. She kept seeing the reproachful eyes of

---

- bolt (BOHLT) make a sudden, swift dash
- reproachful (ri PROHCH ful) disapproving; causing shame

233

Don José as he fell to his death. They seemed to look right at her, and they made her feel very guilty.

Early the next morning, Felipa hurried to the church. There was only one thing to do. She would have to ask for penance, for some kind of punishment that would make up for her evil words.

"Padre," Felipa whispered to the priest. "I am guilty of the death of Don José Vigil." Then she sobbingly told the whole story.

"No," the priest finally said, "you did not cause Don José to die. San Cristóbal would not listen to such a plea. He would not do such a thing. He would never listen to a wicked prayer made by an angry woman."

The old priest looked into Felipa's big brown eyes and went on: "But yes, you *are* guilty. You are guilty of a very wicked prayer. And for that evil act, you must do penance."

"Yes," murmured Felipa, "I know. Without the penance, the rest of my life would be empty."

"Here is what you must do," the priest told her. "You must do penance for your own evil wishes. But more important, you must do penance for Don José, too. You see, he was in some ways an evil man. He had much money, yet he never gave to the poor. But no man is all evil. Right now, could he join us again on earth, Don José would want to do good. That is why your penance must be for him also."

Felipa listened as the priest went on. First she was to go to the mesa and gather Don José's sheep together. Then she was to drive them all over New Mexico, to every village. Everywhere she went, she was to search for indigent people in real need. To each of these people she was to give a single sheep. Felipa was to give the sheep away in the name of Don José, with the blessing of San Cristóbal. She was to beg for bread, and eat nothing else. She was to carry only a cup, and use it only for sheep milk.

"If anyone asks you," the priest finished, "say that the sheep are the sheep of San Cristóbal. Have faith, my daughter. San Cristóbal will guide you. Pray often. And at the end, he will give you a sign. You will know that your penance is over, and that you are free of your sin."

Felipa did as she'd been told. First she went to her house to get a cup. Should she change her clothes? No, she decided. She'd keep

---

- penance (PEN uns) punishment accepted to make up for some evil act
- **padre** (PAH dray) Spanish for *father* or *priest*
- indigent (IN di gent) poor; needy

on what she'd worn to the church, a simple black robe with a hood. Then she headed for the mesa. Her whole body shook as she walked up the dangerous path where Don José had fallen.

On the mesa's flat top, she found the sheep in a group. The faithful dog Sancho had kept them together during the night.

Sancho barked with joy when he saw Felipa coming. He ran up and nuzzled his short brown nose against her leg. Then he led her into some bushes not far away. There on the ground, Felipa saw the bones of three lambs. She knew that coyotes must have taken them during the night.

"You are a good, good dog, Sancho." Felipa scratched the big brown head by her knee. "But some lambs have been lost, am I right? You could not do the whole job, could you? Now you have me to help you. And I have you to help me."

Felipa milked one of the sheep. She held the cup of milk out to Sancho, and he lapped it up quickly. Then they drove the sheep toward the path leading off the mesa. Once safely down, and with Sancho leading, they headed for town. Felipa passed her own house, wondering when she'd ever see it again. A few minutes later they came to the house of Don José. Sancho started to drive the sheep into the corral, as he had always done. Felipa ran forward and headed the sheep back onto the road. She pulled the corral gate shut and urged the sheep on by. Sancho stood next to the corral, his head tipped to one side.

Now the sheep were past Don José's house, and almost to the center of Las Colonias. Felipa looked back at Don José's corral. Sancho was still standing there, watching her.

"Come, Sancho!" Felipa called. "Come! Come!" She clapped her hands together.

For a moment Sancho didn't move. Then all at once he seemed to make up his mind. He rushed toward Felipa, passed her, and took his place far up, in front of the sheep.

The sheep moved through Las Colonias and headed out of town. Felipa tried to count them. Because they were moving and close together, it wasn't an easy job. The first time she counted 172. The second time she got 167. Then she noticed that a large black ewe had dropped back to walk at her side. An hour later, the ewe was still there. Felipa looked at the animal carefully. "I think this sheep wants to be milked," she told herself. "She must be one of the ewes who lost their lambs to the coyotes."

Coming to a grassy spot, Felipa decided that it was time for

• nuzzle (NUZ ul) rub one's nose against

the whole procession to rest. As the other sheep browsed, Felipa milked the large black ewe. She drank the first cup of warm milk herself. The second she gave to Sancho. That was all, and the ewe then wandered off to graze on the thin grass. But as soon as they started down the dusty road again, the ewe came back to Felipa's side.

"You are a good friend, black ewe," Felipa said aloud. "Do you know that I too have lost a child? Can you tell that I share your sadness? Is that why you stay here next to me?"

Before the sun set that day, Felipa had given the black ewe a name: Negrita. In the evening Felipa milked her again, and again the ewe moved away to eat. But as it got dark, and the rest of the sheep settled down for the night, Negrita came back to Felipa and lay down. Felipa lay down, too, using Negrita's soft side as a pillow. She knew that Sancho would stay half awake and watch the sheep.

Soon Felipa was sound asleep. Later she dreamed of Don José's face—smiling at her.

Early the next morning the journey continued, with Negrita still at Felipa's side. About noon they got to the first town, San José. Felipa was surprised to find that everyone was waiting for her. The news of her penance and her journey had traveled on ahead. Many people offered her bread, more than she could have eaten in a week. She asked and asked, but she could find no one poor enough to be given a sheep.

The same reception greeted Felipa in the next village, except that there she gave away her first sheep. And in the town after that she had the same experience. Continuing on, everywhere she went, she found that people had heard of her. On the third day her shoes wore out, and at first the dry desert sand hurt her feet. But she kept going. She traveled down the Rio Grande valley, where she found many poor people. Once she discovered a wrinkled old Indian woman who was starving in a mud hut. "In the name of Don José, and with the blessing of San Cristóbal, I give you this large sheep," Felipa told her. She knew without asking that the woman was a Ute.

The days turned into weeks, and the weeks turned into months. Felipa walked through Santa Cruz, headed north to Chimayo, and then south toward Pogoáqua. Nearly every day, she gave away a sheep. The number of sheep grew smaller and smaller. She went past Tesúque, then over the hills to Santa Fe.

• **browse** (BROUZ) graze; nibble on grass or plants

Finally there were only a few sheep left. There was no need for Sancho to lead them. He now walked on one side of Felipa, with the good sheep Negrita on the other.

In Albuquerque, Felipa gave away her next-to-last sheep. Now only Negrita was left. The next town, Felipa knew, was La Bajada, and for the first time she didn't want to go on. She prayed that there would be no one in La Bajada poor enough to deserve a sheep. But she also knew that if she found the right person, even Negrita would have to go.

Negrita did have to go. Felipa offered her to an emaciated old man who lay on a mat in the shade of a tree. He was almost too weak to stand up.

"Good-bye, Negrita," Felipa said. "You have been a good friend. Good-bye. Good-bye. Good-bye."

As the old man took hold of Negrita, Felipa got down on her knees. She buried her face in Negrita's soft neck. Suddenly feeling tears come to her eyes, she stood up quickly and turned to leave. But all at once, there was Negrita at her side again. The old man had not been strong enough to hold her.

"No, Negrita!" Felipa said. Now the tears were on her cheeks. "You must stay here!" She found a piece of rope and tied Negrita to the tree next to the old man. But when she again started to leave, a strange thing happened. Sancho stayed behind. He growled at the old man; then he growled at Negrita. Suddenly he started to bark. He ran at Negrita, sinking his sharp teeth into one of her back legs. The rope broke, and in an instant both animals were back at Felipa's side.

What should she do? Take Negrita back to the man again? No, Felipa decided. Perplexed, she walked on in silence. She could not force herself to return Negrita to the old man once more. But how long, really, could she keep Negrita? The next village was Socorro (which at the time was the last town in lower New Mexico). Surely, someone there would be poor enough to deserve the last of San Cristóbal's sheep.

Felipa entered Socorro with a heavy heart. As usual, the people already knew she was on her way. They offered her bread and answered her questions. No, they said, there was really no one poor enough to get a sheep. But Felipa didn't feel quite sure that everyone was telling the truth. She then looked into every house. She held her breath at every doorway, but she found no one poor enough to deserve Negrita.

• emaciated (i MAY shee ay tid) very thin

Beyond the town, on the edge of the desert, was one last house. It was a hut, really, adobe, poles, and animal skins. Felipa, with Negrita and Sancho by her side, approached it slowly. A tall man stepped out and stood at the doorway. His face mirrored the hue of the sun-baked desert sand. His wide-brimmed hat was filled with holes, and his clothes were rags.

"Certainly," Felipa told herself, "this is the person."

"In the name of Don José, and with the blessing of San Cristóbal—" Felipa began.

"Ah!" said the man. "So you are Felipa Sandoval!"

Felipa nodded. She watched the man as he smiled at her suddenly.

"No," he said, shaking his head slowly. "You will not give your last sheep to me. I am getting old, but I can still work. I am not as poor as I look."

Felipa's heart rose—then began to plummet again as the man went on:

"You should give your sheep to the child in my hut. He seems to be really in need. I got him from some Navajo Indians yesterday, for just a piece of cheap turquoise. The Navajos told me they got him from the Utes."

Felipa went into the hut. There in the shadows, dressed in Indian clothing, stood her son Manuel.

Feeling her head swimming, Felipa fell to her knees. Was it true? Had Manuel been kept alive by the Utes? Not carried off and killed?

The boy ran toward her arms, and Felipa knew it was true.

This was her son. Her only son. Her son Manuel. She had not held him close to her in a little more than a year.

Bark, bark—it was the dog Sancho, from outside the hut. Felipa pulled the boy toward the door and stepped outside. Negrita came up and nuzzled Felipa's leg as she stood blinking in the bright sunlight. Where was the man? She walked around the hut. Had he simply vanished?

Felipa hurried back to the center of Socorro. She asked about the tall stranger. Even though she described him clearly, the people in town said they had never seen such a man. The hut, they said, had been built years before for goats. No one had ever lived in it. Now even the goats had given it up.

• hue (HYOO) color; shade
• plummet (PLUM it) plunge; fall rapidly

Suddenly Felipa stopped listening. She knew intuitively who the man had been. She knew that San Cristóbal himself had delivered her little boy to her. And she knew, too, as the cloud of her guilt left her, that her penance was over.

For many years, people in New Mexico talked about Felipa Sandoval. They remembered her long walk with the sheep to Socorro. And they remembered even better her journey back home. No one ever forgot the young woman with the kind and joyful face, the little boy, the brown dog, and the black ewe.

Back in Las Colonias, Felipa found only happiness. Her neighbors had cared for her field, and beans were ready to be picked. She and Manuel picked them in peace, happy to be home, and not really caring that their story spread throughout the whole Southwest and then to the rest of the country.

• intuitively (in TOO i tiv lee) by direct insight

ALL THINGS CONSIDERED

1. Felipa's one wrongful act in the story is (a) refusing to marry Don José Vigil. (b) wishing for Don José's death. (c) not giving Negrita to an old man.
2. Felipa undertakes her penance (a) only to please the priest. (b) quite confused about its purpose. (c) willingly.
3. Early in her journey, Felipa dreams she sees Don José's face (a) smiling at her. (b) weeping. (c) laughing at her troubles.
4. Everything in the story might have happened naturally except (a) Don José's death. (b) the boy passing from the Utes to the Navajos to the old man. (c) the tall man being San Cristóbal.
5. The folktale portrays the Spanish-speaking people of the Old Southwest as (a) basically earnest and religious people. (b) people concerned only with material wealth. (c) victims of superstition.

THINKING IT THROUGH

1. Do you think "The Sheep of San Cristóbal" could be a true story? State your opinion and then give one or two reasons to support your answer.
2. The story has several themes. In your opinion, what is the main theme?
3. Felipa's penance can certainly be called a series of *symbolic actions* (see page 208). (a) In the eyes of the padre, what had long been Don José Vigil's greatest fault? (b) How does Felipa's symbolic action of giving away his sheep help to make up for this bad aspect of Don José?
4. Use a good encyclopedia or other reference book to find information on the Ute people of the old Southwest. (a) How did they differ from the Navajos and the Pueblos? (b) Do you think this story gives a fair picture of the Utes?
5. In the English language, San Cristóbal is called St. Christopher. Find out about St. Christopher. (a) For what is he supposed to stand? (b) Why is he a good saint for this particular story?

Critical Thinking

Analogies

An **analogy** (uh NAL uh jee) is a statement that the relationship between two items is in some way similar to the relationship between two other items. You've seen analogies before—even in this book:

- CARPENTER is to HAMMER as ARTIST is to PALETTE.
- PLEASANT is to SWEET as SARCASTIC is to BITTER.
- CRADLE is to BIRTH as HEARSE is to DEATH.

Good readers constantly make analogies as they read; that is, they think about relationships, and relationships between relationships. You certainly made analogies yourself as you read "The Sheep of San Cristóbal":

- DOG is to SANCHO as SHEEP is to NEGRITA.
- VIRTUE is to FELIPA as VICE is to DON JOSÉ.

Here are ten kinds of analogies commonly found on tests. Each is followed by an example from the selection. Complete each with a similar relationship from outside the selection. The first is done as an example.

1. *Like is to like:* BROWSE is to GRAZE as PUPIL is to STUDENT.
2. *Like is to opposite:* FAITH is to DOUBT as . . .
3. *One is to many:* SHEEP is to FLOCK as . . .
4. *Container is to contents:* CUP is to MILK as . . .
5. *Actor is to action:* SANCHO is to BARK as . . .
6. *Place is to area:* ALBUQUERQUE is to NEW MEXICO as . . .
7. *Place is to purpose:* SHRINE is to RELIGION as . . .
8. *Person is to person:* FELIPA is to MANUEL as . . .
9. *Classification is to kind:* HILL is to MESA . . .
10. *Part is to whole:* LEG is to SHEEP as . . .

Composition

1. Suppose you were turning "The Sheep of San Cristóbal" into a play or TV script. The first thing you would do is to decide on the number of scenes. (Whenever there is a change in setting or a jump in time, you will need to start a new scene.) List your scenes on a sheet of paper. Start with "Scene 1: Felipa returns to her house to find her husband dead and her son missing."

2. Which scene in the folktale do you think is the most interesting? Write that scene out in the form of a play. You will probably need to add more dialogue (spoken words) and action to make the scene seem complete.

Richard Wright (1908-1960)

A street in the Far Southwest Side of Chicago in the 1930s

If the following selection appeals to you, you might try looking for the book in a library. It is from *Black Boy*, the first volume of Richard Wright's autobiography, published in 1945. The book is strong stuff. The life Wright led as a child was a tough one, indeed.

Wright was born on a farm near Natchez, Mississippi, in 1908. His family moved here and there, at last settling in Memphis, Tennessee. When his parents separated, his mother had to work long hours to support the family. Wright hung out on the streets and in vacant lots. He learned to amuse the customers in bars by drinking liquor. "I was a drunkard in my sixth year," he tells us, "before I had begun school." Then his mother became very ill, and he spent some time in an orphanage. He quit school after the ninth grade and worked at several low-paying jobs. Always interested in books, he read more and more. He learned that life *could* be different. He began to believe that maybe he *did* have a chance at a happier life, after all. *Black Boy* ends as he leaves the South in 1927, to start a new life in Chicago.

But sadly, there was prejudice in the North, too. Wright still found that he was thought of as a black person first, a person second. After the success of *Black Boy* in 1945, he decided to move to Europe. He spent his last years in France and died in Paris in 1960. The second volume of his autobiography, *American Hunger*, written in the 1940s, was published in 1977.

Richard Wright had an interest that gave his life a turn for the better. What was this interest? How did it help him?

242

from BLACK BOY

by Richard Wright

▶ In this selection, Richard Wright looks back at a moment of truth in his life, an experience that taught him how he *could* behave in the face of danger.

Hunger stole upon me so slowly that at first I was not aware of what hunger really meant. Hunger had always been more or less at my elbow when I played, but now I began to wake up at night to find hunger standing at my bedside, staring at me gauntly. The hunger I had known before this had been no grim, hostile stranger; it had been a normal hunger that had made me beg constantly for bread, and when I ate a crust or two I was satisfied. But this new hunger baffled me, scared me, made me angry and insistent. Whenever I begged for food now my mother would pour me a cup of tea which would still the clamor in my stomach for a moment or two; but a little later I would feel hunger nudging my ribs, twisting my empty guts until they ached. I would grow dizzy and my vision would dim. I became less active in my play, and for the first time in my life I had to pause and think of what was happening to me.

"Mama, I'm hungry," I complained one afternoon.

"Jump up and catch a kungry," she said, trying to make me laugh and forget.

"What's a *kungry?*"

"It's what little boys eat when they get hungry," she said.

"What does it taste like?"

"I don't know."

"Then why do you tell me to catch one?"

"Because you said that you were hungry," she said, smiling.

I sensed that she was teasing me and it made me angry.

"But I'm hungry. I want to eat."

"You'll have to wait."

"But I want to eat now."

- **gauntly** (GAWNT lee) in the manner of a thin, bony person
- **grim** (GRIM) very serious
- **still** (STIL) make calm and quiet
- **clamor** (KLAM ur) noise; excitement

"But there's nothing to eat," she told me.

"Why?"

"Just because there's none," she explained.

"But I want to eat," I said, beginning to cry.

"You'll just have to wait," she said again.

"But why?"

"For God to send some food."

"When is He going to send it?"

"I don't know."

"But I'm hungry!"

She was ironing and she paused and looked at me with tears in her eyes.

"Where's your father?" she asked me.

I stared in bewilderment. Yes, it was true that my father had not come home to sleep for many days now and I could make as much noise as I wanted. Though I had not known why he was absent, I had been glad that he was not there to shout his restrictions at me. But it had never occurred to me that his absence would mean that there would be no food.

"I don't know," I said.

"Who brings food into the house?" my mother asked me.

"Papa," I said. "He always brought food."

"Well, your father isn't here now," she said.

"Where is he?"

"I don't know," she said.

"But I'm hungry," I whimpered, stomping my feet.

"You'll have to wait until I get a job and buy food," she said.

As the days slid past the image of my father became associated with my pangs of hunger, and whenever I felt hunger I thought of him with a deep biological bitterness.

My mother finally went to work as a cook and left me and my brother alone in the flat each day with a loaf of bread and a pot of tea. When she returned at evening she would be tired and dispirited and would cry a lot. Sometimes, when she was in despair, she would call us to her and talk to us for hours, telling us that we now had no father, that our lives would be different from those of other children, that we must learn as soon as possible to take care of ourselves, to dress ourselves, to prepare our own food; that we

---

° **image** (IM ij) mental picture

° pangs (PANGZ) sharp pains

° **flat** (FLAT) apartment

° dispirited (di SPIR i tid) discouraged; low in spirits

must take upon ourselves the responsibility of the flat while she worked. Half frightened, we would promise solemnly. We did not understand what had happened between our father and our mother, and the most that these long talks did to us was to make us feel a vague dread. Whenever we asked why father had left, she would tell us that we were too young to know.

One evening my mother told me that thereafter I would have to do the shopping for food. She took me to the corner store to show me the way. I was proud; I felt like a grownup. The next afternoon I looped the basket over my arm and went down the pavement toward the store. When I reached the corner, a gang of boys grabbed me, knocked me down, snatched the basket, took the money, and sent me running home in panic. That evening I told my mother what had happened, but she made no comment; she sat down at once, wrote another note, gave me more money, and sent me out to the grocery again. I crept down the steps and saw the same gang of boys playing down the street. I ran back into the house.

"What's the matter?" my mother asked.

"It's those same boys," I said. "They'll beat me."

"You've got to get over that," she said. "Now, go on."

"I'm scared," I said.

"Go on and don't pay any attention to them," she said.

I went out of the door and walked briskly down the sidewalk, praying that the gang would not molest me. But when I came abreast of them someone shouted.

"There he is!"

They came toward me and I broke into a wild run toward home. They overtook me and flung me to the pavement. I yelled, pleaded, kicked, but they wrenched the money out of my hand. They yanked me to my feet, gave me a few slaps, and set me home sobbing. My mother met me at the door.

"They b-beat m-me," I gasped. "They t-t-took the m-money."

I started up the steps, seeking the shelter of the house.

"Don't you come in here," my mother warned me.

I froze in my tracks and stared at her.

"But they're coming after me," I said.

"You just stay right where you are," she said in a deadly tone. "I'm going to teach you this night to stand up and fight for yourself."

- molest (muh LEST) bother; annoy
- wrench (RENCH) twist

She went into the house and I waited, terrified, wondering what she was about. Presently she returned with more money and another note; she also had a long heavy stick.

"Take this money, this note, and this stick," she said. "Go to the store and buy those groceries. If those boys bother you, then fight."

I was baffled. My mother was telling me to fight, a thing that she had never done before.

"But I'm scared," I said.

"Don't you come into this house until you've gotten those groceries," she said.

"They'll beat me; they'll beat me," I said.

"Then stay in the streets; don't come back here!"

I ran up the steps and tried to force my way past her into the house. A stinging slap came on my jaw. I stood on the sidewalk, crying.

"Please, let me wait until tomorrow," I begged.

"No," she said. "Go now! If you come back into this house without those groceries, I'll whip you!"

She slammed the door and I heard the key turn in the lock. I shook with fright. I was alone upon the dark, hostile streets and gangs were after me. I had the choice of being beaten at home or away from home. I clutched the stick, crying, trying to reason. If I were beaten at home, there was absolutely nothing that I could do about it; but if I were beaten in the streets, I had a chance to fight and defend myself. I walked slowly down the sidewalk, coming closer to the gang of boys, holding the stick tightly. I was so full of fear that I could scarcely breathe. I was almost upon them now.

"There he is again!" the cry went up.

They surrounded me quickly and began to grab for my hand.

"I'll kill you!" I threatened.

They closed in. In blind fear I let the stick fly, feeling it crack against a boy's skull. I swung again, lamming another skull, then another. Realizing that they would retaliate if I let up for but a second, I fought to lay them low, to knock them cold, to kill them so that they could not strike back at me. I flayed with tears in my eyes, teeth clenched, stark fear making me throw every ounce of

* lamming (LAM ing) striking
* retaliate (ri TAL ee ayt) strike back
* flay (FLAY) beat wildly
* stark (STAHRK) complete; downright

my strength behind each blow. I hit again and again, dropping the money and the grocery list. The boys scattered, yelling, nursing their heads, staring at me in utter disbelief. They had never seen such frenzy. I stood panting, egging them on, taunting them to come on and fight. When they refused, I ran after them and they tore out for their homes, screaming. The parents of the boys rushed into the streets and threatened me, and for the first time in my life I shouted at grownups, telling them that I would give them the same if they bothered me. I finally found my grocery list and the money and went to the store. On my way back I kept my stick poised for instant use, but there was not a single boy in sight. That night I won the right to the streets of Memphis.

- **utter** (UT ur) complete
- frenzy (FREN zee) madness; rage
- **egging** (EG ing) urging
- taunting (TAWNT ing) daring; teasing
- **poised** (POIZD) set and ready

ALL THINGS CONSIDERED _____

1. The hunger described in the first paragraph made the little boy (a) fight with his brother for food. (b) steal things at the store. (c) ache and grow dizzy.
2. The boy's hunger led to a great change in his feelings about his (a) father. (b) brother. (c) friends.
3. Trying to get to the store, the boy was beaten and robbed (a) once. (b) twice. (c) three times.
4. The boy was surprised when his mother (a) gave him a stick and told him to fight. (b) went to the store herself. (c) beat up the neighborhood gang.
5. At the end of the selection, the boy felt (a) defeated. (b) cheated. (c) victorious.

THINKING IT THROUGH _____

1. In your opinion, did the mother do the right thing in her efforts to get the boy to go to the store? Explain.
2. (a) When he left the house for the third time, what else might the boy have done besides fight the gang? (One answer is enough.) (b) How would this other course of action probably have worked out?
3. (a) How does the author use *personification* (see page 44) in the first paragraph of the selection? (b) What are at least three actions described in the personification? (c) In your opinion, does the personification reflect the thoughts of the little boy in the selection, or only those of the 37-year-old man who wrote it years later?
4. The selection has been reprinted several times under the title "Hunger." But the deeper meaning of the story may have little to do with the boy's hunger. In your opinion, what is the message of the story? In other words, what did the boy learn from his experience on the streets?

Literary Skills

Characterization

Fully rounded characters (see page 77) in literature seem to come to life in the reader's mind as unique human beings. For instance, Richard Wright's talent makes his small-boy self rise from the page so that we can feel and share his hunger, fright, confusion, and final triumph. How does the author manage to do this? What skills does he use?

The word **characterization** (kar ik tur i ZAY shun) refers to the methods by which authors develop their characters. If you think about it, you will realize that there are four main methods of characterization:

A. Direct statements by the author. (For instance, Wright tells us directly that the boy was "angry" and "insistent.")

B. Speeches and thoughts of the character. ("'Mama, I'm hungry,' I complained one afternoon.")

C. The character's actions. ("I ran back into the house.")

D. Reactions of other characters to the character. ("A stinging slap came on my jaw.")

Answer the following questions using examples from the selection that are different from those given above:

1. What is a good example of method A—direct statement by the author?

2. (a) What is a good example of method B—the boy's own speeches or thoughts? (b) What more do these words and thoughts tell you about the boy?

3. (a) What is a good example of method C—the boy's actions? (b) What does this action indicate about the boy's state of mind at the time?

4. (a) What is a good example of method D—the reactions of other characters to the boy? (b) What do these reactions show you about the boy?

Composition

1. In a short paragraph, answer this question about the selection: What is the main character's conflict (page 77), and what does he do to resolve it?

2. Think of something you recently saw happen to another person that saddened or amused you. Describe the events in the third person (see page 228), using all four methods of characterization: (A) Comment directly on the subject yourself; (B) show the subject speaking or thinking; (C) show the subject in action; and (D) show the reaction of someone else to the subject. If you choose the right event and use all four methods of characterization well, your story should be a good one.

Robert Frost (1874-1963)

One day in 1909 the State Superintendent of Schools in New Hampshire dropped into a small high school in the tiny town of Derry. His inspection included an English classroom—and a happy surprise. "A class of boys and girls were listening open-mouthed to the teacher," he wrote later. "Slumped down behind a desk at the front of the room was a young man who was talking to the students as he might talk to a group of friends around his own fireside." It didn't take the inspector long to realize that he had discovered "the best teacher in New Hampshire."

Inspector Charles Silver couldn't have known, of course, that he had also discovered a talented young poet named Robert Frost. Neither did he know that his visit was to mark a turning point in Frost's life. Up to that time, Frost had thought of himself as a failure. He had failed at college, dropping out of Harvard after two years to support a growing family. He had failed as a chicken farmer, having spent too much time reading and writing poetry. And most important to him, he had failed to get many of his poems printed.

Then the turning point arrived. With the help of Charles Silver, Frost found a job teaching in a New Hampshire college. He still wanted to write, however, and in 1912 he sold his farm and moved his family to England, an attempt to "get away from it all" and write without pressure. In 1913 his first book of poems was accepted by a London publisher. At the age of 39, Frost was finally on his way. He decided to return to the United States.

Before long Robert Frost was able to live the life he wanted. He bought a small farm in New Hampshire. He taught a little. He traveled a little. He published book after book and collected prize after prize. His hair slowly turned gray with age, and then white with wisdom. "America's beloved poet" lived to be nearly 90.

Frost is often called a "nature poet," but he never liked the term. "I guess I'm just not a nature poet," he said on a TV show in 1952. "I have only written two poems without a human being in them." He might have added that his real subject was *human* nature.

Why did Robert Frost think of himself as a failure when he was in his mid-30s? How old was he when his first book was published?

THREE BY FROST

poems by Robert Frost

▶ Robert Frost has been called "America's beloved poet, ageless and for the ages." Here are three of his best-known poems. The first poem is followed by a short analysis that you should read carefully. The second and third are accompanied by questions that will lead you to your own analysis of each.

THE PASTURE

I'm going out to clean the pasture spring;
I'll only stop to rake the leaves away
(And wait to watch the water clear, I may):
I sha'n't be gone long.—You come too.

I'm going out to fetch the little calf
That's standing by the mother. It's so young
It totters when she licks it with her tongue.
I sha'n't be gone long.—You come too.

"Ways of knowing" is a fitting expression to use when dealing with Robert Frost, for it was he who defined poetry as "saying one thing and meaning another." In other words, a poem can be known in two ways, or on two **levels of meaning**: a surface, "saying" level; and a deeper, "meaning" level.

"The Pasture" illustrates the method Frost used in many of his poems. The speaker, whom we can assume is either Frost or someone very much like him, is a country man who for the most part uses rather simple language. Yet amazingly, the unforced and natural speech also turns out to be lines of pure poetry.

The meaning of "The Pasture"—on the surface or "saying" level—is also rather simple. Here, the speaker invites someone to join him on a leisurely trip to a pasture to do a routine farm chore. On this level, "The Pasture" is so easy that some readers are

---

• fetch (FECH) get and bring back

251

tempted to accept the surface level and dig for nothing deeper. But wait—and remember Frost's caution:

It takes all sorts of in and outdoor schooling
To get adapted to my kind of fooling.

What is Frost really up to in "The Pasture"? Consider these facts:

(1) Frost placed "The Pasture" first in his *Complete Poems*.
(2) Frost placed "The Pasture" first in his *Selected Poems*.
(3) Frost chose *You Come Too* as the title of a collection of poems for young readers.
(4) Frost often opened with "The Pasture" at his poetry readings.
(5) Water, in the work of Frost and many other great writers, is a common symbol of truth.

On a deeper level, the poem is still an invitation—but an invitation of quite another kind. The speaker, or poet, is asking "you," the reader, to join him on a trip into poetry. The aim of that trip is to find certain truths, truths that may well become "clear." The trip will be a short, pleasant one, with some observation of nature along the way. "You come too."

▶ Keep levels of meaning in your mind as you ponder—

THE ROAD NOT TAKEN

Two roads diverged in a yellow wood,
And sorry I could not travel both
And be one traveler, long I stood
And looked down one as far as I
    could
5 To where it bent in the undergrowth;

Then took the other, as just as fair,
And having perhaps the better claim,
Because it was grassy and wanted
    wear;
Though as for that the passing there
10 Had worn them really about the same,

And both that morning equally lay
In leaves no step had trodden black.
Oh, I kept the first for another day!
Yet knowing how way leads on to
    way,
15 I doubted if I should ever come back.

I shall be telling this with a sigh
Somewhere ages and ages hence:
Two roads diverged in a wood, and
    I—
I took the one less traveled by,
20 And that has made all the difference.

WAYS OF KNOWING

1. (a) According to the speaker, why does he finally choose one road over another (lines 6–8)? (b) What does he discover when he starts down his chosen road (lines 9–10)?

2. (a) How serious is the speaker when he says he "kept the first for another day" (line 13)? (b) In your opinion, did he ever come back and start down the road he *didn't* take? Explain.

3. Readers of Frost know that a poem like "The Road Not Taken" must be understood on two levels. The last stanza almost insists that the reader do this. What began as a pleasant walk down woodland roads has now turned into an event that calls for a big "sigh" and has somehow "made all the difference" in the speaker's life. The reader is almost ordered to start looking for symbols. (a) In your opinion, what might the two roads stand for? Your answer can be general or, if you want, it can refer to a specific event in Frost's life. (b) Do you think the speaker feels he has made the right decision or the wrong one? Why?

4. Line 17, "Somewhere ages and ages hence," is unclear to some readers. What does it mean to you?

● diverge (di VURJ) spread apart

▶ What's the most popular poem by America's most popular poet? Probably—

STOPPING BY WOODS ON A SNOWY EVENING

Whose woods these are I think I know.
His house is in the village though;
He will not see me stopping here
To watch his woods fill up with snow.

5 My little horse must think it queer
To stop without a farmhouse near
Between the woods and frozen lake
The darkest evening of the year.

He gives his harness bells a shake
10 To ask if there is some mistake.
The only other sound's the sweep
Of easy wind and downy flake.

The woods are lovely, dark and deep,
But I have promises to keep,
15 And miles to go before I sleep,
And miles to go before I sleep.

• **downy** (DOW nee) soft; fluffy

WAYS OF KNOWING

1. The rhyme scheme in the poem is most unusual. (a) What line in the first stanza does not rhyme with the others? (b) What *does* it rhyme with? (Go on to the second stanza.) (c) Follow the pattern through the rest of the poem. How does the last stanza differ from the first three? (d) Why does the last stanza almost *have* to be different? (e) Some readers think that this rhyme pattern seems to pull the reader through the poem, since each stanza is incomplete without the next. Do you agree?

2. What reason does the speaker give for stopping the horse?

3. What comparison can you make between the time of day and the time of year?

4. In just a few words, how does the speaker seem to feel while "Stopping by Woods on a Snowy Evening"?

5. Does the horse seem to share the speaker's feelings and desires? How do you know?

6. What does the speaker seem to decide to do in the last stanza?

7. In your opinion, what kind of "promises" (line 14) does the speaker mean? To self? To others? To both? Explain.

8. Think about why the last two lines are exactly alike. The next-to-last line probably means just what it says: The speaker has miles to travel before going home to bed. But because the line occurs another time, another meaning is suggested. (a) What might this other meaning be? (b) How is this other meaning related to the rest of the poem?

Ernest Hemingway (1899-1961)

Hemingway aboard a World War II invasion ship, 1944

Quick! List three facts about a famous living American writer.

Could you do it? Maybe. But if you'd lived during the time of Ernest Hemingway, you probably could have done it easily. Wherever he went and whatever he did, Hemingway was always big news. His name was often in the headlines:

HEMINGWAY BREAKS NOSE IN BOXING RING
PLANE CRASH KILLS HEMINGWAY IN AFRICA
GOOD NEWS: HEMINGWAY ALIVE!
HEMINGWAY MARRIES FOR FOURTH TIME
HEMINGWAY YACHT IN U-BOAT CHASE
GUN ACCIDENT INJURES HEMINGWAY

A bear of a man, Hemingway photographed well. All America knew what he looked like. He seemed always in action: skiing in Switzerland, hunting in Africa, fishing from his private yacht, risking his life as a reporter on distant war fronts. Yet somehow during his active life he took the time to write the stories and novels that won him the highest honor a writer can earn, the Nobel Prize.

"All you have to do is write one true sentence," Hemingway discovered when he was starting out. "Write the truest sentence you know." That one sentence, he found, would lead to another, to a paragraph, to a story. He disliked fancy writing; he wanted it pure and simple, lifelike and honest. No other author of our century has had a greater influence upon modern American writers than Ernest Hemingway.

How did Hemingway differ from the stereotype you probably have in your mind labeled "famous author"?

A DAY'S WAIT

by Ernest Hemingway

▶ In this short story, Hemingway deals with one of his favorite subjects—courage—from the viewpoint of a nine-year-old boy. The story is based on a true incident involving Schatz, Hemingway's son. Schatz, who had been living in France, had recently joined his father in America.

He came into the room to shut the windows while we were still in bed and I saw he looked ill. He was shivering, his face was white, and he walked slowly as though it ached to move.

"What's the matter, Schatz?

"I've got a headache."

"You better go back to bed."

"No. I'm all right."

"You go to bed. I'll see you when I'm dressed."

But when I came downstairs he was dressed, sitting by the fire, looking a very sick and miserable boy of nine years. When I put my hand on his forehead I knew he had a fever.

"You go up to bed," I said, "you're sick."

"I'm all right," he said.

When the doctor came he took the boy's temperature.

"What is it?" I asked him.

"One hundred and two."

Downstairs, the doctor left three different medicines in different colored capsules with instructions for giving them. One was to bring down the fever, another a purgative, the third to overcome an acid condition. The germs of influenza can only exist in an acid condition, he explained. He seemed to know all about influenza and said there was nothing to worry about if the fever did not go above one hundred and four degrees. This was a light epidemic of flu and there was no danger if you avoided pneumonia.

Back in the room I wrote the boy's temperature down and made a note of the time to give the various capsules.

"Do you want me to read to you?"

"All right. If you want to," said the boy. He face was very white and there were dark areas under his eyes. He lay still in the

---

- purgative (PUR guh tiv) strong laxative
- **influenza** (in floo EN zuh) disease usually called "flu"

bed and seemed very detached from what was going on.

I read aloud from Howard Pyle's *Book of Pirates;* but I could see he was not following what I was reading.

"How do you feel, Schatz?" I asked him.

"Just the same, so far," he said.

I sat at the foot of the bed and read to myself while I waited for it to be time to give another capsule. It would have been natural for him to go to sleep, but when I looked up he was looking at the foot of the bed, looking very strangely.

"Why don't you try to go to sleep? I'll wake you up for the medicine."

"I'd rather stay awake."

After a while he said to me, "You don't have to stay in here with me, Papa, if it bothers you."

"It doesn't bother me."

"No, I mean you don't have to stay if it's going to bother you."

I thought perhaps he was a little lightheaded and after giving him the prescribed capsules at eleven o'clock I went out for a while.

It was a bright, cold day, the ground covered with a sleet that had frozen so that it seemed as if all the bare trees, the bushes, the cut brush and all the grass and the bare ground had been varnished with ice. I took the young Irish setter for a little walk up the road and along a frozen creek, but it was difficult to stand or walk on the glassy surface and the red dog slipped and slithered and I fell twice, hard, once dropping my gun and having it slide away over the ice.

• slither (SLITH ur) slip and slide

We flushed a covey of quail under a high clay bank with over-hanging brush and I killed two as they went out of sight over the top of the bank. Some of the covey lit in trees, but most of them scattered into brush piles and it was necessary to jump on the ice-coated mounds of brush several times before they would flush. Coming out while you were poised unsteadily on the icy, springy brush they made difficult shooting and I killed two, missed five, and started back pleased to have found a covey close to the house and happy there were so many left to find on another day.

At the house they said the boy had refused to let anyone come into the room.

"You can't come in," he said. "You mustn't get what I have."

I went up to him and found him in exactly the position I had left him, white-faced, but with the tops of his cheeks flushed by the fever, staring still, as he had stared, at the foot of the bed.

I took his temperature.

"What is it?"

"Something like a hundred," I said. It was one hundred and two and four tenths.

"It was a hundred and two," he said.

"Who said so?"

"The doctor."

"Your temperature is all right," I said. "It's nothing to worry about."

"I don't worry," he said, "but I can't keep from thinking."

"Don't think," I said. "Just take it easy."

"I'm taking it easy," he said and looked straight ahead. He was evidently holding tight onto himself about something.

"Take this with water."

"Do you think it will do any good?"

"Of course it will."

I sat down and opened the *Pirate* book and commenced to read, but I could see he was not following, so I stopped.

"About what time do you think I'm going to die?" he asked.

"What?"

"About how long will it be before I die?"

"You aren't going to die. What's the matter with you?"

"Oh, yes, I am. I heard him say a hundred and two."

- flush (FLUSH) drive birds or animals from hiding place
- covey (KUV ee) flock of birds
- **commence** (kuh MENS) begin

"People don't die with a fever of one hundred and two. That's a silly way to talk."

"I know they do. At school in France the boys told me you can't live with forty-four degrees. I've got a hundred and two."

He had been waiting to die all day, ever since nine o'clock in the morning.

"You poor Schatz," I said. "Poor old Schatz. It's like miles and kilometers. You aren't going to die. That's a different thermometer. On that thermometer thirty-seven is normal. On this kind it's ninety-eight."

"Are you sure?"

"Absolutely," I said. "It's like miles and kilometers. You know, like how many kilometers we make when we do seventy miles in the car?"

"Oh," he said.

But his gaze at the foot of the bed relaxed slowly. The hold over himself relaxed too, finally, and the next day it was very slack and he cried very easily at little things that were of no importance.

ALL THINGS CONSIDERED ——————————

1. Schatz doesn't hear the doctor's opinion that his illness is probably "nothing to worry about" because (a) he is too ill to hear anything. (b) the doctor is consulted by phone. (c) the conversation takes place out of Schatz's room.

2. An early hint as to what is wrong with Schatz's thinking comes when the boy (a) thinks the doctor is no good. (b) fears his father has the illness, too. (c) believes it might bother his father to stay in the room.

3. Another hint comes when the boy (a) refuses to let anyone into the room. (b) asks for odd foods. (c) seems uninterested in his father's hunting trip.

4. Schatz's mistake is caused by his lack of (a) courage. (b) knowledge. (c) trust.

5. The BIG IDEA in the story concerns (a) America's failure to adopt the metric system. (b) a father who will go hunting with his son near death. (c) a boy's courage in the face of apparent death.

THINKING IT THROUGH ——————————

1. When Schatz's father tells him not to worry about his temperature, the boy says, "I don't worry, but I can't keep from thinking." Exactly what thoughts and feelings underlie these words?

2. Suppose the same thing had happened to you (a) when you were nine, and (b) a month ago. Would you have behaved as Schatz does? Explain as honestly as you can.

3. Look back at the last sentence of the story. Although the boy doesn't cry during "A Day's Wait," he does cry the next day. How might this behavior be explained?

4. Ernest Hemingway once said that the words a writer *leaves out* are more important than those he *puts in*. Hemingway is famous for saying a lot in a few words. In the first 16 lines of the story, for instance, three conversations take place in three different settings. Do you like this method of telling a story? Or would you have preferred a longer story that contained more details and clues?

Critical Thinking

Fact and Opinion

A **fact,** in simple terms, is something generally known to be true. Most facts can be checked by direct observation or the study of reports by reliable witnesses. An **opinion,** on the other hand, is what a person *thinks, believes, judges,* or *infers* is true, or probably true. The best opinions, of course, are usually those that are most directly based on facts.

The difference between fact and opinion is not always crystal clear. An analysis of "A Day's Wait" will make this point:

1. (a) What opinion of Schatz's did he believe to be a fact? (b) What are two of the facts upon which Schatz based his opinion? (c) What is one important fact that Schatz did not know?

2. Is it a fact that Schatz had an incorrect opinion?

3. Do you think the narrator had an incorrect opinion about Schatz when he went out to hunt?

4. Considering the fact that you just answered the last question with an opinion, can there be such a thing as an opinion of an opinion of an opinion of a set of facts? Explain in detail.

5. Considering your answers to the above questions, would you agree that there can be both facts about opinions and opinions about facts? Explain with examples.

6. Fact: Carlos Baker, considered the nation's leading authority on Hemingway, tells us that "A Day's Wait" is based on a true story. Fact: The story contains the statement that "The germs of influenza can only exist in an acid condition." Does the first fact prove the second? Explain why or why not.

Composition

1. As has been noted, Hemingway is famous for his economy of style: *no wasted words.* Find three short sentences in the story and expand them, as if another author might have written them. For instance, take the sentence, "When the doctor came he took the boy's temperature." It could be written, "When the handsome young doctor came in, he opened his black bag and solemnly took the boy's temperature."

2. Write your opinion of "A Day's Wait" in a single complete sentence. Then write at least three more sentences that support your opinion. Try to be as factual as possible.

VOCABULARY AND SKILL REVIEW

Before completing the exercises that follow, you may wish to review the **bold-faced** words on pages 234 to 262.

I. On a separate sheet of paper, write the term in each line that means the same, or nearly the same, as the word in *italics*.

1. *utter:* kind of insect, complete, small boat, useless
2. *commence:* give in, continue, argue about, begin
3. *browse:* best choice, graze, think deeply, nearly brown
4. *flat:* apartment, apartment house, landlord, monthly rent
5. *clamor:* measurement, noisy excitement, defeat, submit
6. *egging:* farming, judging, breaking, urging
7. *padre:* sister, brother, mother, father
8. *influenza:* liver disease, pneumonia, flu, common cold
9. *image:* cause, kind of perfume, mental picture, excuse
10. *grim:* dirt, short hymn, elf or spirit, very serious

II.
1. In the study of literature, *levels of meaning* refers to (a) a surface and an in-depth understanding. (b) an author's honesty. (c) the vocabulary of a given reader.
2. If you had a hammer *poised*, it would be (a) well hidden. (b) newly repaired. (c) all set and ready to strike.
3. An author's *characterization* is the way he or she (a) writes from personal experience. (b) develops characters. (c) proves that plot is a result of character.
4. The verb *still* is related to (a) the noun *still*, meaning "photograph from a motion picture." (b) the adverb *still*, meaning "yet" or "continuing in time." (c) the adjective *still*, meaning "calm" or "quiet."
5. Which statement is more generally correct? (a) Opinions should be based on facts. (b) Facts should be based on opinions. (c) Opinions should be based on other opinions.
6. Items *7–10* are (a) *analogies.* (b) *images.* (c) *opinions.*
7. THE SHEEP OF SAN CRISTÓBAL is to FOLKTALE as BLACK BOY is to (a) FICTION. (b) AUTOBIOGRAPHY. (c) BIOGRAPHY.
8. SCHATZ is to A DAY'S WAIT as FELIPA is to (a) THE PASTURE. (b) TERRI BUENO. (c) THE SHEEP OF SAN CRISTÓBAL.
9. PROSE is to POETRY as A DAY'S WAIT is to (a) HEMINGWAY. (b) FROST. (c) THE ROAD NOT TAKEN.
10. FACT is to OPINION as TRUTH is to (a) FALSEHOOD. (b) BELIEF. (c) SCIENCE.

III. Read the poem slowly before answering the questions.

WHERE HAVE YOU GONE?

by Mari Evans

Where have you gone

with your confident
walk with
your crooked smile

5 why did you leave
me
when you took your
laughter
and departed

10 are you aware that
with you
went the sun
all light
and what few stars
15 there were?

where have you gone
with your confident
walk your
crooked smile the
20 rent money
in one pocket and
my heart
in another . . .

1. The poem seems to fill up and then overflow with emotion.
What are your feelings about (a) the speaker, and (b) the "you"
in the poem? Go into detail. For instance, can you dislike the
"you" and also sympathize with the speaker's feelings?

2. In just 63 words and 23 short lines, the poet has managed to
outline a dramatic plot and characterize two people. Turn back
to the four methods of *characterization* on page 249. Illustrate
how at least three of them are used in the poem.

3. Discuss the expressions "rent money" (line 20) and "my heart"
(line 22) in terms of fact and opinion.

THE SCARLET IBIS

by James Hurst

▶ Here's a college-level story that should offer you a challenge. Although the editor of this book has read hundreds and hundreds of short stories by American authors, few have had the impact of "The Scarlet Ibis."

It was in the clove of seasons, summer was dead but autumn had not yet been born, that the ibis lit in the bleeding tree. The flower garden was stained with rotting brown magnolia petals and ironweeds grew rank amid the purple phlox. The five o'clocks by the chimney still marked time, but the oriole nest in the elm was untenanted and rocked back and forth like an empty cradle. The last graveyard flowers were blooming, and their smell drifted across the cotton field and through every room of our house, speaking softly the names of our dead.

It's strange that all this is still so clear to me, now that that summer has long since fled and time has had its way. A grindstone stands where the bleeding tree stood, just outside the kitchen door, and now if an oriole sings in the elm, its song seems to die up in the leaves, a silvery dust. The flower garden is prim, the house a gleaming white, and the pale fence across the yard stands straight and spruce. But sometimes (like right now), as I sit in the cool, green-draped parlor, the grindstone begins to turn, and time with all its changes is ground away—and I remember Doodle.

Doodle was just about the craziest brother a boy ever had. Of course, he wasn't a crazy crazy like old Miss Leedie, who was in love with President Wilson and wrote him a letter every day, but

---

- ibis (EYE bis) kind of large wading bird
- clove (KLOHV), or clove hitch: a kind of knot made so that two parts of the rope stick out from a pole in opposite directions
- rank (RANK) vigorously; abundantly
- prim (PRIM) neat; orderly

265

was a nice crazy, like someone you meet in your dreams. He was born when I was six and was, from the outset, a disappointment. He seemed all head, with a tiny body which was red and shriveled like an old man's. Everybody thought he was going to die—everybody except Aunt Nicey, who had delivered him. She said he would live because he was born in a caul and cauls were made from Jesus' nightgown. Daddy had Mr. Heath, the carpenter, build a little mahogany coffin for him. But he didn't die, and when he was three months old Mama and Daddy decided they might as well name him. They named him William Armstrong, which was like tying a big tail on a small kite. Such a name sounds good only on a tombstone.

I thought myself pretty smart at many things, like holding my breath, running, jumping, or climbing the vines in Old Woman Swamp, and I wanted more than anything else someone to race to Horsehead Landing, someone to box with, and someone to perch with in the top fork of the great pine behind the barn, where across the fields and swamps you could see the sea. I wanted a brother. But Mama, crying, told me that even if William Armstrong lived, he would never do these things with me. He might not, she sobbed, even be "all there." He might, as long as he lived, lie on the rubber sheet in the center of the bed in the front bedroom, where the white marquisette curtains billowed out in the afternoon sea breeze, rustling like palmetto fronds.

It was bad enough having an invalid brother, but having one who possibly was not all there was unbearable, so I began to make plans to kill him by smothering him with a pillow. However, one afternoon as I watched him, my head poked between the iron posts of the foot of the bed, he looked straight at me and grinned. I skipped through the rooms, down the echoing halls, shouting, "Mama, he smiled. He's all there! He's all there!" And he was.

When he was two, if you laid him on his stomach, be began to try to move himself, straining terribly. The doctor said that with his weak heart this strain would probably kill him, but it didn't. Trembling, he'd push himself up, turning first red, then a soft purple, and finally collapse back onto the bed like an old worn-out doll. I can still see Mama watching him, her hand pressed tight

---

- caul (KAWL) part of sac or membrane that sometimes covers a baby's head at birth
- marquisette (mahr ki ZET) kind of light fabric
- frond (FROND) kind of large divided leaf, as on some palm trees

across her mouth, her eyes wide and unblinking. But he learned to crawl (it was his third winter), and we brought him out of the front bedroom, putting him on the rug before the fireplace. For the first time he became one of us.

As long as he lay all the time in bed, we called him William Armstrong, even though it was formal and sounded as if we were referring to one of our ancestors, but with his creeping around on the deerskin rug and beginning to talk, something had to be done about his name. It was I who renamed him. When he crawled, he crawled backward, as if he were in reverse and couldn't change gears. If you called him, he'd turn around as if he were going in the other direction, then he'd back right up to you to be picked up. Crawling backward made him look like a doodle-bug, so I began to call him Doodle, and in time even Mama and Daddy thought it was a better name than William Armstrong. Only Aunt Nicey disagreed. She said caul babies should be treated with special respect since they might turn out to be saints. Renaming my brother was perhaps the kindest thing I ever did for him, because nobody expects much from someone called Doodle.

Although Doodle learned to crawl, he showed no signs of walking, but he wasn't idle. He talked so much that we all quit listening to what he said. It was about this time that Daddy built him a go-cart and I had to pull him around. At first I just paraded

him up and down the piazza, but then he started crying to be taken out into the yard and it ended up by my having to lug him wherever I went. If I so much as picked up my cap, he'd start crying to go with me and Mama would call from wherever she was, "Take Doodle with you."

He was a burden in many ways. The doctor had said that he mustn't get too excited, too hot, too cold, or too tired and that he must always be treated gently. A long list of don'ts went with him, all of which I ignored once we got out of the house. To discourage his coming with me, I'd run with him across the ends of the cotton rows and careen him around corners on two wheels. Sometimes I accidentally turned him over, but he never told Mama. His skin was very sensitive, and he had to wear a big straw hat whenever he went out. When the going got rough and he had to cling to the sides of the go-cart, the hat slipped all the way down over his ears. He was a sight. Finally, I could see I was licked. Doodle was my brother and he was going to cling to me forever, no matter what I did, so I dragged him across the burning cotton field to share with him the only beauty I knew, Old Woman Swamp. I pulled the go-cart through the sawtooth fern, down into the green dimness where the palmetto fronds whispered by the stream. I lifted him out and set him down in the soft rubber grass beside a tall pine. His eyes were round with wonder as he gazed about him, and his little hands began to stroke the rubber grass. Then he began to cry.

"For heaven's sake, what's the matter?" I asked, annoyed.

"It's so pretty," he said. "So pretty, pretty, pretty."

After that day Doodle and I often went down into Old Woman Swamp. I would gather wildflowers, wild violets, honeysuckle, yellow jasmine, snakeflowers, and water lilies, and with wire grass we'd weave them into necklaces and crowns. We'd bedeck ourselves with our handiwork and loll about thus beautified, beyond the touch of the everyday world. Then when the slanted rays of the sun burned orange in the tops of the pines, we'd drop our jewels into the stream and watch them float away toward the sea.

There is within me (and with sadness I have watched it in others) a knot of cruelty borne by the stream of love, much as our blood sometimes bears the seed of our destruction, and at times I was mean to Doodle. One day I took him up to the barn loft and

---

- piazza (pee AZ uh) porch or other open area
- bedeck (bi DEK) decorate in a showy way
- loll (LOL) lounge; pass time in a relaxed, idle fashion

showed him his casket, telling him how we all had believed he would die. It was covered with a film of Paris green sprinkled to kill the rats, and screech owls had built a nest inside it.

Doodle studied the mahogany box for a long time, then said, "It's not mine."

"It is," I said. "And before I'll help you down from the loft, you're going to have to touch it."

"I won't touch it," he said sullenly.

"Then I'll leave you here by yourself," I threatened, and made as if I were going down.

Doodle was frightened of being left. "Don't go leave me, Brother," he cried, and he leaned toward the coffin. His hand, trembling, reached out, and when he touched the casket he screamed. A screech owl flapped out of the box into our faces, scaring us and covering us with Paris green. Doodle was paralyzed, so I put him on my shoulder and carried him down the ladder, and even when we were outside in the bright sunshine, he clung to me, crying, "Don't leave me. Don't leave me."

When Doodle was five years old, I was embarrassed at having a brother of that age who couldn't walk, so I set out to teach him. We were down in Old Woman Swamp and it was spring and the sick-sweet smell of bay flowers hung everywhere like a mournful song. "I'm going to teach you to walk, Doodle," I said.

He was sitting comfortably on the soft grass, leaning back against the pine. "Why?" he asked.

I hadn't expected such an answer. "So I won't have to haul you around all the time."

"I can't walk, Brother," he said.

"Who says so?" I demanded.

"Mama, the doctor—everybody."

"Oh, you can walk," I said, and I took him by the arms and stood him up. He collapsed onto the grass like a half-empty flour sack. It was as if he had no bones in his little legs.

"Don't hurt me, Brother," he warned.

"Shut up. I'm not going to hurt you. I'm going to teach you to walk." I heaved him up again, and again he collapsed.

This time he did not lift his face up out of the rubber grass. "I just can't do it. Let's make honeysuckle wreaths."

"Oh yes you can, Doodle," I said. "All you got to do is try. Now come on," and I hauled him up once more.

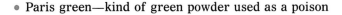

● Paris green—kind of green powder used as a poison

It seemed so hopeless from the beginning that it's a miracle I didn't give up. But all of us must have something or someone to be proud of, and Doodle had become mine. I did not know then that pride is a wonderful, terrible thing, a seed that bears two vines, life and death. Every day that summer we went to the pine beside the stream of Old Woman Swamp, and I put him on his feet at least a hundred times each afternoon. Occasionally I too became discouraged because it didn't seem as if he was trying, and I would say, "Doodle, don't you *want* to learn to walk?"

He'd nod his head, and I'd say, "Well, if you don't keep trying, you'll never learn." Then I'd paint for him a picture of us as old men, white-haired, him with a long white beard and me still pulling him around in the go-cart. This never failed to make him try again.

Finally one day, after many weeks of practicing, he stood alone for a few seconds. When he fell, I grabbed him in my arms and hugged him, our laughter pealing through the swamp like a ringing bell. Now we knew it could be done. Hope no longer hid in the dark palmetto thicket but perched like a cardinal in the lacy toothbrush tree, brilliantly visible. "Yes, yes," I cried, and he cried it too, and the grass beneath us was soft and the smell of the swamp was sweet.

With success so imminent, we decided not to tell anyone until he could actually walk. Each day, barring rain, we sneaked into Old Woman Swamp, and by cotton-picking time Doodle was ready to show what he could do. He still wasn't able to walk far, but we could wait no longer. Keeping a nice secret is very hard to do, like holding your breath. We chose to reveal all on October eighth, Doodle's sixth birthday, and for weeks ahead we mooned around the house, promising everybody a most spectacular surprise. Aunt Nicey said that, after so much talk, if we produced anything less tremendous than the Resurrection, she was going to be disappointed.

At breakfast on our chosen day, when Mama, Daddy, and Aunt Nicey were in the dining room, I brought Doodle to the door in the go-cart just as usual and had them turn their backs, making them cross their hearts and hope to die if they peeked. I helped Doodle up, and when he was standing alone I let them look. There wasn't a sound as Doodle walked slowly across the room and sat down at his place at the table. Then Mama began to cry and ran over to

---

• pealing (PEEL ing) sounding; ringing
• imminent (IM uh nunt) very near; about to happen

him, hugging him and kissing him. Daddy hugged him too, so I
went to Aunt Nicey, who was thanks-praying in the doorway, and
began to waltz her around. We danced together quite well until
she came down on my big toe with her brogans, hurting me so
badly I thought I was crippled for life.

Doodle told them it was I who had taught him to walk, so
everyone wanted to hug me, and I began to cry.

"What are you crying for?" asked Daddy, but I couldn't answer. They did not know that I did it for myself; that pride, whose
slave I was, spoke to me louder than all their voices, and that
Doodle walked only because I was ashamed of having a crippled
brother.

Within a few months Doodle had learned to walk well and his
go-cart was put up in the barn loft (it's still there) beside his little
mahogany coffin. Now, when we roamed off together, resting
often, we never turned back until our destination had been
reached, and to help pass the time, we took up lying. From the
beginning Doodle was a terrible liar and he got me in the habit.
Had anyone stopped to listen to us, we would have been sent off to
Dix Hill.

My lies were scary, involved, and usually pointless, but Doodle's were twice as crazy. People in his stories all had wings and

---

• brogan (BROH gun) kind of heavy shoe

flew wherever they wanted to go. His favorite lie was about a boy named Peter who had a pet peacock with a ten-foot tail. Peter wore a golden robe that glittered so brightly that when he walked through the sunflowers they turned away from the sun to face him. When Peter was ready to go to sleep, the peacock spread his magnificent tail, enfolding the boy gently like a closing go-to-sleep flower, burying him in the gloriously iridescent, rustling vortex. Yes, I must admit it. Doodle could beat me lying.

Doodle and I spent lots of time thinking about our future. We decided that when we were grown we'd live in Old Woman Swamp and pick dog-tongue for a living. Beside the stream, he planned, we'd build us a house of whispering leaves and the swamp birds would be our chickens. All day long (when we weren't gathering dog-tongue) we'd swing through the cypresses on the rope vines, and if it rained we'd huddle beneath an umbrella tree and play stickfrog. Mama and Daddy could come and live with us if they wanted to. He even came up with the idea that he could marry Mama and I could marry Daddy. Of course, I was old enough to know this wouldn't work out, but the picture he painted was so beautiful and serene that all I could do was whisper Yes, yes.

Once I had succeeded in teaching Doodle to walk, I began to believe in my own infallibility and I prepared a terrific development program for him, unknown to Mama and Daddy, of course. I would teach him to run, to swim, to climb trees, and to fight. He, too, now believed in my infallibility, so we set the deadline for these accomplishments less than a year away, when, it had been decided, Doodle could start to school.

That winter we didn't make much progress, for I was in school and Doodle suffered from one bad cold after another. But when spring came, rich and warm, we raised our sights again. Success lay at the end of summer like a pot of gold, and our campaign got off to a good start. On hot days, Doodle and I went down to Horsehead Landing and I gave him swimming lessons or showed him how to row a boat. Sometimes we descended into the cool greenness of Old Woman Swamp and climbed the rope vines or boxed scientifically beneath the pine where he had learned to

---

- iridescent (ir i DES unt) shiny with changing, rainbow-like colors
- vortex (VOR teks) whirling mass
- serene (suh REEN) peaceful; quiet
- infallibility (in fal uh BIL i tee) perfect reliability; sureness of success

walk. Promise hung about us like the leaves, and wherever we looked, ferns unfurled and birds broke into song.

That summer, the summer of 1918, was blighted. In May and June there was no rain and the crops withered, curled up, then died under the thirsty sun. One morning in July a hurricane came out of the east, tipping over the oaks in the yard and splitting the limbs of the elm trees. That afternoon it roared back out of the west, blew the fallen oaks around, snapping their roots and tearing them out of the earth like a hawk at the entrails of a chicken. Cotton bolls were wrenched from the stalks and lay like green walnuts in the valleys between the rows, while the cornfield leaned over uniformly so that the tassels touched the ground. Doodle and I followed Daddy out into the cotton field, where he stood, shoulders sagging, surveying the ruin. When his chin sank down onto his chest, we were frightened, and Doodle slipped his hand into mine. Suddenly Daddy straightened his shoulders, raised a giant knuckly fist, and with a voice that seemed to rumble out of the earth itself began cursing heaven, hell, the weather, and the Republican Party. Doodle and I, prodding each other and giggling, went back to the house, knowing that everything would be all right.

And during that summer, strange names were heard through the house: Château Thierry, Amiens, Soissons, and in her blessing at the supper table, Mama once said, "And bless the Pearsons, whose boy Joe was lost at Belleau Wood."*

So we came to that clove of seasons. School was only a few weeks away, and Doodle was far behind schedule. He could barely clear the ground when climbing up the rope vines and his swimming was certainly not passable. We decided to double our efforts, to make that last drive and reach our pot of gold. I made him swim until he turned blue and row until he couldn't lift an oar. Wherever we went, I purposely walked fast, and although he kept up, his face turned red and his eyes became glazed. Once, he could go no further, so he collapsed on the ground and began to cry.

"Aw, come on, Doodle," I urged. "You can do it. Do you want to be different from everybody else when you start school?"

"Does it make any difference?"

- blighted (BLY tid) stricken; cursed with hardship
- entrails (EN traylz) internal organs: intestines

*The places named are sites of battles during World War I in France.

273

"It certainly does," I said. "Now, come on," and I helped him up.

As we slipped through dog days, Doodle began to look feverish, and Mama felt his forehead, asking him if he felt ill. At night he didn't sleep well, and sometimes he had nightmares, crying out until I touched him and said, "Wake up, Doodle. Wake up."

It was Saturday noon, just a few days before school was to start. I should have already admitted defeat, but my pride wouldn't let me. The excitement of our program had now been gone for weeks, but still we kept on with a tired doggedness. It was too late to turn back, for we had both wandered too far into a net of expectations and had left no crumbs behind.

Daddy, Mama, Doodle, and I were seated at the dining-room table having lunch. It was a hot day, with all the windows and doors open in case a breeze should come. In the kitchen Aunt Nicey was humming softly. After a long silence, Daddy spoke. "It's so calm, I wouldn't be surprised if we had a storm this afternoon."

"I haven't heard a rain frog," said Mama, who believed in signs, as she served the bread around the table.

"I did," declared Doodle. "Down in the swamp."

"He didn't," I said contrarily.

"You did, eh?" said Daddy, ignoring my denial.

"I certainly did," Doodle reiterated, scowling at me over the top of his iced-tea glass, and we were quiet again.

Suddenly, from out in the yard, came a strange croaking noise. Doodle stopped eating, with a piece of bread poised ready for his mouth, his eyes popped round like two blue buttons. "What's that?" he whispered.

I jumped up, knocking over my chair, and had reached the door when Mama called, "Pick up the chair, sit down again, and say excuse me."

By the time I had done this, Doodle had excused himself and had slipped out into the yard. He was looking up into the bleeding tree. "It's a great big red bird!" he called.

The bird croaked loudly again, and Mama and Daddy came out into the yard. We shaded our eyes with our hands against the hazy glare of the sun and peered up through the still leaves. On the topmost branch a bird the size of a chicken, with scarlet feath-

---

- dog days—hot and sultry spell of summer weather
- doggedness (DAW gid nis) determination; stubborness
- reiterate (ree IT uh rayt) repeat

ers and long legs, was perched precariously. Its wings hung down loosely, and as we watched, a feather dropped away and floated slowly down through the green leaves.

"It's not even frightened of us," Mama said.

"It looks tired," Daddy added. "Or maybe sick."

Doodle's hands were clasped at his throat, and I had never seen him stand still so long. "What is it?" he asked.

Daddy shook his head. "I don't know, maybe it's—"

At that moment the bird began to flutter, but the wings were uncoordinated, and amid much flapping and a spray of flying feathers, it tumbled down, bumping through the limbs of the bleeding tree and landing at our feet with a thud. Its long, graceful neck jerked twice into an S, then straightened out, and the bird was still. A white veil came over the eyes and the long white beak unhinged. Its legs were crossed and its clawlike feet were delicately curved at rest. Even death did not mar its grace, for it lay on the earth like a broken vase of red flowers, and we stood around it, awed by its exotic beauty.

"It's dead," Mama said.

"What is it?" Doodle repeated.

"Go bring me the bird book," said Daddy.

- **precariously** (pri KAR ee us lee) unsurely; open to unknown danger
- uncoordinated (un koh OR duh nay tid) not working well or together
- awed (AWD) amazed; very impressed

I ran into the house and brought back the bird book. As we watched, Daddy thumbed through its pages. "It's a scarlet ibis," he said, pointing to a picture. "It lives in the tropics—South America to Florida. A storm must have brought it here."

Sadly, we all looked back at the bird. A scarlet ibis! How many miles it had traveled to die like this, in *our* yard, beneath the bleeding tree.

"Let's finish lunch," Mama said, nudging us back toward the dining room.

"I'm not hungry," said Doodle, and he knelt down beside the ibis.

"We've got peach cobbler for dessert," Mama tempted from the doorway.

Doodle remained kneeling. "I'm going to bury him."

"Don't you dare touch him," Mama warned. "There's no telling what disease he might have had."

"All right," said Doodle. "I won't."

Daddy, Mama, and I went back to the dining-room table, but we watched Doodle through the open door. He took out a piece of string from his pocket and, without touching the ibis, looped one end around its neck. Slowly, while singing softly "Shall We Gather at the River," he carried the bird around to the front yard and dug a hole in the flower garden, next to the petunia bed. Now we were watching him through the front window, but he didn't know it. His awkwardness at digging the hole with a shovel whose handle was twice as long as he was made us laugh, and we covered our mouths with our hands so he wouldn't hear.

When Doodle came into the dining room, he found us seriously eating our cobbler. He was pale and lingered just inside the screen door. "Did you get the scarlet ibis buried?" asked Daddy.

Doodle didn't speak but nodded his head.

"Go wash your hands, and then you can have some peach cobbler," said Mama.

"I'm not hungry," he said.

"Dead birds is bad luck," said Aunt Nicey, poking her head from the kitchen door. "Specially *red* dead birds!"

As soon as I had finished eating, Doodle and I hurried off to Horsehead Landing. Time was short, and Doodle still had a long way to go if he was going to keep up with the other boys when he started school. The sun, gilded with the yellow cast of autumn,

---

• gilded (GIL did) coated with gold
• cast (KAST) shade; appearance

still burned fiercely, but the dark green woods through which we passed were shady and cool. When we reached the landing, Doodle said he was too tired to swim, so we got into a skiff and floated down the creek with the tide. Far off in the marsh a rail was scolding, and over on the beach locusts were singing in the myrtle trees. Doodle did not speak and kept his head turned away, letting one hand trail limply in the water.

After we had drifted a long way, I put the oars in place and made Doodle row back against the tide. Black clouds began to gather in the southwest, and he kept watching them, trying to pull the oars a little faster. When we reached Horsehead Landing, lightning was playing across half the sky and thunder roared out, hiding even the sound of the sea. The sun disappeared and darkness descended, almost like night. Flocks of marsh crows flew by, heading inland to their roosting trees, and two egrets, squawking, arose from the oyster-rock shallows and careened away.

Doodle was both tired and frightened, and when he stepped from the skiff he collapsed onto the mud, sending an armada of fiddler crabs rustling off into the marsh grass. I helped him up, and as he wiped the mud off his trousers, he smiled at me ashamedly. He had failed and we both knew it, so we started back home, racing the storm. We never spoke (What are the words that can solder cracked pride?), but I knew he was watching me, watching for a sign of mercy. The lightning was near now, and

- skiff (SKIF) kind of small boat
- armada (ahr MAH duh) large force
- solder (SAHD ur) mend; join together as new

from fear he walked so close behind me he kept stepping on my heels. The faster I walked, the faster he walked, so I began to run. The rain was coming, roaring through the pines, and then, like a bursting Roman candle, a gum tree ahead of us was shattered by a bolt of lightning. When the deafening peal of thunder had died, and in the moment before the rain arrived, I heard Doodle, who had fallen behind, cry out, "Brother, Brother, don't leave me! Don't leave me!"

The knowledge that Doodle's and my plans had come to naught was bitter, and that streak of cruelty within me awakened. I ran as fast as I could, leaving him far behind with a wall of rain dividing us. The drops stung my face like nettles, and the wind flared the wet, glistening leaves of the bordering trees. Soon I could hear his voice no more.

I hadn't run too far before I became tired, and the flood of childish spite evanesced as well. I stopped and waited for Doodle. The sound of rain was everywhere, but the wind had died and it fell straight down in parallel paths like ropes hanging from the sky. As I waited, I peered through the downpour, but no one came. Finally I went back and found him huddled beneath a red night-shade bush beside the road. He was sitting on the ground, his face buried in his arms, which were resting on his drawn-up knees. "Let's go, Doodle," I said.

He didn't answer, so I placed my hand on his forehead and lifted his head. Limply, he fell backwards onto the earth. He had been bleeding from the mouth, and his neck and the front of his shirt were stained a brilliant red.

"Doodle! Doodle!" I cried, shaking him, but there was no answer but the ropy rain. He lay very awkwardly, with his head thrown far back, making his vermilion neck appear unusually long and slim. His little legs, bent sharply at the knees, had never before seemed so fragile, so thin.

I began to weep, and the tear-blurred vision in red before me looked very familiar. "Doodle!" I screamed above the pounding storm and threw my body to the earth above his. For a long long time, it seemed forever, I lay there crying, sheltering my fallen scarlet ibis from the heresy of rain.

- naught (NAWT) nothing
- spite (SPYT) bitterness; ill will
- evanesce (ev uh NES) fade away; disappear
- vermilion (vur MIL yun) bright scarlet red
- heresy (HER i see) wrongful force or influence

ALL THINGS CONSIDERED ──────────────

1. The narrator makes it clear that his efforts to help Doodle (a) are doomed to failure from the beginning. (b) are done partly because of his own pride. (c) please his parents more than they please himself.

2. Doodle is far from handicapped when it comes to his (a) unusual mathematical ability. (b) artistic talent. (c) very lively imagination.

3. The narrator refers not only to the time period of the story but also to (a) the time of remembering the events and writing the story. (b) a flashback to a period before his birth. (c) Doodle's imagined future in college.

4. At the end of the story, the narrator feels (a) more sorry for himself than for Doodle. (b) relieved that Doodle's troubles are over. (c) partly to blame for Doodle's death.

5. The *mood* (see page 178) of the story is best described as (a) suspenseful. (b) angry. (c) heartrending.

THINKING IT THROUGH ──────────────

1. Why is the story called "The Scarlet Ibis"? Rereading the last sentence will provide a clue.

2. The ending does not come as a complete surprise because it is skillfully foreshadowed. What is an example of this foreshadowing?

3. On page 268, the narrator refers to "a knot of cruelty borne by the stream of love." (a) What does he mean? (b) How is the meaning involved near the end of the story, when "a streak of cruelty within me" is mentioned on page 278?

4. Is the scarlet ibis itself properly called a symbol, a metaphor, or a simile? Explain.

5. "The Scarlet Ibis" is filled with references to nature. (a) In your opinion, do they add to the story, or do they needlessly interrupt the flow of the plot? (b) Why do you think the author mentioned so many plants and birds?

6. Write a sentence that reveals your feelings as you finished the last sentence of the story. Then write at least two other sentences explaining why you felt as you did.

UNIT REVIEW

I. Match the terms in Column A with their definitions in Column B.

A

1. point of view
2. first person
3. third person
4. omniscient
5. symbol
6. analogy
7. characterization
8. fact
9. opinion
10. levels of meaning

B

a) all-knowing
b) something known to be true
c) a "surface" and a "deeper" understanding of a work of literature
d) something that stands for something else
e) how authors bring characters to life
f) judgment or belief
g) the position from which a story is told
h) statement that shows a similar relationship between two sets of items
i) told by a narrator called "I" or "me"
j) told by a storyteller who is *not* a character in the story

II. Nearly all the selections in this unit have dealt with BIG IDEAS about life. Now you are to demonstrate that you have thought deeply about their themes. First pick two of the selections that have themes of interest to you. On your paper, state what you think is the theme (or one of the themes) of each selection you have chosen. Go on to write at least one sentence showing how the theme is illustrated in the selection. Finally, explain why you think the theme is important. The bonus selection, "The Scarlet Ibis," is used as an example. Remember, you are to do *two*.

Example:

THE SCARLET IBIS

One of the themes in "The Scarlet Ibis" is that when we do something for others, we often act from self-interest as well. The narrator makes no secret that one reason he helps Doodle is to remove what he sees as the shame of having a handicapped brother. In my opinion, this theme is very true to life. For instance, people give presents as much to be thanked for their generosity as to make others happy.

SPEAKING UP

The Sound of Sense—and Nonsense

The poet Robert Frost had a lifelong interest in what he called "the sound of sense," or the theory that the *sound* of the spoken language carried a kind of "meaning" quite apart from the words used. By "the sound of sense," Frost meant something other than simple **onomatopoeia** (on uh mat uh PEE uh), or the use of words that sound like what they mean (such as *hiss*, *splash*, and *moan*). Frost pointed out that one could often get some of the meaning of a conversation heard through a thin wall, even though the individual words were indistinct. In the same way, one often can get the emotional meaning of a conversation in a foreign language. Even dogs can "understand" their masters through tone of voice.

▶ In fact, the sound you use when speaking can make the same words "mean" quite different things. Prove this to yourself by reading the following poem in two ways, first as a very sad experience and then as a very happy one:

UFFIA

by Harriet R. White

When sporgles spanned the floreate mead
    And cogwogs glut upon the lea,
Uffia gopped to meet her love
    Who smeeged upon the equat sea.

Dately she walked aglost the sand;
    The boreal wind seet in her face;
The moggling waves yalped at her feet;
    Pangwangling was her pace.

Now try this interesting experiment. Copy the following words on a sheet of paper, and then cut out each word: *peace, justice, freedom, truth, honor, wisdom.* Next copy the paragraph below on your paper, making the blanks about two inches long.

What we need today is not false _____ but old-fashioned

_____. For surely, there is no real _____ without _____.

And as our forefathers knew so well, the price of _____ is a

little _____.

Go on to place the six words you cut out in the six blanks—*in any order.* Read the paragraph in an earnest, serious way. Finally, try reading the paragraph with the words in at least six different orders. Notice that although each reading seems to make sense and even sounds impressive, the meaning is fuzzy, at best. Is it the sound of sense—or nonsense?

WRITING THAT LAST PARAGRAPH

If you did the writing exercises on pages 132 and 197, you have now written two five-paragraph themes. You should know the pattern well. (If not, go back and review the text on page 131.) You should also have discovered that the last paragraph can create problems, since a simple restatement of the main idea usually seems both repetitious and incomplete.

It often happens that when writing a paper, you think of several facts that do not support your main idea, or may even be in opposition to it. If so, turn the last paragraph into one that *admits the other evidence*. Start the paragraph with the word *Admittedly,* (or *Of course,*), and then admit the case for the other side. Continue with a sentence starting with a connecting word such as *however,* followed by a restatement of your main idea. Such a paragraph indicates that you have thoroughly considered your subject matter in a fair way.

Suppose, for instance, that you have written four paragraphs on the idea that small cars are better than big ones. But you have a nagging doubt that the reader will think of an obvious argument against your case. Your final paragraph might read like this:

> *Of course,* statistics do show that small cars are not quite as safe as large ones. *However,* as indicated above, most of the evidence supports my case for the superiority of the small car. Certainly, if *all* cars were small, the big ones wouldn't be on the road to threaten them.

Assignment: Write a five-paragraph theme using one of the three statements below as the main idea. Anything you have read in this book can be used to support your main idea. Remember to follow the *prewriting-writing-revising* procedures on page 132. Use the *Admittedly, . . . However, . . .* pattern for the final paragraph.

(1) I think readers most enjoy characters like themselves.
(2) A good story should make the reader think about something important.
(3) Like it or not, death is a common and fascinating subject in literature.

U N I T · 5

STRANGE
THINGS
DONE

There are strange things done in the midnight sun
  By the men who moil for gold;
The Arctic trails have their secret tales
  That would make your blood run cold. . . .
—from "The Cremation of Sam McGee" by Robert W. Service

In this unit, you will encounter examples of some of our most imaginative fiction—tales that range from the fantastic to the humorous to the seemingly impossible. But no matter how unbelievable a selection may be, you will find yourself wondering, "Could this really happen?"

Some readers view imaginative literature as pure escape, plain fun. Others see it as a way to explore and challenge the "impossible." Whichever view you hold, don't be surprised if your imagination runs wild.

WHO'S CRIBBING?

by Jack Lewis

▶ Suppose you were to write a good story for English and pass it in to your teacher. You expect an "A," or a "B" at the very least. But instead, you get an "F"—because the teacher is certain that exactly the same story was handed in years before by another student. What would you do? If you're as clever as Jack Lewis, you might try using the strange experience as the idea for another story. "Who's Cribbing?" was written in 1952 and is well on its way to becoming a classic. Get set for a flip-flop.

April 2, 1952

Mr. Jack Lewis
90–26 219 St.
Queens Village, N.Y.

Dear Mr. Lewis:

We are returning your manuscript "The Ninth Dimension." At first glance, I had figured it a story well worthy of publishing. Why wouldn't I? So did the editors of *Cosmic Tales* back in 1934 when the story was first published.

As you no doubt know, it was the great Todd Thromberry who wrote the story you tried to pass off on us as an original. Let me give you a word of warning concerning the penalties resulting from plagiarism.

It's not worth it. Believe me.

Sincerely,
Doyle P. Gates
Science Fiction Editor
Deep Space Magazine

- cribbing (KRIB ing) stealing ideas; copying without getting permission
- dimension (di MEN shun) feature of space
- cosmic (KOZ mik) universal; not limited in time or space
- plagiarism (PLAY juh riz um) copying without getting permission

April 5, 1952

Mr. Doyle P. Gates, Editor
Deep Space Magazine
New York, N.Y.

Dear Mr. Gates:

I do not know, nor am I aware of the existence of any Todd Thromberry. The story you sent back was submitted in good faith, and I dislike the suggestion that I plagiarized it.

"The Ninth Dimension" was written by me not more than a month ago, and if there is any similarity between it and the story written by this Thromberry person, it is purely accidental.

However, it has set me thinking. Some time ago, I submitted another story to *Stardust Scientification* and received a penciled note stating that the story was, "too thromberrish."

Who in the world is Todd Thromberry? I don't remember reading anything written by him in the ten years I've been interested in science fiction.

Sincerely,
Jack Lewis

April 11, 1952

Mr. Jack Lewis
90–26 219 St.
Queens Village, N.Y.

Dear Mr. Lewis:

This is a reply to your letter of April 5.

While the editors of this magazine are not in the habit of making open accusations and are well aware of the fact in the writing business there will always be some overlapping of plot ideas, it is very hard for us to believe that you are not familiar with the stories of Todd Thromberry.

While Mr. Thromberry is no longer among us, his stories, like so many other writers', only became widely recognized after his death in 1941. Perhaps it was his work in the field of electricity that supplied him with the bottomless pit of new ideas so obvious

---

- **submit** (sub MIT) send or hand in for approval
- plagiarize (PLAY juh ryz) claim another's writing or ideas as one's own
- **accusation** (ak yoo ZAY shun) charge of wrongdoing

in all his works. Nevertheless, even at this stage of science fiction's development it is clear that he had a style that many of our so-called modern writers might do well to copy. By "copy," I do not mean rewrite word for word one or more of his stories, as you have done. For while you state this has been accidental, surely you must realize that the chance of this actually happening is about a million times as great as the occurrence of four royal flushes on one deal at the poker table.

Sorry, but we're not that stupid.

> Sincerely yours,
> Doyle P. Gates
> Science Fiction Editor
> *Deep Space Magazine*

April 14, 1952

Mr. Doyle P. Gates, Editor
Deep Space Magazine
New York, N.Y.

Sir:

Your accusations are typical of the rag you publish. Please cancel my subscription immediately.

> Sincerely,
> Jack Lewis

April 14, 1952

Science Fiction Society
144 Front Street
Chicago, Ill.

Gentlemen:

I am interested in reading some of the stories of the late Todd Thromberry.

I would like to get some of the magazines that feature his stories.

> Respectfully,
> Jack Lewis

• royal flush—highest hand in poker

April 22, 1952

Mr. Jack Lewis
90–26 219 St.
Queens Village, N.Y.

Dear Mr. Lewis:

So would we. All I can suggest is that you contact the magazines if any are still in business, or haunt your secondhand bookstores.

If you succeed in getting any of these magazines, please let us know. We'll pay you a handsome price for them.

Yours,
Ray Albert
President
Science Fiction Society

May 11, 1952

Mr. Sampson J. Gross, Editor
Strange Worlds Magazine
St. Louis, Mo.

Dear Mr. Gross:

I am enclosing the manuscript of a story I have just completed. As you see on the title page, I call it "Wreckers of Ten Million Galaxies." Because of the great amount of research that went into it, I must set the price on this one at not less than two cents a word.

Hoping you will see fit to use it in your magazine, I remain,

Respectfully,
Jack Lewis

May 19, 1952

Mr. Jack Lewis
90–26 219 St.
Queens Village, N.Y.

Dear Mr. Lewis:

I'm sorry, but at the present time we won't be able to use "Wreckers of Ten Million Galaxies." It's a great tale, though, and if at some future date we decide to use it we will make out the check directly to the living relatives of Todd Thromberry.

That boy sure could write.

Cordially,
Sampson J. Gross
Editor
Strange Worlds Magazine

May 23, 1952

Mr. Doyle P. Gates, Editor
Deep Space Magazine
New York, N.Y.

Dear Mr. Gates:

While I said I would never have any dealings with you or your magazine again, something has happened which is most puzzling.

It seems all my stories are being returned to me by reason of the fact that except for my name, they are exact copies of the stories of this Todd Thromberry person.

In your last letter you described the odds on the accidental occurrence of this in the case of one story. What would you consider the odds on no less than half a dozen of my writings?

I agree with you—out of sight!

Yet in the interest of all humanity, how can I get the idea across to you that every word I have submitted was actually written *by me!* I have never copied any material from Todd Thromberry, nor have I ever seen any of his writings. In fact, as I told you in one of my letters, up until a short while ago I was totally unaware of his very existence.

An idea has occurred to me, however. It's a truly weird idea, and one that I probably wouldn't even suggest to anyone but a science fiction editor. But suppose—just suppose—that this Thromberry person, what with his experiments in electricity and everything, had in some way managed to crack through this time-space barrier mentioned so often in your magazine. And suppose—conceited as it sounds—he had singled out my work as being the type of material he had always wanted to write.

Do you begin to follow me? Or is the idea of a person from a different time looking over my shoulder while I write too fantastic for you to accept?

Please write and tell me what you think of my idea.

Respectfully,
Jack Lewis

May 25, 1952

Mr. Jack Lewis
90–26 219 St.
Queens Village, N.Y.

Dear Mr. Lewis:

We think you should consult a psychiatrist.

Sincerely,
Doyle P. Gates
Science Fiction Editor
Deep Space Magazine

June 3, 1952

Mr. Sam Mines
Science Fiction Editor
Standard Magazines Inc.
New York 16, N.Y.

Dear Mr. Mines:

While the enclosed is not really a manuscript at all, I am submitting this series of letters, carbon copies, and correspondence, in the hope that you might give some belief to this seemingly unbelievable happening.

The enclosed letters are all in proper order and should explain themselves. Perhaps if you publish them, some of your readers might have some idea how all this could have happened.

I call the entire thing "Who's Cribbing?"

Respectfully,
Jack Lewis

June 10, 1952

Mr. Jack Lewis
90–26 219 St.
Queens Village, N.Y.

Dear Mr. Lewis:

Your idea of a series of letters to put across a science fiction idea is an interesting one, but I'm afraid it doesn't quite come off.

It was in the August 1940 issue of *Macabre Adventures* that

- **psychiatrist** (sy KY uh trist) doctor for mental disorders
- macabre (muh KAHB ruh) involving horror

Mr. Thromberry first used this very idea. Strangely enough, the story title also was "Who's Cribbing?"

Feel free to contact us again when you have something more original.

Yours,
Samuel Mines
Science Fiction Editor
Standard Magazines Inc.

ALL THINGS CONSIDERED

1. The story is unusual in that (a) it contains little conflict. (b) there is no description of Todd Thromberry's appearance. (c) the author uses his own name as that of a fictional character.

2. Jack Lewis's problems begin when he (a) steals the writing of others. (b) consults a psychiatrist. (c) is accused of trying to sell a story written by someone else.

3. Who's cribbing? According to the editors, the answer to this question is (a) Todd Thromberry. (b) Jack Lewis. (c) nearly all writers of science fiction.

4. During the exchange of letters, Jack Lewis's problems are (a) made even more confusing. (b) all solved. (c) nearly solved.

5. The surprise at the end of the story is that (a) Todd Thromberry was alive as late as 1940. (b) Jack Lewis is shown to be dishonest. (c) the story "Who's Cribbing?" itself seems to have been written by Thromberry.

THINKING IT THROUGH

1. At one point in the story, Lewis wonders if Todd Thromberry "had in some way managed to crack through this time-space barrier" and "singled out my work as being the type of material he had always wanted to write." Explain in your own words what this means.

2. (a) Have you ever read another story that was told as a series of letters? (b) Why is the use of letters a particularly good idea for *this* story?

3. The basic idea of the story is, of course, impossible. What *else* in the story seems hard to believe?

Reading and Analyzing

Irony of Situation

Have you ever heard the word *irony* (EYE ruh nee) or *ironic* (eye RON ik) used to describe the way people speak? When people speak with irony, or in an ironic way, they say something quite different from what they really mean. Often the spoken words are the direct opposite of the intended meaning. For instance, "Oh, I just *love* that man!" can mean "Oh, I *really dislike* that man!" Or, "We really needed this rain, didn't we?" can mean "We didn't need this rain at all."

In the study of literature, there is more than one type of irony. For example, **irony of situation** occurs when there is a striking difference between what a character expects to happen and what actually does happen. Many stories—such as "Who's Cribbing?"—are rich in irony of situation.

1. (a) In general, what does the character Jack Lewis hope to accomplish in writing the series of letters? (b) Are his expectations realized? (c) Is it, then, accurate to say that his situation throughout the story is ironic?

2. Why do you think the ending of the story is an excellent example of irony of situation? In other words, what does the character expect, and what actually happens?

3. Explain how one other selection in this book involves irony of situation. You might think about "The Eye Catcher" (page 4), "Casey at the Bat" (page 98), "Baxter's Procrustes" (page 169), and "A Day's Wait" (page 257).

Composition

1. There have been many examples of irony of situation in your own life. You prepare for something to happen, and then—oops!—a flip-flop. Describe one such situation in a short paragraph.

2. Imagine you were Melissa Talbot, editor of the science-fiction magazine *It's Fantastic!* Imagine also that Jack Lewis had sent his just-finished story "Who's Cribbing?" to you for publication. Write Mr. Lewis a business letter accepting his story but proposing two small changes. Give good reasons for the changes you propose, but take care not to offend the author. You will have to make up an address for the magazine.

THE STILL ALARM

by George S. Kaufman

▶ George S. Kaufman (1889–1961) spent most of his life in the theater. He wrote, directed, and produced plays. His short play *The Still Alarm* is a masterpiece of a certain kind of irony. Read the author's VITAL NOTE carefully; it tells you just how the play should be read.

(VITAL NOTE: *It is important that the entire play should be acted calmly and politely, in the manner of an English drawing-room comedy. No actor ever raises his voice; every line must be read as though it were an invitation to a cup of tea. If this direction is disregarded, the play has no point at all.*)

The scene is a hotel bedroom. Two windows in the rear wall with a bed between them. A telephone stand is at one end of the bed and a dresser is near the other. In the right wall is a door leading to the hall with a chair nearby. In the left wall is a door to another room; near it is a small table and two chairs.

Ed *and* Bob *are on the stage.* Ed *is getting into his overcoat as the curtain rises. Both are at the hall door.*

Ed: Well, Bob, it's certainly been nice to see you again.

Bob: It was nice to see *you.*

Ed: You come to town so seldom, I hardly ever get the chance to—

Bob: Well, you know how it is. A business trip is always more or less of a bore.

Ed: Next time you've got to come out to the house.

Bob: I want to come out. I just had to stick around the hotel this trip.

Ed: Oh, I understand. Well, give my best to Edith.

Bob (*remembering something*): Oh, I say, Ed. Wait a minute.

Ed: What's the matter?

Bob: I knew I wanted to show you something. (*Crosses to table. Gets roll of blueprints from drawer.*) Did you know I'm going to build?

Ed (*follows to table*): A house?

• drawing room—formal living room or parlor. A "drawing-room comedy" is a humorous play acted in a dignified, serious manner.

Bob: You bet it's a house! *(Knock on hall door.)* Come in! *(Spreads plans.)* I just got these yesterday.

Ed *(sits)*: Well, that's fine! *(The knock is repeated—louder. Both men now give full attention to the door.)*

Bob: Come! Come in!

Bellboy *(enters)*: Mr. Barclay?

Bob: Well?

Bellboy: I've a message from the clerk, sir. For Mr. Barclay personally.

Bob *(crosses to boy)*: I'm Mr. Barclay. What is the message?

Bellboy: The hotel is on fire, sir.

Bob: What's that?

Bellboy: The hotel is on fire.

Ed: This hotel?

Bellboy: Yes, sir.

Bob: Well—is it bad?

Bellboy: It looks pretty bad, sir.

Ed: You mean it's going to burn down?

Bellboy: We think so—yes, sir.

Bob *(a low whistle of surprise)*: Well! We'd better leave.

Bellboy: Yes, sir.

Bob: Going to burn down, huh?

Bellboy: Yes, sir. If you'll step to the window you'll see. (Bob *goes to a window.*)

Bob: Yes, that is pretty bad. H'm *(to Ed)*. I say, you really ought to see this—

Ed *(crosses to window, peers out)*: It's reached the floor right underneath.

Bellboy: Yes, sir. The lower part of the hotel is about gone, sir.

Bob *(still looking out—looks up)*: Still all right up above, though. *(Turns to boy.)* Have they notified the Fire Department?

Bellboy: I wouldn't know, sir. I'm only the bellboy.

Bob: Well, that's the thing to do, obviously *(nods head to each one as if the previous line was a bright idea)* notify the Fire Department. Just call them up, give them the name of the hotel—

Ed: Wait a minute. I can do better than that for you. *(To the boy.)* Ring through to the Chief, and tell him that Ed Jamison told you to telephone him. *(To Bob.)* We went to school together, you know.

Bob: That's fine. *(To the boy.)* Now, get that right. Tell the Chief that Mr. Jamison said to ring him.

Ed: *Ed* Jamison.

Bob: Yes, *Ed* Jamison.

Bellboy: Yes, sir. *(Turns to go.)*

Bob: Oh! Boy! *(Pulls out handful of change; picks out a coin.)* Here you are.

Bellboy: Thank you, sir. (*Exit* Bellboy.)
(*Ed sits at table, lights cigarette, and throws match on rug, then steps on it. There is a moment's pause.*)

Bob: Well! (*Crosses and looks out window.*) Say, we'll have to get out of here pretty soon.

Ed (*going to window*): How is it—no better?

Bob: Worse, if anything. It'll be up here in a few moments.

Ed: What floor *is* this?

Bob: Eleventh.

Ed: Eleven. We couldn't jump, then.

Bob: Oh, no. You never could jump. (*Comes away from window to dresser.*) Well, I've got to get my things together. (*Pulls out suitcase.*)

Ed (*smoothing out the plans*): Who made these for you?

Bob: A fellow here—Rawlins. (*Turns a shirt in his hand.*) I ought to call one of the other hotels for a room.

Ed: Oh, you can get in.

Bob: They're pretty crowded. (*Feels something on the sole of his foot; inspects it.*) Say, the floor's getting hot.

Ed: I know it. It's getting stuffy in the room, too, Phew! (*He looks around, then goes to the phone.*) Hello. Ice water in eleven eighteen. (*Crosses to table.*)

Bob (*at bed*): That's the stuff. (*Packs.*) You know, if I move to another hotel I'll never get my mail. Everybody thinks I'm stopping here.

Ed (*studying the plans*): Say, this isn't bad.

Bob (*eagerly*): Do you like it? (*Remembers his plight.*) Suppose I go to another hotel and there's a fire there, too!

Ed: You've got to take *some* chance.

Bob: I know, but here I'm sure. (*Phone rings.*) Oh, answer that, will you, Ed? (*To dresser and back.*)

Ed (*crosses to phone*): Sure. (*At phone.*) Hello— Oh, that's good. Fine. What? Oh! Well, wait a minute. (*To Bob.*) The firemen are downstairs and some of them want to come up to this room.

Bob: Tell them, of course.

Ed (*at phone*): All right. Come right up. (*Hangs up, crosses, and sits at table.*) Now we'll get some action.

Bob (*looks out of window*): Say, there's an awful crowd of people on the street.

Ed (*absently, as he pores over the plans*): Maybe there's been some kind of accident.

• **plight** (PLYT) bad condition or problem
• **absently** (AB sunt lee) with attention elsewhere
• **pore over** (POHR OH vur) study carefully

Bob (*peering out, suitcase in hand*): No. More likely they heard about the fire. (*A knock at the door.*) Come in.

Bellboy (*enters*): I beg pardon, Mr. Barclay, the firemen have arrived.

Bob: Show them in. (*Crosses to door.*)
(*The door opens. In the doorway appear two* Firemen *in full regalia. The* First Fireman *carries a hose and rubber coat; the* Second *has a violin case.*)

First Fireman (*very apologetically*): Mr. Barclay.

Bob: I'm Mr. Barclay.

First Fireman: We're the firemen, Mr. Barclay. (*They remove their hats.*)

Bob: How de do?

Ed: How de do?

Bob: A great pleasure, I assure you. Really must apologize for the condition of this room, but—

First Fireman: Oh, that's all right. I know how it is at home.

Bob: May I present a friend of mine, Mr. Ed Jamison—

First Fireman: How are you?

Ed: How are you, boys? (Second Fireman *nods.*) I know your Chief.

First Fireman: Oh, is that so? He knows the Chief—dear old Chiefie. (Second Fireman *giggles.*)

Bob (*embarrassed*): Well, I guess you boys want to get to work, don't you?

First Fireman: Well, if you don't mind. We would like to spray around a little bit.

Bob: May I help you?

First Fireman: Yes, if you please. (Bob *helps him into his rubber coat. At the same time the* Second Fireman, *without a word, lays the violin case on the bed, opens it, takes out the violin, and begins tuning it.*)

Bob (*watching him*): I don't think I understand.

First Fireman: Well, you see, Sid doesn't get much chance to practice at home. Sometimes, at a fire, while we're waiting for a wall to fall or something, why, a fireman doesn't really have anything to do, and personally I like to see him improve himself symphonically. I hope you don't resent it. You're not antisymphonic?

Bob: Of course not— (Bob *and* Ed *nod understandingly; the* Second Fireman *is now waxing the bow.*)

- regalia (ri GAY lee uh) signs of royalty, such as special dress (here used ironically)
- symphonically (sim FON ik lee) musically; like a symphony
- antisymphonic (AN ti sim FON ik) against music

First Fireman: Well, if you'll excuse me— *(To window. Turns with decision toward the window. You feel that he is about to get down to business.)*

Bob: Charming personalities.

Ed *(follows over to the window):* How is the fire?

First Fireman *(feels the wall):* It's pretty bad right now. This wall will go pretty soon now, but it'll fall out that way, so it's all right. *(Peers out.)* That next room is the place to fight it from. *(Crosses to door in left wall.* Bob *shows ties as* Ed *crosses.)*

Ed *(sees ties):* Oh! Aren't those gorgeous!

First Fireman *(to* Bob*):* Have you the key for this room?

Bob: Why, no. I've nothing to do with that room. I've just got this one. *(Folding a shirt as he talks.)*

Ed: Oh, it's very comfortable.

First Fireman: That's too bad. I had something up my sleeve, if I could have gotten in there. Oh, well, may I use your phone?

Bob: Please do. *(To* Ed.*)* Do you think you might hold this? *(Indicates the hose.)*

Ed: How?

First Fireman: Just crawl under it. *(As he does that.)* Thanks. *(At phone.)* Hello. Let me have the clerk, please. *(To Second Fireman.)* Give us that little thing you played the night the Equitable Building burned down. *(Back to phone.)* Are you there? This is one of the firemen. Oh, *you* know. I'm in room—ah— *(Looks at* Bob.*)*

Bob: Eleven eighteen.

First Fireman: Eleven eighteen, and I want to get into the next room— Oh, goody. Will you send someone up with the key? There's no one in there? Oh, supergoody! Right away. *(Hangs up.)*

Bob: That's fine. *(To Fireman.)* Won't you sit down?

First Fireman: Thanks.

Ed: Have a cigar?

First Fireman *(takes it):* Much obliged.

Bob: A light?

First Fireman: If you please.

Ed *(failing to find a match):* Bob, have you a match?

Bob *(crosses to table):* I thought there were some here. *(Hands in pockets.)*

First Fireman: Oh, never mind. *(He goes to a window, leans out, and emerges with cigar lighted.* Bob *crosses to dresser; slams drawer. The* Second Fireman *taps violin with bow.)*

First Fireman: Mr. Barclay, I think he's ready now.

Bob: Pardon me.

● **emerge** (i MURJ) come out into view

(They all sit. The Second Fireman *takes center of stage, with all the manner of a concert violinist. He goes into "Keep the Home Fires Burning."* Bob, Ed, *and* First Fireman *wipe brow as lights dim to red on closing eight bars.)*

ALL THINGS CONSIDERED ─────────────

1. According to the author, the play must be acted (a) in an increasingly frantic manner. (b) calmly and politely. (c) realistically.
2. One particularly funny moment occurs when Bob feels his shoes getting warm and Ed (a) insists they leave immediately. (b) cries loudly for help. (c) phones for ice water.
3. At the end of the play, the fire is (a) under control. (b) out. (c) still raging.
4. The last sound in the play is (a) Bob's voice. (b) a violin. (c) the roar of the fire.
5. The humor in the play comes from (a) the fact that the characters do not seem to realize the danger. (b) a lot of jokes. (c) the amazing difference between Bob and Ed.

THINKING IT THROUGH ─────────────

1. Twice during the play, Bob and Ed talk about Bob's blueprints for a new house. What makes a new house the perfect subject of conversation here?
2. One of the funniest parts of the play is when the First Fireman lights his cigar. How is the cigar lighted, and what makes it funny?
3. In your opinion, what is the funniest line in the play? Be prepared to explain why you think the line is amusing and to read it aloud as you think it should be read.
4. An **allusion** (uh LOO zhun) is a passing reference to something in history or literature. In *The Still Alarm*, the playing of a violin during a fire is a hidden allusion to something in history. To what is the author referring? If you do not know, ask your instructor or a history teacher.

299

Reading and Analyzing

Dramatic Irony

On page 293, you looked at situational irony as it occurs in literature. Another type of irony is *dramatic irony*. **Dramatic irony** occurs when the audience knows something important that a character (or characters) does not know.

The term *dramatic irony* is not limited to drama. When reading stories or poems, you also may know something that a character does not know, including the piece's final outcome. You are treated to dramatic irony as you experience the events that almost happen to David Swan (page 117) or watch the great Casey as he heads for what you feel sure will be a strikeout.

The humor in *The Still Alarm,* of course, comes from dramatic irony:

1. (a) When Bob and Ed first learn of the fire, how do they react? (b) What does the audience or reader know that the two characters fail to realize?

2. The dramatic irony increases when the professional firefighters appear. How does their behavior differ from what the average person expects from firefighters?

3. Explain the dramatic irony in *The Legend of Sleepy Hollow* (page 17), "The Tell-Tale Heart" (page 52), or any other selection in this book. Remember, you do not have to be absolutely certain about the forthcoming ending of a story or play to enjoy dramatic irony. A good hunch about the end will do.

Composition

1. The title of the play, *The Still Alarm,* is an odd one that means different things to different people. Try to think of three better titles. Write the three possible titles on your paper and then put a check beside the one you like best.

2. Think of another funny event that could be added to the play. Write it out, using the form of the play. Show where your addition fits in by writing the page number from your book on the top of your paper and using a line from the play as your first line.

Also, have your scene lead into the next line from the play, which you will use as your last line. Your addition should be at least half a page long. If you have trouble getting started, think about the ice water ordered by Ed. Who might bring it up? (It might help to add a female character to the play.) What might that person be like? (For instance, would the person understand either the danger of the fire or the purpose of the ice water?) What pointless conversation might the delivery of the ice water lead to?

Sara Teasdale (1884-1933)

The loveliness of nature—a frequent topic of Teasdale's poetry

Readers of the hopeful poems of Sara Teasdale are tempted to see her as the happiest of human beings. Such readers forget to separate the *speaker* in a poem from the *poet*. Her life was often a troubled one. As she herself put it in a poem called "The Long Hill," after one has achieved a certain height in life, "The rest of the way will be only going down."

Born in St. Louis, Missouri, Sara Teasdale won early success as a poet. She published her first poems as a girl and her first book before she was 25. For years she was in and out of love with a well-known poet named Vachel Lindsay. But she could not bring herself to accept the second-place role of a famous man's wife in the America of the time. Finally, Lindsay married someone else, and

Teasdale rushed into a bad marriage with a businessman named Filsinger. In 1929 she divorced Filsinger and turned again to Lindsay. But it was too late. Lindsay killed himself in 1931, leaving her a lonely, disappointed woman. In 1933 Teasdale, too, committed suicide.

These sad facts help to make the point, once again, that *the speaker in a poem is not to be confused with the poet.* We can safely say, however, that Sara Teasdale must have known *moments* of great beauty. Perhaps she valued these moments all the more because of the numerous disappointments in her life.

How did Sara Teasdale's life differ from the kind of life suggested by many of her poems?

A TEASDALE SAMPLER

poems by Sara Teasdale

▶ The four poems that follow are samples of Sara Teasdale at her best. As you read the poems, remember not to confuse the speaker in the poem with the poet herself.

BARTER

Life has loveliness to sell,
　All beautiful and splendid things,
Blue waves whitened on a cliff,
　Soaring fire that sways and sings,
5 And children's faces looking up,
Holding wonder like a cup.

Life has loveliness to sell,
　Music like a curve of gold,
Scent of pine trees in the rain,
10 　Eyes that love you, arms that hold,
And for your spirit's still delight,
Holy thoughts that star the night.

Spend all you have for loveliness,
　Buy it and never count the cost;
15 For one white singing hour of peace
　Count many a year of strife well lost,
And for a breath of ecstasy
Give all you have been, or could be.

• barter (BAR tur) trade; exchanging one thing for another
• strife (STRYF) troublesome conflict; quarreling

WAYS OF KNOWING

1. "Barter," the title of the poem, means *trade*. Explain just what is to be traded for what.

2. Many readers of the poem find that they remember two lines of the first stanza for a long time. Which two lines do you think these are?

3. If you had to memorize two other outstanding lines in the poem for a test tomorrow, which lines would they be? Try to explain why you like them.

4. Look again at the first two lines of the last stanza. (a) Could the words "spend" and "cost" refer to money? (b) What else besides money could "spend" and "cost" refer to?

5. To make a point, people often exaggerate, or get carried away with the truth. In literature, such *exaggeration*, or *overstatement*, is known as **hyperbole** (hy PUR buh lee). Poets often use hyperbole to add force to their words. Instead of *a long time*, a poet might say *forever*, *for an eternity*, or something like *till all the seas run dry*. What is one example of hyperbole in the last stanza of "Barter"?

6. Think about the advice given in the last stanza. Do you suppose you could ever apply it *literally* (see page 10) to your own life? Explain.

THE FALLING STAR

I saw a star slide down the sky,
Blinding the north as it went by,
Too burning and too quick to hold,
Too lovely to be bought or sold,
Good only to make wishes on
And then forever to be gone.

WAYS OF KNOWING

1. What two words can you think of that accurately describe the mood of the speaker?

2. In what way is line 2 a good example of hyperbole?

3. If you were the speaker and saw the star described, would you really make a wish? Try to explain why or why not. Be honest.

▶ As the profile of Sara Teasdale indicates, the poet knew the sorrows of the earth as well as the splendor of the heavens. Here are two poems that reveal her darker side. Write two good questions about each poem, using the four rules for writing questions given on page 14.

THE LONG HILL

I must have passed the crest a while ago
   And now I am going down—
Strange to have crossed the crest and not to know,
   But the brambles were always catching the hem of my
     gown.

5 All the morning I thought how proud I should be
   To stand there straight as a queen,
Wrapped in the wind and the sun with the world under
   me—
   But the air was dull, there was little I could have seen.

It was nearly level along the beaten track
10   And the brambles caught in my gown—
But it's no use now to think of turning back,
   The rest of the way will be only going down.

I SHALL NOT CARE

When I am dead and over me bright April
   Shakes out her rain-drenched hair,
Tho' you should lean above me broken-hearted,
   I shall not care.

I shall have peace, as leafy trees are peaceful
   When rain bends down the bough,
And I shall be more silent and cold-hearted
   Than you are now.

Before completing the exercises that follow, you may wish to review the **bold-faced** words on pages 287 to 303.

I. On a separate sheet of paper, mark each item *true* or *false*. If it is false, explain what is wrong with the sentence.

1. An *allusion* is a passing reference to something in history or literature.
2. English teachers sometimes ask students to *submit* material to the school literary magazine.
3. A *psychiatrist* is a foot doctor.
4. *Dramatic irony* involves knowing something that a character in a story, poem, or play does not know.
5. If you say something *absently*, you are probably answering an oral test question.
6. Words like *all, never, anything, forever*, and *perfect* are frequently examples of *hyperbole*.
7. The moon can *emerge* from behind a cloud.
8. A *plight* is something often wished for but seldom received.
9. In literature, *irony of situation* occurs when there is a difference between what a character expects to happen and what really happens.
10. Legally, an *accusation* of theft means that the person concerned is in the right.

II. In what way does the following poem involve *irony of situation* from the mother's point of view?

THE ADVERSARY

by Phyllis McGinley

A mother's hardest to forgive.
Life is the fruit she longs to hand you,
Ripe on a plate. And while you live,
Relentlessly she understands you.

- adversary (AD vur ser ee) opponent; foe
- relentlessly (ri LENT lis lee) without pity; harshly

III. Read the poem carefully before answering the questions that follow.

EARTH

by John Hall Wheelock

"A planet doesn't explode of itself," said drily
The Martian astronomer, gazing off into the air—
"That they were able to do it is proof that highly
Intelligent beings must have been living there."

1. The setting of the poem is (a) Mars. (b) Earth. (c) some unknown planet.
2. The time period of the poem is probably (a) about the time of the Civil War. (b) the World War II period. (c) the future.
3. For readers to appreciate the irony in the poem, they must realize that (a) English is not the language of Mars. (b) really "intelligent" people wouldn't blow themselves up. (c) a planet can "explode of itself."
4. The poem suggests seriously that (a) we had better be careful with nuclear power and weapons. (b) there is life on Mars after all. (c) human beings are more intelligent than Martians.

IV. Explain the irony involved in the cartoon below.

• drily (DRY lee) with sly cleverness, especially in an ironic way

THE LADY, OR THE TIGER?

by Frank R. Stockton

▶ The famous tale that follows is one of the most unusual stories ever written. In fact, it breaks RULE NUMBER ONE of storytelling. Remember, in the history of the world, there have been many *strange things done.* . . .

In the very olden time, there once lived a semi-barbaric king. His ideas, though somewhat polished and sharpened by the more civilized ways of distant neighbors, were still raw, savage and reckless, as became the half of him that was still barbaric. He was a man of wild imagination, and his word was law. Whenever he wished, his varied fancies became facts. He was greatly given to self-questioning, and when he and himself agreed upon anything, that thing was done. When everything in his kingdom moved smoothly, his manner was happy and genial; but whenever there was a little trouble, he was happier and more genial still. For nothing pleased him so much as to make the crooked straight, and crush down uneven places.

Among the borrowed ideas by which his barbarism had become softened was that of the public arena. In his arena, both men and beasts displayed their courage. These displays, the king thought, uplifted the minds of his people.

But even here the wild imagination expressed itself. The arena of the king was not built to let his people watch men fight each other with sword and shield. It was not built to settle arguments between religious opinions and hungry jaws. No, its purpose was far better fitted to uplifting the minds of the people. The huge arena, with its many rows of seats, its unseen passages, was a hall of justice. There crime was punished. There goodness was

- **semi-** (SEM ee) prefix meaning half
- **barbaric** (bar BAR ik) wild and cruel; not yet civilized
- became (bi KAYM) suited; fitted
- fancy (FAN see) notion; idea
- **genial** (JEEN yul) pleasant; good-natured
- **barbarism** (BAR buh riz um) state of being barbaric

rewarded. There justice was decided by the completely fair and unprejudiced Law of Chance.

The system was simple. First a person had to be accused of a crime of enough importance to interest the king. Then public notice was given that on a certain day the accused man would appear in the king's arena. When the people of the city had gathered, the king entered. Surrounded by his family and servants, he sat on a throne high up on one side of the arena. Suddenly he gave a signal. A door far beneath him opened, and the accused person stepped out.

Right across from the man on trial were two doors, exactly alike and side by side. It was the duty and the privilege of the person on trial to walk straight to the doors and open one of them. He could open either door he pleased. He was given no help but that of the Law of Chance. If he opened the one, there came out of it a hungry tiger, the wildest and most cruel that could be found. The tiger immediately sprang upon him and tore him to pieces, as punishment for his guilt. The moment that the case of the criminal was so decided, doleful iron bells were rung. Great sighs went up, and the people left the arena with bowed heads and broken

---

• doleful (DOHL ful) sorrowful

hearts. Why did one so young and handsome, or so old and well known, deserve so horrible an end?

But if the accused person opened the other door, there came out of it a lady, always well fitted to the man's age and place in life. In fact, she was always the most perfect wife that his majesty's servants could find among his fair subjects. And to this lady the man was immediately married, as a reward for his innocence. It mattered not that he might already have a wife and family, nor that he might be engaged to a woman of his own choice. The king allowed no such details to interfere with his grand ideas about punishment and reward. The wedding took place right away, and in the arena. Another door opened beneath the king, and a priest, followed by dancing maidens and a group of singers, advanced to where the pair stood side by side. The wedding was short and joyful. Then the happy brass bells rang out, the people cheered and cheered, and the innocent man, following children throwing flowers in his path, led his bride to his home.

This was the king's semi-barbaric method of handing out justice. Its perfect fairness is clear. The criminal could not know out of which doorway would come the lady. He opened either door he pleased. He had not the slightest idea whether, in the next instant, he was to be devoured or married. Sometimes the tiger came out of one door, sometimes out of the other. The king's justice was not only fair, but also fast. The accused person was instantly punished if he found himself guilty. And if innocent, he was rewarded on the spot, whether he liked it or not. There was no escape from the judgments of the king's arena.

The system was a very popular one. The people never knew whether they were to witness a bloody slaughter or a joyous wedding. There was just no way they could know. This gave an interest to the event which it could not otherwise have had. Thus the masses were entertained and pleased. And even the thinking persons in the community could find no reason to say that the plan was unfair. For did not the accused person have the whole matter in his own hands?

This semi-barbaric king had a daughter as blooming as his own lively imagination and with a soul as fiery and as proud as his own. As is usual in such cases, she was the apple of his eye, and was loved by him above all others. And her love? Well . . . among

* fair (FAIR) nice looking
* **subject** (SUB jikt) person under authority of a king or government

309

the king's servants was a handsome young man of that fineness of blood and lowness of station common to story-book heroes who love royal maidens.

This royal maiden was well satisfied with her lover. He was better looking and more brave than anyone else in all the kingdom, and her love for him had enough of barbarism in it to make it very warm, and very, very strong. The love affair moved on happily for many months, until, one day, the king happened to learn of it. He did not waste an instant! He knew his duty in the matter at once. The youth was immediately put into prison, and a day was set for his trial in the king's arena.

This, of course, was an especially important happening in the kingdom. His majesty, as well as all the people, was greatly interested in the preparation for the trial. Never before had such a case occurred—never before had a subject dared to love the daughter of the king!

The tiger cages of the kingdom were searched for the most savage and relentless of beasts, from which the fiercest monster was to be chosen for the arena. And a search was also made among the ranks of maiden youth and beauty throughout the land. The young man was to have a fitting bride, if bride it was to be. Of course, everyone knew that the act of the accused man had, in fact, been done. He had loved the princess, and neither he, she, nor anyone in the kingdom thought of saying anything else. But the king would not think of letting any fact of this kind interfere with the tribunal, in which he took such great delight and satisfaction. No matter how it turned out, the youth's future would be decided. The king was especially interested in finding out whether the young man had done wrong in allowing himself to love the princess.

The day arrived. From far and near the people gathered, and they soon filled the great arena. Outside, more huge crowds, unable to get in, stood against the walls. The king was in his place, opposite the twin portals—so horrible in their likeness to each other!

All was ready. The signal was given. A door beneath the king opened, and the lover of the princess walked into the arena. Tall and handsome, he was greeted with a low hum of wonder and

---

- **station** (STAY shun) place in life
- relentless (ri LENT lis) without pity; harsh and cruel
- tribunal (try BYOON ul) court of justice
- **portal** (POHR tul) door; entrance

Critical Thinking

More Kinds of Analogies

To review, an **analogy** (uh NAL uh jee) is a statement that the relationship between two items is in some way similar to the relationship between two other items. Ten kinds of analogies were introduced on page 241. Here is a more complete list. Each is followed by an example from the selection. Complete each with a similar relationship from outside the selection. The first is done as an example.

1. Like is to like: DOOR is to PORTAL as FAUCET is to SPIGOT.
2. Like is to opposite: BARBARIC is to CIVILIZED as . . .
3. One is to many: MAN is to MASSES as . . .
4. Actor is to action: KING is to RULE as . . .
5. Place is to area: CITY is to KINGDOM as . . .
6. Place is to purpose: HALL OF JUSTICE is to TRIAL as . . .
7. Person is to person: KING is to PRINCESS as . . .
8. Classification is to kind: BEAST is to TIGER as . . .
9. Part is to whole: WALL is to ARENA as . . .
10. Part is to part: HAIR is to EYE as . . .
11. Grammatical form is to grammatical form: HE is to HIS as . . .
12. Worker is to job: PRIEST is to MARRY as . . .
13. Noun is to quality: IRON is to HARD as . . .
14. Cause is to effect: FIRE is to HEAT as . . .
15. Number is to number: ONE is to TWO as . . .
16. Symbol is to thing symbolized: THRONE is to ROYAL POWER as . . .
17. Object is to composition: BELL is to BRASS as . . .
18. Adjective is to noun: HUMAN is to HEART as . . .
19. Action is to object: OPEN is to DOOR as . . .
20. Object is to function: BELL is to RING as . . .

Composition

1. In two paragraphs, write your own ending to "The Lady, or the Tiger?" Include your answer to question 3 in "Thinking It Through." In your ending, tell what the man's reaction is when he opens the door.
2. Imagine you are the author, Frank R. Stockton. Answer this question: Which part of the story did you enjoy writing most, and why?

▶ Two long narrative poems stand above all others as "read-aloud" favorites. One is "Casey at the Bat" (page 98). The other, where there are many *strange things done*, is—

THE CREMATION OF SAM MCGEE

by Robert W. Service

There are strange things done in the midnight sun
   By the men who moil for gold;
The Arctic trails have their secret tales
   That would make your blood run cold;
5 *The Northern Lights have seen queer sights,*
   But the queerest they ever did see
Was that night on the marge of Lake Lebarge
   I cremated Sam McGee.

Now Sam McGee was from Tennessee, where
   the cotton blooms and blows,
10 Why he left his home in the South to roam
   'round the Pole, God only knows.
He was always cold, but the land of gold seemed
   to hold him like a spell;
Though he'd often say in his homely way that
   "he'd sooner live in hell."

- moil (MOIL) work hard
- marge (MARJ) edge; margin
- **homely** (HOHM lee) simple and friendly

On a Christmas Day we were mushing our way
    over the Dawson Trail.
Talk of your cold! through the parka's fold it
    stabbed like a driven nail.
15 If our eyes we'd close, then the lashes froze till
    sometimes we couldn't see;
It wasn't much fun, but the only one to whimper
    was Sam McGee.

And that very night, as we lay packed tight in our
    robes beneath the snow,
And the dogs were fed, and the stars o'erhead
    were dancing heel and toe,
He turned to me, and "Cap," says he, "I'll cash
    in this trip, I guess;
20 And if I do, I'm asking that you won't refuse my
    last request."

Well, he seemed so low that I couldn't say no;
    then he says with a sort of moan:
"It's the cursed cold and it's got right hold till I'm
    chilled clean through to the bone.
Yet 'tain't being dead—it's my awful dread of the
    icy grave that pains;
So I want you to swear that, foul or fair, you'll
    cremate my last remains."

25 A pal's last need is a thing to heed, so I swore I
    would not fail;
And we started on at the streak of dawn; but ah!
    he looked ghastly pale.
He crouched on the sleigh, and he raved all day
    of his home in Tennessee;
And before nightfall a corpse was all that was left
    of Sam McGee.

- mushing (MUSH ing) traveling by dog sled
- cash in—slang for "end the game," or (here) "die"
- foul (FOUL) stormy
- cremate (KREE mate) burn body to ashes after death
- **remains** (ri MAYNZ) corpse; body

There wasn't a breath in that land of death, and I
hurried, horror-driven,
30 With a corpse half hid that I couldn't get rid,
because of a promise given;
It was lashed to the sleigh, and it seemed to say:
"You may tax your brawn and brains,
But you promised true, and it's up to you to
cremate those last remains."

Now a promise made is a debt unpaid, and the
trail has its own stern code.
In the days to come, though my lips were dumb,
in my heart now I cursed that load.
35 In the long, long night, by the lone firelight, while
the huskies, round in a ring,
Howled out their woes to the homeless snows—
O man! how I loathed the thing.

And every day that quiet clay seemed to heavy
and heavier grow;
And on I went, though the dogs were spent and
the grub was getting low;
The trail was bad, and I felt half mad, but I swore
I would not give in;
40 And I'd often sing to the hateful thing, and it
hearkened with a grin.

Till I came to the marge of Lake Lebarge, and a
derelict there lay;
It was jammed in the ice, but I saw in a trice it
was called the "Alice May."
And I looked at it, and I thought a bit, and I
looked at my frozen chum;

- tax (TAKS) put a strain on
- brawn (BRAWN) muscles
- **code** (KOHD) set of rules
- loathe (LOHTH) hate
- spent (SPENT) worn out
- hearken (HAR kun) listen
- derelict (DER uh likt) wrecked and abandoned ship
- trice (TRYS) very short time

Then "Here," said I, with a sudden cry, "is my
    cre-ma-tor-e-um."

45 Some planks I tore from the cabin floor, and I lit
    the boiler fire;
Some coal I found that was lying around, and I
    heaped the fuel higher;
The flames just soared, and the furnace roared—
    such a blaze you seldom see;
And I burrowed a hole in the glowing coal, and I
    stuffed in Sam McGee.

Then I made a hike, for I didn't like to hear him
    sizzle so;
50 And the heavens scowled, and the huskies
    howled, and the wind began to blow.
It was icy cold, but the hot sweat rolled down my
    cheeks, and I don't know why;
And the greasy smoke in an inky cloak went
    streaking down the sky.

I do not know how long in the snow I wrestled
    with grisly fear;
But the stars came out and they danced about
    ere again I ventured near;
55 I was sick with dread, but I bravely said: "I'll just
    take a peep inside.
I guess he's cooked, and it's time I looked;" . . .
    then the door I opened wide.

And there sat Sam, looking cold and calm, in the
    heart of the furnace roar;
And he wore a smile you could see a mile, and
    he said: "Please close that door!
It's fine in here, but I greatly fear you'll let in the
    cold and storm—
60 Since I left Plumtree, down in Tennessee, it's the
    first time I've been warm."

- **crematorium** (kree muh TOHR ee um) furnace for cremating corpses
- grisly (GRIZ lee) horrible
- ere (AIR) before

> *There are strange things done in the midnight sun*
> *By the men who moil for gold;*
> *The Arctic trails have their secret tales*
> *That would make your blood run cold;*
> 65 *The Northern Lights have seen queer sights,*
> *But the queerest they ever did see*
> *Was that night on the marge of Lake Lebarge*
> *I cremated Sam McGee.*

ALL THINGS CONSIDERED

1. The mood of the poem is best described as (a) horrible. (b) humorous. (c) sorrowful.
2. Sam McGee is cremated because (a) he requested it. (b) he had a bad disease. (c) it is the custom in the North.
3. The "quiet clay" in line 37 is (a) earth or gravel. (b) the speaker's conscience. (c) Sam McGee's body.
4. The "cre-ma-tor-e-um" used is (a) a huge campfire. (b) an old railroad engine. (c) the boiler of an old ship.
5. The surprise in the poem is that (a) the speaker is also burned. (b) Sam McGee seems to be alive. (c) the weather suddenly turns warm.

THINKING IT THROUGH

1. As a young man, Robert W. Service left his native Scotland and joined the great Yukon (YOO kon) gold rush in northern Canada. In what ways does the poem show that the author knew the cold land and the hardy people well?
2. "A promise made is a debt unpaid" (line 33) is a famous line. What does it mean, in your own words?
3. (a) Study the rhyme pattern within each stanza. What rhymes with what? (b) In what ways are the first and final stanzas unlike the others?
4. Suppose you were preparing to read the poem aloud to others. Pick three lines that you think need to be read in a special way. Identify them by line number and explain how they should be read.

Literary Skills

Denotation and Connotation

Many words have two kinds of meanings. The **denotation** (dee noh TAY shun) of a word is its usual definition or "dictionary meaning." The **connotation** (kon uh TAY shun) of a word is its "emotional meaning," or all that the word suggests. For instance, the words *corpse, body,* and *remains* have similar denotations, but their connotations are different. The word *corpse* is somehow harsher and uglier than the more polite word *remains.*

To some extent, connotations differ from reader to reader, since people have different associations with certain words. Take the word "moil" in line 2 of the poem. It is an unusual word that to you probably means only "work hard," as defined. Those readers who know the word, however, think that it indicates very stressful and disagreeable work, as does the rhyming word it suggests—*toil.*

Good writers choose words carefully for their connotations. Try to explain what would be lost if the following substitutions were made in "The Cremation of Sam McGee":

1. *making* for "mushing" in line 13

2. *sniffle* or *cry* for "whimper" in line 16

3. *moving* for "dancing" in line 18

4. *fear* for "dread" in line 23

5. *disagreeable* for "ghastly" in line 26

6. *silent* for "dumb" in line 34

7. *unhoused* for "homeless" in line 36

8. *smile* for "grin" in line 40

9. *pulled* for "tore" in line 45

10. *struggled* for "wrestled" in line 53

Composition

1. A rewording using as few of the original words as possible is called a **paraphrase** (PAR uh frayz). Choose a stanza you like from "The Cremation of Sam McGee" (or one assigned by your teacher) for a paraphrase of your own.
2. Many pairs of words have similar denotations but quite different connotations. For example, *corpse* and *remains* is a pair of words in which one word has a more favorable or positive connotation than the other. Think of at least five such pairs. List them on your paper, and, in a sentence or two, explain the difference in the connotations of the words in each pair. If you have trouble getting started, here are some words that need partners: *slender, fat, elderly, politician, bookworm,* and *talkative.*

321

Before completing the exercises that follow, you may wish to review the **bold-faced** words on pages 307 to 321.

I. On a separate sheet of paper, write the *italicized* word that best fills the blank in each sentence.

code	*remains*	*barbarism*	*crematorium*	*station*
genial	*homely*	*subject*	*semi-barbaric*	*portal*

1. _____ means both "unattractive" and "simple and friendly."
2. Abraham Lincoln was born into quite a low _____ in life.
3. No U.S. citizen is the _____ of a king or queen.
4. In ancient times many people lived in a state of _____.
5. Today there are few _____ parts of the world left.
6. Even semi-barbaric people have some sort of a legal _____.
7. _____, *corpse*, and *body* have similar denotations.
8. Few people would want to work in a _____.
9. The name of a school often appears above the _____.
10. CARELESS is to CAREFUL as UNFRIENDLY is to _____.

II. Read this famous poem carefully before answering the questions that follow.

RICHARD CORY

by Edwin Arlington Robinson

Whenever Richard Cory went down town,
We people on the pavement looked at him:
He was a gentleman from sole to crown,
Clean favored, and imperially slim.

5 And he was always quietly arrayed,
And he was always human when he talked;

- favored (FAY vurd) featured
- imperially (im PEER ee ul lee) supremely
- arrayed (uh RAYD) dressed

But still he fluttered pulses when he said,
"Good-morning," and he glittered when he
    walked.

And he was rich—yes, richer than a king—
10 And admirably schooled in every grace:
In fine, we thought that he was everything
To make us wish that we were in his place.

So on we worked, and waited for the light,
And went without the meat, and cursed the
    bread;
15 And Richard Cory, one calm summer night,
Went home and put a bullet through his head.

1. (a) How did you feel as you read the last line? (b) What does the line suddenly tell you about Richard Cory?
2. (a) What connotation does "crown" (line 3) have that the word *head* does not have? (b) What are at least two other words in the poem that have similar connotations?
3. Names often have connotations. What does "Richard" suggest that *Dick* or a name like *Skip* would not?
4. In line 11, what would be lost if *had* were substituted for "was"?
5. How does the connotation of "calm" (line 15) contrast with the surprise in the last line?

III. Discuss the following poem in terms of the connotations of the words "conviction" and "prejudice." You might begin by looking up the dictionary definitions of these two words.

NOTE TO MY NEIGHBOR

by Phyllis McGinley

We might as well give up the fiction
    That we can argue any view.
For what in me is pure Conviction
    Is simple Prejudice in you.

• admirably (AD mur uh blee) excellently
• fine (FYN) summary; conclusion

▶ The amazing Isaac Asimov probably needs no introduction. The author of more than 200 books on many subjects, Asimov is perhaps best known for his science-fiction stories. Here's a short one about a point of law in the year 3011. He calls it—

A LOINT OF PAW

by Isaac Asimov

There was no question that Montie Stein had, through clever fraud, stolen better than a hundred thousand dollars. There was also no question that he was apprehended one day after the statute of limitations had expired.

It was his manner of avoiding arrest during that interval that brought on the epoch-making case of the State of New York *vs*. Montgomery Harlow Stein, with all its consequences. It introduced law to the fourth dimension.

For, you see, after having committed the fraud and possessed himself of the hundred grand plus, Stein had calmly entered a time machine, of which he was in illegal possession, and set the controls for seven years and one day in the future.

Stein's lawyer put it simply. Hiding in time was not fundamentally different from hiding in space. If the forces of law had not uncovered Stein in the seven-year interval, that was their hard luck.

The District Attorney pointed out that the statute of limitations was not intended to be a game between the law and the criminal. It was a merciful measure designed to protect a culprit from indefinitely prolonged fear of arrest. For certain crimes, a

---

- apprehended (ap ri HEN did) arrested; seized
- statute (STACH oot) law. A *statute of limitations* is a law stating that one cannot be arrested for a crime after a certain period of time has gone by, usually seven years.
- epoch (EP uk) period in history. An *epoch-making* event is one that causes a major change.

defined period of apprehension of apprehension (so to speak) was considered punishment enough. But Stein, the D.A. insisted, had not experienced any period of apprehension at all.

Stein's lawyer remained unmoved. The law said nothing about measuring the extent of a culprit's fear and anguish. It simply set a time limit.

The D.A. said that Stein had not lived through the limit.

Defense stated that Stein was seven years older now than at the time of the crime and had therefore lived through the limit.

The D.A. challenged the statement and the defense produced Stein's birth certificate. He was born in 2973. At the time of the crime, 3004, he was thirty-one. Now, in 3011, he was thirty-eight.

The D.A. shouted that Stein was not physiologically thirty-eight, but thirty-one.

Defense pointed out freezingly that the law, once the individual was granted to be mentally competent, recognized solely chronological age, which could be obtained only by subtracting the date of birth from the date of now.

- apprehension (ap ri HEN shun) (1) worry or fear; (2) arrest
- physiologically (fiz ee uh LOJ ik lee) bodily; medically
- competent (KOM pi tunt) qualified; fit and able

The D.A., growing impassioned, swore that if Stein were allowed to go free half the laws on the books would be useless.

Then change the laws, said Defense, to take time travel into account, but until the laws are changed let them be enforced as written.

Judge Neville Preston took a week to consider and then handed down his decision. It was a turning point in the history of law. It is almost a pity, then, that some people suspect Judge Preston to have been swayed in his way of thinking by the irresistible impulse to phrase his decision as he did.

For that decision, in full, was:

"A niche in time saves Stein."

ALL THINGS CONSIDERED

The *allusion* (see page 299) in the last line is to (a) a famous criminal named Stein. (b) Albert Einstein. (c) a familiar saying.

THINKING IT THROUGH

Clearly, the author likes to have fun with the English language. Using the story's title as a model, write two examples of wordplay on your paper. You might rewrite common sayings or book or movie titles.

---

* impassioned (im PASH und) full of feeling
* niche (NICH) (1) hollowed-out place; (2) place or position suitable for a certain person

UNIT REVIEW

I. Match the terms in Column A with their definitions in Column B.

	A		B
1.	paraphrase	**a)**	things working out in unexpected ways
2.	denotation	**b)**	a word's "emotional meaning," all that it suggests
3.	connotation		
4.	irony of situation	**c)**	knowing more than a character knows
5.	dramatic irony	**d)**	a word's usual or "dictionary meaning"
		e)	a restating using as few of the original words as possible

II. This book has suggested several times that the ability to ask questions is at least as important as the ability to answer them. This is true with regard to any subject. Full understanding comes from you yourself realizing what the right questions are, not from answering questions provided by others.

Write ten original questions on this unit that you think are both important and fair. Avoid questions that are too easy as well as questions that few people could answer with the book closed. Vary your questions so that you cover some characters, plots, kinds of literature, and skill terms. Vary the *types* of questions as well, so that you include most of the following:

1. Multiple choice
2. True-false
3. Fill-in
4. Who said, "_____"?
5. Sentence completion
6. Ordering of events in a list
7. Correction of error(s) in a sentence
8. Pairing items in a list of five or more, and explaining the pairing
9. Short answer
10. Essay—paragraph required

SPEAKING UP

Choral reading is reading aloud together, or having various individuals or small groups take different parts in the reading of a piece of literature. Your job now is to make an arrangement of the following selection that puts the speaking talents of everyone in the class to full use. The author, Carl Sandburg (1878–1967), was in many ways the most American of American writers. He wrote a huge biography of Abraham Lincoln and toured the country looking for folk songs, sayings, and tall tales. Start by silently reading—

from THEY HAVE YARNS

by Carl Sandburg

They have yarns
Of a skyscraper so tall they had to put hinges
On the two top stories so to let the moon go by,
Of one corn crop in Missouri when the roots
5 Went so deep and drew off so much water
The Mississippi riverbed that year was dry,
Of pancakes so thin they only had one side,
Of "a fog so thick we shingled the barn and six
    feet out on the fog,"
Of Pecos Pete straddling a cyclone in Texas and
    riding it to the west coast where "it rained out
    under him,"
10 Of the man who drove a swarm of bees across
    the Rocky Mountains and the Desert "and
    didn't lose a bee,"
Of a mountain railroad curve where the engineer
    in his cab can touch the caboose and spit in
    the conductor's eye,
Of the boy who climbed a cornstalk growing so
    fast he would have starved to death if they
    hadn't shot biscuits up to him,
Of the old man's whiskers: "When the wind was
    with him his whiskers arrived a day before he
    did,"

Of the hen laying a square egg and cackling
    "Ouch!" and of hens laying eggs with the
    dates printed on them,
15 Of the ship captain's shadow: it froze to the deck
    one cold winter night,
Of mutineers on that same ship put to chipping
    rust with rubber hammers,
Of the sheep counter who was fast and accurate:
    "I just count their feet and divide by four,"
Of the man so tall he must climb a ladder to
    shave himself,
Of the runt so teeny-weeny it takes two men and a
    boy to see him,
20 Of mosquitoes: one can kill a dog, two of them a
    man,
Of a cyclone that sucked cookstoves out of the
    kitchen, up the chimney flue, and on to the
    next town,
Of the same cyclone picking up wagon-tracks in
    Nebraska and dropping them over in the
    Dakotas,
Of the hook-and-eye snake unlocking itself into
    forty pieces, each piece two inches long, then
    in nine seconds flat snapping itself together
    again,
Of the watch swallowed by the cow—when they
    butchered her a year later the watch was
    running and had the correct time,
25 Of horned snakes, hoop snakes that roll
    themselves where they want to go, and
    rattlesnakes carrying bells instead of rattles on
    their tails,
Of the herd of cattle in California getting lost in a
    giant redwood tree that had hollowed out,
Of the man who killed a snake by putting its tail in
    its mouth so it swallowed itself,
Of railroad trains whizzing along so fast they reach
    the station before the whistle,
Of pigs so thin the farmer had to tie knots in their
    tails to keep them from crawling through the
    cracks in their pens,
30 Of Paul Bunyan's big blue ox, Babe, measuring
    between the eyes forty-two ax-handles and a

plug of Star tobacco exactly,
Of John Henry's hammer and the curve of its
    swing and his singing of it as "a rainbow
    round my shoulder."

        "Do tell!"
        "I want to know!"
    "You don't say so!"
35 "For the land's sake!"
    "Gosh all fish-hooks!"
    "Tell me some more.
    I don't believe a word you say
    but I love to listen
40 to your sweet harmonica
    to your chin-music.
    Your fish stories hang together
    when they're just a pack of lies:
    you ought to have a leather medal:
45 you ought to have a statue
    carved of butter: you deserve
    a large bouquet of turnips."

Now think about the way your class might present a choral reading of "They Have Yarns." In planning your reading, you will have to consider the following:

How large is the group? If everyone read the first few lines together, could an audience understand? If not, how many people should read the beginning? And what about all the lines starting with "Of" in the middle section? Should they be read by individuals, pairs of students, or small groups? Are there certain lines that might be good for particular people to read?

Should students read their parts in the order in which they're lined up, or would it be better to skip around? Should the readers stand in place or take a step forward? Should any actions accompany the words? If so, what?

What else can you think of to make the reading more interesting? For instance, you might want to pause after line 43, as though the performance were over. Then three people could present the three "prizes" at the end to whoever they think did the best jobs.

WRITING: ANYTHING GOES!

The best writing is writing that is of interest to you personally. How do you get started on such a writing assignment? Do you get a case of the blank-paper blahs? Do you sit there like an uninspired fireplug, waiting for someone to open your valves? If so, here are some ways to put some *rush* behind the words.

Prewriting: For this one-page assignment, think of a topic that won't tie your mind in knots. How I *Didn't* Spend My Summer Vacation is a good one. (Make up a tall tale, like bumping into Princess Di on the Riviera.) Others might be: The Art of Shopping, My Advice to New Students, or If I Were 21. Whatever your topic, write some key words in the middle of a sheet of paper. Then, around the key words, scribble whatever pops into your mind. At this point, *anything goes:* bits of description, action, dialogue, even an entirely new subject for your paper.

Writing: When you study your scribbled notes, you'll probably find that you've done some *clustering*. That is, similar notes appear in clusters, or near each other. First decide how you're going to start, marking that note with a ①. Then order your remaining notes ②, ③, ④, ⑤, and so on. If something seems missing, add it. Finally, when you've gone through the whole paper mentally and decided which paragraphs will express which ideas, write it out as clearly and creatively as you can.

Revision: Although the main purpose of revision is to check on clarity and correctness, to some extent anything goes at this point, too. That is, you still can make small creative changes. Add at least three of the following elements to your paper if they are not already there: (1) Express something in terms of light or darkness (*Di's face lit up about 60 watts*). (2) Use music or other sounds in an expression (*Angels harped away in my ears*). (3) Express something about a person in terms of a thing (*Will and Harry attacked the potato chips like two vacuum cleaners*). (4) Express something about a person in terms of a non-thing (*Mom at times just believes in believing*). (5) Use a word that sounds like what it means (*My friend's accusation hit me like a well-aimed splat of truth*). If necessary, rewrite your assignment on a clean piece of paper, including all the improvements you made while revising the original draft.

U N I T · 6

I HEAR AMERICA

This land is your land,
This land is my land
From California
To the New York island;
From the redwood forest
To the Gulf Stream waters;
This land was made for you and me.
© "This Land Is Your Land" by Woody Guthrie

So sang our legendary folksinger, Woody Guthrie. For years he traveled the country over . . . seeing and hearing . . . writing and singing. He knew the nation and its people well: a land of rich natural resources matched by a wealth of human effort.

Many writers have acknowledged the "American spirit," the determination of generations of settlers to make this country a success. Despite failures along the way, most Americans continue to believe they have something to work for.

This unit focuses on both real and fictional people whose spirit seems to characterize Americans—from Paul Revere to newer "settlers" like Jesús Colón; from a northern logger who fails to recognize the power of nature to those who celebrate nature's beauty and understand that its survival is tied to our own.

THE GIFT OF THE MAGI

by O. Henry

▶ Americans are known for their spirit and courage. No matter how bad things look at times, people keep on trying for a better life. That is just what Della Young and her husband, Jim, did. And like many others, they learned that making the effort can be just as important as reaching the goal.

One dollar and eighty-seven cents. That was all. And sixty cents of it was in pennies. Pennies saved one and two at a time by bulldozing the grocer and the butcher until her cheeks burned with embarrassment. Three times Della counted it. One dollar and eighty-seven cents. And the next day would be Christmas.*

There was clearly nothing to do but flop down on the shabby

- **Magi** (MAY jy) the three wise men who, according to the biblical story, made the journey to Bethlehem to present gifts to the Christ child
- bulldozing (BUL dohz ing) bullying; threatening

*This story first appeared in 1905, when a dollar could buy much more than it can now. Think of all sums mentioned as multiplied by ten.

little couch and howl. So Della did it. Which instigates the reflection that life is made up of three stages—sobs, sniffles, and smiles, with sniffles in the lead.

While the woman of the home is gradually coming down from the first stage to the second, take a look at the house. A furnished apartment at eight dollars per week. It did not exactly look like a *poor*house but it certainly brought that word to mind. Nothing worked exactly as it should. In the lobby below was a letter box into which no letter would go, and an electric button from which no mortal finger could tease a ring. And fixed to the box was a card with the name Mr. James Dillingham Young.

The "Dillingham" had been flung to the breeze during a former period of prosperity, when its owner was being paid thirty dollars per week. Now, when the income had shrunk to twenty dollars, the letters of Dillingham looked blurred, as though they were thinking seriously of contracting to a modest and unassuming little D. But whenever Mr. James Dillingham Young came home and reached his apartment above, he was called Jim and greatly hugged by Mrs. James Dillingham Young, already introduced to you as Della. Which is all very good.

Della finished her cry and powdered her cheeks. She stood by the window and looked out dully at a gray cat walking a gray fence in a gray backyard. Tomorrow would be Christmas Day, and she had only one dollar and eighty-seven cents with which to buy Jim a present. She had been saving every penny she could for months, with this result. Twenty dollars a week doesn't go far. Expenses had been greater than she had planned. They always are. Only one dollar and eighty-seven cents to buy a present for Jim. Her Jim. Many a happy hour she had spent planning for something nice for him. Something fine and rare and sterling—something just a little bit near to showing him the honor of being Mrs. James Dillingham Young.

There was a tall wall mirror between the windows of the room. Perhaps you have seen a wall mirror in an eight-dollar apartment. A very thin and very agile woman may, by seeing her reflection in a number of rapid steps, get a fairly good idea of her looks. Della, being slender, had mastered the art.

- **instigate** (IN stuh gayt) bring about; stir up
- **reflection** (ri FLEK shun) serious thought
- **contracting** (kon TRAKT ing) growing smaller
- **unassuming** (un uh SOOM ing) modest; quiet
- **agile** (AJ ul) nimble; well-coordinated

Suddenly she whirled from the window and stood before the glass. Her eyes were shining brightly, but her face lost its color within twenty seconds. Rapidly she pulled down her hair and let it fall to its full length.

Now, the James Dillingham Youngs owned just two things in which they both took a mighty pride. One was Jim's gold watch that had been his father's and his grandfather's. The other was Della's hair. Had the Queen of Sheba* lived in the apartment across the air shaft, Della would have let her hair hang out the window to dry some day just to make fun of her Majesty's jewels and gifts. Had King Solomon been the janitor, with all his treasures piled up in the basement, Jim would have pulled out his watch every time he passed, just to see him pull at his beard with envy.

So now Della's beautiful hair fell about her, rippling and shining like a cascade of brown waters. It reached below her knees and made almost a garment for her. And then she did it up again nervously and quickly. Once she faltered for a minute and stood still while a tear or two splashed on the worn red carpet.

On went her old brown jacket. On went her old brown hat. With a whirl of skirts and with the brilliant sparkle still in her eyes, she fluttered out the door and down the stairs to the street.

Where she stopped, the sign read: "Madame Sofronie. Wigs and Hair Goods of All Kinds." One flight up Della ran, and collected herself, panting. Madame was a large woman, chilly and much too white.

"Will you buy my hair?" asked Della.

"I buy hair," said Madame. "Take your hat off, and let's have a sight at the looks of it."

Down rippled the brown cascade.

"Twenty dollars," said Madame, lifting the hair with a practiced hand.

"Give it to me quick," said Della.

Oh, and the next two hours tripped by on rosy wings. Forget the hashed metaphor. Della was ransacking the stores for Jim's present.

- **cascade** (kas KAYD) waterfall
- trip (TRIP) run gracefully and lightly
- hashed (HASHT) jumbled; all mixed up
- **metaphor** (MET uh for) figure of speech that makes a comparison
- **ransacking** (RAN sak ing) searching furiously

*According to the Bible, the Queen of Sheba traveled from ancient Ethiopia to Israel to visit King Solomon. Amazed by the King's wisdom, she gave him much gold and other valuable gifts. (I Kings 10:1–13.)

She found it at last. It surely had been made for Jim and no one else. There was no other like it in any of the stores, and she had turned all of them inside out. It was a platinum watch chain, simple in design, free of silly and cheap decoration. It was even worthy of The Watch. As soon as she saw it, she knew it must be Jim's. It was like him. Quietness and value—the description applied to both. Twenty-one dollars they took from her for it, and she hurried home with the eighty-seven cents. With that chain on his watch, Jim might be properly anxious about the time in any company. Grand as the watch was, he sometimes looked at it on the sly because of the old leather strap that he used in place of a chain.

When Della reached home, her wild delight gave way a little to good common sense. She got out her hair curlers and lighted the gas stove. Then she went to work repairing the damage made by generosity added to love. Which is always a tremendous task, dear friends—a mammoth task.

Within forty minutes her head was covered with tiny, close-lying curls that made her look wonderfully like a playful school-boy. She studied her reflection in the mirror long and carefully.

"If Jim doesn't kill me," she said to herself, "before he takes a second look at me, he'll say I look like a Coney Island chorus girl.* But what could I do? Oh, what could I do with a dollar and eighty-seven cents?"

At seven o'clock the coffee was made, and the frying pan was on the back of the stove, hot and ready to cook the chops.

Jim was never late. Della held the chain in her hand and sat on the corner of the table near the front door. Then she heard his step on the stair away down on the first flight, and she turned white for just a moment. She had a habit of saying little silent prayers about the simplest everyday things, and now she whispered: "Please, God, make him think I am still pretty."

The door opened, and Jim stepped in and closed it. He looked thin and very serious. Poor fellow—he was only twenty-two. He needed a new overcoat and he was without gloves.

Jim stopped inside the door. He froze suddenly, his eyes fixed upon Della. There was an expression in them that she could not read, and it terrified her. It was not anger, nor disappointment, nor surprise, nor horror, nor any of the feelings she had been prepared for. He simply stood staring at her fixedly with that strange expression on his face.

---

*A night-club dancer at Coney Island, once a busy amusement center on the edge of New York City.

Della wriggled off the table and went for him.

"Jim, darling!" she cried. "Don't look at me that way. I had my hair cut off and sold it, sure! But I did it because I couldn't live through Christmas without giving you a present. It'll grow out again. You won't mind, will you? I just had to do it. My hair grows awfully fast. Say 'Merry Christmas,' Jim, and let's be happy. You don't know what a nice—what a beautiful, nice gift I've got for you."

"You've cut off your hair?" he asked laboriously, with effort, as if he had not really noticed that fact yet, even after the hardest mental work.

"Cut it off and sold it," said Della. "Don't you like me just as well, anyhow? I'm *me* without my hair, aren't I?"

Jim looked about the room curiously.

"You say your hair is gone?" he said, speaking almost like an idiot.

"You needn't look for it," said Della. "It's sold, I tell you—sold and gone, too. It's Christmas Eve, Jim. Be good to me, because the hair went for you. Maybe the hairs of my head were numbered," she went on with a sudden serious sweetness, "but nobody could ever count my love for you. Shall I put the chops on, Jim?"

Out of his trance Jim seemed quickly to wake. He took Della in his arms. For ten seconds let us examine with discreet curiosity some unimportant object in the other direction. Eight dollars a week or a million a year—what is the difference? A mathematician would give you the wrong answer. The Magi brought valuable gifts, but this was not among them. That mysterious sentence will be illuminated later on.

Jim drew a package from his overcoat pocket and threw it on the table.

"Don't make any mistake, Dell," he said, "about me. I don't think there's anything in the way of a haircut or a shampoo that could make me like my girl any less. But if you'll unwrap that package, you may see why you had me going when I first walked in."

Nimble white fingers tore at the string and paper. And then an ecstatic scream of joy. And then—alas!—a rapid change to wild tears and heavy sobs.

- **laboriously** (luh BOHR ee us lee) with much labor and care
- **discreet** (dis KREET) wisely careful
- **illuminate** (i LOO min ayt) make clear
- **nimble** (NIM bul) quick and accurate; agile

For there lay The Combs—the set of combs, side and back, that Della had worshipped for long in a Broadway window. Beautiful combs, pure tortoiseshell with jeweled rims—just the shade to wear in the beautiful vanished hair. They were expensive combs, she knew. She had wanted them more than anything in the world, without the smallest hope of ever owning them. And now they were hers! But the waves of hair that should have held the combs were gone.

Suddenly she hugged them to her throat, and before long she was able to look up with dim eyes and a smile. "My hair grows so fast, Jim," she said.

And then Della leaped up like a little singed cat and cried, "Oh, oh!"

Jim had not yet seen his beautiful present. She held it out to him eagerly upon her opened hand. The platinum seemed to flash with a reflection of her bright and ardent spirit.

"Isn't it something, Jim? I hunted all over town to find it. You'll have to look at the time a hundred times a day now. Give me your watch. I want to see how the chain looks on it."

Instead of obeying, Jim tumbled down on the couch and put his hands under the back of his head and smiled.

"Dell," said he, "let's put our Christmas presents away and keep them awhile. They're too nice to use just now. I sold the watch to get the money to buy your combs. And now, suppose you put the chops on."

The Magi, as you know, were wise men—wonderfully wise men—who brought gifts to the Babe in the manger. They invented the art of giving Christmas presents. Being wise, they no doubt gave wise gifts. And here I have lamely told you the sad little story of two foolish children who most unwisely sacrificed for each other the greatest treasures of their house. But in a last word to the wise of these days, let it be said that of all who gave gifts these two were the wisest. Of all who give and receive gifts, such as they are wisest. Everywhere they are wisest. They are the Magi.

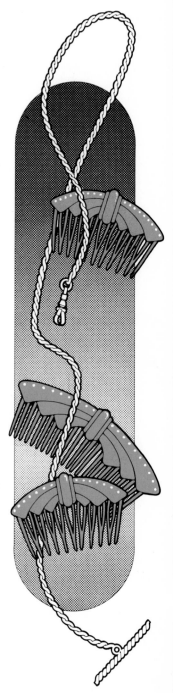

• **ardent** (AHR dunt) very eager; passionate

ALL THINGS CONSIDERED ────────────────────

1. Early in the story, the author is careful to let the reader know vital facts about (a) the letter box and the card. (b) the value placed on Della's hair and Jim's watch. (c) "sobs, sniffles, and smiles."

2. The two main characters are like the Magi in that they (a) make tremendous sacrifices to purchase gifts. (b) give gifts to each other. (c) give gifts to a loved one.

3. When Jim enters the apartment, he stands in shocked silence because (a) he sees Della's present at once. (b) he realizes his present for her is now useless. (c) he has forgotten about Christmas.

4. The story is a good example of O. Henry's literary trademark, (a) the surprise ending. (b) striking realism. (c) the first-person point of view.

5. The story's references to King Solomon and to the Queen of Sheba are called (a) *personifications*. (b) *allusions*. (c) *clichés*.

THINKING IT THROUGH ────────────────────

1. What clues help you foresee the ending of the story?

2. In the last paragraph of the story, the author states that Della and Jim had acted "unwisely." Yet in the very next sentence, he calls them the "wisest" of all who gave gifts. (a) In what way can the presents of Jim and Della be considered mistakes? (b) In what way can their actions be thought most admirable?

3. O. Henry's writing seems old-fashioned to some modern readers. One reason for this is his use of big, fancy words to describe ordinary situations. An example is the remark that Della's howling "instigates the reflection" that life has three stages. (a) What is another example of this flowery language? (b) Why do you think O. Henry chose to write this way?

4. Look back at the discussion of *metaphor* on page 30. Then look at one of the narrator's direct comments to the reader on page 336: "Forget the hashed metaphor." It refers to the sentence that comes just before it: "Oh, and the next two hours tripped by on rosy wings." In what way is the metaphor in that sentence "hashed," or mixed up?

5. After Jim's last speech on page 339, the story just stops—and O. Henry goes on with a long final paragraph that expresses the story's theme. (a) What *is* the theme? (b) How do you feel the story would hold up if it had been written in the 1980s?

Reading and Analyzing: Review

If you wish to review the meaning of any term in *italics* in this exercise, refer to the Glossary of Terms at the back of this book.

1. In what way is the ending of "The Gift of the Magi" an example of *irony of situation?*

2. The description of Della's hair is an example of effective *imagery.* (a) To what does O. Henry twice compare the hair? (b) How does this comparison help create a clear visual *image?*

3. In your own words, what *conclusion* does O. Henry draw in the last paragraph of the story?

4. Some modern readers object to O. Henry's *tone.* Such readers feel that O. Henry doesn't really care about his characters, but instead treats them like puppets who are led to do certain things for the sake of a clever plot. Do you agree? Explain.

5. Tone also can reveal an author's attitude toward his or her readers. Some readers dislike O. Henry's writing because they feel the author to be more of a show-off than a good writer. These readers feel that O. Henry is constantly shouting between the lines, "Look at ME! Aren't I the most wonderfully clever writer you ever read?" Do you agree? What is your opinion of O. Henry's attitude?

6. Why can the selling of the hair and the watch be called *symbolic actions?* In other words, what do the two actions symbolize about Della and Jim?

7. In what way does O. Henry use the card on the letter box (page 335) as a *symbol?*

8. The footnote on page 334 informs you that "The Gift of the Magi" was first printed in 1905. What *inference* might you make about the month of year in which the story was published?

Composition

1. Read in the Bible (Matthew 2:1–16) about the Magi, or wise men. Then answer these questions: (a) What was Herod's lie to the wise men? (b) Why were the Magi wise not to return to Herod?

2. A footnote on page 334 noted the difference in the value of money between 1905 and today. What other differences between 1905 and today do you find in the story? Think particularly about the following questions: Does Della seem to be a working woman? Is extremely long hair a popular style for women today? Does Della pay any sales tax at the store? Do many modern men carry or value pocket watches?

Walt Whitman (1819-1892)

"Wake up, America!" Walt Whitman's poetry seems to shout. "Wake up and look around. Wake up and listen. Wake up to a new life in a world that is wonder-full."

If any American deserves the title "People's Poet," it is Walt Whitman. He thought of himself as the poet of democracy. Everything inspired Whitman. Everything had meaning for him. His aim was to tell Americans about themselves in a way that would make them, too, feel fully alive.

Whitman was born into a farm family on Long Island, near New York City. At 11, he dropped out of school and went to work for a printer. In the years that followed, he worked as a carpenter, teacher, and newspaper writer and editor. These different trades and his travels around the United States gave him firsthand knowledge of the people he was later to celebrate in his poetry.

In 1850 Whitman suddenly quit a job as an editor and went back to live with his mother and father. Once a well-known figure in newspaper and political circles, he simply dropped out of sight. Then followed the five "dark years" in his life. Apparently he worked now and then as a carpenter, but most of the time he must have written poetry. In 1855 the "dark years" came to an end. In that year he gave the world *Leaves of Grass,* which, with its new and different poetic style, became perhaps the most important single collection of poems by an American poet. In its content too, *Leaves of Grass* marks a turning point in American poetry, for it touches on all aspects of life, including subjects not previously found in verse. In 1856 an expanded edition appeared, after which Whitman continued to work on the volume, adding and dropping poems throughout most of his life.

Whitman was over 40 when the Civil War began, but he insisted on doing his part. He spent the war years nursing and comforting injured soldiers. By the end of the war, more than 80,000 wounded soldiers had met the big friendly man who usually dressed in a shabby wide-brimmed hat and an open shirt and jacket. The war service, however, affected Whitman's own health. Then, in 1873, he suffered a stroke and spent his last years as an invalid.

What experiences in Walt Whitman's life helped qualify him for the title "People's Poet"?

342

WHITMAN: PEOPLE'S POET

poems by Walt Whitman

▶ Walt Whitman has been praised many times for his love of the common people and for his ability to celebrate ordinary work. Both these characteristics are obvious in—

I HEAR AMERICA SINGING

I hear America singing, the varied carols I hear,
Those of mechanics, each one singing his as it
    should be blithe and strong.
The carpenter singing his as he measures his
    plank or beam,
The mason singing his as he makes ready for
    work, or leaves off work,
5 The boatman singing what belongs to him in his
    boat, the deck hand singing on the
    steamboat deck,
The shoemaker singing as he sits on his bench,
    the hatter singing as he stands.
The woodcutter's song, the plowboy on his way
    in the morning, or at noon intermission or at
    sundown,
The delicious singing of the mother, or of the
    young wife at work, or of the girl sewing or
    washing,
Each singing what belongs to him or her and to
    none else,
10 The day what belongs to the day—at night the
    party of young fellows, robust, friendly,
Singing with open mouths their strong melodious
    songs.

- blithe (BLYTH) happy; cheerful
- mason (MAY son) stone worker
- hatter (HAT ur) hat maker
- **robust** (roh BUST) strong; healthy

WAYS OF KNOWING

1. In your opinion, why does the poet use "carols" instead of the word *songs* in line 1?
2. In what way are the eight occupations mentioned in lines 2–7 alike?
3. In what way does the song of each person belong "to him or her and to none else" (line 9)?
4. The poem was written about 125 years ago. Do you suppose people now sing at work as much as they used to? Explain why, or why not.

▶ Whitman's outstanding service in the Civil War was not limited to nursing wounded soldiers. This poem about the death of Abraham Lincoln, a tragedy that occurred only six days after the war ended, was meant to comfort the whole nation.

O CAPTAIN! MY CAPTAIN!

O Captain! my Captain! our fearful trip is done,
The ship has weather'd every rack, the prize we
    sought is won,
The port is near, the bells I hear, the people all
    exulting,
While follow eyes the steady keel, the vessel grim
    and daring;
5 But O heart! heart! heart!
    O the bleeding drops of red,
        Where on the deck my Captain lies,
           Fallen cold and dead.

- weather (WETH ur) last through; endure
- rack (RAK) hardship; torture
- **exulting** (ig ZULT ing) rejoicing; showing joy
- **keel** (KEEL) "backbone" of a ship

O Captain! my Captain! rise up and hear the
    bells;
10 Rise up—for you the flag is flung—for you the
    bugle trills,
For you bouquets and ribbon'd wreaths—for you
    the shores a-crowding
For you they call, the swaying mass, their eager
    faces turning;
Here Captain! dear father!
    This arm beneath your head!
15   It is some dream that on the deck,
      You've fallen cold and dead.

My Captain does not answer, his lips are pale and
    still,
My father does not feel my arm, he has no pulse
    nor will,
The ship is anchor'd safe and sound, its voyage
    closed and done,
20 From fearful trip the victor ship comes in with
    object won;
    Exult O shores, and ring O bells!
    But I with mournful tread
      Walk the deck my Captain lies,
      Fallen cold and dead.

WAYS OF KNOWING

1. The whole poem must be read as an *extended metaphor* (see page 44). Explain the underlying meaning of each of the following: (a) "Captain" (line 1); (b) "fearful trip" (line 1); (c) "ship" (line 2); (d) "prize" (line 2); (e) "port" (line 3); (f) "steady keel" (line 4); and (g) all of line 19.
2. In stanzas 2 and 3, what does the speaker imagine doing to or for the "Captain"?
3. Why tell others to "exult" (line 21) when the speaker is so sad?

- trill (TRIL) play music with a quivering sound
- **will** (WIL) wishes; desires
- **object** (OB jekt) purpose; goal
- tread (TRED) step; walk

As an alternative to *answering* questions, another way to show your understanding of a literary work is to think of good questions to *ask*. You might ask questions of the teacher or of other students.

Write two questions about the following Whitman poem:

1. A question that tests understanding on a rather simple level. Anyone who has read the poem thoughtfully should be able to answer it.
2. A question that requires some insight to answer. Ask yourself: What understanding might be missed in a fast or careless reading?

WHEN I HEARD THE LEARN'D ASTRONOMER

When I heard the learn'd astronomer,
When the proofs, the figures, were ranged in
    columns before me,
When I was shown the charts and diagrams, to
    add, divide, and measure them,
When I sitting heard the astronomer where he
    lectured with much applause in the lecture
    room,
How soon unaccountable I became tired and sick,
Till rising and gliding out I wandered off by
    myself,
In the mystical moist night air, and from time to
    time,
Looked up in perfect silence at the stars.

- ranged (RAYNJD) set forth; arranged
- **unaccountable** (un uh KOWN tuh bul) for no apparent reason
- **mystical** (MIS ti kul) mysterious; having a hidden meaning

VOCABULARY AND SKILL REVIEW ⸺⸺⸺⸺⸺⸺

Before completing the exercises that follow, you may wish to review the **bold-faced** words on pages 334 to 346.

I. On a separate sheet of paper, write the term in each line that means the same, or nearly the same, as the word in *italics*.

1. *cascade:* cliff, waterfall, small hill, canyon
2. *robust:* skillful, intelligent, crafty, strong and healthy
3. *mystical:* clouded over, mysterious, starry, defeated
4. *ransacking:* packing, backpacking, following, searching
5. *exulting:* rejoicing, quitting, leaving, crying
6. *contracting:* decaying, adding, growing smaller, maddening
7. *Magi:* magic, kind of hat, spicy food, wise men
8. *agile:* small drill, nimble and athletic, small, red
9. *instigate:* stir up, kind of school, joyful, put an end to
10. *illuminate:* cover, pale and weak, make clear, forget

II. 1. A *discreet* person is (a) careful in a wise way. (b) needlessly foolish. (c) very proud.

2. An *ardent* person is (a) very wise. (b) timid and fearful. (c) eager or passionate.

3. To consider the *will* of another is to (a) think of that person's desires. (b) envy the person. (c) estimate the weight of the person.

4. An *unaccountable* happening is (a) not counted as serious. (b) too confusing to count. (c) unexplained.

5. A *metaphor* is a kind of (a) comparison. (b) plot. (c) conflict.

6. *Laboriously* stems from the word (a) *laboratory.* (b) *Labrador.* (c) *labor.*

7. Time for *reflection* is time for (a) play or athletics. (b) serious thought. (c) eating without hurrying.

8. A serious *object* is a serious (a) goal or purpose. (b) look or expression. (c) story or book.

9. RAPID is to SLOW as *NIMBLE* is to (a) FAST. (b) AWKWARD. (c) UNMOVING.

10. BACKBONE is to BODY as *KEEL* is to (a) BUILDING. (b) ANIMAL. (c) SHIP.

LITTLE THINGS ARE BIG

by Jesús Colón

▶ When Jesús Colón came to the mainland from Puerto Rico, it didn't take him long to learn about prejudice. It was bad for blacks. It was bad for Puerto Ricans. And, as he realizes in this selection, it was bad for everybody. The selection is from his book *A Puerto Rican in New York*.

It was very late at night on the eve of Memorial Day. She came into the subway at the 34th Street station. I am still trying to remember how she managed to push herself in, with a baby on her right arm, a valise in her left hand, and two children, a boy and girl about three and five years old, trailing after her. She was a nice-looking white lady in her early twenties.

At Nevins Street, Brooklyn, we saw her preparing to get off at the next station, Atlantic Avenue, which happened to be the place where I too had to get off. Just as it had been a problem for her to get on the subway, it was going to be a problem for her to get off. She had two small children to take care of, a baby on her right arm and a medium-sized valise in her left hand.

And there I was, also preparing to get off at Atlantic Avenue, with no bundles to take care of—not even the usual book under my arm, without which I feel that I am not completely dressed.

As the train was entering the Atlantic Avenue station, some white man stood up from his seat and helped her out of the car, placing the children on the long, deserted platform. There were only two adult persons on the long platform sometime after midnight on the eve of Memorial Day.

I could see the steep, long concrete stairs going down to the Long Island Railroad or into the street. Should I offer my help as the American white man had done at the subway door, placing the two children outside the subway car? Should I take care of the girl and the boy? Should I take them by their hands until they reached the end of the steep, long concrete stairs of the Atlantic Avenue station?

• **valise** (vuh LEES) small suitcase

348

Courtesy is a characteristic of the Puerto Rican. And here I was—a Puerto Rican. Hours past midnight, valise, two white children, and a white lady with a baby on her arm badly needing somebody to help her until she got down the long concrete stairs.

But how could I, a black and a Puerto Rican, approach this white lady? I knew she very likely might be prejudiced against blacks and everybody with foreign accents. And we were in a deserted subway station, very late at night.

What would she say? What would be the first reaction of this white American woman, perhaps coming from a small town, with a valise, two children and a baby on her right arm? Would she say, "Yes, of course, you may help me"? Or would she think that I was just trying to get too familiar? Or would she think worse than that perhaps? What would I do if she let out a scream as I went toward her to offer my help?

Was I misjudging her? So many slanders are written every day in the newspapers against the blacks and Puerto Ricans. I hesitated for a long, long minute. The ancestral manners that the most illiterate Puerto Rican passes on from father to son were struggling inside me. Here was I, way past midnight, face to face with a situation that could very well explode into an outburst of prejudice.

It was a long minute. I passed on by her as if I saw nothing. As if I didn't care about her need. Like a rude animal walking on two legs, I just moved on. I half ran down the long subway platform, leaving the children and the valise and her with the baby on her arm. I took the steps of the long concrete stairs in twos until I reached the street. The cold air slapped my warm face.

This is what racism and prejudice and artificial divisions can do to people and to a nation!

Perhaps the lady was not prejudiced after all. Or not prejudiced enough to scream at the coming of a black man toward her in a lonely subway station a few hours past midnight.

If you were not that prejudiced, I failed you, dear lady. I know that there is a chance in a million that you will read these lines. I am willing to take that millionth chance. If you were not that

---

- **characteristic** (kar ik tuh RIS tik) special quality
- **slander** (SLAN dur) lie; harmful statement
- **ancestral** (an SES tral) coming from an ancestor
- **illiterate** (i LIT ur it) unable to read
- **racism** (RAY siz um) racial prejudice

prejudiced, I failed you, lady, I failed you, children. I failed my-self to myself.

I buried my courtesy early on Memorial Day morning. But here is a promise that I make to myself here and now: If I am ever faced with a situation like that again, I am going to offer my help regardless of how the offer is going to be received.

Then I will have my courtesy with me again.

ALL THINGS CONSIDERED

1. The author's age at the time of the event described seems to be about (a) 14. (b) 25. (c) 50.
2. Jesús Colón states that the Puerto Rican people (a) dislike big cities. (b) are courteous. (c) do not believe a woman should travel alone.
3. The author decides not to help the woman because (a) he thinks she would refuse help from anyone. (b) she manages to handle the situation easily. (c) he thinks his actions might be mis-judged.
4. At the end of the experience, the author feels (a) sure that his decision was right. (b) disappointed in himself. (c) too tired to help anyone.
5. The title, "Little Things Are Big," probably means that (a) seemingly unimportant events can lead to lasting thoughts. (b) many small problems can add up to one big problem. (c) small children can be big problems.

THINKING IT THROUGH

1. The author suggests that people "coming from a small town" might be more prejudiced than New Yorkers. What is your opinion? Explain.
2. (a) What promise does the author make himself at the end of the selection? (b) In your opinion, is the promise a wise one? (c) Do you believe he will keep it? Explain your thinking.

Literary Skills: Review

If you wish to review the meaning of any term in *italics* in this exercise, refer to the Glossary of Terms.

1. Why is the *setting* so important in this particular selection?
2. Would you describe the narrator as a *stereotyped character?* Explain your answer.
3. What *stereotyped* ideas about people might be involved in the white woman's thinking?
4. There is one main *conflict* in this short selection. (a) What is the conflict? (b) How does Colón resolve the problem?
5. In your opinion, where in the selection does the *climax* occur?

6. Which portion of the selection can correctly be called the *resolution?*
7. In your judgment, what is the *theme* of the selection? In other words, what does the narrator learn about life from his experience?
8. "The cold air slapped my warm face." In what way is this sentence from the selection an example of *personification?*
9. "I buried my courtesy early on Memorial Day morning." (a) What words in the quoted sentence represent a *figure of speech?* (b) Is it a *metaphor* or a *simile?*
10. Exactly what is the *point of view* in the selection?

Composition

1. Use these five vocabulary words from the selection in five sentences of your own. Although your sentences must be about the selection, you should not simply copy from the book. The words are these: *valise, characteristic, slander, ancestral,* and *illiterate* (pages 348–349).

2. "Little Things Are Big" concerns what a character does *not* do. Think of an interesting time in your own life when you did *not* do something you might have done. Describe the incident in detail and state what you learned from the experience.

351

Henry Wadsworth Longfellow (1807-1882)

An 1826 sketch of Boston and the South Boston Bridge

At the time of his death, and for many years after, Henry Wadsworth Longfellow had no rival as America's best-loved poet. His poetry often appeared in magazines. His books were in constant demand. Schoolchildren read dozens of his poems, and often had to memorize several.

Longfellow's popularity is easy to understand. He saw beauty everywhere—in an old ship against the moon in Boston Harbor, in the forests, in the fields. He was interested in the common life of the common people, from the village blacksmith to the well-traveled sailor. He usually wrote rather simple, melodious poems that nearly everyone could understand. But most of all, he calmed the nerves of the nation. In an age when life was often hard, Longfellow told his American readers to work hard and to accept whatever fate had to offer.

Longfellow's life was mostly a comfortable one. He grew up in Maine, sailed through college at an early age, and went to Europe for further study. After that he managed to keep two careers going at the same time—first as a poet, and second as a professor of foreign languages. He had money, friends, and fame. He lived to see his poetry translated into 24 languages. But as he told his readers, "Into each life some rain must fall." In 1861 his wife burned to death when her dress accidentally caught fire. Longfellow's own struggle out of sorrow is reflected in some of his best poems.

In his own day, what features of Longfellow's poetry most appealed to his readers?

THE LONGFELLOW LEGACY

poems by Henry Wadsworth Longfellow

▶ In the spring of 1775, trouble was brewing in this country between the colonists and their British rulers. The Revolutionary War had not yet started, but all that seemed needed to set it off was a spark. The situation in Massachusetts was especially bad. The British troops waited nervously in Boston, expecting the worst. Meanwhile, the colonists collected a large supply of weapons in Concord, a town in nearby Middlesex County. The colonists expected that the British army would be sent to Concord to try to capture the arms. They also expected that the British would start the move in the quiet of the night. But what route to Concord would the British choose? Would they take the long overland route? Or would they start the trip by sailing across Boston Harbor? These were the questions that puzzled Paul Revere and other patriots.

from PAUL REVERE'S RIDE

Listen, my children, and you shall hear
Of the midnight ride of Paul Revere,
On the eighteenth of April, in Seventy-five;
Hardly a man is now alive
5 Who remembers that famous day and year.*

He said to his friend, "If the British march
By land or sea from the town to-night,
Hang a lantern aloft in the belfry arch
Of the North Church tower as a signal light,—
10 One, if by land, and two, if by sea;
And I on the opposite shore will be,
Ready to ride and spread the alarm
Through every Middlesex village and farm,
For the country folk to be up and to arm."

● **belfry** (BEL free) bell tower
*Longfellow's poem was written about 80 years after the events described.

15 Then he said, "Good night!" and with muffled oar
Silently rowed to the Charlestown shore,
Just as the moon rose over the bay,
Where swinging wide at her moorings lay
The Somerset, British man-of-war;
20 A phantom ship, with each mast and spar
Across the moon like a prison bar,
And a huge black hulk, that was magnified
By its own reflection in the tide.

Meanwhile, his friend, through alley and street,
25 Wanders and watches with eager ears,
Till in the silence around him he hears
The muster of men at the barrack door,
The sound of arms, and the tramp of feet,
And the measured tread of the grenadiers,
30 Marching down to their boats on the shore. . . .

On the opposite shore walked Paul Revere.
Now he patted his horse's side,
Now gazed at the landscape far and near,
Then, impetuous, stamped the earth,
35 And turned and tightened his saddle-girth;
But mostly he watched with eager search
The belfry-tower of the Old North Church,
As it rose above the graves on the hill,
Lonely and spectral and sombre and still.
40 And lo! as he looks, on the belfry's height
A glimmer, and then a gleam of light!
He springs to the saddle, the bridle he turns,
But lingers and gazes, till full on his sight
A second lamp in the belfry burns!

- moorings (MOOR ingz) ropes to fasten a ship
- man-of-war—warship
- spar (SPAR) pole attached to mast
- hulk (HULK) old ship
- muster (MUS tur) roll call
- grenadier (gren uh DEER) foot soldier
- impetuous (im PECH oo us) eager; violent
- girth (GURTH) strap that holds saddle on horse
- spectral (SPEK trul) ghostlike
- **sombre** (SOM bur) spelled somber; dark and gloomy

45 A hurry of hoofs in a village street,
A shape in the moonlight, a bulk in the dark,
And beneath, from the pebbles, in passing, a spark
Struck out by a steed flying fearless and fleet:
That was all! And yet, through the gloom and the light,
50 The fate of a nation was riding that night;
And the spark struck out by that steed, in his flight,
Kindled the land into flame with its heat.

It was twelve by the village clock,
When he crossed the bridge into Medford town. . . .

55 It was one by the village clock,
When he galloped into Lexington. . . .

It was two by the village clock,
When he came to the bridge in Concord town.
He heard the bleating of the flock,
60 And the twitter of birds among the trees,
And felt the breath of the morning breeze
Blowing over the meadows brown.
And one was safe and asleep in his bed
Who at the bridge would be first to fall,
65 Who that day would be lying dead,
Pierced by a British musket-ball.

You know the rest. In the books you have read,
How the British Regulars* fired and fled,—
How the farmers gave them ball for ball,
70 From behind each fence and farm-yard wall,
Chasing the red-coats down the lane,
Then crossing the fields to emerge again
Under the trees at the turn of the road,
And only pausing to fire and load.

- bulk (BULK) object; shape
- fleet (FLEET) very fast
- **bleating** (BLEET ing) cry of sheep

*These were regular army troops.

75 So through the night rode Paul Revere;
And so through the night went his cry of alarm
To every Middlesex village and farm,—
A cry of defiance and not of fear,
A voice in the darkness, a knock at the door,
80 And a word that shall echo forevermore!
For, borne on the night-wind of the Past,
Through all our history, to the last,
In the hour of darkness and peril and need,
The people will waken and listen to hear
85 The hurrying hoof-beats of that steed,
And the midnight message of Paul Revere.

WAYS OF KNOWING _____

1. Without looking back, try to tell the story of "Paul Revere's Ride" in your own words. If you have trouble, reread the poem and then give it a second try.

2. Lines 51–52 provide an example of figurative language. Longfellow does not mean that sparks from the horseshoes truly started a huge fire. What does the line mean?

3. In the closing lines of the poem, Longfellow states that Paul Revere's ride will be important "forevermore." What reason does the poet have to believe that Paul Revere's ride will continue to be meaningful in the future?

4. Try to find a map of the old Boston area in an American history book or other source. If you can, locate Boston, the North Church, Charlestown, and Concord. Why do you think the British chose to start the trip as they did?

5. Read further about Paul Revere in an American history book or an encyclopedia. (a) What important fact did Longfellow change in the poem? (b) Can you find some additional facts that Longfellow left out of the poem? If so, what are they?

Write three questions about the following poem by Longfellow. If you can, include the terms *mood, theme, comparison, metaphor,* and *simile,* as well as the phrase *relation to the poet's life.*

- **borne** (BORN) carried
- **peril** (PER ul) danger

from THE DAY IS DONE

The day is done, and the darkness
  Falls from the wings of Night,
As a feather is wafted downward
  From an eagle in his flight.

5 I see the lights of the village
  Gleam through the rain and the mist,
And a feeling of sadness comes o'er me
  That my soul cannot resist:

A feeling of sadness and longing,
10   That is not akin to pain,
And resembles sorrow only
  As the mist resembles the rain.

Come, read to me some poem,
  Some simple and heartfelt lay,
15 That shall soothe this restless feeling,
  And banish the thoughts of day.

Such songs have power to quiet
  The restless pulse of care,
And come like the benediction
20   That follows after prayer.

Then read from the treasured volume
  The poem of thy choice,
And lend to the rhyme of the poet
  The beauty of thy voice.

25 And the night shall be filled with music,
  And the cares, that infest the day,
Shall fold their tents, like the Arabs,
  And as silently steal away.

- wafted (WAFT id) blown along smoothly
- akin (uh KIN) related
- **heartfelt** (HART felt) sincere; meaningful
- lay (LAY) short song or story-poem
- benediction (ben i DIK shun) blessing; state of grace
- **infest** (in FEST) trouble; disturb

Jack London (1876-1916)

Prospectors on the Chilcoot Pass during the Klondike Gold Rush, 1898

Jack London was born in San Francisco. He grew up there and in nearby Oakland, always the toughest boy in the toughest of neighborhoods. At 15 he was a high-school dropout, a married man, and known as the "Prince of the Oyster Pirates." He worked in a canning factory and tramped around the United States. At 18 he sailed the Pacific as a crew member on a sealing ship. At 20 he joined the gold rush in the Yukon, a region of northern Canada and the setting of "To Build a Fire." Like the characters in his stories and novels, London seemed always in motion.

However, London found the time to read a good deal. When he was about 21, he decided to be a writer, and he thought a college education would be necessary. For three months he studied 19 hours a day to pass the entrance exams for the University of California. He succeeded—but then found college too slow for him. For the second time in his life he became a dropout.

London wrote about 150 short stories, selling his first one in 1899. In 1903 *The Call of the Wild*, a novel about a dog, made him famous. From then until his death, he averaged four books a year. He also served as a war reporter in the Far East and Mexico. He was the first American author to earn more than a million dollars from his writing, but he spent it quickly and finally suffered financial disaster. Few other writers ever packed more living into 40 years of life.

The brief biography you have just read gives several details about London's life before the age of 21. In your opinion, in what way might these experiences have enriched his fiction?

TO BUILD A FIRE

by Jack London

▶ The man was master of his fate until luck turned against him. Here's a classic of short fiction that you'll remember for a long, long time.

Day had broken cold and gray, exceedingly cold and gray, when the man turned aside from the main Yukon trail and climbed the high earth-bank. Ahead of him a dim and little-traveled trail led eastward through the fat spruce timberland. It was a steep bank, and he paused for breath at the top, excusing the act to himself by looking at his watch. It was nine o'clock. There was no sun nor hint of sun, though there was not a cloud in the sky. It was a clear day, and yet there seemed to be a subtle gloom over the face of things that made the day dark, and that was due to the absence of sun. This fact did not worry the man. He was used to the lack of sun. It had been days since he had seen the sun, and he knew that a few more days must pass before that cheerful orb would just peep above the hills and dip immediately from view.

The man flung a look back along the way he had come. The Yukon River lay a mile wide and hidden under three feet of ice. On top of this ice were as many feet of snow. It was all pure white, rolling in gentle undulations where the piles of ice had formed. North and south, as far as his eye could see, it was unbroken white, except for a small dark line that curved and twisted out of sight. This dark hairline was the trail—the main trail that led south five hundred miles to the Chilcoot Pass, Dyea, and salt water, and that led north seventy miles to Dawson, and still on to the north to St. Michael, on Bering Sea, a thousand miles and half a thousand more.

But all this—the mysterious, far-reaching hairline trail, the absence of sun, the tremendous cold, and the strangeness of it all—made no impression on the man. It was not because he was long used to it. He was a newcomer in the land, a *chechaquo*. This was his first winter. The trouble with him was that he was without imagination. He was quick and alert in the things of life, but only in the things, and not in their meanings. Fifty degrees below zero meant eighty-odd degrees of frost. Such fact impressed him as being cold and uncomfortable, and that was all. It did not lead him to meditate about his

- subtle (SUT ul) faint and mysterious
- orb (OHRB) round object
- undulation (un juh LAY shun) wavy form or outline
- **hairline** (HAIR lyn) very thin line
- **meditate** (MED i tayt) think deeply; ponder

actly fifty degrees below zero. That there should be anything more to it than that was a thought that never entered his head.

As he turned to go on, he spat speculatively. There was a sharp little explosion that startled him. He spat again. And again, in the air, before it could fall to the snow, the spittle popped. He knew that at fifty below spittle exploded on the snow, but this spittle had popped in the air. Undoubtedly it was colder than fifty below. How much colder he did not know. But the temperature did not matter. He was bound for the old claim on the left fork of Henderson Creek, where the men were already. They had come over mountains from the Indian Creek country, while he had come the other way. He had wanted to take a look at the possibilities of getting out logs in the spring from the islands in the Yukon. He would be in camp by six o'clock. That was a bit after dark, it was true, but the men would be there, a fire would be going, and a hot supper would be ready. As for lunch, he pressed his hand against the bundle under his jacket. It was also under his shirt, wrapped up in a handkerchief and lying against the naked skin. It was the only way to keep the biscuits from freezing. He smiled to himself as he thought of those biscuits, each cut open and sopped in bacon grease, and each enclosing a generous slice of fried bacon.

frailty as a creature of temperature. Neither did he think about the weakness of all people, able only to live within certain narrow limits of heat and cold. From there on it did not lead him to thoughts of immortality and man's place in the universe. Fifty degrees below zero stood for a bit of frost that hurt and that must be guarded against by the use of mittens, earflaps, warm boots, and thick socks. Fifty degrees below zero was to him just ex-

---

- **immortality** (im or TAL i tee) unending life
- speculatively (SPEK yuh lah tiv lee) thinking about possibilities
- spittle (SPIT ul) saliva; what one spits

He plunged in among the big spruce trees. The trail was faint. A foot of snow had fallen since the last sled had passed, and he was glad he was without a sled, traveling light. In fact, he carried nothing but the lunch wrapped in the handkerchief. He was surprised, however, at the cold. It certainly was cold, he told himself. He rubbed his numb nose and cheekbones with his mittened hand. He was a warm-whiskered man, but the hair on his face did not protect the high cheekbones and the eager nose from the frosty air.

At the man's heels trotted a dog, a big husky. It was almost a wolf-dog, gray-coated and without any real difference from its brother, the wild wolf. The animal was saddened by the tremendous cold. It knew that this was no time for traveling. Its instinct told it a truer tale than was told to the man by the man's judgment. In truth, it was not just colder than fifty below zero. It was colder than sixty below, than seventy below. It was seventy-five below zero. Since the freezing point is thirty-two above zero, it meant that there were one hundred and seven degrees of frost. The dog did not know anything about thermometers. Possibly in its brain there was no sharp awareness of a condition of very cold such as was in the man's brain. But the beast had its instinct. It experienced a vague apprehension about the cold that made it sneak along at the man's heels. It questioned every movement of the man, as if expecting him to go into camp or to find shelter somewhere and build a fire. The dog had learned fire. Now it wanted fire, or else to dig under the snow and curl up away from the air.

The frozen moisture of the dog's breath had settled on its fur in a fine powder of frost, and its muzzle and eyelashes were whitened by its snowy breath. The man's red beard and mustache were likewise frosted, but more solidly. The ice on his face increased with every warm, moist breath he took. Also, the man was chewing tobacco, and the ice made his lips so stiff that he was unable to clear his chin when he spat out the juice. The result was that an icy brown beard was increasing its length on his chin. If he fell down it would shatter like glass into small pieces. But he did not mind it, really. It was the penalty all tobacco-chewers paid in that country. And he had been out before in two cold snaps. They had not been so cold as this, he knew. But by the thermometer at Sixty Mile he knew they had been fifty below and fifty-five.

He held on through the woods for several miles, crossed a wide flat place, and dropped down a bank to the frozen bed of a small stream. This was Henderson Creek, and he knew he was ten miles from the fork. He looked at his watch. It was ten o'clock. He was making four miles an hour, and he calculated that he would arrive at the fork at half-past twelve. He decided to celebrate that event by eating his lunch there.

- apprehension (ap ri HEN shun) worry; fear of a coming event
- muzzle (MUZ ul) mouth and nose of animal

The dog dropped behind again at his heels, with its tail drooping, as the man swung along the creekbed. The furrow of the old sled trail was plainly visible, but a dozen inches of snow covered the marks of the last runners. In a month no man had come up or down that silent creek. The man held steadily on. He was not much given to thinking, and just then he had nothing to think about. He knew that he would eat lunch at the fork and that at six o'clock he would be in camp with the men. There was nobody to talk to; and, had there been, speech would have been impossible because of the ice on his mouth. So he continued monotonously to chew tobacco and to increase the length of his brown beard.

Once in a while the thought reiterated itself that it was very cold and that he had never experienced such cold. As he walked along he rubbed his cheekbones and nose with the back of his mittened hand. He did this automatically, now and again changing hands. But rub as he would, the instant he stopped his cheekbones went numb, and the following instant the end of his nose went numb. He was sure to frost his cheeks; he knew that. He wished he had made a nose strap of the sort Bud wore in cold snaps. Such a strap passed across the cheeks, as well, and saved them. But it didn't matter much, after all. What were frosted cheeks? A bit painful, that was all. They were never serious.

Empty as the man's mind was of thoughts, he was keenly observant. He noticed the changes in the creek, the curves and bends and logjams, and always he sharply noted where he placed his feet. Once, coming around a bend, he shied quickly, like a startled horse, curved away from the place where he had been walking, and took several steps back along the trail. The creek, he knew, was frozen clear to the bottom— but he knew also that there were springs that bubbled out from the hillsides and ran along under the snow and on top of the ice of the creek. He knew that the coldest snaps never froze these springs, and he knew likewise their danger. They were traps. They hid pools of water under the snow that might be three inches deep, or three feet. Sometimes a skin of ice half an inch thick covered them, and in turn was covered by the snow. So when one broke through he kept on breaking through, sometimes wetting himself to the waist.

That was why he had shied in such panic. He had felt the softness under his feet and heard the crack of a snow-hidden ice-skin. And to get his feet wet in such a temperature meant trouble and danger. At the very least it meant delay, for he would be forced to stop and build a fire. Then he would have to bare his feet while he dried his socks and boots. He stood and studied the creek bed and its banks and decided that the flow of water seemed to come from the right. He reflected awhile, rubbing his nose and cheeks. Then he moved to the left, walking carefully

---

- reiterate (ree IT uh rayt) repeat tiresomely
- shy—draw back
- **reflect** (ri FLEKT) think

and testing each step. Once clear of the danger, he took a fresh chew of tobacco and swung along at his four-mile gait.

In the next two hours he came upon several similar traps. Usually the snow above the hidden pools had a sunken, solid appearance that advertised the danger. Once again, however, he had a close call, and another time, suspecting danger, he made the dog go on in front. The dog did not want to go. It hung back until the man shoved it forward, and then it went quickly across the white, unbroken surface. Suddenly it broke through, floundered to one side, and got away to safety. It had wet its feet and legs, and almost immediately the water turned to ice. It made quick efforts to lick the ice off its legs, then dropped down in the snow and began to bite out the ice that had formed between the toes. This was a matter of instinct. To permit the ice to remain would mean sore feet. It did not know this. It just obeyed the mysterious orders that came from somewhere deep inside it. But the man knew, having made a judgment on the subject, and he removed the mitten from his right hand and helped tear out the ice pieces. He did not uncover his fingers more than a minute, and was astonished at the swift numbness that hit them. It certainly was cold. He pulled on the mitten hastily, and beat the hand savagely across his chest.

At twelve o'clock the day was at its brightest. Yet the sun was too far south on its winter journey to appear in the sky. The man walked under a clear sky at noon and cast no shadow. At half-past twelve, to the minute, he arrived at the fork of the creek. He was pleased at the speed he had made. If he kept it up, he would certainly be with the men by six. He unbuttoned his jacket and shirt and drew forth his lunch. The action took no more than a quarter of a minute, yet in that brief time the numbness laid hold of the exposed fingers. He did not put the mitten on right away, but instead struck the fingers a dozen sharp smashes against his leg. Then he sat down on a snow-covered log to eat. The sting that followed the striking of his fingers against his leg stopped so quickly that he was startled. He had had no chance to take a bite of biscuit. He struck the fingers again and returned them to the mitten, baring the other hand for the purpose of eating. He tried to take a mouthful, but the ice on his face prevented it. He had forgotten to build a fire and thaw out. He chuckled at his foolishness, and as he chuckled he noted the numbness creeping into the bare fingers. Also, he noted that the stinging which had first come to his toes when he sat down was already passing away. He wondered whether the toes were warm or numb. He moved them inside the boots and decided that they were numb.

He pulled the mitten on hurriedly and stood up. He was a bit frightened. He stamped up and down until the stinging returned into the feet. It certainly was cold, was his thought. That man from Sulphur Creek had spoken the truth when telling how cold it sometimes got in this country. And he had laughed at him at the time! That

---

• **gait** (GAYT) manner of walking or running

showed one must not be too sure of things. There was no mistake about it— it was cold. He walked up and down, stamping his feet and swinging his arms, until he felt the returning warmth. Then he got out matches and proceeded to make a fire. From the bushes where high water of the spring had left a supply of twigs, he got his firewood. Working carefully from a small beginning, he soon had a roaring fire. He thawed the ice from his face, and in the protection of the fire he ate his biscuits. For the moment the cold was defeated. The dog took satisfaction in the fire, too, stretching out close enough for warmth and far enough away to escape being burned.

When the man had finished, he filled his pipe and took his comfortable time over a smoke. Then he pulled on his mittens. He settled the ear-flaps of his cap about his ears, and took the creek trail up the left fork. The dog was disappointed. It didn't want to leave the fire. This man did not know cold. Possibly all the man's ancestors had known nothing of cold, of real cold, of cold one hundred and seven degrees below the freezing point. But the dog knew. All its ancestors had known, and the knowledge had come down to it. It knew that it was not good to walk abroad in such fearful cold. This was the time to lie snug in a hole in the snow and wait for better weather. There was no great intimacy between the dog and the man. The one was the slave of the other. The only caresses it ever received were the caresses of the whip. So the dog made no effort to communicate its apprehension to the man. It was not concerned about the safety of the man. It was for its own sake that it wanted back toward the fire. But the man whistled, and spoke to it with the sound of a whip, and the dog swung in at the man's heel and followed after.

The man took a chew of tobacco and proceeded to start a new amber beard. Also, his moist breath quickly covered with white his mustache and eyebrows. There did not seem to be so many dangerous springs on the left fork of the Henderson, and for half an hour the man saw no signs of any. And then it happened. At a place where there were no signs, where the snow was soft and unbroken, the man broke through. It was not deep. He wet himself halfway to the knees before he floundered out.

He was angry, and cursed his luck aloud. He had hoped to get into camp with the men at six o'clock. This would delay him an hour, for he would have to build a fire and dry out his socks and boots. This was imperative at that low temperature—he knew that much. He turned aside to the bank, which he climbed. On top, tangled in the bushes around the trunks of several small spruce trees, was some dry firewood. There were sticks and twigs, but also larger branches and fine, dry, last-year's grasses. He threw down several large pieces on top of the snow. This served for a foundation and prevented the young flame from drowning itself

---

- **intimacy** (IN tuh muh see) very close friendship, even love
- **imperative** (im PER uh tiv) really necessary; essential

in the snow it otherwise would melt. The flame he got by touching a match to a small piece of birch bark that he took from his pocket. This burned even more easily than paper. Placing it on the foundation, he fed the young flame with dry grass and with the tiniest dry twigs. He worked slowly and carefully, keenly aware of his danger. Gradually, as the flame grew stronger, he increased the size of the twigs with which he fed it. He squatted in the snow, pulling the twigs out from the brush and feeding them directly to the flame. He knew there must be no failure. When it is seventy-five below zero, a man must not fail in his first attempt to build a fire—that is, if his feet are wet. If his feet are dry, and he fails, things are different. He can run along the trail for half a mile and regain his circulation. But the circulation of wet and freezing feet cannot be regained by running when it is seventy-five below. No matter how fast he runs, the wet feet will freeze harder and harder.

All this the man knew. The old-timer on Sulphur Creek had told him about it in the fall, and now he was glad for the advice. Already all feeling had gone out of his feet. To build the fire he had been forced to remove his mittens, and the fingers had quickly gone numb. His walking speed of four miles an hour had kept his heart pumping blood to the surface of his body and to all the extremities. But the instant he stopped, the action of the pump slowed down.

The cold of space had settled down on the unprotected tip of the planet. And he, being on that unprotected tip, received the full force of the blow. The blood of his body drew back before it. The blood was alive, like the dog, and like the dog it wanted to hide away and cover itself up from the fearful cold. So long as he walked four miles an hour, he pumped that blood to the surface. But now it ebbed away and sank down into the recesses of his body. The extremities were the first to feel its absence. His wet feet froze faster, and his bare fingers numbed faster, though they had not yet begun to freeze. Nose and cheeks were already freezing, while the skin of all his body chilled as it lost its blood.

- extremities (ik STREM i teez) hands and feet; parts farthest away
- ebb (EB) flow back or away
- recess (ri SES) interior place

CHECKPOINT

Stop here and consider what you have read so far.

1. We learn from the story that in the Far North (a) it sometimes gets too cold to snow. (b) the winter sun never rises into the sky. (c) wild dogs sometimes attack people.
2. We also learn that in very cold weather (a) spittle pops before it hits the ground. (b) tobacco will not burn. (c) footsteps sound unusually loud.
3. The man's destination is (a) his farm and family. (b) the town of Dawson. (c) a camp where his friends are waiting.
4. The temperature at the time of the story is (a) 75°F below freezing. (b) 75°F below zero. (c) 107°F below zero.
5. The man's chief worry as he walks along is (a) snow sliding down the bank. (b) hidden springs under the snow. (c) wild animals.
6. When the man stops to eat lunch, he has to (a) feed the dog as well. (b) thaw out the frozen food. (c) build a fire.
7. The man's worst piece of bad luck is (a) getting his feet wet. (b) losing his dog. (c) not being able to light his fire.
8. Of the following, the author seems to favor (a) the man's judgment. (b) the dog's instinct. (c) the man's imagination.
9. At this point in the story, what do you think will happen next? What might this lead to? How might the story end?

But he was safe. Toes and nose and cheeks would be only touched by the frost, for the fire was now beginning to burn with strength. He was feeding it with twigs the size of his finger. In another minute he would be able to feed it with branches the size of his wrist. Then he could remove his wet boots and socks. While they dried, he could keep his naked feet warm by the fire, rubbing them at first, of course, with snow. The fire was a success. He was safe. He remembered the advice of the old-timer on Sulphur Creek, and smiled. The old-timer had been very serious in laying down the law that no man must travel alone in the Klondike* after fifty below. Well, here he was. He had had the accident. He was alone, and he had saved himself. Those old-timers were rather too fearful, some of them, he thought. All a man had to do was to keep his head, and he was all right. Any man who was a man could travel alone. But it was surprising, the speed with which his cheeks and nose were freezing. And he had not thought his fingers could go lifeless in so short a time. Lifeless they were, for he could hardly make them move together to grip a

---

*The Klondike (KLON dyk) is an area in northern Canada, next to Alaska.

twig, and they seemed far from his body and from him. When he touched a twig, he had to look and see whether or not he had hold of it. The wires were pretty well down between him and his finger-ends.

All of which counted for little. There was the fire, snapping and growing and promising life with every dancing flame. He started to untie his boots. They were coated with ice. The thick German socks were like sheaths of iron halfway to the knees. The boot laces were like rods of steel all twisted and knotted as by some conflagration. For a moment he tugged with his numb fingers. Then, realizing the folly of his effort, he drew his knife.

But before he could cut the strings, it happened. It was his own fault or, rather, his mistake. He should not have built the fire under the spruce tree. He should have built it in the open. But it had been easier to pull the twigs from the brush and drop them directly on the fire. The tree under which he had done this carried a lot of snow on its branches. No wind had blown for weeks, and each branch was fully loaded. Now he had a growing fire, and he had been moving about under the tree. The heat and motion were not much, so far as he was concerned, but they were enough to bring about the disaster. High up in the tree one branch dumped its load of snow. This fell on the boughs beneath, making them dump their snow. This continued, spreading out over the whole tree. It grew like an avalanche, and it descended without warning upon the man and the fire. The fire was blotted out! Where it had burned was a mantle of fresh and disordered snow.

The man was shocked. It was as though he had just heard his own sentence of death. For a moment he sat and stared at the spot where the fire had been. Then he grew very calm. Perhaps the old-timer on Sulphur Creek was right. If he had only had a companion he would have been in no danger now. The other person could have built the fire. Well, it was up to him to build the fire over again, and this second time there must be no failure. Even if he succeeded, he would most likely lose some toes. His feet must be badly frozen by now, and there would be some time before the second fire was ready.

Such were his thoughts, but he did not sit and think them. He was busy all the time they were passing through his mind. He made a new foundation for a fire, this time in the open, where no treacherous tree could blot it out. Next, he gathered dry grasses and tiny twigs. He could not bring his fingers together to pull them out, but he was able to gather them by the handful. In this way he got many rotten twigs and bits of green moss that he didn't want, but it was the best he could do. He worked methodically, even collecting an armful of the larger branches to be used later when the fire gathered strength.

- **sheath** (SHEETH) protective covering
- conflagration (kon fluh GRAY shun) huge fire
- mantle (MAN tul) something that covers
- methodically (muh THOD ik lee) orderly; systematically

And all the while the dog sat and watched him. There was a certain wishful look in its eyes, for it looked upon him to build a fire, and the fire was slow in coming.

When all was ready, the man reached in his pocket for a second piece of birch bark. He knew the bark was there. Though he could not feel it with his fingers, he could hear its crisp sound as he reached for it. Try as he would, he could not get hold of it. And all the time, in his mind, was the knowledge that each instant his feet were freezing. This thought might have put him in a panic, but he fought against it and kept calm. He pulled on his mittens with his teeth. He swung his arms back and forth, beating his hands with all his might against his sides. He did this sitting down, and he stood up to do it. All the while the dog sat in the snow, its tail curled around warmly over its feet, and its sharp wolf-ears pricked forward eagerly as it watched the man. And the man, as he beat his feet and waved his arms and hands, felt a great wave of envy. He knew that the dog was warm and safe in its natural covering.

After a time he was aware of the first far-away signals of feeling in his beaten fingers. The faint tingle grew stronger till it grew into a stinging ache that was excruciating, but the man greeted it with satisfaction. He stripped the mitten from his right hand and brought forth the birch bark. The bare fingers were quickly going numb again. Next he pulled out his bunch of matches. But the tremendous cold had already driven the life out of his fingers. In his effort to separate one match from the others, the whole bunch fell in the snow. He tried to pick it out of the snow, but failed. The dead fingers could neither touch nor grasp. He was very careful. He drove the thought of his freezing feet, and nose, and cheeks, out of his mind. He put his whole soul into getting the matches. He watched his hands, using the sense of vision in place of that of touch. When he saw his fingers on each side of the bunch, he closed them. That is, he tried to close them, for the wires were down, and the fingers did not obey. He pulled the mitten on the right hand, and beat it fiercely against his knee. Then, with both mittened hands, he scooped the bunch of matches, along with much snow, into his lap. Yet he was no better off.

After some trouble he managed to get the bunch between the heels of his mittened hands. In this way he carried it to his mouth. The ice snapped and broke when by a tremendous effort he opened his mouth. He drew the lower jaw in, and curled the upper lip out of the way. Then he scraped the bunch with his upper teeth in order to separate a match. He succeeded in getting one, which he dropped on his lap. He was no better off. He could not pick it up. Then he devised a way. He picked it up in his teeth and scratched it on his leg. Twenty times he scratched before he succeeded in lighting it. As it flamed he held it with his teeth to the birch bark. But the burning fumes went up

---

• excruciating (ik SKROO shee ay ting) very painful

his nostrils and into his lungs, causing him to cough spasmodically. The match fell into the snow and went out.

The old-timer on Sulphur Creek was right, he thought in the sad moment that followed. After fifty below, a man should travel with a partner. He beat his hands, but failed to regain any feeling. Suddenly he bared both hands, removing the mittens with his teeth. He caught the whole bunch of matches between the heels of his hands. His arm muscles were not frozen, and he could press the hand-heels tightly against the matches. Then he scratched the bunch along his leg. It roared into flame, seventy matches at once! There was no wind to blow them out. He kept his head to one side to escape the fumes and held the blazing bunch to the birch bark. As he so held it, he became aware of feeling in his hand. His flesh was burning. He could smell it. Deep down below the surface he could feel it. The feeling turned into pain that grew and grew. And still he endured it, holding the flame of the matches clumsily to the bark that would not light easily because his own burning hands were in the way.

At last, when he could endure no more, he jerked his hands apart. The blazing matches fell sizzling into the snow, but the birch bark was on fire. He began laying dry grasses and the tiniest twigs on the flame. He could not pick and choose, for he had to lift the fuel between the heels of his hands. Small pieces of rotten wood and green

moss clung to the twigs, and he bit these off as well as he could with his teeth. He cherished the flame carefully and awkwardly. It meant life to him. The lack of blood on the surface of his body now made him begin to shiver, and he grew more awkward. A large piece of green moss fell directly on the little fire. He tried to poke it out with his fingers, but his shivering body made him poke too far, and he disturbed the center of the little fire. The burning grasses and tiny twigs separated and scattered. He tried to poke them together again, but in spite of the effort, his shivering got away with him, and the twigs were hopelessly scattered. Each twig gave a puff of smoke and went out. The fire had failed. He had failed. As he looked apathetically about him, his eyes chanced on the dog. The animal was sitting across the ruins of the fire from him, in the snow, slightly lifting one front foot and then the other.

The sight of the dog put a wild idea into his head. He remembered the tale of the man, caught in a blizzard, who killed a steer and crawled inside the dead body, and so was saved. He would kill the dog now. He would bury his hands in the warm body until the numbness went out of them. Then he could build another fire. He spoke to the dog, calling it to him. But in his voice was a strange note of fear that frightened the animal, who had never known the man to speak in such a way before. Something was the matter. The dog felt the

- spasmodically (spaz MOD ik lee) in sudden bursts
- apathetically (ap uh THET ik lee) with little or no feeling

danger. It knew not what danger, but somewhere, somehow, in its brain there rose a distrust of the man. It flattened its ears down at the sound of the man's voice. It would not come to the man. He got on his hands and knees and crawled toward the dog. This unusual posture again made the dog suspicious, and the animal sidled away.

The man sat up in the snow for a moment and struggled for calmness. Then he pulled on his mittens, by using his teeth, and got to his feet. He glanced down, in order to make sure that he was really standing up, for the absence of feeling in his feet left him separated from the earth. His standing up in itself started to drive the webs of suspicion from the dog's mind. And when he spoke an order with the sound of a whip in his voice, the dog obeyed once again and came to him. As it came within reaching distance, the man lost his control. His arms flashed out to the dog. Then he discovered that his hands

could not grasp, that there was neither bend nor feeling in the fingers. He had forgotten for the moment that they were frozen and that they were freezing more and more. All this happened quickly. But before the animal could get away, he had its body in his arms. He sat down in the snow, and in this way held the dog, while it snarled and whined and struggled.

But it was all he could do, hold its body in his arms and sit there. He realized that he could not kill the dog. There was no way to do it. With his helpless hands he could neither draw nor hold his knife. Nor could he choke the animal. He let it go, and it plunged wildly away, with tail between legs, and still snarling. It stopped forty feet

• sidle (SYD ul) move sideways; edge along slyly

away and looked at him curiously, with ears sharply forward. The man looked down at his hands in order to locate them, and found them hanging on the ends of his arms. It struck him as curious that one should have to use his eyes in order to find out where his hands were. He began swinging his arms back and forth, beating the mittened hands against his sides. He did this for five minutes, very hard. His heart pumped enough blood up to the surface to put a stop to his shivering. But no feeling returned to the hands. They hung like weights on the ends of his arms.

A certain dull fear of death came to him now. This fear quickly became poignant as he realized that it was no longer a matter of just freezing his fingers and toes. It was no longer a matter of losing his hands and feet. No, it was a matter of life and death, with the chances against him. This threw him into a panic, and he turned and ran up the creek bed along the old, dim trail. The dog joined in behind and kept up with him. He ran blindly, without any real purpose in mind, filled with a fear such as he had never known in his life. Slowly, as he plowed and floundered through the snow, he began to see things again. The banks of the creek. The old logjams. The sky. The running made him feel better. He did not shiver. Maybe, if he ran on, his feet would thaw out. Anyway, if he ran far enough, he would reach camp and the men. Without doubt he would lose some fingers and toes and some of his face.

But the men would take care of him, and save the rest of him when he got there. And at the same time there was another thought in his mind that said he would never get to the camp. It was too many miles away. The freezing had too great a start on him, and he would soon be stiff and dead. This second thought he tried to keep in the background. Sometimes it pushed itself forward and demanded to be heard, but he forced it back and tried to think of other things.

It struck him as curious that he could run at all. His feet were so frozen that he could not feel them when they struck the earth and took the weight of his body. He seemed to himself to glide along above the surface. He seemed to have no connection with the earth. Somewhere he had once seen a winged Mercury,* and he wondered if Mercury felt as he felt when skimming over the earth.

His idea of running until he reached camp had one thing wrong with it: he lacked the endurance. Several times he stumbled, and finally he fell. When he tried to rise, he failed. He must sit and rest, he decided. The next time he would try only to walk and keep on going. As he sat and regained his breath, he noted that he was feeling quite warm and comfortable. He was not shivering, and it even seemed that a warm glow had come to his chest. And yet, when he touched his nose or cheeks, there was no feeling. Running would not thaw them out. Nor would it thaw out his hands and feet. Then the

---

● poignant (POIN yunt) sharp; keenly felt
*Mercury (MUR kyu ree) was the ancient Roman god who served as messenger of the gods and is often pictured with wings on his heels.

thought came to him that the frozen portions of his body must be growing larger. He tried to keep this thought down, to forget it, to think of something else. He was aware of the panicky feeling that it caused, and he was afraid of the panic. But the thought came again, and kept on coming, until he had a vision of his body totally frozen. This was too much. He made another wild run along the trail. Once he slowed down to a walk, but the thought of the freezing made him run again. And all the time the dog ran with him, at his heels. When he fell down a second time, it curled its tail over its front feet and sat facing him, curiously eager. The warmth and safety of the animal angered him, and he cursed it till it flattened down its ears appeasingly. This time the shivering came more quickly upon the man. He was losing in his battle with the frost. It was creeping into his body from all sides. The thought of it drove him on, but he ran no more than a hundred feet, when he staggered and fell. It was his last panic. When he had recovered his breath and control, he sat up and thought about meeting death with dignity. However, the idea did not come to him in such terms. His idea of it was that he had been making a fool of himself. He had been running around like a chicken with its head cut off—such was the simile that occurred to him. Well, he was bound to freeze anyway, and he might as well take it with dignity. With this new-found peace of mind came the first drowsiness. A good

idea, he thought, to sleep off to death. It was like taking an anesthetic. Freezing was not so bad as people thought. There were lots worse ways to die.

He pictured the men finding his body next day. Suddenly he found himself with them, coming along the trail and looking for himself. And, still with them, he came around a turn in the trail and found himself lying in the snow. He did not belong with himself anymore, for even then he was out of himself, standing with the men and looking at himself in the snow. It certainly was cold, was his thought. When he got back to the States he could tell the folks what real cold was. He drifted on from this to a vision of the old-timer on Sulphur Creek. He could see him quite clearly, warm and comfortable, and smoking a pipe.

"You were right, old hoss. You were right," the man mumbled to the old-timer of Sulphur Creek.

Then the man drowsed off into what seemed to him the most comfortable and satisfying sleep he had ever known. The dog sat facing him and waiting. The brief day drew to a close in a long, slow twilight. There were no signs of a fire to be made, and besides, never in the dog's experience had it known a man to sit like that in the snow and make no fire. As the twilight drew on, its need for the fire mastered it. It lifted its feet up and down. It whined softly, then flattened its ears down, expecting to be scolded by the man. But the man remained silent. Later, the dog

---

- appeasingly (uh PEEZ ing ly) in a manner to please or obey
- anesthetic (an is THET ik) substance that lessens pain

whined loudly. And still later it crept close to the man and caught the scent of death. This made the animal bristle and back away. A little longer it delayed, howling under the stars that leaped and danced and shone brightly in the cold sky. Then it turned and trotted up the trail in the direction of the camp it knew, where were the other men, men with food and fire.

ALL THINGS CONSIDERED

1. At the beginning of the story, the man feels (a) terrified by the forces of nature. (b) doubtful about his chances. (c) quite sure of himself.
2. The man builds his first fire (a) when he stops to eat. (b) when the dog gets wet. (c) when he wets his feet.
3. During the whole story, the man starts to build (a) one fire. (b) two fires. (c) three fires.
4. As the man slips off toward death, he (a) watches the dog leave. (b) feels strangely peaceful. (c) dreams of his wife and children.
5. The author seems to have the *least* admiration for the (a) dog. (b) old-timer on Sulphur Creek. (c) man.

THINKING IT THROUGH

1. (a) At what point in the story did you think the man would die? (b) What gave you this idea? (c) Did you realize the man would die before or after he reached the same conclusion?
2. What is the *irony* in the sentence, "Those old-timers were rather too fearful, some of them, he thought"?
3. Consider the *tone* of the story. (a) What seems to be London's attitude toward the man? Is he entirely sympathetic, somewhat sympathetic, or not sympathetic at all? (b) What do you think accounts for London's attitude?
4. Jack London is good at creating memorable *images*. One visual image is that of the snow falling from the spruce tree, first from a single branch high up, then spreading down and around the tree. (a) What is another visual image that remains in your mind? (b) What third image, one that appeals to another sense, do you recall? (c) Taken together, what *mood* do these three images suggest?
5. Locate at least five specific details of *setting* from the story. In what way does setting add to the general mood that is conveyed by the story?

• **bristle** (BRIS ul) raise hair in alarm

Literary Skills: Review

If you wish to review the meaning of any term in *italics* in this exercise, refer to the Glossary of Terms.

1. As the story nears its end, most readers feel that the man will die. They feel this way because of London's skillful use of *foreshadowing*. Give at least three examples.
2. Although Jack London writes simply, he does use an occasional figure of speech. Which of the following sentences, (a) or (b), contains a *simile*? Which contains a *metaphor*?

Explain the metaphor.

a. The wires were pretty well down between him and his finger-ends.
b. The boot laces were like rods of steel all twisted and knotted as by some conflagration.

3. Logically, why couldn't "To Build a Fire" have been written in the *first person*?
4. Logically, why was Jack London forced to make only little use of one of the four main methods of *characterization*?

Composition

1. Like some other stories, "To Build a Fire" is full of factual information. Report at least two interesting facts you learned from the story.
2. Because "To Build a Fire" is quite long, you can write about it in the same way you would write a book report. Write a report at least one page long. Remember the following guidelines and apply them to your paper on London's story:
   (a) *Do* comment on the *way* the author writes. For instance, does he use interesting figurative language? Does he establish a definite mood? Does he construct a clear setting? Explain and give examples.
   (b) *Do* explain how the author changed your way of thinking, or at least tell what he made you think about.
   (c) *Do* explain what the author taught you, especially about people.
   (d) *Do* tell what kind of readers would probably like the story, and what kind would not.

   (a) *Don't* begin with a sentence that reads this way: I liked "To Build a Fire" because it was interesting. The second part of such a sentence really tells the reader nothing. If you found something "interesting," of course you "liked" it!
   (b) *Don't* use words like "interesting" or "boring" without explaining the reasons for your opinions.
   (c) *Don't* devote more than half your report to telling what happened. Of course you have to write about the characters and their problems, but remember that a good report is much more than a summary.

374

VOCABULARY AND SKILL REVIEW

Before completing the exercises that follow, you may wish to review the **bold-faced** words on pages 348 to 373.

I. On a separate sheet of paper, mark each item *true* or *false*. If it is false, explain what is wrong with the sentence.
1. You probably would see a *valise* in a busy bus station.
2. Some churches have a *gait* in their steeple.
3. Some churches have a *belfry* in their steeple.
4. A sharp knife is often slipped into a *sheath.*
5. A dog often will *bristle* when attacked by another.
6. Because of the *intimacy* sometimes shared with pets, children may view their animals as close friends.
7. Some people like to just sit and *meditate* for a while when they get home from work.
8. Gorgeous sunsets are brilliant, colorful, and *somber.*
9. Playfulness is not a *characteristic* of most puppies and kittens.
10. *Racism* can be the result of *ancestral* likes and dislikes.

II. On a separate sheet of paper, write the *italicized* word that best fills the blank in each sentence.

slander	*borne*	*bleating*	*infest*	*hairline*
illiterate	*peril*	*heartfelt*	*reflect*	*immortality*

1. Sometimes only a _____ of difference separates an "A" from a "B" on a report card.
2. _____ people would not be doing this exercise.
3. Seeds often are _____ by the wind to other places.
4. A newspaper that knowingly prints _____ may have to pay a fine.
5. Sometimes the everlasting beauty in nature causes people to wish for _____ .
6. Small children, like sheep, are sometimes said to be _____ .
7. Many of Longfellow's poems are _____ messages of inspiration.
8. Statistics assure us there is less _____ in plane travel than in travel by car.
9. To _____ on something is to think about it.
10. Mice and roaches often _____ old apartment buildings.

III. Demonstrate your command of literary analysis and termi-
nology by answering five questions on the following poem.

FUTILITY

by Mary S. Hawling

I try to capture rhythm with
The makeshift words that limit me:
The wind has more success than I
By simply bending down a tree.

I seek for color, and must be
Content with some cold, distant name:
Yet swiftly, as the night walks near,
The sky is surging bronze and flame.

I struggle for a single line
To measure an emotion by:
A wild bird, effortless, takes wing
And writes a poem across the sky.

1. In a sentence of your own, what is the *theme* of the poem?
2. Upon what main *conflict* is the poem based?
3. What is an example of *personification* in the poem?
4. What *metaphor* can you find that is not also an example of *personification?*
5. Think about the *mood* of the poem and the degree to which you share it. (a) What do you have in common with the speaker? (b) In what way (if any) do you feel different from the speaker?

- futility (fyoo TIL i tee) lack of success; uselessness
- makeshift (MAYK shift) substitute; temporary

IV. Benjamin Franklin (1706–1790) became a famous American for several reasons. One reason is that he annually wrote and published *Poor Richard's Almanac* over a period of 25 years. *Poor Richard* was among the most popular of early American almanacs.

Here are ten of Poor Richard's sayings. (Most of them did not originate with Franklin; he took them from other sources and often polished them up in witty "Poor Richard" language.) (a) Tell whether each of them contains any figurative language—and if so, try to identify the figurative language as *metaphor, simile, personification,* or *hyperbole.* There is room for some difference of opinion. (b) Explain in your own words the underlying meaning of each saying.

Example:

Tart words make no friends; a spoonful of honey will catch more flies than a gallon of vinegar.

(a) The saying contains figurative language. The first part illustrates personification, and perhaps hyperbole. The second part is a metaphor. (b) The saying means that sweet words are more effective than bitter words.

1. The things which hurt, instruct.
2. Early to bed and early to rise, makes a man healthy, wealthy, and wise.
3. The sleeping fox catches no poultry.
4. Beware of little expenses; a small leak will sink a great ship.
5. Fish and visitors stink after three days.
6. A country man between two lawyers, is like a fish between two cats.
7. The worst wheel of the cart makes the most noise.
8. Be slow in choosing a friend, slower in changing.
9. At the *working* man's house, Hunger looks in, but dares not enter.
10. Sally laughs at everything you say. Why? Because she has fine teeth.

Alice Walker (Born 1944)

Alice Walker, recent winner of both the Pulitzer Prize and the National Book Award, became a writer at age eight. Her story is an interesting one.

One day in 1952, an eight-year-old Georgia girl named Alice was shot accidentally in the right eye with a BB gun by one of her brothers. The family had little money, and the best medical attention was not available. The eye went blind. The pain ceased after a few days, but the scar tissue remained. "For a long time I thought I was ugly and disfigured," the author states. "This made me shy and timid, and I often reacted to insults that were not intended. . . . I believe, though, that it was from this period . . . that I really began to see people and things."

Ironically, the loss of an eye enabled the girl to "see." She spent a lot of time alone, outside the house, away from family and friends. Soon she found herself writing down thoughts and impressions in a notebook, and she discovered that the writing made her feel better. "I think writing really helps you heal yourself," she says now. "I think if you write long enough you will be a healthy person." She also started to read a great deal. "Books became my world because the world I was in was very hard."

Writing and reading helped erase the mental scars, but the scarred eye remained until Alice was 14, when an operation removed the disfigurement. Other changes followed fast. By graduation time she was not only class valedictorian but also voted "Most Popular." Her partial blindness qualified her for a special scholarship for the handicapped to Spelman College. She later transferred to Sarah Lawrence College, graduating in 1965.

Walker continued to write in notebooks at Sarah Lawrence and soon found herself writing poetry at a furious pace. She showed the poems to one of her teachers, the poet Muriel Rukeyser. With Rukeyser's help and encouragement, the poems became Alice Walker's first book, *Once* (1968).

Author of poems, novels, short stories, and works of nonfiction, Alice Walker is recognized today as one of America's leading writers. Of general interest are a book of essays, *In Search of Our Mothers' Gardens,* and a biography of her "spirit helper," *Langston Hughes: American Poet.*

In what two ways did loss of sight in one eye prove not to be a "handicap" for Walker?

EVERYDAY USE
for your grandmama

by Alice Walker

▶ This story is a sensitive look at how people view their heritage—and how they might apply that heritage to everyday life. The narrator is a proud woman whose two daughters, Maggie and Dee, see their shared heritage in entirely different ways.

I will wait for her in the yard that Maggie and I made so clean and wavy yesterday afternoon. A yard like this is more comfortable than most people know. It is not just a yard. It is like an extended living room. When the hard clay is swept clean as a floor and the fine sand around the edges lined with tiny, irregular grooves, anyone can come and sit and look up into the elm tree and wait for the breezes that never come inside the house.

Maggie will be nervous until after her sister goes: She will stand hopelessly in corners, homely and ashamed of the burn scars down her arms and legs, eying her sister with a mixture of envy and awe. She thinks her sister has held life always in the palm of one hand, that "no" is a word the world never learned to say to her.

You've no doubt seen those TV shows where the child who has "made it" is confronted, as a surprise, by her own mother and father, tottering in weakly from backstage. (A pleasant surprise, of course: What would they do if parent and child came on the show only to curse out and insult each other?) On TV mother and child embrace and smile into each other's faces. Sometimes the mother and father weep, the child wraps them in her arms and leans across the table to tell how she would not have made it without their help. I have seen these programs.

Sometimes I dream a dream in which Dee and I are suddenly brought together on a TV program of this sort. Out of a dark and soft-seated limousine I am ushered into a bright room filled with many people. There I meet a smiling, gray, sporty man like Johnny Carson who shakes my hand and tells me what a fine girl I have. Then we are on the stage and Dee is embracing me

---

- awe (AW) wonderment; admiration
- confronted (kun FRUNT id) set face to face

with tears in her eyes. She pins on my dress a large orchid, even though she has told me once that she thinks orchids are tacky flowers.

In real life I am a large, big-boned woman with rough, man-working hands. In the winter I wear flannel nightgowns to bed and overalls during the day. I can kill and clean a hog as mercilessly as a man. My fat keeps me hot in zero weather. I can work outside all day, breaking ice to get water for washing; I can eat pork liver cooked over the open fire minutes after it comes steaming from the hog. One winter I knocked a bull calf straight in the brain between the eyes with a sledge hammer and had the meat hung up to chill before nightfall. But of course all this does not show on television. I am the way my daughter would want me to be: a hundred pounds lighter, my skin like an uncooked barley pancake. My hair glistens in the hot bright lights. Johnny Carson has much to do to keep up with my quick and witty tongue.

But that is a mistake. I know even before I wake up. Who ever knew a Johnson with a quick tongue? Who can even imagine me looking a strange white man in the eye? It seems to me I have talked to them always with one foot raised in flight, with my head turned in whichever way is farthest from them. Dee, though. She would always look anyone in the eye. Hesitation was no part of her nature.

"How do I look, Mama?" Maggie says, showing just enough of her thin body enveloped in pink skirt and red blouse for me to know she's there, almost hidden by the door.

"Come out into the yard," I say.

Have you ever seen a lame animal, perhaps a dog run over by some careless person rich enough to own a car, sidle up to someone who is ignorant enough to be kind to him? That is the way my Maggie walks. She has been like this, chin on chest, eyes on ground, feet in shuffle, ever since the fire that burned the other house to the ground.

Dee is lighter than Maggie, with nicer hair and a fuller figure. She's a woman now, though sometimes I forget. How long ago was it that the other house burned? Ten, twelve years? Sometimes I can still hear the flames and feel Maggie's arms sticking to me, her hair smoking and her dress falling off her in little black papery flakes. Her eyes seemed stretched open, blazed open by the flames reflected in them. And Dee. I see her standing off under the sweet gum tree she used to dig gum out of; a look of concentration on her face as she watched the last dingy gray board of the house fall in toward the red-hot brick chimney. Why don't you do a dance around the ashes? I'd wanted to ask her. She had hated the house that much.

I used to think she hated Maggie, too. But that was before we raised the money, the church and me, to send her to Augusta to school. She used to read to us without pity; forcing words, lies, other folks' habits, whole lives upon us

---

- tacky (TAK ee) too showy; not fashionable
- sidle (SYD ul) move sideways; edge along slyly

two, sitting trapped and ignorant underneath her voice. She washed us in a river of make-believe, burned us with a lot of knowledge we didn't necessarily need to know. Pressed us to her with the serious way she read, to shove us away at just the moment, like dimwits, we seemed about to understand.

Dee wanted nice things. A yellow organdy dress to wear to her graduation from high school; black pumps to match a green suit she'd made from an old suit somebody gave me. She was determined to stare down any disaster in her efforts. Her eyelids would not flicker for minutes at a time. Often I fought off the temptation to shake her. At sixteen she had a style of her own: and knew what style was.

I never had an education myself. After second grade the school was closed down. Don't ask me why: In 1927 colored asked fewer questions than they do now. Sometimes Maggie reads to me. She stumbles along good-naturedly but can't see well. She knows she is not bright. Like good looks and money, quickness passed her by. She will marry John Thomas (who has mossy teeth in an earnest face) and then I'll be free to sit here and I guess just sing church songs to myself. Although I never was a good singer. Never could carry a tune. I was always better at a man's job. I used to love to milk till I was hooked in the side in '49.

Cows are soothing and slow and don't bother you, unless you try to milk them the wrong way.

I have deliberately turned my back on the house. It is three rooms, just like the one that burned, except the roof is tin; they don't make shingle roofs anymore. There are no real windows, just some holes cut in the sides, like the portholes in a ship, but not round and not square, with rawhide holding the shutters up on the outside. This house is in a pasture, too, like the other one. No doubt when Dee sees it she will want to tear it down. She wrote me once that no matter where we "choose" to live, she will manage to come see us. But she will never bring her friends. Maggie and I thought about this and Maggie asked me, "Mama, when did Dee ever *have* any friends?"

She had a few. Furtive boys in pink shirts hanging about on washday after school. Nervous girls who never laughed. Impressed with her they worshiped the well-turned phrase, the cute shape, the scalding humor that erupted like bubbles in lye. She read to them.

When she was courting Jimmy T she didn't have much time to pay to us, but turned all her faultfinding power on him. He *flew* to marry a cheap city girl from a family of ignorant flashy people. She hardly had time to recompose herself.

When she comes I will meet—but there they are!

- organdy (OR gun dee) kind of thin, crisp cotton cloth
- pumps (PUMPS) kind of low-cut shoes for women
- furtive (FUR tiv) sly; shifty
- recompose (re kum POHZ) pull oneself together; become calm again

Maggie attempts to make a dash for the house, in her shuffling way, but I stay her with my hand. "Come back here," I say. And she stops and tries to dig a well in the sand with her toe.

It is hard to see them clearly through the strong sun. But even the first glimpse of leg out of the car tells me it is Dee. Her feet were always neat-looking, as if God himself had shaped them with a certain style. From the other side of the car comes a short, stocky man. Hair is all over his head a foot long and hanging from his chin like a kinky mule tail. I hear Maggie suck in her breath. "Uhnnnh," is what it sounds like. Like when you see the wriggling end of a snake just in front of your foot on the road. "Uhnnnh."

Dee next. A dress down to the ground, in this hot weather. A dress so loud it hurts my eyes. There are yellows and oranges enough to throw back the light of the sun. I feel my whole face warming from the heat waves it throws out. Earrings gold, too, and hanging down to her shoulders. Brace-

lets dangling and making noises when she moves her arm up to shake the folds of the dress out of her armpits. The dress is loose and flows, and as she walks closer, I like it. I hear Maggie go "Uhnnnh" again. It is her sister's hair. It stands straight up like the wool on a sheep. It is black as night and around the edges are two long pigtails that rope about like small lizards disappearing behind her ears.

"Wa-su-zo-Tean-o!" she says, coming on in that gliding way the dress makes her move. The short stocky fellow with the hair to his navel is all grinning and he follows up with "Asalamalakim, my mother and sister!" He moves to hug Maggie but she falls back, right up against the back of my chair. I feel her trembling there and when I look up I see the perspiration falling off her chin.

"Don't get up," says Dee. Since I am stout it takes something of a push. You can see me trying to move a second or two before I make it. She turns, showing white heels through her sandals, and goes back to the car. Out she peeks next with a Polaroid. She stoops down quickly and lines up picture after picture of me sitting there in front of the house with Maggie cowering behind me. She never takes a shot without making sure the house is included. When a cow comes nibbling around the edge of the yard she snaps it and me and Maggie *and* the house. Then she puts the Polaroid in the back seat of the car, and comes up and kisses me on the forehead.

Meanwhile Asalamalakim is going through motions with Maggie's hand. Maggie's hand is as limp as a fish, and probably as cold, despite the sweat, and she keeps trying to pull it back. It looks like Asalamalakim wants to shake hands but wants to do it fancy. Or maybe he don't know how people shake hands. Anyhow, he soon gives up on Maggie.

"Well," I say. "Dee."

"No, Mama," she says. "Not 'Dee,' Wangero Leewanika Kemanjo!"

"What happened to 'Dee'?" I wanted to know.

"She's dead," Wangero said. "I couldn't bear it any longer, being named after the people who oppress me."

"You know as well as me you was named after your aunt Dicie," I said. Dicie is my sister. She named Dee. We called her "Big Dee" after Dee was born.

"But who was *she* named after?" asked Wangero.

"I guess after Grandma Dee," I said.

"And who was she named after?" asked Wangero.

"Her mother," I said, and saw Wangero was getting tired. "That's about as far back as I can trace it," I said. Though, in fact, I probably could have carried it back beyond the Civil War through the branches.

"Well," said Asalamalakim, "there you are."

"Uhnnnh," I heard Maggie say.

"There I was not," I said, "before 'Dicie' cropped up in our family, so why should I try to trace it that far back?"

He just stood there grinning, looking down on me like somebody inspecting a Model A car. Every once in a while he and Wangero sent eye signals over my head.

"How do you pronounce this name?" I asked.

"You don't have to call me by it if you don't want to," said Wangero.

"Why shouldn't I?" I asked. "If that's what you want us to call you, we'll call you."

"I know it might sound awkward at first," said Wangero.

"I'll get used to it," I said. "Ream it out again."

Well, soon we got the name out of the way. Asalamalakim had a name twice as long and three times as hard. After I tripped over it two or three

---

• cowering (KOU ur ing) crouching in fear
• ream (REEM) enlarge; open up (here used figuratively)

times he told me to just call him Hakim-a-barber. I wanted to ask him was he a barber, but I didn't really think he was, so I didn't ask.

"You must belong to those beef-cattle peoples down the road," I said. They said "Asalamalakim" when they met you, too, but they didn't shake hands. Always too busy: feeding the cattle, fixing the fences, putting up salt-lick shelters, throwing down hay. When the white folks poisoned some of the herd the men stayed up all night with rifles in their hands. I walked a mile and a half just to see the sight.

Hakim-a-barber said, "I accept some of their doctrines, but farming and raising cattle is not my style." (They didn't tell me, and I didn't ask, whether Wangero (Dee) had really gone and married him.)

We sat down to eat and right away he said he didn't eat collards and pork was unclean. Wangero, though, went on through the chitlins and corn bread, the greens and everything else. She talked a blue streak over the sweet potatoes. Everything delighted her. Even the fact that we still used the benches her daddy made for the table when we couldn't afford to buy chairs.

"Oh, Mama!" she cried. Then turned to Hakim-a-barber. "I never knew how lovely these benches are. You can feel the rump prints," she said, running her hands underneath her and along the bench. Then she gave a sigh and her hand closed over Grandma Dee's butter dish. "That's it!" she said. "I knew there was something I wanted to ask you if I could have." She jumped up from the table and went over in the corner where the churn stood, the milk in it clabber by now. She looked at the churn and looked at it.

"This churn top is what I need," she said. "Didn't Uncle Buddy whittle it out of a tree you all used to have?"

"Yes," I said.

"Uh huh," she said happily. "And I want the dasher, too."

"Uncle Buddy whittle that, too?" asked the barber.

Dee (Wangero) looked up at me.

"Aunt Dee's first husband whittled the dash," said Maggie so low you almost couldn't hear her. "His name was Henry, but they called him Stash."

"Maggie's brain is like an elephant's," Wangero said, laughing. "I can use the churn top as a centerpiece for the alcove table," she said, sliding a plate over the churn, "and I'll think of something artistic to do with the dasher."

When she finished wrapping the dasher the handle stuck out. I took it for a moment in my hands. You didn't even have to look close to see where hands pushing the dasher up and down to make butter had left a kind of sink in the wood. In fact, there were a lot of

---

- doctrine (DOK trin) belief; theory
- collards (KOL urdz) kind of green vegetable
- chitlins (CHIT lins) hog intestines used as food
- clabber (KLAB ur) sour, thick milk
- dasher (DASH ur) plunger with paddles for stirring
- alcove (AL kohv) opening off a room

small sinks; you could see where thumbs and fingers had sunk into the wood. It was beautiful light yellow wood, from a tree that grew in the yard where Big Dee and Stash had lived.

After dinner Dee (Wangero) went to the trunk at the foot of my bed and started rifling through it. Maggie hung back in the kitchen over the dishpan. Out came Wangero with two quilts. They had been pieced by Grandma Dee and then Big Dee and me had hung them on the quilt frames on the front porch and quilted them. One was in the Lone Star pattern. The other was Walk Around the Mountain. In both of them were scraps of dresses Grandma Dee had worn fifty and more years ago. Bits and pieces of Grandpa Jarrell's Paisley shirts. And one teeny faded blue piece, about the size of a penny matchbox, that was from Great Grandpa Ezra's uniform that he wore in the Civil War.

"Mama," Wangero said sweet as a bird. "Can I have these old quilts?"

I heard something fall in the kitchen, and a minute later the kitchen door slammed.

"Why don't you take one or two of the others?" I asked. "These old things was just done by me and Big Dee from some tops your grandma pieced before she died."

"No," said Wangero. "I don't want those. They are stitched around the borders by machine."

"That'll make them last better," I said.

"That's not the point," said Wangero. "These are all pieces of dresses Grandma used to wear. She did all this stitching by hand. Imagine!" She held the quilts securely in her arms, stroking them.

"Some of the pieces, like those lavender ones, come from old clothes her mother handed down to her," I said, moving up to touch the quilts. Dee (Wangero) moved back just enough so that I couldn't reach the quilts. They already belonged to her.

"Imagine!" she breathed again, clutching them closely to her bosom.

"The truth is," I said, "I promised to give them quilts to Maggie, for when she marries John Thomas."

She gasped like a bee had stung her.

"Maggie can't appreciate these quilts!" she said. "She'd probably be backward enough to put them to everyday use."

"I reckon she would," I said. "God knows I been saving 'em for long enough with nobody using 'em. I hope she will!" I didn't want to bring up how I had offered Dee (Wangero) a quilt when she went away to college. Then she had told me they were old-fashioned, out of style.

"But they're *priceless!*" she was saying now, furiously; for she has a temper. "Maggie would put them on the bed and in five years they'd be in rags. Less than that!"

"She can always make some more," I said. "Maggie knows how to quilt."

Dee (Wangero) looked at me with hatred. "You just will not understand. The point is these quilts, *these* quilts!"

"Well," I said, stumped. "What would *you* do with them?"

"Hang them," she said. As if that

• rifling (RYF ling) searching; going through hurriedly

385

was the only thing you *could* do with quilts.

Maggie by now was standing in the door. I could almost hear the sound her feet made as they scraped over each other.

"She can have them, Mama," she said, like somebody used to never winning anything, or having anything reserved for her. "I can 'member Grandma Dee without the quilts."

I looked at her hard. She had filled her bottom lip with checkerberry snuff and it gave her face a kind of dopey, hangdog look. It was Grandma Dee and Big Dee who taught her how to quilt herself. She stood there with her scarred hands hidden in the folds of her skirt. She looked at her sister with something like fear but she wasn't mad at her. This was Maggie's portion. This was the way she knew God to work.

When I looked at her like that something hit me in the top of my head and ran down to the soles of my feet. Just like when I'm in church and the spirit of God touches me and I get happy and shout. I did something I never had done before: hugged Maggie to me, then dragged her on into the room, snatched the quilts out of Miss Wangero's hands and dumped them into Maggie's lap. Maggie just sat there on my bed with her mouth open.

"Take one or two of the others," I said to Dee.

But she turned without a word and went out to Hakim-a-barber.

"You just don't understand," she said, as Maggie and I came out to the car.

"What don't I understand?" I wanted to know.

"Your heritage," she said. And then she turned to Maggie, kissed her, and said, "You ought to try to make something of yourself, too, Maggie. It's really a new day for us. But from the way you and Mama still live you'd never know it."

She put on some sunglasses that hid everything above the tip of her nose and her chin.

Maggie smiled; maybe at the sunglasses. But a real smile, not scared. After we watched the car dust settle I asked Maggie to bring me a dip of snuff. And then the two of us sat there just enjoying, until it was time to go in the house and go to bed.

• checkerberry (CHEK ur BER ee) kind of small red berry (wintergreen)

ALL THINGS CONSIDERED _____

1. Although the narrator "never had an education," she (a) has read a great deal. (b) is a sensitive and imaginative person. (c) has managed to educate both daughters well.

2. Dee is characterized as (a) bright and bold, but not a very likable person. (b) sympathetic and tender where her family is concerned. (c) the daughter who truly understands the "spirit" of the quilts.

3. Dee has changed her name (a) because she has recently married. (b) to avoid confusion with her aunt and grandmother. (c) to erase the heritage of slavery.

4. The narrator's action at the end indicates that she (a) believes Dee has money enough to buy her own quilts. (b) believes Maggie appreciated the quilts in a better way than Dee. (c) wants to keep the quilts close to home.

5. At the end of the story, (a) both daughters really get what they want. (b) Dee is happier than Maggie. (c) Maggie is happier than Dee.

THINKING IT THROUGH _____

1. The author, Alice Walker, was once tremendously impressed by a quilt she saw in the Smithsonian Institution, a museum in Washington, D.C. It was a work of amazing beauty, sewed together by probably uneducated black women many years ago. In what way does this fact relate to the story?

2. (a) In what ways are Maggie and Dee different? (b) What is one admirable quality about each?

3. The quilts in "Everyday Use" stand out as *symbols*. (a) What do they symbolize? (b) What is the difference between the ways in which the two daughters see the symbols?

4. Why is the story called "Everyday Use," and why is it *"for your grandmama"*?

5. Look back at the dialogue on the last pages of the story. What three or four speeches seem to you the most meaningful? Why?

EPILOGUE

AMERICA THE BEAUTIFUL

by Katharine Lee Bates

▶ A few works of literature are so familiar that they commonly slide by without notice. "America the Beautiful," for instance, is itself a beautiful poem. Try to forget about the music in your head and think about the words.

O beautiful for spacious skies,
  For amber waves of grain,
For purple mountain majesties
  Above the fruited plain!
5   America! America!
  God shed His grace on thee
And crown thy good with brotherhood
  From sea to shining sea!

O beautiful for pilgrim feet,
10   Whose stern, impassioned stress
A thoroughfare for freedom beat
  Across the wilderness!
    America! America!
  God mend thine every flaw,
15 Confirm thy soul in self-control,
    Thy liberty in law!

- epilogue (EP uh log) part added to a literary work
- impassioned (im PASH und) determined; filled with passionate feeling
- thoroughfare (THUR oh fair) passage; way through

O beautiful for heroes proved
    In liberating strife,
Who more than self their country loved,
20   And mercy more than life!
        America! America!
        May God thy gold refine
Till all success be nobleness
And every gain divine!

25 O beautiful for patriot dream
    That sees beyond the years
Thine alabaster cities gleam
    Undimmed by human tears!
        America! America!
30   God shed His grace on thee
And crown thy good with brotherhood
    From sea to shining sea!

WAYS OF KNOWING

1. Notice the pattern of each stanza. The first four lines celebrate some part of our national experience. In your own words, what part of that experience is covered in each stanza?

2. The last four lines of each stanza express hope for the present and the future. What are some of these hopes?

3. Why is it correct to call "America the Beautiful" a *poem* as well as a *song*? Think of as many reasons as you can. Don't forget striking images. Don't forget figurative language, or lines that mean more than their words literally mean. Point out examples.

- strife (STRYF) violent quarreling; war
- alabaster (AL uh bas tur) kind of decorative white stone

UNIT REVIEW

I. Match the terms in Column A with their definitions in Column B.

A

1. imagery
2. tone
3. symbol
4. climax
5. theme
6. personification
7. foreshadowing
8. first-person point of view
9. irony of situation
10. resolution

B

a) things working out in unexpected ways

b) the part of the story that sometimes follows the climax

c) the most exciting part of a story, at or near the end

d) the meaning or message of a piece of literature

e) the attitude (usually inferred) of an author toward both subject matter and reader

f) clues deliberately planted by an author to enable the reader to predict what may or will happen

g) told by a narrator who is an *I/me* character in a story

h) giving human qualities to non-human subjects

i) something that stands for something else

j) language that appeals to the five senses

II. Below are ten terms that may describe your reactions to the selections in this unit. Choose five terms, connect each to a different selection, and then explain your feelings or thoughts in a few sentences. For example, you might choose the first term, "sympathy," for one of your five pieces, connect it to Alice Walker's "Everyday Use," and then go on to write about why you feel *sympathetic* toward both of the sisters in Walker's story.

1. sympathy
2. fright
3. admiration
4. anger
5. boredom
6. pity
7. confusion
8. curiosity
9. disappointment
10. bliss

SPEAKING UP

Students of literature sometimes share a common complaint. You read something that you find personally meaningful. It may move you emotionally or be fascinating food for thought. Then, instead of asking you about your personal reactions, questions in your textbook deal at some length with literary analysis, calling specifically on your command of terms: *simile, cliché, denotation, imagery, theme, tone,* and the like.

Naturally, the purpose of these questions is to help you understand and be able to discuss the selections in your book. But you should not leave any work of literature that you truly value without the chance to express your personal reactions.

Your task right now is to **prepare a short talk** (at least two or three minutes) on your reaction to a favorite selection in this book. The main purpose of the talk is to explain why you found the selection personally meaningful. Remember the following points:

- Be positive, not negative.
- Choose your selection with this point in mind: The reason for your interest should also be of interest to others. For instance, if you liked "To Build a Fire," it might be because you once had a scary experience on a cold, snowy day.
- Think of a strong way to start. The "hook" (see page 131) is as important in speaking as in writing. Your beginning probably will deal with a personal experience rather than with the selection itself.
- Go through your talk in your mind, writing some key words on a few cards and placing the cards in an appropriate sequence. But remember, your job is to talk in an interesting way, not to read a prepared speech.
- Remember that enthusiasm is the secret of a good talk. If you are absorbed in a subject you really want to share with others, you won't have to worry about what to do with your hands, about eye contact, about talking loudly enough, or about any of the other so-called problems of speaking.

Your talk may be shared with the whole class or with a small group, as your teacher directs.

WRITING ABOUT YOUR REACTIONS

Assignment: Turn your short talk on your personal reaction to a selection (page 391) into a composition at least 250 words long.

Prewriting: Because most of the necessary steps have already been taken in connection with the "Speaking Up" assignment on page 391, this assignment is not as hard a task as it may first appear. Try to profit from your earlier experience. If anything went wrong, how can you correct it now? For instance, you may be able to find a better "hook" or a better way to connect your personal experience with the selection. Or you may have done some further thinking on what you learned from your reading. One thing is certain: You will have to think through your talk and decide where each new paragraph in your composition should start. In the spoken version of our language, paragraphs hardly exist.

Writing: When you have notes on what is to be the paragraph pattern of your paper, you will be ready to start writing. Keep in mind that paragraphs do not alone make the difference between speech and writing. When you presented your subject orally, you really didn't have to think about complete sentences or correct punctuation. Now you do. Try to make your writing "sound" like you, but make sure it reflects the part of you that uses correct grammar and punctuation.

Revising: As with previous writing assignments, the more time you can let go by between *writing* and *revising,* the better. By now you should have little trouble with the revision process, since you know your own strengths and weaknesses as a writer. But don't just correct your weaknesses; use your strengths as well. Here and there try to add a needed detail, a fresh image, or an original figure of speech.

When you are certain that your revised draft represents your best work, write your final copy. Be sure to include all of your improvements.

Glossary of Terms

This glossary defines terms that you have studied. The page references shown with the terms indicate where the terms are first defined and discussed. Turn to those pages if you need to review the lessons.

Allusion p. 299 An *allusion* in a work of literature is a passing reference to some person, place, or event in history or in another work of literature.

Analogy p. 241 An *analogy* is a statement that the relationship between two items is in some way similar to the relationship between two other items.

Biography p. 63 A *biography* is the story of a person's life, written by another person. Biography is one of the most popular forms of nonfiction.

Cause and Effect p. 124 A *cause* is an event or idea that leads to a certain result, which is called an *effect. Cause and effect* is a common pattern of thinking, and of writing.

Character Clues p. 77 *Character clues* are speeches, thoughts, and actions that indicate indirectly what a character is like. An author is more likely to provide clues about a character than to describe that character directly.

Characterization p. 249 The word *characterization* refers to the methods by which authors develop their characters. There are four main methods of characterization: (1) direct statements made by the author, (2) the speeches and thoughts of a character, (3) a character's actions, and (4) the reactions of other characters.

Choral Reading p. 328 *Choral reading* is reading aloud together, or having various individuals or small groups take different parts in the reading of a piece of literature.

Chronological Order pp. 68, 149 When the details of a story or composition are given in their normal sequence of time, they are in *chronological order*, that is, the order in which they occur.

Cliché p. 10 A *cliché* is an overused figurative expression. The expression, "He was the apple of my eye," is a common cliché.

Climax p. 77 The *climax*, or most exciting part of a story, comes at or near the story's end. (See also *Plot.*)

Comparison and Contrast p. 164 A *comparison* shows how two (or more) things, ideas, or feelings are alike. A *contrast*, on the other hand, shows how they are different. (Note: The word *comparison* is sometimes used to establish both similarities and differences.)

Conclusion p. 114 A *conclusion* is a major inference requiring considerable thought and observation. (See also *Inference.*)

Conflict p. 77 All plots depend on *conflict*, or the meeting of opposing forces. Characters in stories can be in conflict with—or struggling against—(1) other characters, (2) themselves ("inner conflict"), (3) things, or (4) nature. (See also *Plot.*)

Connotation p. 321 Many words have two kinds of meanings. The *connotation* of a word is its "emotional meaning," or what the word suggests. (See also *Denotation.*)

Denotation p. 321 Many words have two kinds of meanings. The *denotation* of a word is its usual or "dictionary" meaning. (See also *Connotation.*)

Dialogue p. 105 *Dialogue* is spoken language in a work of literature.

Episode p. 123 In literature, an *episode* is a unit of action.

Extended Metaphor p. 44 An *extended metaphor* is a figurative comparison that continues throughout much or all of a poem, or other work of literature.

Fact p. 262 A *fact* is something generally known to be true. Most facts can be checked by direct observation or the study of reports by witnesses. (See also *Opinion.*)

Fiction p. 63 *Fiction* is literature in which an author creates imaginary characters and events. Short stories and novels are two popular forms of fiction. (See also *Nonfiction.*)

Figurative Language p. 10 *Figurative language* is language that says one thing and means another. For instance, when you say "Hold your horses!" to someone, you really want that person to slow down. Literature is rich in figurative language. Some common forms are *metaphor, simile, hyperbole,* and *personification.* (See also *Literal Language.*)

Figures of Speech p. 30 *Figures of speech* are specific forms of figurative language. Most figures of speech compare two unlike things. The two main kinds of comparison used in literature are called *metaphor* and *simile.* (See also *Figurative Language.*)

Flashback p. 149 A *flashback* is an interruption of chronological order to insert a scene that happened before the time frame of a story. Authors often use this device to provide important background information.

Folk Literature p. 140 *Folk literature* is a term applied to stories that have been told many times. Folktales are usually passed along orally from generation to generation.

Foreshadowing p. 141 *Foreshadowing* is a technique used by authors to allow readers to predict what will happen in a work of literature. Authors may foreshadow events by providing certain hints or clues that suggest what action is to come.

A *prediction,* in general, is a judgment about what will happen in the future. Good readers use foreshadowing in order to make reasonable predictions. This skill prepares readers to accept an event when it finally does happen.

Hyperbole p. 303 *Hyperbole* is exaggeration or overstatement in a literary work. Poets, in particular, often use hyperbole to add force to their words.

Hypothesis/Hypotheses p. 209 A *hypothesis* is a possible solution to a problem or an explanation of an event. Frequently, there are several possible solutions or explanations. These are called *hypotheses.* The process of finding hypotheses and then seeking facts from reading to support those hypotheses is a common approach when analyzing literature.

Imagery p. 59 *Imagery* is the use of language that appeals to any or all of the five senses. Writers use *images* to help readers experience what is being described. For example, a **visual image** helps a reader form a vivid mental picture of how something looks.

Inference p. 114 An *inference* is an understanding of something that is only suggested, not stated directly, by an author. (See also *Conclusion.*)

Irony pp. 293, 300 When people speak with *irony,* or in an *ironic* way, they say something quite different from what they really mean. Often, the spoken words are the direct opposite of the intended meaning.

In the study of literature, there is more than one kind of irony. **Irony of situation** occurs when there is a striking difference between what a character expects to happen and what actually does happen. **Dramatic irony** occurs when an audience (including readers) knows something important that a character (or characters) does not know.

Levels of Meaning p. 251 A work of literature can be understood in two ways, or can have two *levels of meaning:* a "surface" level and a "deeper" level. Whereas the surface meaning may be rather simple and is based only on what is said, the deeper meaning usually requires some "digging."

Literal Language p. 10 *Literal language* is language that means exactly what it says. (See also *Figurative Language.*)

Main Idea p. 68 The central thought of a paragraph, or of a longer piece, is called the *main idea.* The main idea is often stated in a single sentence. (See also *Supporting Details.*)

Metaphor p. 30 A *metaphor* is a figure of speech that makes a comparison directly, without using extra words to show that the comparison is being made. Sometimes a word or expression is simply substituted for another. For example, notice how the simple substitution by the word *plows* sets up a comparison in this metaphor: "The ship plows through the sea." The way a ship *moves* through water is being compared to the way a tractor *plows* through soil. (See also *Simile*.)

Monologue p. 103 A *monologue* is a long speech spoken in the way a person would normally talk.

Mood and Tone p. 178 The *mood* of a piece of literature is the feeling it gives a reader. For instance, a story can be depressing, hilarious, disturbing, or peaceful.

The word *tone* refers to the author's attitude toward the subject matter, the characters, and the reader. The tone of a story includes all the unstated understandings between author and reader. An author's attitude, or tone, frequently serves to convey the mood of a piece of literature.

Narrative Poem p. 98 A *narrative poem* is a poem that tells a story. "Casey at the Bat" is an example of a narrative poem.

Narrator p. 58 The *narrator* of a story is the person who tells the story. (See also *Point of View*.)

Nonfiction p. 63 *Nonfiction* is literature that tells about real characters and events. *Biography* is a popular form of nonfiction. (See also *Fiction*.)

Onomatopoeia p. 281 *Onomatopoeia* is the use of words that sound like what they mean. Onomatopoetic words usually imitate natural sounds. Examples are *hiss*, *splash*, and *moan*.

Opinion p. 262 An *opinion* is what a person thinks, believes, judges, or infers is true, or probably true. The best opinions are usually those that are most directly based on facts. (See also *Fact*.)

Oral Interpretation p. 102 *Oral interpretation* means reading aloud with expression.

Pantomime p. 72 To *pantomime* is to act out silently. Pantomiming is a good exercise when working to improve techniques of oral interpretation.

Paraphrase p. 321 To *paraphrase* is to restate something using as few of the original words as possible.

Personification p. 44 *Personification* is figurative language in which nonhuman subjects are given human qualities. "An angry sea" is an example.

Plot p. 77 A *plot* is what happens in a work of literature. The plot usually focuses on some *conflict*, or the meeting of opposing forces. The basic elements of plot include the *rising action*, a *climax*, and a final *resolution*. The action in a work of literature can be viewed also as posing and then answering a series of *plot questions*.

Plot Question p. 77 A *plot question* is a question that is raised in a work of literature by an action in the plot. The action that answers this question can either end the story or lead to still other questions. For example, in "Appointment in Baghdad," this plot question is raised: Why is the young man in such a rush? The story quickly reveals this answer: He is trying to escape Death.

Point of View p. 228 *Point of view* is the position from which a work of literature is presented. The two most common points of view are the *first person* and the *third person*.

In the **first-person point of view**, the storyteller (or *narrator*) is one of the characters. The narrator refers to himself or herself as "I" and presents *only* what he or she knows and observes.

In the **third-person point of view**, the storyteller is completely outside the story. Being an outsider, the narrator calls all the characters "he" or "she" and *never* refers to himself or herself. Some third-person storytellers are **omniscient**, or "all-knowing." The omniscient narrator can enter the minds of *any* of the characters. Other narrators take a **limited** third-person point of view, limiting themselves to the feelings and thoughts of a *single* character, usually the main character.

Prediction p. 141 A *prediction* is a judgment about what will happen in the future. (See also *Foreshadowing*.)

Resolution p. 77 Some stories continue past the climax with a section of falling action, or a *resolution*. (See also *Plot*.)

Rhyme Scheme pp. 3, 62 *Rhyme scheme* is the pattern of rhymes in a poem. **End rhymes** occur at the end of lines. **Internal rhymes** are words that rhyme within single lines.

Rising Action p. 77 The events in a plot that lead to a climax make up the *rising action*. To build excitement, a writer tries to make each plot problem more interesting than the one before it. (See also *Plot*.)

Rounded Characters p. 77 *Rounded characters* are distinct individuals rather than types. As with real people, readers can't predict exactly what rounded characters will do when faced with certain problems. (See also *Stereotypes*.)

Satire p. 177 A *satire* is a literary work that pokes fun at some idea or human weakness. However, the aim of satire is usually serious, intended to teach the reader some lesson about life.

Setting p. 77 The *setting* of a story is the time and the place of the action. A setting might include a natural event, such as a snowstorm.

Simile p. 30 A *simile* is a figure of speech that makes a comparison by using a special word, usually *like* or *as*, to show that the comparison is being made. "Strong as a bull" is a common example. (See also *Metaphor*.)

Stanza p. 3 A *stanza* is a group of lines in a poem that may be like at least one other group in (1) number of lines, (2) approximate length of lines, or (3) rhyme scheme, or pattern.

Stereotypes pp. 77, 165 In literature, *stereotypes* are one-dimensional characters one has met before in one's reading. Their thoughts and actions are easily predictable. The kind old grandmother and the football hero who always manages the last-minute touchdown are examples of stereotypes. (See also *Rounded Characters*.)

In life, a *stereotype* is the standard "picture in our heads" that a certain word brings to mind. Because the "picture in our heads" is of no particular person or thing, the stereotype is usually proved false when it comes to individual cases.

Story-Within-a-Story p. 140 A *story-within-a-story* is one story contained within another story. A character from the outer story usually tells the **inner story** to another character.

Supporting Details p. 68 The *supporting details* in a paragraph or longer piece are the examples or reasons upon which the main idea is based. (See also *Main Idea*.)

Symbol and Symbolic Action p. 208 A *symbol* is something that stands for something else. A symbol in a work of literature must really appear *in* that work of literature. It is usually something one can see and touch; what it stands for tends to be an idea, a feeling, or a quality. For example, a flag might represent the idea of freedom.

A *symbolic action* is an act that suggests something more about a person. In "The Gift of the Magi," for example, Della's cutting and selling of her hair is *symbolic* of her love for her husband.

Theme p. 78 A *theme* is the meaning or message of a piece of literature. Some stories and poems have more than one theme, and others have a theme of only minor importance.

Index of Authors and Titles

Page numbers in **bold-faced** type indicate profiles (short biographies).

Acknowledgments

We thank the following authors, agents, and publishers for their permission to reprint copyrighted material:

FORREST J. ACKERMAN AGENCY—for permission to adapt "Who's Cribbing?" by Jack Lewis. Copyright © 1952 by Better Publications, Inc.

ISAAC ASIMOV and THE MAGAZINE OF FANTASY AND SCIENCE FICTION—for "A Loint of Paw" by Isaac Asimov. © 1957 by Mercury Press, Inc. Reprinted from *The Magazine of Fantasy and Science Fiction.*

ATHENEUM PUBLISHERS—for "Eating Poetry" from *Reasons for Moving* by Mark Strand. Copyright © 1966 by Mark Strand.

DODD, MEAD & COMPANY, INC. and McGRAW-HILL RYERSON LIMITED—for "The Cremation of Sam McGee" from *The Collected Poems of Robert Service* by Robert Service. Copyright 1907, 1909, 1912 by Dodd, Mead & Company. Copyright 1916, 1921 by Dodd, Mead & Company, Inc. Copyright 1940 by Robert Service.

DON DOUGHERTY, SATURDAY REVIEW—for cartoons by Don Dougherty. Reprinted from *Saturday Review.* Copyright © 1978 by Don Dougherty, Saturday Review. Copyright © 1979 by Don Dougherty, Saturday Review.

NORMA MILLAY ELLIS—for "Afternoon on a Hill" and "Lament" from *Collected Poems* by Edna St. Vincent Millay, published by Harper & Row. Copyright 1917, 1921, 1945, 1948 by Edna St. Vincent Millay and Norma Millay Ellis.

MARI EVANS—for "Where Have You Gone?" from *I Am a Black Woman*, published by Wm. Morrow & Company. Copyright © 1970.

SAMUEL FRENCH, INC.—for "The Still Alarm" by George S. Kaufman. Copyright 1925 by George S. Kaufman. Copyright 1930 by Brady & Wiman Productions Corporation. Copyright 1952 (in renewal), 1957 (in renewal) by George S. Kaufman. *CAUTION:* Professionals and amateurs are hereby warned that "The Still Alarm," being fully protected under the copyright laws of the United States of America, the British Empire, including the Dominion of Canada, and all other countries of the Copyright Union, is subject to a royalty. All rights, including professional, amateur, motion pictures, recitation, public reading, radio and television broadcasting and rights of translation in foreign languages are strictly reserved. Amateurs may give stage productions of this play upon payment of a royalty of Ten Dollars for each performance one week before the play is to be given to Samuel French, Inc., at 25 West 45th St., New York, N.Y. 10036, or 7623 Sunset Blvd., Hollywood, Calif., or if in Canada to Samuel French (Canada) Ltd., at 80 Richmond Street East, Toronto, M5C, 1P1, Canada.

GINN AND COMPANY (XEROX CORPORATION)—for "The Legend of Sleepy Hollow" by Washington Irving. Adapted from the radio script by Margaret Blackburn and others of a Colorado College of Education Radio Workshop, from *Discovery Through Reading of The Ginn Basic Reading Program* by David H. Russell and others. Copyright © 1952, 1963 by Ginn and Company.

MALCOLM HANCOCK, SATURDAY REVIEW—for cartoon by Malcolm Hancock. Reprinted from *Saturday Review.* Copyright © 1977 by Saturday Review.

HARCOURT BRACE JOVANOVICH, INC.—for "Fog" from *Chicago Poems* by Carl Sandburg. Copyright 1916 by Holt, Rinehart and Winston, Inc. Copyright 1944 by Carl Sandburg.—for excerpt from "They Have

Yarns" from *The People, Yes* by Carl Sandburg. Copyright 1936 by Harcourt Brace Jovanovich, Inc. Copyright 1964 by Carl Sandburg.—for "Everyday Use" by Alice Walker. Copyright © 1973 by Alice Walker. Reprinted from her volume *In Love & Trouble* by permission of Harcourt Brace Jovanovich, Inc.

HARPER & ROW, PUBLISHERS, INC.—for excerpt from *Black Boy* by Richard Wright. Copyright 1937, 1942, 1944, 1945 by Richard Wright.

SIDNEY HARRIS—for cartoon by Sidney Harris. Copyright © 1986 by Sidney Harris.

HILL AND WANG (A DIVISION OF FARRAR, STRAUS & GIROUX, INC.)—for "The Story-Teller" from *A Winter Day and Other Poems* by Mark Van Doren. Copyright © 1935 by Mark Van Doren. Renewed copyright © 1962 by Mark Van Doren.

HOLT, RINEHART AND WINSTON, PUBLISHERS—for "The Pasture," "Stopping by Woods on a Snowy Evening," and "The Road Not Taken" by Robert Frost. From *The Poetry of Robert Frost* edited by Edward Connery Lathem. Copyright 1916, 1923, 1939, © 1967, 1969 by Holt, Rinehart and Winston. Copyright 1944, 1951 by Robert Frost.

JAMES HURST—for "The Scarlet Ibis" by James Hurst. Copyright *The Atlantic Monthly* July 1960. By permission of the author.

INTERNATIONAL PUBLISHERS—for permission to adapt "Little Things Are Big" from *A Puerto Rican in New York* by Jesús Colón, published by Mainstream Publishers. Copyright © 1961.—for "To Satch" (originally titled "American Gothic: To Satch") by Samuel Allen (Paul Vesey). From *Poets of Today*, published by International Publishers.

ALFRED A. KNOPF, INC.—for "Triad," "November Night" and "On Seeing Weather-Beaten Trees" from *Verse* by Adelaide Crapsey. Copyright 1922 by Algernon S. Crapsey and renewed 1950 by the Adelaide Crapsey Foundation.—for "Mother to Son" from *Selected Poems of Langston Hughes* by Langston Hughes. Copyright 1926 by Alfred A. Knopf, Inc. and renewed 1954 by Langston Hughes.—for "Motto," "Warning," and "Harlem" from *The Panther and the Lash: Poems of Our Times* by Langston Hughes. Copyright 1951 by Langston Hughes. Copyright © 1967 by Arna Bontemps and George Houston Bass.—for excerpt from *The Woman Warrior: Memoirs of a Girlhood Among Ghosts*, by Maxine Hong Kingston. Copyright © 1975, 1976 by Maxine Hong Kingston. Reprinted by permission of Alfred A. Knopf, Inc.

FREDERICK LAING—for permission to adapt "The Eye Catcher" (originally titled "The Beau Catcher") by Frederick Laing.

LITTLE, BROWN AND COMPANY—for "Song of the Open Road" from *Verses from 1929 On* by Ogden Nash. Copyright 1932 by Ogden Nash. Originally published in *The New Yorker*.—for "The Hippopotamus" from *Verses from 1929 On* by Ogden Nash. Copyright 1935 by Ogden Nash.

LUDLOW MUSIC, INC.—for "This Land Is Your Land," words and music by Woody Guthrie. © Copyright 1956 (renewed 1984), 1958 (renewed 1986) and 1970 by The Richmond Organization and Ludlow Music, Inc., New York, NY. Used by permission.

MACMILLAN PUBLISHING COMPANY, INC.—for "The Falling Star" from *Collected Poems* by Sara Teasdale. Copyright 1930 by Sara Teasdale Filsinger, renewed 1958 by Guaranty Trust Co. of New York, Executor.—for "Barter" from *Collected Poems* by Sara Teasdale. Copyright 1917 by Macmillan Publishing Co., Inc., renewed 1945 by Mamie T. Wheless.—for "I Shall Not Care" from *Collected Poems* by Sara Teasdale. Copyright 1915 by Macmillan Publishing Co., Inc., renewed 1943 by Mamie T. Wheless.—for "The Long Hill" from *Collected Poems* by Sara Teasdale. Copyright 1920 by Macmillan Publishing Co., Inc., renewed 1948 by Mamie T. Wheless.

HAROLD MATSON COMPANY, INC.—for permission to adapt "Duel" by Richard Matheson. © 1971 by Richard Matheson. Reprinted by permission of Harold Matson Company, Inc.

RONA MAYNARD—for "The Fan Club" by Rona Maynard. Reprinted from *Read* magazine by permission of the author.

EVE MERRIAM—for "Umbilical" from *Finding a Poem* by Eve Merriam. Copyright © 1970 by Eve Merriam. All rights reserved. Reprinted by permission of Marian Reiner for the author.

WILLIAM MORROW & COMPANY, INC.—for "The World Is Not a Pleasant Place to Be" from *My House* by Nikki Giovanni. Copyright © 1972 by Nikki Giovanni. By permission of William Morrow & Company.

SHERYL NELMS—for "Cumulus Clouds" by Sheryl Nelms. First published in *Modern Maturity*, August-September 1985.

NEW DIRECTIONS PUBLISHING CORPORATION.—for "The Secret" from *Poems 1960–1967* by Denise Levertov. Copyright © 1964 by Denise Levertov Goodman. Reprinted by permission of New Directions Publishing Corp.

THE NEW YORK TIMES COMPANY—for "Futility" by Mary S. Hawling, of August 25, 1931. Copyright © 1931 by The New York Times Company. Reprinted by permission.

NEWS AMERICA SYNDICATE—for "A Monster at the Wheel" by Ann Landers, from the Ann Landers column of August 22, 1984. Copyright by News America Syndicate. Reprinted by permission of News America Syndicate and the *Independent Journal*.

ALAN E. NOURSE—for "The Canvas Bag" from *The Counterfeit Man: More Science Fiction Stories* by Alan E. Nourse. Copyright © 1952, 1953, 1954, 1955, 1956, 1963 by Alan E. Nourse. Adapted by permission of the author.

HAROLD OBER ASSOCIATES, INC.—for "Dream Boogie," "Request," "Tell Me," "Blues at Dawn," "Figurette," "Argument," and "Island" from *Montage of a Dream Deferred* by Langston Hughes. Copyright © 1951 by Langston Hughes.

G. P. PUTNAM'S SONS—for "Snow" from *Everything and Anything* by Dorothy Aldis. Copyright © 1955 by Dorothy Aldis.

CHARLES SCRIBNER'S SONS—for "A Day's Wait" from *Winner Take Nothing* by Ernest Hemingway. Copyright 1933 by Charles Scribner's Sons, renewal © 1961 by Mary Hemingway.—for "Earth" from *The Gardener and Other Poems* by John Hall Wheelock. Copyright © 1961 by John Hall Wheelock.—for "Richard Cory" from *Children of the Night* by Edwin Arlington Robinson.

MILO SHEPARD—for "To Build a Fire" from *Lost Face* by Jack London.

THIRD PRESS INTERNATIONAL—for "Haiku" from *Love Poems* by Sonia Sanchez. Copyright © 1973 by Sonia Sanchez.

UNITED FEATURE SYNDICATE, INC.—for "Peanuts" cartoon by Charles Schulz. Copyright © 1961 by United Feature Syndicate, Inc.

VIKING PENGUIN, INC.—for "The Adversary" from *Times Three* by Phyllis McGinley. Copyright © 1959 by Phyllis McGinley. Originally published in *The New Yorker*.—for "Note to My Neighbor" from *Times Three* by Phyllis McGinley. Copyright © 1951 by Phyllis McGinley. Originally published in *The New Yorker*. Reprinted by permission of Viking Penguin, Inc.

401

ACKNOWLEDGMENTS

JERRY VOGEL MUSIC COMPANY, INC.— for "Trees" by Joyce Kilmer. Copyright 1913, renewed 1941. Copyright assigned to Jerry Vogel Music Company, Inc.

WORKMAN PUBLISHING CO.—for cartoon by B. Kliban, reprinted from *Tiny Footprints*. Copyright © 1978 by B. Kliban.

Every effort has been made to locate the author of "Crabby Old Woman" to obtain permission to reprint the poem. If either the author or heirs are located subsequent to publication, they are hereby entitled to due compensation.

The following selections are in the public domain. Some have been slightly adapted for the modern reader by Globe Book Company: Katherine Lee Bates, "America the Beautiful"; Ann Bradstreet, "To My Dear and Loving Husband"; Terri Bueno, "The Sheep of San Cristóbal"; Charles W. Chesnutt, "Baxter's Procrustes"; Chief Joseph, "No More Forever"; Emily Dickinson, "I'm Nobody!" "A Word," "I Never Saw a Moor," "The Sky Is Low," "Some Keep the Sabbath"; Adages by Ralph Waldo Emerson; Benjamin Franklin, from *Poor Richard's Almanac*; Bret Harte, "The Outcasts of Poker Flat"; Nathaniel Hawthorne, "David Swan"; O. Henry, "The Last Leaf," "The Gift of the Magi"; Walter Hubbell, "On the Path of the Poltergeist"; Henry Wadsworth Longfellow, from "Paul Revere's Ride," from "The Day Is Done"; Edgar Allan Poe, "The Tell-Tale Heart," "Annabel Lee"; Maureen Scott, "The Girl in the Lavender Dress"; Frank R. Stockton, "The Lady, or the Tiger?"; Ernest L. Thayer, "Casey at the Bat"; Henry David Thoreau, from *Walden*, adages by Thoreau; Traditional version of "Appointment in Baghdad"; Mark Twain, "How to Tell a Story," "The Wounded Soldier," "An Encounter with an Interviewer"; Harriet R. White, "Uffia"; Walt Whitman, "I Hear America Singing," "O Captain! My Captain!" "When I Heard the Learn'd Astronomer."

Photo Acknowledgments

Photo Researchers/National Audubon Society/Keith Gunnar: xii; Photo Researchers/Mary Evans Picture Library: 11; Historical Pictures Service, Chicago: 16 (left); Sleepy Hollow Restorations: 16 (right); Monkmeyer Press/Albrecht: 43; Library of Congress: 46 (left); Frederic Lewis: 46 (right); Springer/Bettmann Film Archive: 47 (left); Frederic Lewis/P.L. Sperr: 47 (right); Monkmeyer Press/Strickler: 74; Peter Simon: 96; Monkmeyer Press/ Michal Heron: 115; Brown Brothers: 116 (left); Library of Congress: 116 (right); Photo Researchers/Michael Uffer: 134; Smithsonian Institution: 150; Historical Pictures Service, Chicago: 168 (left); The Western Reserve Historical Society: 168 (right); Culver Pictures: 179; The Bettmann Archive: 182; Photo Researchers/Vivienne: 198; The Bettmann Archive: 200 (left); Culver Pictures: 200 (right); UPI/Bettmann Archive: 227; Culver Pictures: 242 (left); AP/Wide World Photos: 242 (right); The Bettmann Archive: 250; Brown Brothers: 256 (left); Culver Pictures: 256 (right); Photo Researchers/National Audubon Society/Grant M. Haist: 284; Brown Brothers: 301 (left); H. Armstrong Roberts: 301 (right); The Port of New York Authority: 332; Culver Pictures: 342; Library of Congress: 352 (left); Historical Pictures Service, Chicago: 352 (right); The Bettmann Archive: 358 (left); Brown Brothers: 358 (right); Chicago Historical Society: 360; Wide World Photos: 378. **Cover:** Library of Congress (Mark Twain); © 1986 Thomas Victor and courtesy of Alfred A. Knopf, Inc. (Maxine Hong Kingston); AP/Wide World Photos (Langston Hughes); Culver Pictures (O. Henry); Brown Brothers (Sara Teasdale); William R. Morrow, Publishers (Mari Evans); The Bettmann Archive (Bret Harte); Frederic Lewis/American Stock Photos (Ernest Hemingway); Library of Congress (Edgar Allan Poe).

Illustrators

Ted Burwell: 19, 22, 23, 26, 28, 57, 213, 216, 219, 221, 223, 225, 316; Peter Catalanato: 80, 84, 87; Ron Dilg: 54, 56, 230; Julie Evans: 144, 147; Ken Hamilton: 152, 160; Karen Kretchman: 232, 235, 238; Glee LoScalzo: 203, 205, 334, 339; Eileen McKeating: 5, 7, 181, 254–255; Steve Moore: 382, 386; Karen Pritchett: 109, 111, 267, 269, 271, 275, 277; Bob Sabin: 258; Don Schlegel: 34, 37, 40, 173, 360, 365, 370; Robert Shore: 349; Gerald Smith: 2–3, 187, 308, 311; Cindy Spenser: 245, 247; Marsha Tidy: 137, 139, 346; Kevin Walter: 210, 325.

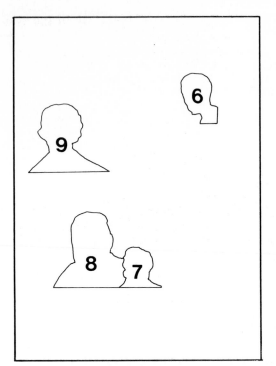

Back Cover

Front Cover

Authors on the Cover:

1. Mark Twain
2. Maxine Hong Kingston
3. Langston Hughes
4. O. Henry
5. Sara Teasdale
6. Mari Evans
7. Bret Harte
8. Ernest Hemingway
9. Edgar Allan Poe